550+
PSAT®
Practice Questions

Second Edition

The Staff of The Princeton Review

PrincetonReview.com

Penguin
Random
House

The Princeton Review
110 East 42nd Street, 7th Floor
New York, NY 10017
E-mail: editorialsupport@review.com

Published in the United States by Penguin Random House LLC, New York, and in Canada by Random House of Canada, a division of Penguin Random House Ltd., Toronto.

Some of the content in 550+ PSAT Practice Questions, 2nd Edition has previously appeared in Workout for the PSAT, 2nd Edition, published as a trade paperback by Random House, an imprint and division of Penguin Random House LLC, in 2015.

ISBN: 978-0-451-48748-3
ISSN: 2333-9322

Editor: Aaron Riccio
Production Editors: Liz Rutzel and Jim Melloan
Production Artist: Craig Patches

Printed in the United States of America on partially recycled paper.

10 9 8 7 6 5 4 3 2 1

Second Edition

Editorial
Rob Franek, Editor-in-Chief
Casey Cornelius, VP Content Development
Mary Beth Garrick, Director of Production
Selena Coppock, Managing Editor
Meave Shelton, Senior Editor
Colleen Day, Editor
Sarah Litt, Editor
Aaron Riccio, Editor
Orion McBean, Associate Editor

Penguin Random House Publishing Team
Tom Russell, VP, Publisher
Alison Stoltzfus, Publishing Director
Jake Eldred, Associate Managing Editor
Ellen Reed, Production Manager
Suzanne Lee, Designer

Acknowledgments

Special thanks to Amy Minster and Elizabeth Owens.

Thanks also to Chris Aylward, Brian Becker, Clarissa Constantine, Lori DesRochers, Zoe Gannon, Cat Healey, Erik Kolb, Aaron Lindh, Kathryn Menefee, Anne Morrow, Alexander Palmer, Garrison Pierzynski, Stephen Shuck, and Jess Thomas.

—Jonathan Chiu
National ACT & SAT Content Director
The Princeton Review

The Princeton Review would also like to acknowledge the hard work of its production team, from the creativity and flexibility of Craig Patches to the sharp eyes and dedication of Liz Rutzel and Jim Melloan.

Contents

Get More (Free) Content! vi

Part I: Orientation 1

1 Your Guide to Getting the Most Out of This Book 3

2 What You Need to Know for the PSAT 7

3 All About National Merit Scholarships 13

Part II: Reading Test 19

4 Reading Test Drill 1 21

5 Reading Test Drill 1: Answers and Explanations 37

6 Reading Test Drill 2 49

7 Reading Test Drill 2: Answers and Explanations 65

8 Reading Test Drill 3 75

9 Reading Test Drill 3: Answers and Explanations 91

Part III: Writing and Language Test 101

10 Writing and Language Test Drill 1 103

11 Writing and Language Test Drill 1: Answers and Explanations....... 119

12 Writing and Language Test Drill 2 127

13 Writing and Language Test Drill 2: Answers and Explanations 141

14 Writing and Language Test Drill 3 149

15 Writing and Language Test Drill 3: Answers and Explanations....... 163

Part IV: Math Test 171

16 Math Test Drill 1 173

17 Math Test Drill 1: Answers and Explanations 195

18 Math Test Drill 2 207

19 Math Test Drill 2: Answers and Explanations 229

20 Math Test Drill 3 239

21 Math Test Drill 3: Answers and Explanations 259

Part V: Practice Test 273

22 Practice Test 275

23 Practice Test: Answers and Explanations 325

Appendix: Reading Tips 355

Get More (Free) Content

1 Go to **PrincetonReview.com/cracking.**

2 Enter the following ISBN for your book: 9780451487483.

3 Answer a few simple questions to set up an exclusive Princeton Review account. (If you already have one, you can just log in.)

4 Click the "Student Tools" button, also found under "My Account" from the top toolbar. You're all set to access your bonus content!

Need to report a potential **content** issue?

Contact **EditorialSupport@review.com.**
Include:

- full title of the book
- ISBN number
- page number

Need to report a **technical** issue?

Contact **TPRStudentTech@review.com**
and provide:

- your full name
- email address used to register the book
- full book title and ISBN
- computer OS (Mac/PC) and browser (Firefox, Safari, etc.)

The **Princeton Review**®

Once you've registered, you can...

- Take a full-length practice PSAT, SAT, and/or ACT

- Get valuable advice about the college application process, including tips for writing a great essay, where to apply for financial aid, and our "College Insider" guide

- If you're still choosing between colleges, use our searchable rankings of *The Best 382 Colleges* to find out more information about your dream school

- Download and print bubble sheets and an extra warm-up drill for the Writing and Language and Math sections

- Check to see if there have been any corrections or updates to this edition

- Get our take on any recent or pending updates to the PSAT

Look For These Icons Throughout The Book

 MORE GREAT BOOKS

 COLLEGE ADVISOR APP

Part I
Orientation

1   Your Guide to Getting the Most Out of This Book
2   What You Need to Know for the PSAT
3   All About National Merit Scholarships

Chapter 1
Your Guide to Getting the Most Out of This Book

WHAT'S INSIDE

Hello, and welcome to *550+ PSAT Practice Questions, 2nd Edition*! In these pages you'll find more than 500 practice questions to help you prepare for the PSAT. These questions showcase all the features of the PSAT: Reading, Writing & Language, and Math. Working through these problems in conjunction with our detailed, technique-filled explanations is a great way to familiarize yourself with the challenges of the PSAT.

Which PSAT?

It's true, there are several iterations of the PSAT, from the PSAT 8/9 to the PSAT 10 and the PSAT/NMSQT. The PSAT 8/9 is, as you might have guessed, a version of the PSAT that is geared toward 8th and 9th graders. This book does not deal with this version of the test.

A Rose By Any Other Name
To be honest, we're not entirely sure how to pronounce PSAT/NMSQT. You could call it *pee-sat-nim-squit*, but we think it's easier to just call it the PSAT, so that's what we'll do throughout this book.

The PSAT 10 and PSAT/NMSQT are essentially the same, and are what we're talking about when we use the term PSAT in these pages. What's different is that the PSAT 10 is offered in the Spring (as opposed to the Fall) and does not qualify students for the National Merit Scholarships, so if you think you've got a shot at one of those—and we'll talk more about this in Chapter 3—make sure you're ready for the PSAT/NMSQT.

What Is The Princeton Review?

The Princeton Review is the nation's leading test-preparation company. In just a few years, we became the nation's leader in SAT preparation, primarily because our techniques work. We offer courses and private tutoring for all of the major standardized tests, and we publish a series of books to help in your search for the right school. If you would like more information about how The Princeton Review can help you, go to **PrincetonReview.com** or call 800-2-Review.

HOW TO USE THIS BOOK

There are three drills for each of the three sections that you will see on the PSAT: Reading, Writing & Language, and Math. These are designed to test the skills required for each section. There is also a Practice Test at the end of the book, which not only tests your skills, but provides a taste of the test-day experience.

Work through this book at your own pace. We recommend taking at least one of each drill first, so you can see where you might want more practice, and to then take the Practice Test under test-like conditions (time yourself!) to see how you handle the endurance and concentration required by the PSAT. After that, you can return to the drill section to continue practicing any areas that you still feel uncomfortable with. You can also string drill sections back to back to continue practicing the timing of the overall test.

When You Take a Drill
Here are some guidelines for taking these tests.

- Time yourself strictly. Use a timer, watch, or stopwatch that will ring, and do not allow yourself to go over time for any section. If you try to do so at the real test, your scores will likely be canceled.
- Always take a practice drill using an answer sheet with bubbles to fill in, just as you will for the real test. You need to be comfortable transferring answers to the separate sheet because you will be skipping around a bit.
- Each bubble you choose should be filled in thoroughly, and no other marks should be made in the answer area.
- As you fill in the bubble for a question, check to be sure you are on the correct number on the answer sheet. If you fill in the wrong bubble on the answer sheet, it will not matter if you worked out the problem correctly in the test booklet. All that matters to the machine scoring the test is the No. 2 pencil mark.

Bubble Sheets
Bubble sheets can be printed out from your online student tools, so don't be shy about filling them in! For more information on accessing these, see page vi.

PRINCETON REVIEW TECHNIQUES AND STRATEGIES
Think about the last time you set out to accomplish something: Whether it's taking a photo, recording a song, building a cabinet, or writing a screenplay, you probably used all the tools at your disposal to get the job done. The PSAT is no different from any other task—just as you wouldn't attempt to film a movie without a video camera or a boom mike, you wouldn't want to take this test without the skills and strategies that will best help you to succeed. This book is what we at The Princeton Review affectionately call "drill and kill" in that we are offering you gobs of practice problems and detailed answers and explanations. In some of those explanations, we will use Princeton Review strategies and jargon that might sound foreign to you. So before we go any further, let's introduce some of the shorthand terms that you might see in your PSAT practice problems.

This book is focused on providing you with an opportunity to practice your skills on PSAT-like questions. If you're looking for more hands-on experience learning these strategies, check out *Cracking the PSAT/NMSQT, 2018 Edition*, and *Are You Ready for the SAT and ACT?*

ZONEF (FROZEN)—This acronym stands for Zero, One, Negative, Extreme, and Fraction, and it refers to a few special numbers that you should test out when checking to see what will satisfy an algebraic expression.

POE—There are many more wrong answers on the PSAT than there are credited answers, so on some of the more difficult questions, you'll be well served by not trying to find the best answer, but rather finding the wrong answers and using POE, the process of elimination. Even if you aren't quite sure of the correct answer, you can guess strategically by eliminating a few choices that you know are incorrect and then taking your best guess.

PITA or **Plugging In the Answers**—Plugging In the Answers (PITA) converts algebra problems into arithmetic problems. No matter how good you are at algebra, you're better at arithmetic. Why? Because you use arithmetic every day, every time you go to the store, estimate the price of new pair of sneakers, or tip a waiter. Chances are you rarely use algebra in your day-to-day activities. Plug in real numbers to make a problem concrete rather than abstract.

Ballparking—Ballparking helps you eliminate answer choices and increase your odds of zeroing in on the correct answer by eliminating any answer choices that are "out of the ballpark." For example, use quick estimations to eliminate one or two answer choices that are simply way too big or way too small.

FOIL—When faced with two sets of parentheses in a quadratic equation, use this acronym to help you remember to multiply every term in the first set by every term in the second set. FOIL stands for First, Outer, Inner, and Last. So, for example, if you see $(x + 4)(x + 3)$, you would multiply the first terms $(x \cdot x)$, the outer terms $(x \cdot 3)$, the inner terms $(4 \cdot x)$, and finally, the last terms $(4 \cdot 3)$.

FANBOYS—for, and, nor, but, or, yet, so. A comma plus any of these is the equivalent of STOP punctuation.

GOOD LUCK!

We know that the PSAT might seem intimidating, but you're already headed in the right direction. And we'll be with you every step of the way.

Lord of the Dings
Even if you run out of time for POE, you should still fill in every remaining bubble—there's no penalty for incorrect answers, so you can only improve your score. We recommend picking a Letter of the Day (LOTD) and just using that for every question that's still blank when time is up.

One More Step
In addition to the techniques and strategies mentioned above, we've also included an appendix of tools and terminology for tackling the Reading section. You'll find this section on page 355.

Chapter 2
What You Need
to Know for the
PSAT

HOW DO I SIGN UP FOR THE PSAT?

You don't have to do anything to sign up for the PSAT; your school will do all the work for you. Test registration fees can vary from school to school, but shouldn't be more than $16; be sure to check with your school counselor if you have questions about how much the PSAT will cost you.

What About Students with Special Needs?

If you have a diagnosed learning difference, you will probably qualify for special accommodations on the PSAT. However, it's important that you get the process started early. The first step is to speak to your school counselor who handles learning differences. Only he or she can file the appropriate paperwork. You'll also need to gather some information (documentation of your condition) from a licensed practitioner and some other information from your school. Then your school counselor will file the application for you. You will need to apply for accommodations only once; with that single application you'll qualify for accommodations on the PSAT, SAT, SAT Subject Tests, and AP Exams. The one exception to this rule is that if you change schools, you'll need to have a counselor at the new school refile your paperwork.

Does the PSAT Play a Role in College Admissions?

No! The PSAT plays no role in college admissions. It's really just a practice test for the SAT. The one exception is for that very small group of students, about 4 percent of all students nationwide, whose PSAT scores qualify them for National Merit recognition. (We'll tell you more than you ever wanted to know about that in Chapter 3.) Recognition as a commended scholar, semifinalist, or finalist for National Merit is a fairly impressive addition to your college admissions portfolio, and is something that you should certainly pursue if you are seriously in contention for it.

WHAT DOES THE PSAT TEST?

As you begin your prep, it's useful to remember that the PSAT is not a test of aptitude, how good of a person you are, or how successful you will be in life. The PSAT simply tests how well you take the PSAT. That's it. And performing well on the PSAT is a skill, one that can be learned like any other. The Princeton Review was founded more than 30 years ago on this very simple idea, and—as our students' test scores show—our approach is the one that works.

All of these changes to tests that you hear could heavily influence your college admission strategy can be extremely daunting. However, remember that any standardized test is a coachable test. A beatable test. Just remember:

The PSAT doesn't measure the stuff that matters. It measures neither intelligence nor the depth and breadth of what you're learning in high school. It doesn't predict college grades as well as your high school grades do, and many schools are still hesitant to use the score from your essay in their application decisions at all: That's why it's now optional. Colleges know there is more to you as a student—and as a person—than what you do on a single test administered on a Saturday morning.

WHO WRITES THE PSAT?

The PSAT is administered by the College Board. You might think that the people at the College Board are educators, professors of education, or teachers. They are not. They are people who just happen to make a living writing tests. In fact, they write hundreds of tests, for all kinds of organizations.

The folks at the College Board aren't really paid to educate; they are paid to prepare tests. While you (or your school) will be paying them to take the PSAT, you are not their customer. The actual customers the College Board cater to are the colleges, which get the information they want at no cost. This means that you should take everything the College Board says with a grain of salt and realize that its testing "advice" is not always the best advice. (Getting testing advice from the College Board is a bit like getting baseball advice from the opposing team.)

Every test reflects the interests of the people who write it. If you know who writes the test, you will know a lot more about what kinds of answers will be considered "correct" answers on that test.

WHAT IS ON THE PSAT?

Category	PSAT (also referred to as the PSAT/NMSQT or the PSAT 10)
Time	2 hours and 45 minutes
Components	• Evidence-Based Reading and Writing: Reading; Writing & Language • Math
Number of Questions, Time by Section	Reading: 47 Qs, 60 mins Writing & Language: 44 Qs, 35 mins Math: 48 Qs, 70 mins
Important Features	• Emphasis on reasoning in addition to a strong focus on the knowledge, skills, and understanding important to college and career readiness and success • Emphasis on the meaning of words in extended contexts and on how word choice shapes meaning, tone, and impact • Rights-only scoring (a point for a correct answer but no deduction for an incorrect answer; blank responses have no impact on score)
Score Reporting	• Some scores will be reported on the same scale used for the SAT. This scale ranges from 320 to 1520 for total score, 160–760 for two section scores, and 10–40 for test scores.
Subscore Reporting	Subscores for every test, providing added insight for students, parents, educators, and counselors
Answer Choices	4 answer choices (for multiple-choice questions)

You should expect these questions to be complex, purportedly aligned with what introductory college courses and vocational training programs offer. Reading passages lean toward history and science-based material. The Writing and Language section may test your ability to demonstrate a full understanding of the source's ideas, not just a specific set of stand-alone editing skills.

You'll also find that the Math section focuses on a more specific set of problem-solving and analytical topics, and it includes higher-level content (like trigonometry). You will have to contend with grid-in questions, and you will face topics that are both specifically geared to test your ability to use a calculator and for which calculators are not permitted.

The Math Test is divided into two sections, one with the calculator, with 31 questions over the course of 45 minutes, and one without, with 17 questions administered in 25 minutes. Because of the tight time limit, particularly in the non-calculator section, it's important that you review the explanations for the problems in this book that you solved correctly, as you may discover techniques that help to shave seconds from your solutions. A large part of what's being tested is your ability to use the appropriate tools in a strategic fashion, and while there may be multiple ways to solve a given problem, you'll want to focus on the most efficient.

SCORING ON THE PSAT

The PSAT is scored on a scale of 320 to 1520, which is the sum of two section scores that range from 160 to 760. The two sections are the Evidence-Based Reading and Writing section and the Mathematics section. Wrong answers to multiple-choice questions are not penalized, so you're advised never to leave a question blank—even if that means blindly picking a letter and bubbling it in for any uncompleted questions before time runs out.

In addition to the overall total score and the section scores, you'll find several subscores on your PSAT score report:

An **Analysis in History/Social Studies** and **Analysis in Science** cross-test score is generated based on questions from all three of the subject tests (Math included!), and these assess the cross-curricular application of the tested skills to other contexts. Relax! This doesn't mean that you have to start cramming dates and anatomy—every question can be answered from the context of a given reading passage or the data included in a table or figure. The only changes have to do with the content of the passages and questions themselves.

Additionally, the Math test is broken into several categories. The **Heart of Algebra** subscore looks specifically at how well students understand how to handle algebraic expressions, work with a variety of algebraic equations, and relate real-world scenarios to algebraic principles. **Problem Solving and Data Analysis** focuses more on interpretation of mathematical expressions, graphical analysis, and data interpretation. Your ability to not only understand what a problem is asking, but to represent it in your own words, will come in handy here. **Passport to Advanced Mathematics** questions showcase the higher-level math that's been added to the test, from quadratics and their graphs to the creation and translation of functions.

Finally, there is an **Additional Topics** domain that's filled with what you might consider wild-card material. Although these questions might not correlate directly to a subscore, six of these miscellaneous types will show up on the redesigned test. In the Verbal portions of the test, the **Command of Evidence** subscore measures how well you can translate and cite specific lines that back up your interpretation, while the **Relevant Words in Context** subscore ensures that you can select the best definition for how a word is used in a passage. The Writing & Language section additionally measures **Expression of Ideas**, which deals with revising language in order to make more logical and cohesive arguments, and **Standard English Conventions**, which assesses your ability to conform to the basic rules of English structure, punctuation, and usage.

Are You Ready for the SAT?

If you want to start preparing for the SAT, pick up a copy of our *Cracking the SAT Premium*, which is chock full of content review, strategy, and realistic practice questions!

Study

If you were getting ready to take a biology test, you'd study biology. If you were preparing for a basketball game, you'd practice basketball. So, if you're preparing for the PSAT (and eventually the SAT), study the PSAT.

What Does the PSAT Score Mean for My SAT Score?

The SAT is scored on a 1600 scale, whereas the PSAT is scored on a 1520 scale. However, because the PSAT and SAT are aligned by the College Board to be scored on the same scale, your PSAT score indicates the approximate SAT score you would earn were you to have taken the SAT on that same day.

How Much Should I Prepare for the PSAT?

If you're in that very small percentage of students who are in contention for National Merit recognition, it may be worth your while to put in a good deal of time to prepare for this test. After all, your extra hard work may well put you in a better position for National Merit recognition. Otherwise, you should prepare enough so that you feel more in control of the test and have a better testing experience. (Nothing feels quite as awful as being dragged through a testing experience feeling like you don't know what you're being tested on or what to expect—except perhaps dental surgery.) The other reason to prepare for the PSAT is that it will give you some testing skills that will help you begin to prepare for the tests that actually count, namely the SAT and SAT Subject Tests.

The bottom line is this: the best reason to prepare for the PSAT is that it will help you get an early start on your preparation for the SAT.

Chapter 3
All About National Merit Scholarships

You may sometimes see the PSAT referred to as the PSAT/NMSQT. The NMSQT part stands for National Merit Scholarship Qualifying Test. That means that the PSAT serves as the test that will establish whether or not you are eligible for National Merit recognition. This chapter will help you figure out what that may mean for you.

WHAT IS THE NATIONAL MERIT SCHOLARSHIP PROGRAM?

You might think that the PSAT is simply a warm-up for the SAT, but the National Merit Scholarship Program makes the PSAT an important test in its own right.

The mission of National Merit Scholarship Corporation (NMSC) is to recognize and honor the academically talented students of the United States. NMSC accomplishes this mission by conducting nationwide academic scholarship programs. The enduring goals of NMSC's scholarship programs are the following:

- To promote a wider and deeper respect for learning in general and for exceptionally talented individuals in particular
- To shine a spotlight on brilliant students and encourage the pursuit of academic excellence at all levels of education
- To stimulate increased support from organizations that wish to sponsor scholarships for outstanding scholastic talent.

The National Merit Scholarship Program is an academic competition for recognition and scholarships that began in 1955. High school students enter the National Merit Program by taking the Preliminary SAT/National Merit Scholarship Qualifying Test (PSAT/NMSQT) and by meeting published program entry and participation requirements.

How Do I Qualify for National Merit?

To participate in the National Merit Scholarship Program, a student must:

1. Take the PSAT/NMSQT in the specified year of the high school program and **no later than** the third year in grades 9 through 12, regardless of grade classification or educational pattern;
2. Be enrolled as a high school student (traditional or homeschooled), progressing normally toward graduation or completion of high school, and planning to enroll full time in college no later than the fall following completion of high school; and
3. Be a citizen of the United States; or be a U.S. lawful permanent resident (or have applied for permanent residence, the application for which has not been denied) and intend to become a U.S. citizen at the earliest opportunity allowed by law.

The Index

How does your PSAT score qualify you for National Merit? The National Merit Scholarship Corporation uses a Selection Index, which is twice the sum of your Math, Critical Reading, and Writing Skills scores.

Remember that those scores are each on a scale of 8–38, so if you add the maximum scores together (114) and then multiply by 2, you'll see that the highest possible Selection Index Score is 228.

These qualifying score cutoff differs from state to state and year to year, and NMSC is very tight-lipped about releasing official information. Historically, cutoff scores can range anywhere from 210–222, as different states have different cutoff scores for National Merit consideration. Check with your school counselor for what the PSAT cut-off score was in your state the previous year.

The Awards and the Process

In the fall of their senior year, about 50,000 students will receive one of two letters from NMSC: either a Letter of Commendation or a letter stating that they have qualified as semifinalists for National Merit.

Commended Students　Roughly two-thirds of these students (about 34,000 total students each year) will receive a Letter of Commendation by virtue of their high scores on the test. This looks great on your college application, so if you have a reasonable chance of receiving this recognition, it is definitely worth your time to prepare for the PSAT. Make no mistake, though, these letters are not easy to get. They are awarded to students who score between the 95th and the mid-99th percentiles.

If you receive this honorable mention from NMSC, you should be extremely proud of yourself. Even though you will not continue in the process for National Merit scholarships, this commendation does make you eligible for special scholarships sponsored by certain companies and organizations, which vary in their amounts and eligibility requirements.

Semifinalists　The other third of these students—those 16,000 students who score in the upper 99th percentile in their states—will be notified that they are National Merit semifinalists. If you qualify, you will receive a letter announcing your status as a semifinalist, along with information about the requirements for qualification as a finalist. These include maintaining high grades, performing well on your SAT, and getting an endorsement from your principal.

Becoming a National Merit semifinalist is quite impressive, and if you manage it, you should certainly mention it on your college applications.

Finalists   The majority of semifinalists (more than 90 percent) go on to qualify as finalists. Students who meet all of the eligibility requirements will be notified in February of their senior year that they have qualified as finalists. This means that they are now eligible for scholarship money, though it does not necessarily mean that they will receive any. In fact, only about half of National Merit finalists actually win scholarships. What determines whether a student is awarded money or not? All winners are chosen from that Finalist group based on their abilities, skills, and accomplishments—without regard to gender, race, ethnic origin, or religious preference. A variety of information is available for NMSC selectors to evaluate: the Finalist's academic record, information about the school's curricula and grading system, two sets of test scores, the high school official's written recommendation, information about the student's activities and leadership, and the Finalist's own essay. This year, there will be 7,500 Merit Scholarship winners and 1,200 Special Scholarship recipients. Unlike the Merit Scholarships, which are given by the NMSC, the Special Scholarship recipients will receive awards from corporate sponsors and are selected from students who are outstanding, but not National Merit finalists.

Though the amounts of money are not huge, every little bit helps, and the award itself looks very impressive in your portfolio. So if you think you are in contention for National Merit recognition, study hard.

But I am Not a Junior in High School Yet…

If you are not yet a junior, and you are interested in National Merit, you will have to take the test again your junior year in order to qualify.

A certain number of schools give the PSAT to students in their sophomore year—and sometimes even earlier. These schools hope that earlier exposure to these tests will help their students perform better in later years. If you are not yet in your junior year, the PSAT will not count for National Merit scholarship purposes, so it is really just a trial run for you. However, it is still a good idea to go into the test prepared in order to feel and perform your best.

What If I am in a Three-Year or Other Nonstandard Course of Study?

If you are going to spend only three years in secondary school, you have two options for when to take the PSAT for National Merit purposes: You can take it either in your next-to-last year or in your last year of secondary school. However, our advice is this: If you are in any program other than a usual four-year high school, be sure to talk to your guidance counselor. He or she will consult with NMSC and help ensure that you take the PSAT at the right time. This is important because not taking the PSAT at the right time can disqualify you from National Merit recognition.

What If I Miss the PSAT Administration My Junior Year?

If you are not concerned about National Merit scholarships, there is no reason to do anything in particular—except, perhaps, to obtain a few PSAT booklets to practice on, just to see what fun you missed.

However, if you want to be eligible for National Merit recognition, then swift action on your part is required. If an emergency arises that prevents you from taking the PSAT, you should write to the National Merit Scholarship Corporation *immediately* to request alternate testing dates. If your request is received soon enough, it should be able to accommodate you. (NMSC says that this kind of request must absolutely be received by April 1 following the missed PSAT administration.) You will also need a signature from a school official.

For More Information

If you have any questions or problems, the best person to consult is your school guidance counselor, who can help make sure you are on the right track. If you need further help, contact your local Princeton Review office at 800-2-REVIEW or **PrincetonReview.com**. Or, you can contact National Merit directly:

National Merit Scholarship Corporation
1560 Sherman Avenue, Suite 200
Evanston, IL 60201-4897
(847) 866-5100
NationalMerit.org

Part II
Reading Test

4   Reading Test Drill 1
5   Reading Test Drill 1: Answers and Explanations
6   Reading Test Drill 2
7   Reading Test Drill 2: Answers and Explanations
8   Reading Test Drill 3
9   Reading Test Drill 3: Answers and Explanations

Chapter 4
Reading Test
Drill 1

Reading Test

60 MINUTES, 47 QUESTIONS

Turn to Section 1 of your answer sheet to answer the questions in this section.

DIRECTIONS

Each passage or pair of passages below is followed by a number of questions. After reading each passage or pair, choose the best answer to each question based on what is stated or implied in the passage or passages and in any accompanying graphics (such as a table or graph).

Questions 1-9 are based on the following passage.

The following is excerpted from the Texas Declaration of Independence, in which Texas declared its independence from Mexico in the Texas Revolution.

When a government has ceased to protect the lives, liberty, and property of the people, from whom its legitimate powers are derived, and for the
Line advancement of whose happiness it was instituted,
5   and so far from being a guarantee for the enjoyment of those inestimable and inalienable rights, becomes an instrument in the hands of evil rulers for their oppression.
   When the Federal Republican Constitution of their
10 country, which they have sworn to support, no longer has a substantial existence, and the whole nature of their government has been forcibly changed, without their consent, from a restricted federal republic, composed of sovereign states, to a consolidated
15 central military despotism, in which every interest is disregarded but that of the army and the priesthood, both the eternal enemies of civil liberties, the ever ready minions of power, and the usual instruments of tyrants.
20   When, long after the spirit of the constitution has departed, moderation is at length so far lost by those in power, that even the semblance of freedom is removed, and the forms themselves of the constitution discontinued, and so far from their petitions and
25 remonstrances being regarded, the agents who bear them are thrown into dungeons, and mercenary armies sent forth to force a new government upon them at the point of the bayonet.

   When, in consequence of such acts of malfeasance
30 and abdication on the part of the government, anarchy prevails, and civil society is dissolved into its original elements. In such a crisis, the first law of nature, the right of self-preservation, the inherent and inalienable rights of the people to appeal to first principles, and
35 to take their political affairs into their own hands in extreme cases, enjoins it as a right towards themselves, and a sacred obligation to their posterity, to abolish such a government, and create another in its stead, calculated to rescue them from impending dangers,
40 and to secure their future welfare and happiness.
   Nations, as well as individuals, are amenable for their acts to the public opinion of mankind. A statement of a part of our grievances is therefore submitted to an impartial world, in justification of the
45 hazardous but unavoidable step now taken, of severing our political connection with the Mexican people, and assuming an independent attitude among the nations of the earth.
   The Mexican government, by its colonization
50 laws, invited and induced the Anglo-American population of Texas to colonize its wilderness under the pledged faith of a written constitution, that they should continue to enjoy that constitutional liberty and republican government to which they had been
55 habituated in the land of their birth, the United States of America.
   In this expectation they have been cruelly disappointed, inasmuch as the Mexican nation has acquiesced in the late changes made in the government
60 by General Antonio Lopez de Santa Anna, who having

CONTINUE

overturned the constitution of his country, now offers us the cruel alternative, either to abandon our homes, acquired by so many privations, or submit to the most intolerable of all, tyranny.

65 It has sacrificed our welfare to the state of Coahuila, by which our interests have been continually depressed through a jealous and partial course of legislation, carried on at a far distant seat of government, by a hostile majority, in an unknown tongue, and this 70 too, notwithstanding, we have petitioned in the humblest terms for the establishment of a separate state government, and have, in accordance with the provisions of the national constitution, presented to the general Congress a republican constitution, which was, 75 without just cause, contemptuously rejected.

We, therefore, the delegates with plenary powers of the people of Texas, in solemn convention assembled, appealing to a candid world for the necessities of our condition, do hereby resolve and declare, that our 80 political connection with the Mexican nation has forever ended, and that the people of Texas do now constitute a free, Sovereign, and independent republic.

1

The tone of the passage is best described as

A) passive.

B) inspiring.

C) hateful.

D) accusatory.

2

As used in line 6, "inestimable" most nearly means

A) worthy.

B) infinite.

C) respectful.

D) desirable.

3

The description in the second paragraph (lines 9–19) indicates that what the authors value most in a government is

A) a weak centralized government with stronger with autonomous territories.

B) a militarily strong government.

C) a government with strong moral and religious convictions.

D) a transparent government that engages in hostile behavior toward sovereign states.

4

In paragraph 6 (lines 49–56), the author explains the ways in which the Mexican government encouraged colonists in order to

A) demonstrate the positive relationship the state of Texas once shared with the government of Mexico.

B) illustrate the unethical behavior Americans have experienced from foreigners historically.

C) compare the United States government and the Mexican government.

D) establish the initial understanding those who immigrated to Texas had of Mexico.

5

The passage most strongly suggests that authors of the document and the Mexican government share which of the following assumptions?

A) The state of Texas is under the rule of the Mexican government.

B) Compromise is necessary in order to repair the mistrust created by each side's actions.

C) The creation and maintenance of a Federal Republican Constitution is the best way in which to ensure everyone's rights are guaranteed.

D) The importance of the federal government and the priesthood cannot be overstated.

CONTINUE

6

Which choice provides the best evidence for the answer to the previous question?

A) Lines 1–8 ("When a … oppression")

B) Lines 41–42 ("Nations, as … mankind")

C) Lines 49–56 ("The Mexican … America")

D) Lines 65–75 ("It has … rejected")

7

The position General Santa Anna takes in the seventh paragraph (lines 57–64) is best described as that of

A) a democratically appointed leader of an unstable nation.

B) a strong and fearless leader of an army.

C) an uncompromising ruler.

D) a bloodthirsty dictator.

8

The authors include the description of their grievances against the Mexican government in paragraph 8 (lines 65–75) primarily in order to

A) explain their decision to secede from the Mexican nation.

B) begin a dialogue that results in political change within the Mexican government.

C) demonstrate to the world that the Mexican government is an illegal and unethical entity.

D) bolster their claim that they would be better fit to establish a strong federal government than those who are currently in power.

9

As used in line 77, "convention" most nearly means

A) trend.

B) habit.

C) conference.

D) contract.

CONTINUE ▶

Questions 10-19 are based on the following passage.

The following passage discusses some of the early, lesser-known governments, documents, and people that shaped the formation of the United States of America.

It is difficult for many to imagine an American government that does not begin with George Washington as the president. But from the moment
Line we declared independence from the rule of the British
5 Monarchy, and even before, America had to be run by someone or something. A successful revolution and construction of a country does not happen without deliberation. Hence, neither the first functioning government of the United States of America nor its
10 first president is the one we are most familiar with today. In fact, there are quite a few more governments and presidents of the United States of which many may not be aware.

For all intents and purposes, and despite the
15 contrary opinion of the British Monarchy, the governing body of the American colonies prior to and during the American Revolution was the Continental Congress. The Continental Congress was a convention of delegates from all Thirteen Colonies formed in
20 1774 when it met from September 5 to October 26. Although the Declaration of Independence would not be signed for two years, it was this Congress that wrote and issued the redress of grievances to King George and began an economic boycott of Great Britain.
25 Because of the actions entered into by the Continental Congress and the democratic approach it adopted in its function, it is viewed by some as the first active autonomous government of the United States.

There were 56 delegates in all who attended the
30 first meeting of the Continental Congress. From among the notable men in attendance, which included Benjamin Franklin, George Washington, and John Adams, a land-owner and public official from Virginia named Peyton Randolph was elected as president
35 of the Congress. Since, as was stated previously, the Continental Congress was at this point functioning as a democratic, autonomous government for the united colonies, Randolph is considered by many to be the

first president of the United States. Randolph did
40 not serve in this capacity for long. On May 5, 1775, Randolph suffered from acute apoplexy, bleeding within the internal organs, and passed away. He was succeeded as president by John Hancock. It was Hancock who served as president during the writing
45 and issue of the Declaration of Independence to the British Monarchy, which is why his signature was both first and most prominent.

The Second Continental Congress, which followed the First Continental Congress, convened on May
50 10, 1775. This Congress outlasted its predecessor as it continually met throughout the course of the American Revolution, and by issuing the Declaration of Independence on July 4, 1776, claimed sovereignty over the whole of the colonies. The Second Continental
55 Congress remained the governing body of the nascent nation until March 1, 1781, when it adopted the Articles of Confederation.

The Articles of Confederation was a type of precursor to the Constitution of the United States
60 of America. It formally established the Congress of the Confederation as the governing body of the United States of America. That body was maintained from 1781 to 1789. Although the Congress of the Confederation was paramount to the successful end
65 of the American Revolution, once peace and American freedom were attained, its significance was dramatically decreased. Under the Articles of Confederation, the Congress had little control over the individual states or commonwealths, especially in regards to tax collection
70 and debt consolidation at the federal and state level.

Because such a discordant system of varying powers was unsustainable, the Congress of the Confederation drafted and enacted the modern day Constitution of the United States, laying the
75 groundwork for a stronger central government than currently existed. Under that constitution, the Congress of the Confederation became the Congress of the United States, half of the legislative branch of the three-branched government. It is this same Congress
80 that we elect today, although it now represents a few more states than its predecessors.

CONTINUE ➤

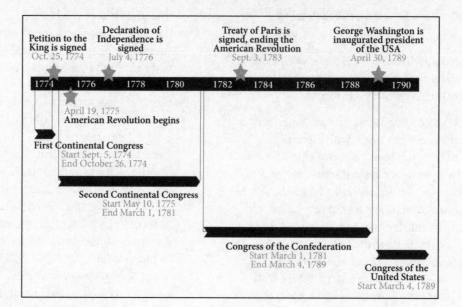

The phrase "For all intents and purposes" in line 14 serves primarily to

A) demonstrate that the Continental Congress' power was effectively recognized domestically.

B) indicate that the one true authority over the colonies was the King of England.

C) allow the author to straddle both sides of the American Revolution without preferring one to the other.

D) state the purpose of the formation of the Continental Congress.

According to the passage, it can be inferred that which of the following influenced the dissolution of the Congress of the Confederation?

A) The Congress was unable to exert a strong federal authority.

B) The Articles of Confederation were not as well written as the Constitution.

C) A single legislature was deemed undemocratic by the leaders of the American Colonies.

D) It was overthrown by a group of delegates who established a three branch government and produced the Constitution.

Which of the following provides the most support for the answer to the previous question?

A) Lines 48-57 ("The Second … Confederation")

B) Lines 58-60 ("The Articles … America")

C) Lines 71-79 ("Because such … government")

D) Lines 76-80 ("Under that … today")

The purpose of the third paragraph (lines 29–47) is chiefly to

A) support the assertion made earlier that George Washington is not considered by all as the first president of the United States.

B) explain the origin of the common phrase "put your John Hancock" on something when asked to sign a document.

C) demonstrate the close bond that existed between many of the founding fathers even before the start of the American Revolution.

D) assert that if it had not been for Peyton Randolph's untimely death, he would have been elected as President of the United States rather than George Washington.

CONTINUE

14

The passage most strongly suggests which of the following is true of John Hancock?

A) He was the sole author of the Declaration of Independence.

B) He was president during the creation of two important documents in American history.

C) He served as president of the Continental Congress until his death.

D) He served as president in both the original and the second Continental Congress.

15

As used in line 45, "issue" most nearly means

A) copy.

B) delivery.

C) concern.

D) installment.

16

As used in line 16, "body" most nearly means

A) form.

B) physique.

C) entity.

D) bulk.

17

In context, the word "successful" in line 6 refers mainly to America's

A) victory over the British.

B) implementation of democracy.

C) establishment of a functioning government.

D) foreign diplomacy.

18

According to the information in the passage, the author most likely would agree that our modern-day Congress differs from the Congress of the Confederation in all of the following ways EXCEPT

A) it now represents a greater number of states.

B) its existence was established by a document.

C) it was granted a greater amount of authority over the states.

D) it lasted for a longer period of time.

19

Which claim about American history is best supported by the graphic?

A) George Washington's first act as president was to institute the Congress of the United States.

B) The Congress of the United States ended in 1791.

C) It was more than fourteen years after the American Revolution began and almost six after it ended that George Washington became president of the United States.

D) October 25, 1774, is the date the Continental Congress took power through the Petition to the King.

CONTINUE ▶

Questions 20-28 are based on the following passage.

The following passage discusses the issues surrounding internet regulation and the concept of net neutrality.

It is quite common that the government moves slower than the times in terms of law implementation and regulation. This is in no way a criticism; it is only fitting and proper that a government, chosen and guided by the people, should first examine the needs and protections of its people prior to imposing restriction on any aspect of life. Furthermore, it is often the case that a government is unable to create restriction on any given object or action until it is comprehensively understood and its implications made clear.

Take the internet. When it was still a nascent technology, it would have been difficult to imagine all the ways in which the internet would become involved in our personal, public, and professional lives. It would also have been unimaginable to some that the internet would play such a fundamentally central role in our daily lives. The regulation of the internet has been slow in coming, progressing in fits and starts. The latest topic of governmental interest is whether or not the internet constitutes a public utility, and, if so, whether or not it should be regulated as such.

The term public utility refers to a service that is consumed by the widespread public, such as natural gas, electricity, water, and sewage. Generally, government agencies provide such services in a monopolized way, meaning there is no competitive market for utilities. Although they can be privatized depending on the supply and demand needs of a specific region, they are strictly regulated by the government. This regulation is necessary to ensure that these resources are made available in an equitable and affordable fashion due to their necessity.

Up until this point, the internet has not been considered a public utility by the United States government. Although restrictions have been placed on internet use by the government, this is has been limited to criminal internet activity, such as piracy, gambling, or harassment. Currently, internet is provided by a small handful of internet providers, which are not strongly regulated in their provision of internet and exist for capital gain. This creates the opportunity for such providers to exploit their customers as customers try to attain internet access to

all available data. Regulating the internet would ensure fair provision of the internet. This idea is called "net neutrality," which means that internet providers should act as a neutral gateway to internet content, as opposed to a gatekeeper that can control speed and access by content demand as they so choose or based on fees.

The Federal Communications Commission (FCC), which is a separate government entity charged with regulating interstate communications by radio, television, wire, satellite, and cable, announced in 2014 that it is in favor of creating a net neutrality approach to regulation of the internet. The following statement was given by FCC Chairman Tom Wheeler on the matter:

"Using this authority, I am submitting to my colleagues the strongest open internet protections ever proposed by the FCC. These enforceable, bright-line rules will ban paid prioritization, and the blocking and throttling of lawful content and services. I propose to fully apply—for the first time ever—those bright-line rules to mobile broadband. My proposal assures the rights of internet users to go where they want, when they want, and the rights of innovators to introduce new products without asking anyone's permission."

Where this issue becomes tricky is not in the decision of whether or not to regulate the provision of the internet, but how to enforce that regulation. The internet is unlike any other technology. Aspects such as internet speed and accessibility at the individual level are almost impossible to monitor, especially for a government that acts many steps behind the progress of this technology.

20

The primary purpose of the passage is to

A) provide a better understanding of what government utility regulation is and the difficulty in applying it to new technologies.

B) convince the reader that net neutrality is unlikely to ever take place due to current government regulation of illegal electronic activity.

C) argue against the need for regulation of one of the few free spaces left to the American consumer.

D) explain the FCC's stance when it comes to net neutrality.

CONTINUE

21

In the context of the passage, the author's use of the phrase "Take the internet" in line 12 is primarily meant to convey

A) the most difficult new technology the government has attempted to regulate.

B) a technology of greater interest to the writer than television, radio, or cable.

C) an example of a technology that government regulation has not yet caught up with.

D) an instance of a technology that has drastically transformed the average American day over the last twenty years.

22

The author mentions natural gas and sewage (line 25) in order to

A) clarify what a commonly used and regulated service is.

B) to help the reader understand why they are not overcharged for the use of these services.

C) to illustrate everyday services that were also once unregulated, like the internet.

D) to provide a comprehensive lists of the items that have been monopolized in our marketplace.

23

As used in line 43, "exploit" most nearly means

A) achieve.

B) mistreat.

C) explore.

D) utilize.

24

The quotation (lines 59–68) indicates that what the FCC values most about net neutrality is

A) the public's ability to move freely in society.

B) the creativity that the use of the internet helps to enhance.

C) the ability for broadband to be mobile.

D) the equal access to content for equivalent payment rates.

25

The passage most strongly suggests which of the following about the FCC?

A) The FCC has only recently begun to consider the need to regulate criminal activity on the internet.

B) It is unlikely the FCC will be able to convince the United States government to enforce regulating the internet as a public utility.

C) The FCC has been regulating such public utilities as natural gas, electricity, and water for some time now as those utilities are not as recent.

D) The FCC is unlikely to effectively implement and oversee the proposed regulations of the internet.

26

Which choice provides the best support for the answer to the previous questions?

A) Lines 7–11 ("Furthermore it … clear")

B) Lines 23–25 ("The term … sewage")

C) Lines 34–36 ("Up until … government")

D) Lines 72–76 ("Aspects such … technology")

27

The passage suggests that regulation of the internet is necessary for all of the following reasons EXCEPT

A) speed.

B) equal access.

C) file protection.

D) online betting.

28

As used in line 69, "tricky" most nearly means

A) magical.

B) devious.

C) artful.

D) difficult.

CONTINUE ➡

Questions 29-37 are based on the following passage.

The following passage is excerpted from the article "Antarctica Yields Two Unknown Dinosaur Species," published by the National Science Foundation on June 9, 2004.

In December 2003, against incredible odds, researchers working in separate sites, thousands of miles apart in Antarctica found what they believe
Line are the fossilized remains of two species of dinosaurs
5 previously unknown to science.

One of the two finds, which were made less than a week apart, is an early carnivore that would have lived many millions of years after the other, a plant-eating beast, roamed the Earth. One was found at the sea
10 bottom, the other on a mountaintop.

Working on James Ross Island off the coast of the Antarctic Peninsula, veteran dinosaur hunters Judd Case, James Martin, and their research team believe they have found the fossilized bones of an entirely
15 new species of carnivorous dinosaur related to the enormous meat-eating tyrannosaurs and the equally voracious, but smaller and swifter, velociraptors that terrified movie-goers in the film *Jurassic Park.*

Features of the animal's bones and teeth led the
20 researchers to surmise the animal may represent a population of carnivores that survived in the Antarctic long after they had been succeeded by other predators elsewhere on the globe.

Case, the dean of science and a professor of biology
25 at Saint Mary's College of California who discovered the bones, said the shape of the teeth and features of the feet are characteristic of a group of dinosaurs known as theropods, which includes the tyrannosaurs, as well as all other meat-eating dinosaurs. The
30 theropods, or "beast-footed" dinosaurs, make up a large and diverse group of now-extinct animals with the common characteristic of walking on two legs like birds. Recent research has shown that birds are direct descendants of theropods.

35 The remains include fragments of an upper jaw with teeth, isolated individual teeth and most of the bones from the animal's lower legs and feet. The creature likely inhabited the area millions of years ago when the climate and terrain were similar to
40 conditions in today's Pacific Northwest and radically different than they are today.

Martin, curator of vertebrate paleontology at the South Dakota School of Mines & Technology, said the size and shape of the ends of the lower-leg and foot
45 bones indicate that in life the animal was a running dinosaur roughly 1.8 to 2.4 meters (6 to 8 feet) tall.

The team believes that the body of the dinosaur may have been scavenged by marine lizards after it died, coming to rest on the ocean bottom, where it was
50 found among the remains of creatures similar to those that feasted on its body.

At the same time, thousands of miles away, a research team led by William Hammer of Augustana College in Rock Island, Ill. was working in the
55 Antarctic interior on a mountaintop roughly 3,900 meters (13,000 feet) high and near the Beardmore Glacier. They found embedded in solid rock what they believe to be the pelvis of a primitive sauropod, a four-legged, plant-eating dinosaur similar to better-known
60 creatures such as brachiosaurus and diplodocus. Now known as Mt. Kirkpatrick, the area was once a soft riverbed before millions of years of tectonic activity elevated it skyward.

Also a veteran dino hunter known for his
65 discovery of *Cryolophosaurus ellioti* in 1991, Hammer had returned to the site of that find to continue his work, which had been halted in part because the *Cryolophosaurus* excavation had dug far into a cliff face, creating a potentially dangerous overhang.
70 Specialized workers were flown into the research camp at Beardmore Glacier to remove the overhang and make it safer to continue the excavations.

Based on field analysis of the bones, Hammer and his fellow researchers believe the pelvis—roughly one
75 meter (three feet) across—is from a primitive sauropod that represents one of the earliest forms of the emerging dinosaur lineage that eventually produced animals more than 30 meters (100 feet) long.

Basing his estimates on the bones excavated at the
80 site, Hammer suggests the new, and as-yet-unnamed creature was between 1.8 and 2.1 meters (six and seven feet) tall and up to nine meters (30 feet) long.

CONTINUE ➔

Characteristics of Vertebrate Groups

	Mammals	Birds	Modern Reptiles	Theropod Dinosaurs
Number of ear bones	3	1	1	1
Legs directly under body	yes	yes	no	yes
Produce milk	yes	no	no	no
Constant body temperature	yes	yes	no	yes
Live birth	yes	no	some	no
Skin covering	hair	feathers/scales	scales	feathers/scales

29

As used in line 20, "surmise" most nearly means

A) total.

B) amaze.

C) know.

D) conjecture.

30

The passage most strongly suggests that Case and Martin used which of the following to determine the species of dinosaur they discovered?

A) The location where the dinosaur remains were discovered

B) Skeletal and oral aspects of the remains

C) The time period the dinosaur was most likely to have lived during

D) The pelvic measurement of the dinosaur

31

Which choice provides the best evidence for the answer to the previous question?

A) Lines 11-18 ("Working on … *Jurassic Park*")

B) Lines 19-23 ("Features of … globe")

C) Lines 37-41 ("The creature … today")

D) Lines 73-78 ("Based on … long")

32

The author refers to the film *Jurassic Park* (line 18) primarily to

A) introduce the reader to one of the author's favorite films from childhood.

B) impress upon the reader the importance of such a discovery, as it brings us one step closer to creating a real-life *Jurassic Park*.

C) associate the discovery of the scientists to a representation of dinosaurs that the reader may be familiar with.

D) help the reader better understand the time period in which the dinosaur discovered was most likely to have lived.

33

According to the passage, Case, Martin, and Hammer all have what in common?

A) They all specialize in carnivorous dinosaur skeletal excavation.

B) They were funded by the same grant, which accounts for their closely timed discoveries.

C) They all believe that Antarctica is the best remaining site for dinosaur excavation.

D) They are all affiliated with educational institutions.

CONTINUE ➡

34

In the eighth paragraph (lines 47–51), the author includes the description of where the remains of the dinosaur were discovered primary in order to

A) provide a description of the primary predator of theropods.

B) account for the location where the remains of the theropod was found.

C) illustrate the dangers of working in such a remote site.

D) transition into the other discovery by Hammer of a primitive marine lizard, thereby connecting the two discoveries.

35

With which of the following statements would the author most likely agree?

A) It is uncommon for two distinct discoveries of dinosaur skeletal remains to occur not only within such close physical proximity but also time period.

B) Because the dinosaur discovered by Hammer is an older dinosaur species than that discovered by Martin and Case, it is a more scientifically important discovery.

C) Antarctica is one of the more popular sites for dinosaur excavation due to its desolate landscape.

D) We now know that dinosaurs who walked on two legs are direct descendants of birds.

36

As used in line 63, "elevated" most nearly means

A) enlightened.

B) prominent.

C) raised.

D) advanced.

37

Which of the following can be reasonably inferred from information in the passage and the graphic?

A) The newly discovered dinosaur species are more closely related to mammals than reptiles.

B) Marine lizards are direct descendants of theropods, and they share the same number of ear bones.

C) Tyrannosaurs maintained a constant body temperature.

D) The newly discovered dinosaurs lived concurrently with modern birds.

CONTINUE ▶

Questions 38-47 are based on the following passages.

Both Passage 1 and Passage 2 discuss vaccines and relative benefits and risks of administering them to children.

Passage 1

Despite the first vaccination having been administered in the United States as long ago as 1800, it still remains one of the most divisive topics in the United States today. But the fact that vaccinations have continued to be administered at increasing rates despite such strong, long-held opposition is an indicator of their efficacy.

Physicians strongly encourage families to follow the prescribed vaccination schedule for their young children for a variety of reasons. But there is one reason that is more prominent than others: vaccines work. According to the American Academy of Pediatrics, "most child vaccines are 90%-99% effective in preventing disease." And by "effective" these physicians don't just mean that the vaccines have cut down on the rate of flu and measles infection, which is like a more severe version of the chicken pox. It is estimated that between 1994 and 2014 alone 732,000 American children were saved from death due to vaccinations, and 322 million cases of childhood illnesses were prevented.

This is not to say that there are no drawbacks to vaccinations whatsoever. On the contrary, physicians are quick to acknowledge that vaccinations do not come without risk. However, this risk is strictly minimal. Adverse reactions, such as anaphylaxis, illness, or even death, occur so infrequently it is difficult to determine exact numbers. The American Academy of Pediatrics estimates the number to somewhere between "one per several hundred thousand to one per million vaccinations." For the sake of the general population, this number is not great enough to argue against widespread vaccination.

It is believed that if enough people were to become vaccinated against any one disease, that disease could eventually be eradicated. This would work out well for both those who are pro-vaccine and anti-vaccine; because vaccines are so effective, there would no longer be a need for them. Speaking as an American with children of my own, it is in our best interest to bring everyone around to the idea of mandatory child vaccination.

Passage 2

The Greek philosopher Socrates is credited with having said "I know that I know nothing." These are wise words from a wise man, and should be kept in mind whenever dealing with "scientific fact." The truth is that despite the leaps and bounds we have made over the course of human history, especially in the medical sciences, we in truth know very little. And there is never a time that this fact is as salient as when it comes to the health of the most vulnerable in our society.

This is exactly the problem with a vaccine, which is defined as a preparation of killed microorganisms, living attenuated organisms, or living fully virulent organisms. There is a great deal that is unknown about vaccines, both in terms of the general public and the scientific community. The general public knows very little about what goes into vaccines and how they function, while the scientific community knows very little about the range of effects vaccines may have.

Although vaccinations have been in use for some time, the composition of them has changed drastically over the last several decades. Certain flu vaccines have been found to contain trace amounts of thimerosal, an organic mercury compound, which may have adverse neurological impacts on young children. Aluminum, which is found in many vaccines, can also cause neurological damage to humans in excess amounts. Because the recommended vaccine schedule calls for so many vaccines to be administered in quick succession, it is difficult to tell what amount of aluminum may exist in the child's body and for how long. Some vaccines even contain the carcinogen formaldehyde, even though no studies have been conducted to determine the long-term effect of its use on future health. The short term effects of formaldehyde are known, however, and can include cardiac impairment, central nervous system depression, anaphylactic shock, and comas in some who receive it.

The question is not "do vaccines help?" Undoubtedly they do, that we know. The question is, or at least it should be "do vaccines harm?" The answer here is equally clear: undoubtedly they do. We just don't know to what extent.

CONTINUE

38

Passage 1 most strongly suggests that which of the following is true of the author?

A) She believes more research is needed to convince those who are anti-vaccine that vaccines are indeed safe.

B) She thinks that the worldwide use of vaccines would eliminate all instances of childhood death.

C) She herself is likely to vaccinate her own children.

D) She was vaccinated as a child.

39

Which choice provides the best evidence for the answer to the previous question?

A) Lines 4–7 ("But the … efficacy")

B) Lines 17–21 ("It is … prevented")

C) Lines 39–41 ("Speaking as … mandatory")

D) Lines 57–60 ("The general … have")

40

As used in line 26, "adverse" most nearly means

A) other.

B) contradictory.

C) confrontational.

D) undesirable.

41

What claim about vaccination is best supported by the third paragraph (lines 22–33) in Passage 1?

A) Vaccines should be used despite the fact that they do harm some individuals.

B) Scientists give a wide range of numbers of those harmed from vaccines in order to avoid accountability for the harmful effects of vaccines.

C) Physicians are very strict regarding the vaccination schedule parents should adhere to for their children.

D) The goal of administering any vaccine is to eliminate a specific type of disease once and for all.

42

The author of Passage 2 refers to Socrates in order to

A) use a prominent scholar the reader is familiar with to validate her argument.

B) illustrate a point that is discussed throughout the remainder of the passage.

C) explain how one man has greatly influenced our approach to scientific and medical research.

D) dismiss the notion that it is safe to use drugs before they are approved by the FDA.

43

As used in line 50, "salient" most nearly means

A) relevant.

B) smart.

C) related.

D) welcome.

44

The author of Passage 2 refers to formaldehyde in order to

A) demonstrate the ways in which doctors manipulate patients and parents into accepting vaccines with harmful chemicals.

B) assert that a vaccine without formaldehyde may be safe to use, but those that contain it should be avoided.

C) provide an example of an ingredient found in vaccines that has known and possibly unknown harmful side-affects.

D) offer proof that vaccines can kill the patients who receive them.

45

In the final paragraph of Passage 2, the author

A) undermines her argument.

B) offers a concession.

C) quotes scientific evidence.

D) compares doctors who vaccinate to those who do not.

CONTINUE ▶

46

The central ideas of the passages differ in that Passage 1

A) reviews the positive aspects of vaccinations, while Passage 2 examines specific instances of vaccinations having been harmful after being administered.

B) is against the uninformed use of vaccinations, while Passage 2 states the benefits of vaccinations far outweigh the risks.

C) offers an argument in favor of vaccines, while Passage 2 contends that our understanding of vaccines is deficient.

D) is ambivalent regarding the use of vaccinations on the recommended schedule, while Passage 2 states not enough is known of the long-term effects of vaccines.

47

Both passages contain which of the following?

A) A definition

B) A simile

C) A question

D) A quotation

STOP

If you finish before time is called, you may check your work on this section only.
Do not turn to any other section.

Chapter 5
Reading Test
Drill 1: Answers
and Explanations

ANSWERS AND EXPLANATIONS

Section 1—Reading Test

1. **D** The people of Texas are declaring their independence because they feel they have been misled by the Mexican government. In the passage, the people charge the Mexican government with wrongdoing, so the tone of the passage is one of blaming. The best answer is (D), *accusatory*, since that is the only answer choice that is synonymous with blaming.

2. **B** The first paragraph of the passage uses the words *inestimable* and *inalienable* to describe the rights of the people. By using these adjectives, the authors of this declaration are stating that these rights have a value unable to be estimated and that these rights should be guaranteed. In context, the word *inestimable* means something similar to "immeasurable." Choices (A), (C), and (D) do not mean "immeasurable," which leaves (B). *Infinite* is the most similar word to "immeasurable," so it is the best answer.

3. **A** In the second paragraph, the people of Texas claim that *their government has been forcibly changed… from a restricted federal republic, composed of sovereign states, to a consolidated central military despotism*. The authors of this declaration are upset by this and believe that a tyrannical government now governs them. Therefore, the authors of this passage would not value a *militarily strong government* since that would be reflective of a *consolidated central military despotism* (eliminate (B)). Furthermore, they would not value a government that *engages in hostile behavior towards sovereign states* (eliminate (D)). Since they are upset that *their government has been forcibly changed, without their consent*, the authors would value the government they had before—one that was a *restricted federal republic, composed of sovereign states*. This makes (A) the best answer. There is no mention that they desire for their government to have strong *religious convictions—priesthood* is mentioned negatively in the passage as *an eternal enemy of civil liberties* (eliminate (C)).

4. **D** The sixth paragraph states that the Mexican government wanted the *Anglo-American population of Texas to colonize its wilderness* and lists the things the government used to induce the colonists to come: They would ensure constitutional liberty for the colonists and a government of the type the colonists were used to having in the USA. Therefore, the purpose of this paragraph is to explain why the colonists came (i.e., the expectations the colonists had once they immigrated to Texas). The next paragraph reveals that they were *cruelly disappointed* when their expectations were not met. Therefore, (D) is the correct answer. There is no evidence in the passage to support (A). The previous relationship the state of Texas had with the government of Mexico is never revealed. The sixth paragraph does not contain historical examples of how Americans have experienced *unethical behavior* from foreigners, so the purpose of this paragraph would not be to illustrate unethical behavior (eliminate (B)). The colonists are being assured that they should continue to enjoy the liberty and government they're used to having, but the purpose of this paragraph is not to compare the two governments (eliminate (C)).

5.   **A**   The only choice that would be an assumption shared by both the authors of the document and the recipients of it is the idea that the state of Texas is under Mexican rule, as in (A). The Mexican government invited and induced these people to colonize their land and promised a government like the one they had in the USA (lines 45–56), and the authors wrote the document to formally declare the end of their political connection with the Mexican nation (lines 76–82). All other answer choices can be eliminated. Based on the seventh paragraph, the Mexican government does not desire to ensure everyone's rights, as in (C); based on the whole passage, neither side would share the assumptions made in (B) or (D).

6.   **D**   The answer to the previous question is best supported by (D) since these lines contain support for an assumption that both the authors and recipients of the document would share—that the state of Texas is under the rule of the Mexican government. Choices (A) and (B) are incorrect because neither mention the Mexican government. Choice (C) is incorrect since these lines suggest that the people will enjoy the same liberties they had in their nation of origin.

7.   **C**   In the seventh paragraph, General Santa Anna is described as someone who has *overturned the constitution of his country* and has declared two options (*either to abandon our homes…or submit to… tyranny*). Choice (A) is incorrect because the general is not described in the passage as a leader who was democratically appointed—he *overturned the constitution of his country*. There is no mention of an actual army, so even though his title is *General*, there is no support in the passage for (B). Killing people is not mentioned in this paragraph, so there is not textual support that he is *bloodthirsty*, which eliminates (D). Therefore, the best answer is (C). He is *uncompromising* since he gave the people *the cruel alternative*—either leave or submit to tyranny.

8.   **A**   The authors have listed their grievances against the Mexican government in order to support the decision they have come to in the final paragraph of the passage: *we [the people of Texas]…do hereby resolve and declare that our political connection with the Mexican nation has forever ended*. Therefore, (A) is the correct answer. The people of Texas are not interested in beginning a dialogue—their petitions have already been *contemptuously rejected* (eliminate (B)). Their purpose is not to expose the Mexican government as illegal and unethical to the world—this declaration is intended for the Mexican government, not the world (eliminate (C)). Finally, (D) is incorrect because the authors are not trying to claim that they themselves would be better rulers; they are using the grievances to establish why they are now declaring themselves as a free, sovereign, and independent republic.

9.   **C**   The authors state in the last paragraph of the passage that the people of Texas have *assembled* or come together in a serious discussion and have to decide to declare the end of their political connection with Mexico. In context, the word *convention* means something similar to "discussion" or the idea of coming together. Choices (A), (B), and (D) do not mean "discussion," which leaves (C). *Conference* is the most similar word to "discussion," so it is the best answer.

10.   **A**   The paragraph describes the formation and actions of the Continental Congress. The paragraph also states that the Continental Congress was the governing body of the colonies *despite the contrary opinion of the British Monarchy* and that only *some* view it as the first government of the United States. This information taken together indicates that the Continental Congress was acting

as a governing body, but it was technically not the recognized government by all at the time. The phrase *for all intents and purposes* accounts for the functional role of the Continental Congress in enacting policies such as the boycott, while allowing for its lack of official authority. Therefore, (A) is the best answer. Choice (B) contains the extreme language *one true authority* and refers to the King of England, which is not being described by this phrase. Choice (C) refers to the American Revolution, which had not yet occurred during the time this passage discusses. Choice (D) is a deceptive answer, as it contains words from the phrase but does not explain the reason for the phrase. Although the passage does discuss the formation of the Continental Congress, the phrase *intents and purposes* refers to the Congress itself, not its formation.

11. **A** The Congress of the Confederation is discussed in the last two paragraphs. The author states the Congress had *little control over the … states or commonwealths* and that it *drafted and enacted the modern day Constitution* because *such a discordant system … was unsustainable.* Based on these lines, it is clear that the Congress of the Confederation purposefully created a stronger federal Congress in order to consolidate authority over the states, which it had previously lacked. Choice (B) is deceptive, as it names both of the documents discussed in this area of the passage, but it refers to the quality of the documents rather than their purpose/function. Choices (C) and (D) are not supported by the passage and are deceptive based on the later discussion of our current model of government. Choice (A) is the correct answer, as it addresses the lack of centralized power held by the Congress of the Confederation.

12. **C** Choice (A) refers to the formation of the Congress of the Confederation, not to its dissolution. Choice (B) refers only to the Articles of Confederation, not to the Congress of the Confederation or its dissolution. The statement in (D) refers to the transformation of the Congress of the Confederation into the Congress of the United States, but it does not indicate what led to the dissolution of the Congress of the Confederation. Choice (C) correctly references the lack of a strong, centralized power that led to the dissolution of the Congress of the Confederation, making it the best answer choice.

13. **A** The third paragraph focuses primarily on the delegates and the president of the initial Continental Congress, Peyton Randolph, who is described as *considered by many to be the first president of the United States.* This discussion references the earlier statement made by the author in the first paragraph that the first president of the United States is not *the one we are most familiar with today*, who is referenced earlier as George Washington. Choice (A) is the best answer, as it correctly states the paragraph is included to support that earlier statement. Choice (B) is incorrect, as it focuses on John Hancock, who is not the chief focus of this paragraph. Choice (C) is not supported by the paragraph, as there is no indication that there was a *close bond* among the founding fathers, only a political one. Choice (D) is not supported because it goes too far; the paragraph does not indicate anything about the likelihood of subsequent election results.

14. **D** The passage states that John Hancock succeeded Randolph as the president of the initial Continental Congress, during which time the Declaration of Independence was signed and sent, and that he was the first to sign that document. Choice (A) contains extreme language and is not supported by the passage; it states that Hancock *oversaw the writing* of the Declaration of Independence, not that he was the sole author of it. Since the passage states that he *oversaw the writing* of the Declara-

tion of Independence only, (B) can be eliminated. Hancock's death is not discussed in the passage, only Randolph's is, so eliminate (C) as well. That leaves (D). The passage clearly states that Hancock served as president of the first Continental Congress, but it may seem unclear whether or not Hancock served as president of the Second Continental Congress. However, since the author says Hancock was president during the *writing and issue* of the Declaration of Independence and that the document was written during the Second Continental Congress, it can be reasonably inferred that (D) is correct.

15. **B**   In this sentence, the author is discussing the writing of the Declaration of Independence and the subsequent step taken with it, saying that something was done with it *to the British Monarchy*. Since the Declaration of Independence was sent to the British monarchy, the best word will mean something close to "sent" or "given." Since (A), (C), and (D) all have meanings that differ from the meaning of the word "given," they can be eliminated. The choice that best matches this meaning is (B), *delivery*.

16. **C**   In this sentence, *body* refers to the Second Continental Congress. Since the Continental Congress is a group that acts as a single thing, *body* in this context refers to something that means "unit" or "object." Choices (A) and (B) are physical descriptions, so they can be eliminated. Choice (D) means "large," which does not match the meaning of "unit" or "object." The best match to the meaning "unit" or "object" is (C).

17. **A**   In this sentence, *successful* refers to the end of the American Revolution. Choice (B) can be eliminated because the passage states after the Revolution ended, peace and American freedom were attained. The passage does not say democracy was established at this time. Choice (C) can be eliminated because *successful* is not referring to the creation of the subsequent American government. Choice (D) can be eliminated because there is no mention of foreign diplomacy in the passage. Since (A) is the only choice that refers to the end of the war, it is the best answer.

18. **B**   Since this question asks about how the modern-day Congress differs from the Congress of the Confederation, focus on the last two passages which discuss those two entities and POE as you can. The passage states that the current Congress *represents a few more states than its predecessors*, so eliminate (A). The Constitution *laid the groundwork for a stronger central government* and that under that document, *the Congress of the Confederation became the Congress of the United States*, so eliminate (C). Since the passage states that the Congress of the United States *is the same Congress that we elect today*, (D) can be eliminated as well. While it is true that the modern-day Congress was established by a document, the Constitution, it is also true that the Congress of the Confederation was established by a document as well: The Articles of the Confederation. Since both Congresses were established by documents, they do not differ on this point. The correct answer is (B).

19. **C**   This is a very open-ended question, so rely on POE. According to the graphic, the Congress of the United States began on March 4, 1789, while George Washington was inaugurated president of the United States on April 30, 1789. Therefore, the Congress of the United States already existed before the beginning of Washington's presidency, so eliminate (A). The Congress of the United States does not have an end date listed in the graphic, so eliminate (B). The American Revolution

began on April 19, 1775, and Washington was inaugurated on April 30, 1789, which is more than fourteen years later. The war ended with the signing of the Treaty of Paris on September 3, 1783, which is slightly less than six years before Washington's inauguration. These findings both support (C). Because the Continental Congress was established in September of 1784, any power they had would have begun at that point and not in October with the Petition to the King. That eliminates (D), making (C) the best answer.

20. **A** This question is focused on the passage in its entirety and the reason it was written. Because this is an open-ended question, use POE to eliminate incorrect answer choices. Although the author does explain what the FCC's stance is when it comes to net neutrality, (D) is too limited and not the primary purpose of the passage, so eliminate it. The author does not make an argument in this passage, but merely provides factual information to the reader in an unbiased manner, so eliminate (C). Likewise, the author does not try to convince the reader of anything, including the likelihood of net neutrality occurring, so eliminate (B) as well. That leaves (A), which states the author is trying to provide a better understanding of what regulation is and the challenges it faces in this instance. That is supported by the neutral tone and subject matter of the passage, so it is the best answer.

21. **C** The phrase, *Take the internet* connects the first and second paragraph, functioning as a link between the two. The first paragraph discusses the slow response of the government in regards to regulation. The second paragraph discusses how this has occurred with the internet specifically. Choice (A) is incorrect because it contains extreme language and is not supported by the passage; at no point does the passage state that the internet is the *most difficult* technology for the government to regulate. Choice (B) is incorrect, as it contains the deceptive language *television, radio, and cable*, which are mentioned later in the passage and are not relevant to this question. The passage does not discuss the influence of the internet on the *average American day*, so (D) should be eliminated as well. Choice (C) states the phrase provides an example of something that government regulation has not caught up with, which establishes a link between the first two paragraphs. Therefore, (C) is the best answer.

22. **A** In this sentence, the author provides the definition of what a public utility is and clarifies by including the phrase *such as natural gas, electricity, water, and sewage;* consequently, these items are examples of public utilities. Choice (B) contains the deceptive language *overcharged*, which is not discussed until later in the paragraph and is not why the author mentions the two examples in this sentence. Choice (C) is not supported by the passage, as the author never states if these utilities were once unregulated. The words *such as* implies examples, but it does not indicate that all utilities are limited to these examples, so eliminate (D). Only (A) correctly identifies the two examples in the question as clarification for the reader, so it is the best answer.

23. **B** In the previous sentence, internet providers are characterized as *existing for capital gain*. In the following sentence, government regulation would *ensure fair provision*. So currently, the unregulated internet may not be provided in a fair way. In the sentence, *exploit* most nearly means take advantage of. Since (A), (C), and (D) do not match the meaning "take advantage of," they can be eliminated. The only answer choice that means "to take advantage of" is (B).

24. **D** In the provided quote, the FCC states that it wants to ensure that better service is not provided to those who can pay more (*paid prioritization*) and that internet providers do not block lawful content. Choice (A) is deceptive since the quote does reference people being able to *go where they want, when they want.* However, the author is applying that freedom to the internet, not literal movement of the public. The same is true of (B), as the quote contains a reference to *innovators.* Although that is mentioned at the end of the quote, it is not what the FCC is mainly concerned with, so eliminate (B). Choice (C) also contains deceptive language since the quote contains the word *mobile*, which refers to broadband as opposed to people. Only (D) contains the main concerns of the FCC, so it is the best answer.

25. **D** For open-ended questions, use POE to eliminate incorrect answers. Choice (A) states that the need to regulate criminal activity on the internet has been a recent consideration. However, earlier in the passage the author states that restrictions have been limited to criminal activity up to this point, so (A) is incorrect. Choice (B) is deceptive, as the passage does state that it will be difficult to enforce regulation, but not that the FCC will have trouble convincing the government to do so. Choice (C) can be eliminated, as the FCC regulates communications, not other public utilities. The best answer is (D), which is supported when the passage states that the tricky part of internet regulation is *how to enforce that regulation.*

26. **D** The previous question asked about the FCC. Choice (A) references a line that is about the U.S. government in general, and not the FCC specifically, so it is not the best support for the previous answer. Choice (B) references public utilities that are regulated, and it is not relevant to the regulation of the internet. Choice (C) refers to the fact that the internet has only recently been under consideration as a utility by the government, which does not offer any insight into the difficulty of regulating it. Choice (D) describes why the internet is so difficult for the government to regulate, which supports the previous answer that the internet is difficult to regulate. Therefore, the most supportive answer is (D).

27. **C** On EXCEPT questions, the best approach is to start with POE based on what you have already read. The passage referred to two different types of regulation—criminal and commercial. In the paragraph discussing criminal regulation, the author mentions *gambling*, so (D) will not be correct. In the paragraphs discussing the need for commercial regulation, the concerns are over internet providers providing slower internet and blocking content for those who pay less. This eliminates (A) and (B). The only thing that is not mentioned in the passage that should be regulated is (C), *file protection.* Therefore, (C) is the best answer.

28. **D** In the sentence, the author is stating that regulating internet provision is not very easy to do. So in this context, *tricky* means not easy. Because (A), (B), and (C) do not match those meanings at all, they will not be the correct answer. The only possible answer for this question is (D), *difficult.*

29. **D** The sentence is stating that based on features of animals, the researchers were able to draw conclusions about what type of dinosaur it was. Therefore, *surmise* means to draw conclusions. Choices (A) and (B) are not words that mean to draw conclusion, so they are incorrect. When comparing (C) and (D), (C) is clearly a more definite word. To know something is to be certain about it. Since the researchers are only making educated guesses based on their findings, the best choice is (D), *conjecture.*

30. **B** In the fifth paragraph, the passage states that Case and Martin believed the finding could be classified as a theropod based on the *shape of the teeth and features of the feet*. Since teeth and feet count as oral and skeletal characteristics, the best supported answer is (B). Although the location, (A), and the time period, (C), are both mentioned in regards to this finding, they are included as pieces of additional information rather than support for the type of dinosaur. Choice (D) refers to a pelvis bone, which pertains to the discovery discussed later in the passage. The best answer here is (B).

31. **B** The answer to the previous question is (B), *skeletal and oral aspects of the remains*. Choice (A) does discuss the type of dinosaur the researchers believe they found, but does not offer any evidence of why that conclusion was made. Choice (B) is from the beginning of the fourth paragraph and references the physical features of the skeletal remains, which offers strong support for the answer to the previous question. Choice (C) discusses the environment that the creature would have inhabited, but nothing about what characteristics likely identify the dinosaur. Choice (D) is from a paragraph that describes the findings of William Hammer, not those of Case and Martin, so this choice can be eliminated. The best answer here is (B).

32. **C** The author mentions the film *Jurassic Park* at the end of a sentence discussing dinosaurs that the newly discovered remains are likely related to. Thus, the author is offering the example of *Jurassic Park* to try to illustrate for the reader a clearer picture of the newly discovered dinosaur. Choice (A) is not supported by the passage, as the author does not state whether he liked or disliked the film. The author does not imply that *Jurassic Park* is anything but a film, so (B) is also incorrect. No time period is mentioned in relation to the film *Jurassic Park*, so (D) does not make sense as an answer. The best supporting answer is (C), in that the author is offering an example to help relate the discovery to something more familiar to the reader.

33. **D** The passage does not provide a great deal of information about the specific researchers, so this is a good POE opportunity. Based on the job descriptions of the three researchers, all have differing specialties. Also, only the team lead by Case and Martin discovered the remains of a carnivorous dinosaur; the team lead by Hammer discovered a plant-eating dinosaur. So (A) is not correct. The passage does not mention grants or funding, so (B) should also be eliminated. Although the passage clearly states that both discoveries were located in Antarctica, there is nothing in the passage that supports the claim that the researchers held the belief it was the "best" place for their research. Eliminate (C). Each of the three researchers had an educational institution included in the job description provided, so (D) is best supported.

34. **B** This paragraph gives a description of where the remains were found, which was on the sea floor. Since this was a land-dwelling dinosaur, the author offers an explanation from the research team as to how the remains could have ended up in that location. The purpose of this explanation is best indicated by (B). Choice (A) is not supported by the passage since marine lizards are not referred to as the primary predator of theropods. Choice (C) does not make sense, as there is no danger mentioned to the researchers themselves in this paragraph. The passage does not go on to discuss the discovery of a marine lizard, so (D) is also incorrect.

35. **A** This is a very open-ended argument, so use POE. The passage describes the two discoveries as occurring against incredible odds, which is consistent with (A). Keep it. The passage does note that the dinosaur Hammer's team discovered lived millions of years before the other, but no mention of relative significance is made. Eliminate (B). The passage discusses Antarctica, but only to state that it is the location where both discoveries occurred. Eliminate (C). The author mentions birds in relation to dinosaurs, stating that birds are direct descendants of theropods. Choice (D) is deceptive, as it includes language-similar phrasing, but says the opposite: Dinosaurs are descendants of birds. Eliminate (D).

36. **C** This sentence is discussing how Mt. Kirkpatrick was a riverbed until tectonic activity resulted in it becoming more *skyward*. In this context, *elevated* is used to mean "pushed" or "sent" toward the sky. Because (A) and (B) do not match these meanings at all, they can be eliminated. Between (C) and (D), (C) is a more literal match to "pushed" or "sent" toward the sky. The best answer is (C).

37. **C** Although theropods shared more characteristics with mammals than reptiles, this does not prove that theropods (including the newly discovered species) are more closely related to mammals. Choice (A) is incorrect. The passage states that birds are the direct descendants of theropods, eliminating (B). There is no evidence in either the passage or graphic for (D). However, the graphic does state that theropods (including tyrannosaurs) maintained a constant body temperature. Choice (C) is correct.

38. **C** According to the author of the first passage, vaccines are beneficial and the risks minimal. While she clearly argues in favor of vaccines and believes that children should be vaccinated, she does not address the best way to convince those who are anti-vaccine of this fact. This makes (A) unsupported and therefore incorrect. Although the author clearly believes that the use of vaccines would help to decrease instances of childhood diseases and deaths resulting from those diseases, the author does not address *all instances of childhood death*. This makes (B) extreme and therefore incorrect. The author does state at the end of the passage that the author has a family and is in favor of mandatory vaccination, which would indicate that the author is likely to vaccinate her own children, as stated in (C). The passage provides no information regarding the author's vaccine history, so (D) is not correct. The best answer is (C).

39. **C** The correct answer to the previous question is (C), she herself is likely to vaccinate her own children. The author is clearly in favor of vaccinations, so the line reference that will best support this choice is one that directly references her own children. The only way to show this is the last line, which states that the author is *an American with children of [her] own*. She then goes on to say that she is in favor of mandatory vaccination, so it cannot be that she is against vaccinations for her own children. This makes (C) the best answer. While all other answer choices are pro-vaccine, they do not specifically support how the author feels about vaccines for her own children.

40. **D** The reactions that are being listed in this sentence, *anaphylaxis, illness, or even death,* are harmful ones. Since vaccines are meant to protect people from harmful illnesses, these *adverse reactions* are not what the doctors are hoping to accomplish through vaccinations. The best meaning for the word *adverse* in this context is "unwanted," "unintended," or "harmful." Choices (A), (B), and (C) do not match either of these meanings. *Undesirable* matches "unwanted" or "unintended," making (D) the best answer.

41.   **A**   The third paragraph in the first passage discusses the fact there can be harmful drawbacks to vaccines. However, the author makes it clear that these drawbacks are not serious or widespread enough to deter people from vaccinating their children. The answer that best matches this stance is (A). Choice (D) is supported by information in the fourth paragraph, not the third paragraph, so it can be eliminated. Both (B) and (C) are deceptive. Choice (B) discusses the wide range of the number of people harmed, but not only is that mentioned in a different paragraph, it is also not indicated that physicians are attempting to avoid accountability. Eliminate (B). Although the vaccination schedule brought up in (C) is also mentioned, it too is referenced in another part of the passage, and it is not stated that physicians are strict about it.

42.   **B**   In Passage 2, Socrates is mentioned when the author includes a quote from him. The author uses this quote to introduce the idea that people may not always know as much as they think they do, which is a central theme of the author's argument. Since the FDA is never mentioned in the passage, (D) cannot be correct. It is also never stated that Socrates influenced scientific and medical research in any way, so (C) can also be eliminated. The author does not mention Socrates because he is a well-known scholar, but because the quote is appropriate for the point she is making. So (A) is also not the best answer. Since the author is using the quote to introduce the reasoning behind her argument, the best supported answer is (B).

43.   **A**   When the author says *there is never a time that this fact is as salient as when it comes to the health of the most vulnerable in our society*, she is referring to how relevant Socrates's quote still is when it comes to vaccines and children's health. What she means by *salient* is "pertinent." So the correct answer will match the meaning of *pertinent*, as in (A), *relevant*.

44.   **C**   Formaldehyde is mentioned in the third paragraph of Passage 2, in which the author lists potentially harmful ingredients that are included in various vaccines. It is used as an example of one of these ingredients, and it is described as having very harmful short-term effects and unknown long-term effects. Since the author is including formaldehyde as a harmful ingredient in the short term and possibly the long term, (B) cannot be correct. The author does not cite any specific instances when a vaccine containing formaldehyde resulted in the death of a patient, so eliminate (D). The author does not state that she thinks doctors actively manipulate, only that they aren't as knowledgeable as they may seem when it comes to vaccines, so (A) is also incorrect. The answer that best matches the information provided is (C), that formaldehyde has known effects, the short-term ones, and unknown effects, the possible long-term ones.

45.   **B**   This question is very open-ended, so the best approach to use is POE. In the last paragraph, the author states that while she believes vaccines can help, she thinks it is possible they may cause an unknown amount of harm. There is no scientific evidence offered, so eliminate (C). No doctors are mentioned in the final paragraph, so (D) cannot be correct. Although the author does acknowledge that vaccines can be helpful, she goes on to say that they may cause known harm. So while she makes a concession, she does not undermine her own argument in the end. This eliminates (A) and best supports (B).

46. **C** The first passage focuses on the benefits of vaccines. Choices (B) and (D) do not match this information for Passage 1, so they are both incorrect. The second passage focuses on the lack of knowledge regarding the possible harm that can come from vaccines. However, the passage does not provide any specific instances of vaccinations having caused harm, so (A) is incorrect for the central idea of Passage 2. This leaves (C) as the best answer for the central idea for both passages.

47. **D** In the first passage, the author quotes the American Academy of Pediatrics multiple times: *most child vaccines are 90%-99% effective in preventing disease* and *one per several hundred thousand to one per million vaccinations.* In the second passage, the author quotes Socrates at the beginning: *I know that I know nothing.* The correct answer is (D), as both passages contain a quotation.

Chapter 6
Reading Test
Drill 2

Reading Test

60 MINUTES, 47 QUESTIONS

Turn to Section 1 of your answer sheet to answer the questions in this section.

DIRECTIONS

Each passage or pair of passages below is followed by a number of questions. After reading each passage or pair, choose the best answer to each question based on what is stated or implied in the passage or passages and in any accompanying graphics (such as a table or graph).

Questions 1-9 are based on the following passage.

The following is an excerpt from *The Social Contract,* a book written by Jean-Jacques Rousseau in 1762. Rousseau was a Genevan writer, philosopher, and composer whose philosophical writings profoundly influenced modern political thinking.

Let us take it that men have reached the point at which the obstacles to their survival in the state of nature overpower each individual's resources for
Line maintaining himself in that state. So this primitive
5 condition can't go on; the human race will perish unless it changes its manner of existence.

Now, men can't create new forces; they can only bring together ones that already exist and steer them. So their only way to preserve themselves is to unite
10 a number of forces so that they are jointly powerful enough to deal with the obstacles. They have to bring these forces into play in such a way that they act together in a single thrust.

For forces to *add up* in this way, many people have
15 to work together. But for each, man's force and liberty are what he chiefly needs for his survival; so how can he put them into this collective effort without harming his own interest and neglecting the care he owes to himself? This difficulty, in the version of it that arises
20 for my present subject, can be put like this:

Find a form of association that will bring the whole common force to bear on defending and protecting each associate's person and goods, doing this in such a way that each of them, while united himself with all,
25 still obeys only himself and remains as free as before.

There's the basic problem that is solved by the social contract. The clauses of this contract settled by the nature of the act that the slightest change would make them all null and void; so that although they may never
30 have been explicitly stated, they are everywhere the same and everywhere tacitly accepted and recognized, until the social compact is violated and each individual regains his original rights and resumes his natural liberty, while losing the liberty-by-agreement which
35 had been his reason for renouncing them.

Properly understood, these clauses come down to one—the total alienation of each associate, together with all his rights, to the whole community. This may seem drastic, but three features of it make it
40 reasonable.

I. Because each individual gives himself *entirely*, what is happening here for any one individual is the same as what is happening for each of the others, and, because this is so, no one has any interest in making
45 things tougher for everyone but himself.

II. Because the alienation is made without reserve, i.e., without anything being held back, the union is as complete as it can be, and no associate has anything more to demand. To see why the association *has to* be
50 done in this way, consider what the situation would be if the individuals retained certain rights. In the absence of any superior to decide issues about this, each individual would be his own judge across the board; this would continue the state of nature, and the
55 association would necessarily become inoperative or tyrannical.

CONTINUE ▶

III. Each man in giving himself to everyone gives himself to no one; and the right over himself that others get is matched by the right that he gets over 60 each of them. So he gains as much as he loses, and *also* gains extra force for the preservation of what he has.

Filtering out the inessentials, we'll find that the social compact comes down to this: Each of us puts his person and all his power in common under the 65 supreme direction of the general will, and, in our corporate capacity, we receive each member as an indivisible part of the whole.

1

As used in line 13, "thrust" most nearly means

A) shove.

B) direction.

C) gist.

D) assault.

2

The passage most strongly suggests that which of the following is true of the author?

A) He believes that when people unite together, they are stronger than when they remain separate.

B) He thinks that people should not be as selfish as their nature inherently makes them.

C) He trusts that once a group comes together in shared understanding, they will never break their word.

D) He asserts that once society develops to the point of capitalism and corporations, we will have more to bind us together.

3

Which choice provides the best evidence for the answer to the previous question?

A) Lines 7–8 ("Now, men … them")

B) Lines 15–19 ("But for … himself?")

C) Lines 57–61 ("Each man … has")

D) Lines 63–67 ("Each of … whole")

4

As used in line 31, "tacitly" most nearly means

A) delicately.

B) skillfully.

C) obviously.

D) implicitly.

5

Over the course of the passage, the main focus of the narrative shifts from

A) the natural state of humanity to the socially evolved relationships humanity can create.

B) the capacity for violence that humanity has to the capacity for mercy that humanity has.

C) the desire to express one's independence to the desire to fit in.

D) the negative aspects of the social contract to the positive aspects of the social contract.

6

The "forces" the author refers to throughout the passage refer to

A) armies of men.

B) solely the physical power one person has over another.

C) the ability of the group to coerce members into joining.

D) the physical and mental capacities that we are all naturally endowed with.

The passage most strongly suggests that what be done in order for people to unite together?

A) They must be willing to give up all liberties.

B) They must enter into an agreement in which individual rights are committed for the sake of communal right.

C) They must bring their forces to bear upon one another, so that the strongest force can prevail and unite the community together.

D) They must put their survival and the survival of their families above all else.

What claim about force and liberty is best supported by the passage?

A) Force and liberty are the most valued assets in a system of commercial exchange.

B) By giving up force and liberty, a person ultimately sacrifices his or her natural claims to independence and becomes a slave to the will of the people.

C) If someone freely gives his or her force and liberty in order attain a shared force and liberty, then nothing is being given up.

D) Force and liberty are of little importance, as they are found primarily in nature and have little to do with civilized, structured society.

The central idea of the passage is that

A) it is better to have known what it is to be free and then be enslaved than to have never known freedom at all.

B) it is in man's best interest to conform to society, or else he risks being stripped of his liberty.

C) it is not enough to merely live in harmony with one another; a legal contract must be entered into to ensure that way of life will endure.

D) by relinquishing individual rights to a communal power, the rights of all are enhanced and even more greatly secured.

CONTINUE

Questions 10-18 are based on the following passage.

The following passage discusses the cultural significance of the number 13 both historically and in the present day.

Every culture comes with its own superstitions and taboos. Certain things that seem so innocuous to us in the modern day that they hardly warrant emotion were
Line once viewed with irrational fear. And sometimes, this
5 fear carried on even into the modern day. Such is the case with Friday, the number 13, and Friday the 13th.

Historically, in many cultures, Friday has been treated as an unlucky day. This is especially true of Western, Christian cultures. The original references
10 to Friday as an unlucky day are based on two biblical occurrences believed to have taken place on a Friday: the day that Adam and Eve ate from the tree of knowledge and the crucifixion of Jesus. This superstition was believed most firmly by Christian
15 maritime cultures, who associated bad luck in sailing with Friday. It was strongly believed that any ship that departed from harbor on a Friday would have ill-luck during the voyage, and commercial sailing schedules were set around this belief.
20 The fear of the number 13 is much more common across the globe, and much more standard than is the fear of Friday. It is what is called a specific phobia, because sufferers are afraid of 13 specifically, rather than a larger range of fears. This phobia is called
25 *triskaidekaphobia*. This fear also has biblical roots for the western, Christian cultures that fear it (which, interestingly enough, does not include Italian culture). There were 13 people present at the Last Supper, which occurred the day before Jesus' death, and to
30 this day, many believe that sitting down to a table of 13 people will bring death. Also, the number 13 was highly inconvenient for church officials in the Middle Ages when it came to the number of moon cycles in a year. The Greco-Roman calendar was based primarily
35 on a twelve-moon year, as a typical century has 63 years with twelve moons and 37 with 13 moons. As all official religious events were scheduled on a twelve-moon year, the inclusion of a 13th moon proved very problematic for the monks. It was they who were in
40 charge of keeping the calendar, and the discrepancy caused many issues throughout the year for them. Hence, the number was viewed as a highly unlucky one for the more educated members of Christian societies. But obviously the fear spread and continues to this

45 day. It is not uncommon for buildings to omit the 13th floor of buildings or rooms numbered 13 by referring to them as 12A, M (for the 13th letter of the alphabet), or skipping that number in the floor numbering pattern altogether. The number is also avoided as an
50 interstate highway number.

But it is the combination of Friday and the number 13 that constitutes one of the most well-known superstitions still in existence today. The superstition of Friday the 13th has also been given a name due to
55 the widespread belief in it: *paraskevidekatriaphobia*. And it truly is a combination of the two discrete fears that make this fear what it is. As anthropologist Phillips Stevens, Jr. put it, "There were 13 people at the table and the 13th was Jesus. The last supper was
60 on a Thursday, and the next day was Friday, the day of crucifixion. When 13 and Friday come together, it is a double whammy."

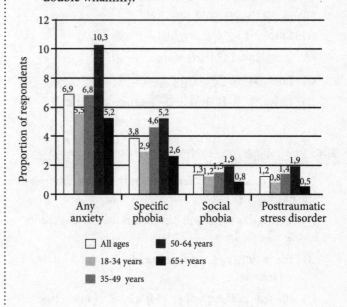

10

As used in line 3, "warrant" most nearly means

A) ensure.

B) arrest.

C) licenses.

D) deserve.

11

Which of the following supports the belief that the number 13 is unlucky?

A) Judas was the last person to attend the Last Supper, becoming the 13th guest at dinner.

B) The fact that there were more often 13 moons in a year made the twelve-year calendar an unfortunate choice.

C) The number 13 was an inconvenient astronomical occurrence for the religious authority.

D) Adam and Eve are believed to have partaken of the fruit of knowledge on a Friday.

12

Which choice provides the best evidence for the answer to the previous question?

A) Lines 9-13 ("The original … Jesus")

B) Lines 28-31 ("There were … death")

C) Lines 31-34 ("Also, the … year")

D) Lines 34-36 ("The Greco-Roman … moons")

13

It can be reasonably inferred from the information in the passage that

A) to this day ships will not set sail on a Friday if it is at all avoidable.

B) the majority of superstitions are based on biblical references.

C) the fear of the number 13 is more common than is the fear of Friday.

D) the Greco-Roman calendar was altered centuries ago to accommodate the differing number of moons that occur each year.

14

The central idea of the passage is

A) a common fear is based on two separate fears that trace their origin to the same root cause.

B) it is more common to fear the number 13 than it is to fear Friday.

C) without the influence of religious authority during the Middle Ages, it is doubtful whether or not the fear of Friday the 13th would ever have existed.

D) of all cultures, maritime cultures tend to be the most religious and most superstitious.

15

As used in line 52, "constitutes" most nearly means

A) establishes.

B) starts.

C) charters.

D) conditions.

16

In the context of the passage, the author's use of the phrase "which, interestingly enough, does not include Italian culture" (lines 26–27) is primarily meant to convey

A) confusion over what number is considered to be unlucky by the Italians.

B) curiosity in a seemingly odd exception to the cultures that share a belief in the unlucky nature of 13.

C) distrust in Italy due to its lack of conformity to other cultures' beliefs.

D) interest in why the seed of the Roman Empire would not be aware of the biblical origins of a belief.

CONTINUE ➡

17

The author most likely includes the names of the phobias associated with certain fears in the passage in order to

A) indicate that they are highly complex conditions that require names in order to properly reference them.

B) demonstrate the prevalent nature of the fears.

C) impress upon the reader the importance of knowing the correct names and definitions when discussing various topics in order to avoid confusion.

D) share with the reader little-known facts in order to maintain their interest in an otherwise dry subject matter.

18

Which of the following is supported by the passage and the graph?

A) *Triskaidekaphobia* is most common among those 50 to 64 years of age.

B) Because it is the combination of two fears, the fear of Friday the 13th occurs at twice the rate as the fear of the number 13 or the fear of Friday.

C) Specific phobias are unique to Western, predominantly Christian cultures.

D) Those 65 years and older are least likely to be plagued by specific phobias, because they are less likely to subscribe to Western values.

CONTINUE

Questions 19-28 are based on the following passages.

Both Passage 1 and Passage 2 discuss a mysterious event in American history.

Passage 1

History is full of puzzles that strike a chord in the human imagination, regardless of how unsolvable they may be. No event illustrates the lure of the unknowable
Line more than the disappearance of the *Mary Celeste*.
5   The *Mary Celeste* was an American merchant brigantine. On November 7, 1872, it set sail from New York harbor in route to Genoa to deliver 1,701 barrels of crude alcohol. The ship was captained by Benjamin Briggs and carried a crew of seven men, as well
10 Brigg's wife and young daughter. It was discovered on December 4 completely abandoned.

    Although it appeared that the sails and rigging of the ship had received minimal damage and that two hatch doors had been broken, it was in otherwise
15 completely sailable condition. The cargo was mostly intact, there was a six-month supply of food and water, and there were no visible signs of panic, violence, or fire. The ship's sole lifeboat was missing along with navigational equipment and many of the ship's papers,
20 but the passengers' valuables were still present. The sea log was present, with the last entry having been made ten days previously. But not a single soul was found on board, nor was one ever seen or heard from again.

    What would make an entire crew, and a captain
25 with his wife and child aboard, abandon a sailable ship with no evident reason? Did the crew mutiny and then abandon the ship? Did pirates attack and leave the cargo? Many reasons have been put forth but none has ever been widely accepted, and it would be very
30 difficult for any to be proven correctly.

Passage 2

The enigmatic history of the *Mary Celeste* has long intrigued historians and maritime experts since 1872. Many theories have been postulated regarding its abandonment, ranging from the levelheaded to the
35 ludicrous. In terms of the latter, it has been suggested that the ship was abandoned for such reasons as underwater sonic earthquakes, giant squid attacks, and even drunken mutiny (did the crew mutiny itself?).

    The most likely reason seems clear now, but it
40 would have easily slipped by the hasty investigation that took place after the *Mary Celeste's* discovery. When

discovered, it was found that nine of the 1,701 alcohol cargo barrels were constructed of red oak, while the rest were constructed of white oak. All nine of the
45 red oak barrels were emptied—the only barrels to be found so. Although it is possible that the alcohol was drunk by the crew, it is doubtful such a large amount of unrefined alcohol could be so quickly. And even if the crew did drink the alcohol, would they then kill
50 the captain and his family only to abandon the ship entirely? There is a more likely explanation for both the disappearance of the alcohol and all aboard. Because red oak is more porous than white oak, it would have been very easy for alcoholic fumes to escape from the
55 barrels and buildup down in the hold. If a great enough buildup occurred, then the hatch doors would be forced ajar. If this occurred, the most likely reaction of the captain and crew would be to abandon ship for fear of the explosive capability of such a buildup of gas.

60   In such a case, it would be common practice to load into the lifeboat, tether it to the ship, and float a safe distance away until the risk of explosion appeared to abate. Due to the complete disappearance of the crew, with little taken with them, it is probably that the
65 tether keeping the ship and lifeboat connected was not made strongly enough, resulting in the loss of the ten souls aboard.

19

Which of the following is mentioned by both of the authors?

A) The number of cargo barrels aboard

B) The name of the captain of the *Mary Celeste*

C) The date the *Mary Celeste* set sail

D) The natural phenomenon behind the disappearance

CONTINUE ➤

20

Passage 1 most strongly suggests which of the following about the *Mary Celeste*?

A) There was no identifiable reason that the crew could not have completed the voyage with the boat as it was discovered.

B) The *Mary Celeste* serves as strong evidence as to why women and children should not be taken as passengers on possibly dangerous expeditions.

C) The majority of reasons suggested for the dereliction of the *Mary Celeste* should be dismissed as meritless.

D) It would not be difficult to discover the true reason behind the disappearance of those aboard the *Mary Celeste* if there were motivation to do so.

21

Which choice provides the best evidence for the answer in the previous question?

A) Lines 8–10 ("The ship … daughter")

B) Lines 12–15 ("Although it … condition")

C) Lines 28–30 ("Many reasons … correctly")

D) Lines 33–35 ("Many theories … ludicrous")

22

The main rhetorical effect of the series of the three questions in the last paragraph (lines 24–30) of Passage 1 is to

A) stress the mysterious nature of the desertion of the *Mary Celeste*.

B) demonstrate the ignorance of maritime historians, both in the 1800s and the modern day.

C) point out that you never know what is behind the actions of a certain individual or group.

D) increase the intensity of the need to determine the true story of the *Mary Celeste*.

23

As used in line 31, "enigmatic" most nearly means

A) straightforward.

B) interesting.

C) disappointing.

D) perplexing.

24

The author of Passage 2 references "giant squid" (line 37) in order to

A) contradict an opinion offered in the previous passage.

B) provide an instance of a natural occurrence.

C) give an example of an assertion made earlier in the paragraph.

D) offer a detailed description of an alternative theory.

25

In the context of Passage 2, the author's use of the phrase "did the crew mutiny itself" (line 38) is primarily meant to convey

A) confusion over how everyone on board the *Mary Celeste* disappeared.

B) mockery of those who are not intelligent enough to have solved the mystery of the *Mary Celeste*.

C) disbelief in a proposed solution to the puzzle of a derelict ship.

D) lost hope in the certainty of the inevitable death of the crew that was lost at sea.

26

As used in line 57, "ajar" most nearly means

A) off.

B) open.

C) shut.

D) gouged.

CONTINUE ▶

27

Which of the following choices best supports Passage 2's author's reasoning that the passengers on board the *Mary Celeste* left temporarily and had intended to return?

A) Lines 18–20 ("The ship's … present")

B) Lines 20–22 ("The sea … previously")

C) Lines 22–23 ("But not … again")

D) Lines 24–26 ("What would … reason?")

28

The central ideas of the two passages differ in that Passage 1

A) discusses a historical description of a mystery, while Passage 2 discusses the various ways a ship may be abandoned.

B) discusses the individual souls who were lost at sea, while Passage 2 discusses the way in which alcohol can emit noxious fumes.

C) discusses the facts of an unsolved maritime disappearance, while Passage 2 discusses a probable reason for the abandonment of a specific ship.

D) discusses the cargo-related cause of the loss of a crew and captain, while Passage 2 discusses the background of an ill-fated ship.

CONTINUE ➡

Questions 29-37 are based on the following passage.

The following passage discusses three diseases that have the unique characteristic of leaving signs of their pathology on the human skeleton.

When studying ancient human remains, it is often difficult to tell how the people of those remains were met with their end. Unless there are clear signs of how
Line death may have occurred, it can be impossible. When
5 people die from natural causes, rarely is there evidence of the affliction or disease left on the skeletal remains. Luckily, for paleopathologists, this is not always the case.

Paleopathology is the study of ancient diseases. Certain diseases that were common in the ancient
10 world, and still are today, leave clear signs of their pathology on the skeleton itself. The three primary diseases for which this phenomenon is known to occur most often are leprosy, tuberculosis, and syphilis.

Leprosy is a chronic infectious disease that is
15 caused by the parasite *Mycobacterium leprae* and dates back to 4000 B.C. Once leprosy has been contracted, it begins to breakdown the skin and nerve cells, resulting in a lack of sensation and greater occurrence of injury. Injury commonly results in the loss of
20 fingers and toes, due to the lack of pain reception and high utility of those body parts. The disease will then attack the skeleton itself, infecting bone marrow. This weakens the skeleton, leading to a common pattern of deformation.

25 Leprosy is not highly contagious. It is spread through long-term contact with individuals who have it, either through long-term contact with infected skin or through infected skin cells or ejected mucous being released into the environment. Because the parasite
30 has a low rate of contagion and takes years of close contact to spread, it is common to find groupings of skeletal remains with signs of leprosy in isolated, small populations rather than large, dispersed ones.

Tuberculosis, another disease that leaves clear
35 marks on the skeleton, is much older, more contagious, and deadlier than leprosy. Dating as far back at 10,200 B.C., tuberculosis was most likely first contracted from ingesting infected animal products. Once a human is infected, that person can easily spread the disease by
40 releasing infected mucous into the air when coughing. The symptoms of tuberculosis are chronic cough accompanied with bloody sputum, fever, night sweats, and weight loss.

Tuberculosis has a long period of maturation, up
45 to two decades, during which the body goes through cycles of weakening and recovery. From its onset, the bacteria that causes tuberculosis penetrates into the growth areas of spongy bone tissue, the cancellous tissue, near the knee and hip joints and the spine.
50 During a weakening period, the bacteria will begin to slowly destroy the bone in those areas; during recovery periods, the bone will heal itself. These alternating cycles lead to calcified lesions on those areas of the skeleton, clearly indicating the presence of the
55 disease to paleopathologists. Tuberculosis can also be established through DNA testing, a unique attribute.

Compared to the previous two diseases, syphilis is far and away the most contagious and deadly and the most clearly marked on skeletal remains of
60 the untreated. Syphilis progresses over four stages: primary, secondary, latent, and tertiary. The first three stages present with relatively minimal and simple symptoms; in primary there is the presentation of a single chancre (a ulceration with no sensation),
65 in secondary there is a rash that presents on the hands and feet, and in latent there is no presentation of symptoms. But the tertiary stage, which occurs anywhere from three to fifteen years after infection, presents with symptoms that include gummas (soft,
70 tissue like balls of inflammation on the body), nervous system decay, seizure, dementia, and aneurysm.

Despite the seemingly innocuous symptoms of the first stages, indications of syphilis on the skeleton begin immediately after infection. During the primary
75 and secondary stages, the bone marrow of the infected swells, producing lesions on the bone. This is typically seen on the skull and tibiae. In the later stages, the bone literally begins to decay, resulting in pore-shaped lesions that have been described as looking like
80 "worm-holes" by paleopathologists.

Paleopathology, though limited in its application to very specific diseases, plays an important role in both deciphering the past and helping to prepare for the future. The three diseases listed above are still very
85 much a concern for both the developed and developing worlds today. With a greater understanding of the history, rates, and pattern of infection of these diseases, we will be better enabled to combat them more effectively now and in the future.

CONTINUE ▶

Instances of Leprosy 2010

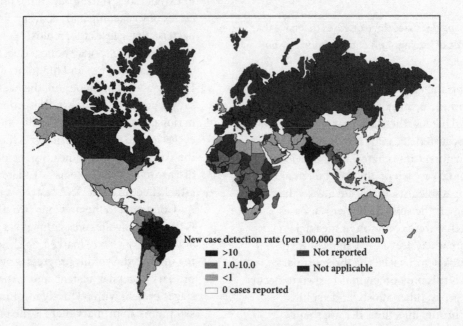

New case detection rate (per 100,000 population)

- ■ >10
- ■ 1.0-10.0
- ■ <1
- □ 0 cases reported
- ■ Not reported
- ■ Not applicable

29

The tone of the passage is best described as

A) pedantic.

B) judgmental.

C) descriptive.

D) conciliatory.

30

Based on the information in the first paragraph (lines 1–7), it can be reasonably inferred that

A) it is easy to identify the cause of death for ancient human remains when the cause of death was not natural.

B) paleopathology is considered a lucky profession by many in the archaeology field.

C) ancient populations often died of undiagnosed cancers that left no marks on the skeleton.

D) a cause of death cannot be determined for some skeletal remains.

31

As used in line 18, "sensation" most nearly means

A) stir.

B) fuss.

C) perception.

D) wonder.

32

As used in line 36, "contracted" most nearly means

A) diminished.

B) restricted.

C) commissioned.

D) caught.

33

In the fifth paragraph (lines 34–43), the author draws a distinction between

A) tuberculosis in animals and humans.

B) tuberculosis and leprosy.

C) tuberculosis and syphilis.

D) knee and hip joints and the spine.

CONTINUE ▶

34

The author's reference to the "unique attribute" in lines 56-57 primarily serves to

A) indicate that tuberculosis is the most distinctive paleopathological disease.

B) imply that other paleopathological diseases cannot be verified through DNA testing.

C) explain why tuberculosis is the most commonly found paleopathological disease.

D) counter the assertion that syphilis is the most easily identifiable paleopathological disease.

35

In discussing the last paleopathological disease reviewed, syphilis, the author of the passage suggests that

A) it is easier to identify indicators of syphilis on ancient human remains than the indicators of other paleopathological diseases.

B) if syphilis is treated and cured by the latent period, both the skeleton and body experience little to no symptoms of its presences.

C) syphilis takes a longer time to progress than tuberculosis does, despite being more deadly.

D) the three major stages of tuberculosis are the primary, secondary, and tertiary.

36

Which of the following line references provides the most support for the answer to the previous question?

A) Lines 57–60 ("Compared to … untreated")

B) Lines 61–63 ("The first … symptoms")

C) Lines 67–71 ("But the … aneurysm")

D) Lines 72–74 ("Despite the … infection")

37

Which of the following can be reasonably inferred from the information in the passage and the graphic?

A) Due to its low contagion rate, it is unlikely the number of leprosy cases in the United States will increase in future years.

B) Due to its low contagion rate, it is likely that the current number of leprosy cases that exist in the United States will decrease in future years.

C) Due to its high contagion rate, it is likely that the occurrence of leprosy in India will remain greater than 10 cases per 100,000 people.

D) Due to its high contagion rate, occurrences of leprosy are likely to increase across central and western Africa.

CONTINUE ▶

Questions 38–47 are based on the following passage.

The following passage is excerpted from the article "How to grow mussels," originally published by the National Science Foundation on September 25, 2014.

Blue mussels, *mytilus edulis*, live on northern Atlantic shores in the area between high and low tides. "Mussels are one of the most significant filter-
Line feeders in the marine environment," said Brian Beal, a
5 marine ecologist at the University of Maine at Machias. "They are responsible not only for efficiently producing high-quality protein but for cleaning the waters around them through their feeding activities."

Because many creatures—especially humans—
10 enjoy eating blue mussels, farmers grow mussels using aquaculture, or aquatic farming. More than 650,000 pounds of blue mussels were cultured and harvested in Maine in 2012, according to the state's Department of Marine Resources.

15 Young mussels may be cultivated in the wild, or they may grow on ropes that are submerged in culture tanks, where they are protected from storms and predators. Once the mussels reach a certain size, they are moved into ocean pens to mature.

20 But practitioners often struggle in their efforts to increase the number, size, and overall health of their mussels. Like many farmers, they turn to science and engineering to improve their harvest.

Beal, along with a team of National Science
25 Foundation (NSF)-funded researchers at the University of Maine at Machias and the Downeast Institute, is investigating the growing conditions and practices that will reliably yield healthy and plentiful blue mussels.

"Our goal is to develop methods in the hatchery
30 to create consistent quantities of seed-size mussel juveniles," Beal said. "At present, mussel farmers rely on wild settlement, which can be very spotty from year to year and from place to place." Maine's annual harvest of cultured blue mussels commonly varies by
35 hundreds of thousands of pounds.

Young mussels go through several stages of development. After swimming for their first few weeks of life, mussel larvae adhere to an underwater surface such as a rope. They attach themselves using byssus
40 threads, which are flexible strands of protein.

"A narrow range of seawater temperatures combined with relatively high salinities results in healthy, active juveniles," Beal said, "and different phytoplankton diets fed to the swimming larvae affect
45 their ability to settle effectively onto substrates such as rope."

Beal's team plans to use what they learn about blue mussel development to optimize how many and how well larvae secure themselves to rope used in
50 aquaculture. They are now conducting field studies to examine the effects of stocking densities on mussel growth and survival.

The researchers also are investigating exactly when to transition the young mussels into ocean pens and
55 where in the pens they grow best.

With better understanding of their cultivation, the researchers and their partner New DHC, an aquaculture company, hope to improve commercial prospects for sustainably grown blue mussels.

60 "A consistent seed supply also will allow aquaculturists to create business plans that project their annual production more realistically," Beal explained.

The collaboration is supported by the NSF
65 Partnerships for Innovation program, which stimulates regional innovation based on science and engineering discoveries.

In speaking of Beal, NSF program director Sally Nerlove said, "His life's work is of tremendous potential
70 importance to the economy and the ethos of region, and, at the same time, his accomplishments track the evolution of the NSF Partnerships for Innovation program."

38

The quote included in the second paragraph (lines 3–8) primarily serves to

A) establish the main motivation behind the commercial farming of blue mussels.

B) demonstrate the important role a species plays that the reader may not be aware of.

C) encourage the reader to decrease their personal consumption of blue mussels.

D) indicate the expertise of a scientist quoted later in the passage.

CONTINUE ➤

39

According to the fourth paragraph (lines 15–19), growing mussels in culture tanks helps to

A) enhance their size.

B) increase their maturity.

C) prepare them for the wild.

D) protect them from harm.

40

As used in line 19, "mature" most nearly means

A) marinate.

B) mellow.

C) develop.

D) stabilize.

41

What claim about blue mussels is best supported by the passage?

A) Were it not for their commercial importance, researchers would not be interested in sustainable growth for mussels.

B) Blue mussels grow best in ocean pens rather than the open water.

C) Mussels have multiple natural predators.

D) Immediately after birth, mussels must attach to a physical object to increase their chances of survival.

42

Which choice provides the best evidence for the answer to the previous question?

A) Lines 9–11 ("Because many … farming")

B) Lines 39–40 ("They attach … protein")

C) Lines 53–55 ("The researchers … best")

D) Lines 56–59 ("With better … mussels")

43

The passage most strongly suggests that researchers from the University of Maine at Machias and the Downeast Institute share which assumption?

A) Mussels prefer to attach to rope as opposed to other materials after maturing past the larvae stage of development.

B) Blue mussels are the most important species for maintaining a clean ocean environment.

C) Because farmers are unwilling to wait for mussels to fully develop, they often sacrifice a great deal of their potential crop as seed supply.

D) Wild settlement is not the most reliable method for farming blue mussels.

44

What is the primary purpose of the ninth paragraph (lines 41–46)?

A) Illustrate the way in which blue mussel development differs from other ocean life such as phytoplankton

B) Review previously known information that has been utilized by the mussel farming industry for decades

C) Provide an example of the insight the researchers have gained on aspects of mussel development

D) Offer a comprehensive review of the developmental needs of mussels determined by the research team

45

The stance that Brian Beal takes in the passage could best be described as

A) an environmentalist fighting for a species' survival.

B) a capitalist searching for the most efficient answer to a problem.

C) an academic writing a book on a scientific matter for public consumption.

D) a scholar investigating a series of hypotheses.

CONTINUE ▶

As used in line 54, "transition" most nearly means

A) shift.

B) evolve.

C) modify.

D) alter.

The central idea of the passage is that

A) a more efficient aqua-farming approach for raising blue mussels would greatly benefit the mussel species, commercial farming productivity, and the marine environment.

B) if something is not done soon, it is likely that blue mussels will soon be extinct due to overconsumption by humans.

C) the larger a mussel is, the better it is at filter-feeding the environment around it.

D) the optimal conversion point between larvae development, where mussels attach to rope, to ocean pens is one question researchers are focused on.

STOP

**If you finish before time is called, you may check your work on this section only.
Do not turn to any other section.**

Chapter 7
Reading Test
Drill 2: Answers
and Explanations

ANSWERS AND EXPLANATIONS

Section 1—Reading Test

1. **B** The second paragraph of the passage describes the need for men to *bring together* forces and *steer them...in such a way that they act together in a single thrust*. All forces should work together as a single force or unit, so in context, the word *thrust* means something similar to "movement." Choices (A), (C), and (D) do not mean "movement," which leaves (B). *Direction* is the most similar word to "movement," so it is the best answer.

2. **A** Choice (A) captures the main idea of the passage and is reiterated in lines 57–61 *(Each man...he has.)*—that uniting together will result in a stronger whole. The author does state that *man's force and liberty are what he chiefly needs for his survival* and raises the question of *how can he put them into this collective effort without harming his own interest and neglecting the care he owes to himself*. However, the author never says that this is selfish or that *selfishness* is an *inherent quality* in man, so eliminate (B). Eliminate (C) because there is nothing in the passage to support that the group will never break its word. Choice (D) is incorrect because it introduces terms that are never discussed in the passage.

3. **C** The answer to the previous question is best supported by (C) since these lines summarize the author's belief that when people unite together, they are stronger than when they remain separate. Choices (A) and (B) fail to discuss the strength benefit gained by coming together, so both answers should be eliminated. Choice (D) is incorrect because this sentence only discusses coming together but doesn't draw any conclusions about being stronger as the result of coming together.

4. **D** Earlier in this sentence, the author writes that *although they may never have been explicitly stated*, the clauses of this contract were *tacitly accepted and recognized*. If the clauses were not clearly or directly stated, then they must have been accepted in an understood or implied manner, without being spoken. In context, the word *tacitly* means "understood" or "unspoken." Choices (A), (B), and (C) do not mean "understood" or "unspoken," which leaves (D). *Implicitly* is the most similar word to "understood" and "unspoken," so it is the best answer.

5. **A** In the second sentence of the passage, the author states that the human race has reached a point from where it *can't go on*, which is the natural state of humanity. The author goes on to propose a way to improve the natural state of humanity: uniting together, which is a socially evolved relationship. Therefore, (A) is the correct answer. Choice (B) is incorrect because *violence* and *mercy* are topics never discussed in the passage. Choice (C) is incorrect because the author never mentions any *desire to fit in*. Finally, (D) is incorrect because the narrative isn't about comparing the positive and negative aspects of the social contract; it's about why a social contract is imperative.

6. **D** The "forces" the author refers to are not actual *armies of men*, so eliminate (A). The author never mentions asserting physical power over someone nor does the author mention a group pressuring individuals to join it, so (B) and (C) are incorrect. By POE, (D) is left, so it is the best answer.

7. **B** The author says in lines 41–45 *(Because each individual…everyone but himself.)* that individuals do give up their rights; however, there is more to uniting together than just giving up their rights (eliminate (A)). Whatever an individual gives to a group he gets back *(So he gains as much as he loses.)*, so the individual understands that he is sacrificing his rights for the good of the group. Therefore, (B) is the best answer. The author is encouraging people to work together, not fight against one another, so eliminate (C). Choice (D) contradicts the main idea of the passage since the author explicitly states in the three features (lines 41–61) that working together will result in not only better results for the whole community but also for each individual.

8. **C** Choices (A) and (B) are incorrect because the author never discusses *commercial exchange* or becoming *a slave*. The entire passage is about the author's desire to create a stronger civilized society by individuals willingly giving up their forces and liberties to the group, so (D) should be eliminated, making (C) the correct answer.

9. **D** The answer to this question should be in line with the answers to questions 2, 3, 5, 7, and 8. The central idea of the passage is that an individual will *gain as much as he loses* as when he does so the group is *jointly powerful enough to deal with the obstacles*. Therefore, the best answer is (D). Choices (A) and (C) are incorrect because the author never discusses enslavement or a *legal* contract. Choice (B) is counter to what the author says. Individuals are not being stripped of their liberties, rather individuals voluntarily give up their liberties to form a stronger group.

10. **D** The sentence in question describes how *certain things* seem harmless *to us in the modern day* and that an emotional response to them is hardly even necessary, yet to many cultures these same things have traditionally caused *irrational fear*. Since emotion is hardly required, the word *warrant*, in context, means something similar to "requires." Choices (A), (B), and (C) do not mean "requires," which leaves (D). *Deserve* is the most similar word to "requires," so it is the best answer.

11. **C** Choice (A) should be eliminated because *Judas* is never mentioned in this passage. (Don't bring outside knowledge into the test. The answer will be supported by the provided text.) Choice (B) can be disproven by the passage: *As all official religious events were scheduled on a twelve moon year, the inclusion of a 13th moon proved very problematic for the monks.* However, this sentence as well as a previous sentence *(Also, the number 13 was highly inconvenient…when it came to the number of moon cycles in a year.)* offer reasons that the number 13 is unlucky and do support (C). Although (D) is mentioned in the text, it does not answer the question being asked—why is the number 13 unlucky, not a certain day of the week—and should be eliminated. Therefore, (C) is the correct answer.

12. **B** Choice (A) is incorrect because those lines support why the day Friday is considered unlucky, not the number 13. Since the previous answer was about 13 being an inconvenient astronomical occurrence, (C) should be eliminated, because those lines are referring to Biblical, not astronomical, reasons why 13 is an unlucky number. Choice (D) does not offer specific support for why the number 13 is unlucky, rather those lines provide information about the moon cycles. Choice (B) does provide the necessary support for the previous answer and is the correct answer.

13. **C** The only answer that can be supported by information from the text is (C). Choice (A) makes an assumption beyond the scope of the passage—paragraph 2 only states that commercial sailing schedules *were set* around departing on Friday. There is no mention about "to this day." Choices (B) and (D) are incorrect since there is no reference to either one in the passage. Choice (C) is supported by the first sentence of paragraph 3 (*The fear of the number 13...than is the fear of Friday.*) and is the correct answer.

14. **A** The quote in the last paragraph by anthropologist Phillips Stevens, Jr. provides a nice summary of the passage since it discusses the fear of Friday the 13th by explaining the two fears that form it and discussing their origins, both of which stem from a religious event. Therefore, (A) is the best answer. Choice (B) is supported by the passage; however, it is only a detail and not the central idea expressed by the passage. Choices (C) and (D) do not summarize the central idea of the passage, nor can they be supported by text from the passage.

15. **A** The sentence in question describes how the combination of two superstitions (Friday and the number 13) has "set up" or "created" *one of the most well-known superstitions still in existence today*. In context, the word *constitutes* means something similar to "sets up." Choices (B), (C), and (D) do not mean "sets up," which leaves (A). *Establishes* is the most similar word to "sets up," so it is the best answer.

16. **B** Eliminate (A) because the author is not discussing what number is considered to be unlucky by Italians. Choice (C) is incorrect because is there no evidence about the author's personal opinion to suggest that he or she distrusts Italy. Finally, eliminate (D) because the author does not state that Italy is not aware of the biblical origins of this fear, just that they do not share this belief with other western, Christian cultures. The author uses the word *interestingly*, so he or she finds it curious that Italy, the "odd exception," does not agree with what is otherwise a widely shared belief. Therefore, the best answer is (B).

17. **B** In the third paragraph, the author states that the fear of the number 13 is so common that "it has been given a name: *triskaidekaphobia*." The author states in the final paragraph that "The superstition of Friday the 13th has also been given a name due to the widespread belief in it: *paraskevidekatriaphobia*." Since the fears are so prevalent, there has been a need to have a specific name for these two fears. Therefore, (B) is the correct answer. There is no mention of these fears being *highly complex conditions* (eliminate (A)) or that the author is providing the names of the phobias because he or she is concerned about the importance of others knowing the names (eliminate (C)). The author is not providing the scientific names to share little-known facts—the fears are very common and widespread—so eliminate (D). The best answer is (B).

18. **A** Check to see which of the answer choices are supported by information both in the passage and in the graph. While the fear of Friday the 13th is the combination of two fears, there is no evidence in the passage or in the graph to suggest it occurs at twice the rate of those singular fears. Choice (B) can be eliminated. While specific fears do occur in Western cultures, there is no evidence that these fears are unique to them, so (C) can be eliminated. According to the graph, those 65 and older are least likely to have specific phobias, but there's no evidence that this has anything to do with their relationship to Western values. Therefore, (D) is incorrect. The passage states that *triskaidekaphobia* is a specific phobia, and specific phobias occur most often among those 50 to 64 years of age. Choice (A) is correct.

19. **A** The correct answer must be mentioned in both passages. Use POE to check each answer. Only Passage 1 mentions the name of the captain of the *Mary Celeste* (eliminate (B)) and the date that the ship set sail (eliminate (C)). Only Passage 2 discusses the possible natural phenomenon behind the disappearance (the porousness of the cargo barrels), so (D) is incorrect. The author of Passage 1 states that the *Mary Celeste* was carrying *1,701 barrels of crude alcohol*. The author of Passage 2 states that *nine of the 1,701 alcohol cargo barrels were constructed of red oak*. Thus, (A) is correct.

20. **A** The author of Passage 1 states that other than some minimal damage, the ship was in *completely sailable condition* when it was found. Furthermore, *the cargo was mostly intact, there was a six-month supply of food and water, and there were no visible signs of panic, violence, or fire*. Therefore, the passage suggests that no identifiable reason can be given, based on what was found, for why the voyage could not have been completed, as in (A). Passage 1 makes no reference as to whether or not women and children should be taken as passengers on expeditions (eliminate (B)). The passage is not suggesting that the reasons for abandoning the ship are meritless—just that no reason has ever been widely accepted and that any reason would be very difficult to prove (eliminate (C)). The passage also does not suggest that there is a lack of motivation to discover the true reason for the disappearance of the ship, so (D) is incorrect, making (A) the best answer.

21. **B** Only (B) provides the best evidence for the previous question since it contains information that the ship was found in *completely sailable condition*. Therefore, those who discovered the abandoned ship could find no identifiable reason that the crew could not have completed the voyage. Choices (A), (C), and (D) do not provide support for the answer to the previous question and should be eliminated.

22. **A** The author concludes the three questions with the comment, *many reasons have been put forth but none has ever been widely accepted*. Thus, the author is emphasizing the mysterious nature of the ship's abandonment, which makes (A) the best answer. There is no reason to believe that the author thinks the historians are ignorant; the author's tone is neutral and there is no evidence in Passage 1 to support this (eliminate (B)). The author is not using the series of questions to make a general claim about the motivations of individuals or groups of people, rather the author wants to stress the uncertainty surrounding the disappearance of the ship's passengers and crew by listing possible scenarios, so eliminate (C). Choice (D) is incorrect because the author states in the last sentence of the passage that any of the reasons would be difficult to prove, so the author is not advocating that the *true* story needs to be determined since it's unlikely that it could be.

23. **D** The sentence in question states that the history of the *Mary Celeste* has *intrigued* historians and experts since 1872. Following this sentence, the author states that *many theories have been postulated regarding its abandonment*. The word *enigmatic* is describing history, and the history of the ship has *intrigued* these people. Since many theories have developed, the historians and experts are "puzzled" by the ship's abandonment. Therefore, the word *enigmatic*, in context, means something similar to "puzzling." Choices (A) and (C) do not mean "puzzling" and should be eliminated. Though (B) is tempting (the historians are interested in the ship's history), (D) provides a closer match to "puzzling." These people find the history of the ship's abandonment more than just interesting; they find the history intriguing and have developed many theories to account for the abandonment. Thus, since *perplexing* is the most similar word to "puzzling" and captures the author's intended meaning, (D) is the best answer.

24. **C** At the beginning of this sentence, the author of Passage 2 uses the phrase *in terms of the latter* to refer to the *ludicrous* theories that have been postulated regarding the ship's abandonment. One such ridiculous reason is that there were *giant squid attacks*. Therefore, the author uses the *giant squid* reference in order to provide an example of the *ludicrous* theories some have developed, making (C) the best answer. Eliminate (A) because the phrase is supporting, not contradicting, previous information in the passage. The author doesn't suggest that a giant squid attacking a ship is a natural occurrence; the author presents that and the other theories as rather unlikely occurrences (eliminate (B)). Choice (D) is incorrect because the phrase referenced does not offer a detailed description.

25. **C** All the theories mentioned in the last sentence of this paragraph are theories the author believes to be absurd, so the author does not use the phrase "*did the crew mutiny itself*" to convey confusion or lost hope (eliminate (A) and (D)). The author may be mocking; however, the author is not mocking people who can't solve the mystery, so (B) is also incorrect. Since the author feels it is unlikely that any of these *ludicrous* theories are the reason for the ship's abandonment, the author used the phrase in parentheses to express his or her disbelief in this theory as a viable solution. Therefore, (C) is correct.

26. **B** Prior to the sentence in question, the author states that alcoholic fumes could have easily escaped from barrels, and those fumes could have built up down in the hole. The author then states that if the pressure from the buildup became great enough, the hatch doors would be forced to do something. If the pressure is building behind the hatch doors, the word *ajar*, in context, means something similar to "wide open." Choices (A), (C), and (D) do not mean "wide open," which leaves (B). *Open* does mean "wide open," so (B) is the best answer.

27. **A** The author of Passage 2 states that in a case in which there was a fear of explosion on a ship, *it would be common to load into the lifeboat, tether it to the ship, and float a safe distance away until the risk of explosion appeared to abate*. The author of Passage 1 indicated that only the ship's lifeboat, navigational equipment, and many of the ship's papers were missing, yet the valuables of the passengers were still present. This provides strong support that the passengers on board the *Mary Celeste* intended to return to the ship. Therefore, (A) is the best answer. Choice (B) does not provide a reason as compelling as (A), so eliminate it. Choice (C) does not address the fact that the passengers intended to return and cannot support the author's reasoning. Choice (D) is asking a question and not providing support for Passage 2's author's reasoning, so eliminate it.

28. **C** Use POE and focus on one passage at a time. Start with Passage 1. The central idea of Passage 1 is to describe the unsolved mystery of the *Mary Celeste*. Eliminate (B) because the central idea of Passage 1 is not to discuss the individuals lost at sea, and eliminate (D) because Passage 2, not Passage 1, discusses the cargo-related cause of the ship's abandonment. The central idea of Passage 2 is to describe a likely scenario, related to the cargo onboard, that could account for the ship's abandonment. Compare (A) and (C) since those are the two choices remaining. Choice (A) is incorrect because the central idea of Passage 2 is not to discuss various ways the ship may have been abandoned, but rather to discuss one specific way. Choice (C) accurately expresses the central idea of Passage 2, so it best explains the differences between the two passages.

29. **C** The passage discusses the function and purpose of the field of paleopathology and reviews factual information of three diseases related to that field. The author is positive regarding the field of paleoanthropology at the end of the passage and is neutrally toned during the rest of it. Anything that goes against the idea of the author being positive or neutral can be eliminated, such as (B), *judgmental*. Although the author does present a great deal of information, she does so in a very accessible way, rather than an overly educated or ostentatious way, so eliminate (A), *pedantic*. Choice (D) does not make sense with this passage; for the author to be *conciliatory*, she would have to be appeasing or apologizing for something, and there is no indication of that in the passage. The best answer is (C), *descriptive*. The author gives us a great deal of descriptive detail on a field and what it studies.

30. **D** The first paragraph is introducing the topic of the passage, paleopathology. It states that without clear indications of disease on ancient human remains, it is difficult to determine the cause of death with certainty. Choice (A) is off-topic; the author only refers to determining the cause of death based on natural causes. Choice (B) references *lucky* from the passage, stating that paleopathologists are themselves lucky. This is deceptive, as the passage says *luckily for paleopathologists*, not that they are in fact lucky, so eliminate (B). Choice (C) is not supported by the text of the passage since at no point does the author mention any diseases other than paleopathological ones. Choice (D) correctly states that the cause of death can't be determined in the case of some remains, which is supported by the paragraph's emphasis that *unless there are clear signs of how death…occurred*, a cause of death may be impossible to determine. Therefore, (D) is the best answer.

31. **C** The sentence is discussing the symptoms of leprosy and the breakdown of *the skin and nerve cells*. The following sentence states that injuries occur because of the *lack of pain reception*. So the loss that is occurring here is the ability to feel or sense pain. Therefore, *sensation* must mean "feeling" or "pain reception." Choices (A), (B), and (D) all refer to a different use of the word "sensation" than "feeling," so they can be eliminated. This leaves (C), which best matches the meaning of "feeling."

32. **D** The sentence reads *tuberculosis was most likely first contracted from ingesting infected animal products*. The following sentence goes on to say *once a human is infected…*. Therefore, *contracted* most closely matches the meaning of *infected* in the following sentence. Choices (A), (B), and (C) do not match the meaning of *infected*, so they cannot be the correct meaning of the word *contracted* in this context. The best match is (D), *caught*, which can be used synonymously with the word "infected" when regarding infections and diseases.

33. **B** The fifth paragraph introduces the disease tuberculosis and provides background information on the disease. In order to answer this question, compare the answer choices against the information provided in the paragraph and use POE for answer choices that do not match. Choice (A) refers to *tuberculosis in animals and humans*. Although both animals and humans are mentioned, we are only told about the spread of the disease between the two and not the distinction between the disease in them. Eliminate (A). Choice (B) refers to *tuberculosis and leprosy*. In the first sentence of the paragraph, the author mentions both by comparing tuberculosis to leprosy and noting how they differ. Therefore, (B) is strongly supported by the paragraph. Choice (C) is incorrect as it references *syphilis*, which has not yet been discussed in detail and is not mentioned in this paragraph at all. *Knee and hip joints and the spine* are

not mentioned in this paragraph but in the following one. In that paragraph, they are treated as a connected list of skeletal areas affected by tuberculosis and are not contrasted to one another.

34. **B** In this context, the word *unique* is used to mean that something is specific to tuberculosis. That something is the fact that DNA testing can be used to determine the presence of tuberculosis in human remains. Since this is specific to tuberculosis, it can be inferred that DNA testing cannot be used in the same manner for other paleopathological diseases. Choice (A) is extreme and unsupported by the passage; tuberculosis itself is not unique, just the fact that it can be tested for through DNA. Eliminate (A). Choice (B) is supported by the text of the passage as that is what the phrase implies. The passage does not say what the most commonly found paleopathological disease is, so get rid of (C). This statement is about tuberculosis, not about syphilis, so get rid of (D) as well.

35. **A** There is a great deal of information regarding syphilis, so the best approach to this question is POE. Choice (A) states that it is easier to identify syphilis from indications on human remains than other paleopathological diseases, which is supported by the opening sentence of the seventh paragraph. Choice (B) refers to curing syphilis, which is not mentioned in the passage. It also states no symptoms appear on the skeleton if syphilis is treated and cured by the latent period, but the passage says that skeletal changes occur immediately after infection. So get rid of (B). Choice (C) references how long it takes syphilis to progress compared to tuberculosis. Since the passage provides a large time range for the progress of both diseases in the passage, it cannot be determined which one is faster than the other as the timing can vary for both. Since (C) is not supported by the passage, eliminate it. Choice (D) refers to only three stages of syphilis when the passage states that there are four: *primary, secondary, latent, and tertiary.* So (D) cannot be correct.

36. **A** Since the correct answer to the previous question is that syphilis is more easily identifiable from human remains than other diseases, the answer will be a line that contains that information in it. The only line that does this is (A), the first sentence of the seventh paragraph. According to that sentence, syphilis is *contagious and deadly, and the most clearly marked on skeletal remains.* Choice (B) discusses the symptoms of the first three stages, not the indicators on the skeleton. Choice (C) refers only to the non-skeletal symptoms of the tertiary stage of syphilis, so it is irrelevant. Choice (D) refers to the timing of the indications on the skeleton, not how clearly they appear as compared with other diseases. The best answer here is (A).

37. **A** Read the question carefully! The question asks what can be inferred based on information in both the passage and the graphic. Since the graphic presents data on leprosy only, eliminate answer choices based on what doesn't match the information in the passage. The passage states that *leprosy is not highly contagious.* Based on that fact, (C) and (D) can be eliminated since they both incorrectly state that leprosy has a high contagion rate. Now compare (A) and (B). Both are focused on the United States, which currently does not experience any rate of leprosy. Since it would be impossible to decrease from a rate of 0, (B) does not make sense. The best answer is (A).

38. **B** The quote in the second paragraph provides background information on blue mussels, especially the beneficial role they play in the environment. Therefore, the answer will likely be connected to the positive role of mussels. Since this quote only discusses mussels, and not the people studying them, it does

not indicate anything about a scientist. Eliminate (D). This quote is only informative and does not contain any reference to human behavior, let alone a change to that behavior, so (C) cannot be the correct answer. Later in the passage it discusses the farming of blue mussels due to their popularity as a food item, so (A) is also incorrect. Commercial farming raises mussels to sell, not to help the environment. Choice (B) refers to the important role played by mussels and accounts for the purpose of giving the reader this background information as the reader may not be aware of it. Choice (B) is the best answer.

39. **D** The only information provided on the culture tanks is that when grown in them, mussels are *protected from storms and predators*. Choices (A), (B), and (C) all contain deceptive language from the passage. In the same paragraph, it states that mussels can also be grown in the wild OR culture tanks, so get rid of (C). *Maturity* is also mentioned in the same paragraph, but in relation to ocean pens rather than culture tanks. So get rid of (B) as well. The following paragraph discusses the size of mussels, but does not say that is why they are grown in culture tanks, so eliminate (A). The only choice that fits with protecting the mussels is (D).

40. **C** This paragraph is discussing the process of cultivating, or growing, young mussels. The sentence says that mussels are *moved into ocean pens to mature* after they *reach a certain size*. This sentence is about the growth of mussels, so the word *mature* means growth, in this context. As (A), (B), and (D) do not match this meaning of the word *mature*, the only possible answer is (C).

41. **C** This is a very open-ended question, so take each answer choice one at a time. Choice (A) contains extreme language, stating that researchers would not be interested in mussels if it weren't for their commercial importance. However, at the beginning of the passage, the environmental importance of the mussels is discussed in a quote made by a researcher. Since there is evidence of another interest in mussels and no evidence that commercial farming is the most important aspect of mussels, eliminate (A). Choice (B) also contains extreme language, discussing how *mussels grow best*. The passage is discussing the research being conducted on growing mussels, and there is no evidence that a "best" method has been discovered. In the third paragraph, the author says that *many creatures—especially humans—enjoy eating blue mussels*, which clearly supports (C). In the eighth paragraph, the passage describes mussels as *swimming for their first few weeks of life*, which would indicate that they do not immediately adhere to an object after birth, as in (D).

42. **A** The correct answer to the previous question is that mussels have multiple natural predators. In the third paragraph, the author says that *many creatures—especially humans—enjoy eating blue mussels*, which clearly supports that answer. Choice (A) correctly identifies this line as the best support for the answer to the previous question. The remaining answer choices do not offer line references that support the answer to the previous question. Choice (B) discusses how mussels attach to objects, (C) discusses the use of pens for best growing practices, and (D) discusses the improvement of commercial prospects for mussels.

43. **D** The passage states that Beal and a team from the two institutions listed in the question are *investigating the growing conditions and practices that will reliably yield healthy and plentiful blue mussels*. The passage then goes on to quote Beal as referring to *our goal*, which is to develop methods to enhance consistent quantities of mussels. He states that currently *mussel farmers rely on wild settlement, which can be very*

spotty from year to year and from place to place. The assumption indicated here is that wild settlement is not the most consistent method for raising mussels, and the use of the phrase "our goal" indicates this belief is true for the whole group. The best answer that matches this information is (D), *wild settlement is not the most reliable method for farming blue mussels.* Choice (C) is not supported by the passage, as the behavior of the farmers is not discussed, only the current farming practices. Choice (B) refers to the environmental aspect of mussels, which was discussed only by Beal earlier in the passage. Choice (A) refers to the mussels' preference for rope as an adherence object, which is never stated.

44. **C** Paragraph nine reviews the variables that lead to healthy mussel growth and behavior identified by Beal and his team. The following paragraph then discusses that *Beal's team plans to use what they learn about blue mussel development to optimize how many and how well larvae secure themselves to rope used in aquaculture.* The information presented in paragraph nine constitutes at least some of what Beal's team has learned. Choice (A) is deceptive, as the paragraph does not compare mussels with phytoplankton; it states that mussels eat phytoplankton. Choice (B) does not make sense, as the farming industry is not discussed in these paragraphs. Choice (D) is extreme due to the word *comprehensive*: This is a short list of findings the research team has discovered. By comparison, (C) refers to the findings as an example of what the researchers have found, making it the best answer.

45. **D** Brian Beal is the main researcher focused on in the passage. He is quoted several times as giving background information on mussels and describing the research questions he and his team study and the purpose of those questions. Although he does mention the environmental benefits of mussels, his research is dedicated to helping enhance consistent commercial farming of mussels. Although this is partly to help keep mussels from being over-harvested, (A) is too limited in its focus on the environment. Although Beal is searching for an efficient way to farm mussels consistently, he himself is not the one who intends to profit. This makes the use of *capitalist* in (B) incorrect. Beal is an *academic*, but he is studying mussels to solve a problem, not to write a book on them, so (C) is not correct. As the passage indicates, Beal and his team are *conducting field studies to examine the effects of stocking densities on mussel growth and survival*, which best matches a scholar testing hypotheses. Therefore, the best answer is (D).

46. **A** This sentence discusses the timing of transitioning mussels into ocean pens, which would mean a physical movement of the mussels into the pens. The closest meaning of *transition* is physical movement. Choices (B), (C), and (D) are all closer in meaning to "change" than to "movement," so they are all incorrect. The only choice that matches the meaning of "movement" is *shift*, making (A) the correct answer.

47. **A** This passage discusses blue mussels and their various values and the issues that have been experienced when commercially farming them. It reviews the findings of a research team attempting to increase the consistency of mussel farming practices. Only (A) contains a general statement that addresses these aspects of the passage. Choice (B) is too limited, as it only touches on the consumption of mussels. Choice (C) is also too limited, as it only refers to the ability of mussels to filter feed and makes a claim that is not substantiated in the passage. The information in (D) is correct, but it only discusses a single research question the team in the passage is focused on as opposed to the central idea of the entire passage.

Chapter 8
Reading Test
Drill 3

Reading Test

60 MINUTES, 47 QUESTIONS

Turn to Section 1 of your answer sheet to answer the questions in this section.

Questions 1-9 are based on the following passage.

"The Joy Luck Club" from THE JOY LUCK CLUB by Amy Tan, copyright © 1989 by Amy Tan. Used by permission of G. P. Putnam's Sons, an imprint of Penguin Publishing Group, a division of Penguin Random House LLC. All rights reserved. This novel tells the story of four immigrant families in San Francisco.

My father has asked me to be the fourth corner at the Joy Luck Club. I am to replace my mother, whose seat at the mah jong table has been empty since she
Line died two months ago. My father thinks she was killed
5   by her own thoughts.

"She had a new idea inside her head," said my father. "But before it could come out of her mouth, the thought grew too big and burst. It must have been a very bad idea."

10   The doctor said she died of a cerebral aneurysm. And her friends at the Joy Luck Club said she died just like a rabbit: quickly and with unfinished business left behind. My mother was supposed to host the next meeting of the Joy Luck Club.

15   The week before she died, she called me, full of pride, full of life: "Auntie Lin cooked red bean soup for Joy Luck. I'm going to cook black sesame-seed soup."

"Don't show off," I said.

"It's not showoff." She said the two soups were
20   almost the same, *chabudwo*. Or maybe she said *butong*, not the same thing at all. It was one of those Chinese expressions that means the better half of mixed intentions. I can never remember things I didn't understand in the first place.

25   My mother started the San Francisco version of the Joy Luck Club in 1949, two years before I was born. This was the year my mother and father left China with one stiff leather trunk filled only with fancy silk dresses. There was no time to pack anything else, my mother had
30   explained to my father after they boarded the boat. Still his hands swam frantically between the slippery silks, looking for his cotton shirts and wool pants.

When they arrived in San Francisco, my father made her hide those shiny clothes. She wore the
35   same brown-checked Chinese dress until the Refugee Welcome Society gave her two hand-me-down dresses, all too large in sizes for American women. The society was composed of a group of white-haired American missionary ladies from the First Chinese Baptist
40   Church. And because of their gifts, my parents could not refuse their invitation to join the church. Nor could they ignore the old ladies' practical advice to improve their English through Bible study class on Wednesday nights and, later, through choir practice
45   on Saturday mornings. This was how my parents met the Hsus, the Jongs, and the St. Clairs. My mother could sense that the women of these families also had unspeakable tragedies they had left behind in China and hopes they couldn't begin to express in their
50   fragile English. Or at least, my mother recognized the numbness in these women's faces. And she saw how quickly their eyes moved when she told them her idea for the Joy Luck Club.

Joy Luck was an idea my mother remembered
55   from the days of her first marriage in Kweilin, before the Japanese came. That's why I think of Joy Luck as

CONTINUE

her Kweilin story. It was the story she would always
tell me when she was bored, when there was nothing
to do, when every bowl had been washed and the
60 Formica table had been wiped down twice, when my
father sat reading the newspaper and smoking one Pall
Mall cigarette after another, a warning not to disturb
him. This is when my mother would take out a box
of old ski sweaters sent to us by unseen relatives from
65 Vancouver. She would snip the bottom of a sweater
and pull out a kinky thread of yarn, anchoring it to
a piece of cardboard. And as she began to roll with
one sweeping rhythm, she would start her story. Over
the years, she told me the same story, except for the
70 ending, which grew darker, casting long shadows into
her life, and eventually into mine.

1

Which choice best summarizes the passage?

A) A woman's mother dies, leading the woman to
   consider her mother's life.

B) An immigrant couple struggling to establish a new
   home finds a community in a local church.

C) A man and his wife rush to pack their home and
   flee their country before invading forces arrive.

D) A woman looking for friendship begins a mah
   jong club.

2

What does the passage suggest about how the
narrator's father views his wife's death as compared
with how the narrator views her mother's death?

A) The narrator is less sad about the empty space at
   the Joy Luck Club than her father.

B) The narrator is more devastated by the loss of her
   mother than is her father by the loss of his wife.

C) The narrator is more satisfied by the explanation
   of a medical professional than is her father.

D) The narrator has more difficulty accepting that her
   mother died quickly than does her father.

3

Which choice provides the best evidence for the
answer to the previous question?

A) Lines 2–4 ("I am…ago")

B) Lines 4–5 ("My father…thoughts")

C) Lines 11–13 ("Her friends…behind")

D) Lines 13–14 ("My mother…Club")

4

The italicized words in lines 20–21 serve mainly to

A) demonstrate the narrator's mastery of her parents'
   native language.

B) exemplify differences between spoken Chinese
   and spoken English.

C) highlight cultural differences between the narrator
   and her parents.

D) offer two commonly confused Chinese words.

5

It can reasonably be inferred that the narrator's
father's hands "swam frantically" (line 31) because

A) he was desperate to find his own clothes.

B) he was struggling to stay afloat in the water.

C) he couldn't communicate with his wife about what
   they needed to pack.

D) he was waving at his wife on the San Francisco
   docks.

6

Which choice provides the best evidence for the
answer to the previous question?

A) Lines 25–26 ("My mother…born")

B) Lines 27–28 ("This was…dresses")

C) Lines 34–37 ("She wore…women")

D) Lines 40–41 ("And because…church")

CONTINUE

7

As used in line 48, "unspeakable" most nearly means

A) impossible.

B) subtle.

C) scandalous.

D) appalling.

8

As used in line 50, "fragile" most nearly means

A) brittle.

B) crisp.

C) shaky.

D) antiquated.

9

The main purpose of lines 68–71 is to

A) foreshadow something negative that is going to happen to the narrator.

B) illustrate the narrator's mother's creativity by showing how she changes the story's ending every time she tells it.

C) offer an explanation for a confusing memory the narrator had from her childhood.

D) resolve a conflict between the narrator and her mother.

CONTINUE

Questions 10-18 are based on the following passage and supplementary material.

…Over the past decade, an abundance of psychology research has shown that experiences bring
Line people more happiness than do possessions. The
5 idea that experiential purchases are more satisfying than material purchases has long been the domain of Cornell psychology professor Thomas Gilovich. Since 2003, he has been trying to figure out exactly how and why experiential purchases are so much better than
10 material purchases. In the journal *Psychological Science* last month, Gilovich and [psychologist Matthew] Killingsworth, along with Cornell doctoral candidate Amit Kumar, expanded on the current understanding that spending money on experiences "provide[s]
15 more enduring happiness." They looked specifically at anticipation as a driver of that happiness; whether the benefit of spending money on an experience accrues before the purchase has been made, in addition to after. And, yes, it does.

20   Essentially, when you can't live in a moment, they say, it's best to live in anticipation of an experience. Experiential purchases like trips, concerts, movies, et cetera, tend to trump material purchases because the utility of buying anything really starts accruing before
25 you buy it.

Waiting for an experience apparently elicits more happiness and excitement than waiting for a material good (and more "pleasantness" too—an eerie metric). By contrast, waiting for a possession is more likely
30 fraught with impatience than anticipation. "You can think about waiting for a delicious meal at a nice restaurant or looking forward to a vacation," Kumar told me, "and how different that feels from waiting for, say, your pre-ordered iPhone to arrive. Or when the
35 two-day shipping on Amazon Prime doesn't seem fast enough."…

Experiential purchases are also more associated with identity, connection, and social behavior. Looking back on purchases made, experiences make people
40 happier than do possessions. It's kind of counter to the logic that if you pay for an experience, like a vacation, it will be over and gone; but if you buy a tangible thing, a couch, at least you'll have it for a long time.

Actually most of us have a pretty intense capacity
45 for tolerance, or hedonic adaptation, where we stop appreciating things to which we're constantly exposed. iPhones, clothes, couches, et cetera, just become background. They deteriorate or become obsolete. It's the fleetingness of experiential purchases that endears
50 us to them. Either they're not around long enough to become imperfect, or they are imperfect, but our memories and stories of them get sweet with time. Even a bad experience becomes a good story.

When it rains through a beach vacation, as Kumar
55 put it, "People will say, well, you know, we stayed in and we played board games and it was a great family bonding experience or something." Even if it was negative in the moment, it becomes positive after the fact. That's a lot harder to do with material
60 purchases because they're right there in front of you. "When my Macbook has the colorful pinwheel show up," he said, "I can't say, well, at least my computer is malfunctioning!"…

That means making purchasing an experience,
65 which is terrible marketing-speak, but in practical terms might mean buying something on a special occasion or on vacation or while wearing a truly unique hat. Or tying that purchase to subsequent social interaction. Buy this and you can talk about buying it,
70 and people will talk about you because you have it.

"Turns out people don't like hearing about other people's possessions very much," Kumar said, "but they do like hearing about that time you saw Vampire Weekend."…

75   "There are actually instances of positivity when people are waiting for experiences," Kumar said, like talking to other people in the concert line about what songs Vampire Weekend might play. So there is opportunity to connect with other people. "We know
80 that social interaction is one of the most important determinants of human happiness, so if people are talking with each other, being nice to one another in the line, it's going to be a lot more pleasant experience than if they're being mean to each other which is
85 what's (more) likely to happen when people are waiting for material goods."…

CONTINUE ➤

Figure 1

Consumers' Belief that Money is Well-spent
(1 = not at all; 7 = very much)

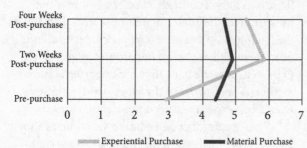

Experiential Purchase   Material Purchase

Figure 2

Consumer Purchase Satisfaction

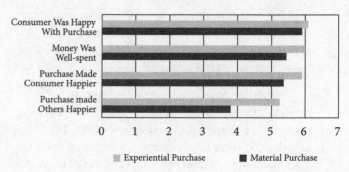

Experiential Purchase   Material Purchase

10

As used in line 6, "material" most nearly means

A) sensible.

B) consequential.

C) actual.

D) physical.

11

In line 15, the author places the phrase "provide[s] more enduring happiness" in quotes in order to

A) define the idea researchers intended to disprove.

B) provide a summary of research findings.

C) highlight a foundational belief behind the research.

D) question the current understanding of a topic.

12

According to the passage, waiting for a possession and waiting for an experience differ from the purchaser's perspective regarding

A) efficiency and indifference.

B) eeriness and pleasantness.

C) happiness and excitement.

D) agitation and enthusiasm.

13

Which choice provides the best evidence for the answer to the previous question?

A) Lines 22–25 ("Experiential purchases … it")

B) Lines 26–28 ("Waiting for … metric")

C) Lines 29–30 ("By contrast…anticipation")

D) Lines 34–36 ("Or when… enough")

14

As used in line 52, "sweet" most nearly means

A) candied.

B) cherished.

C) delicious.

D) luscious.

15

The author indicates that an experience that is bad in the moment

A) will forever be remembered as a disappointment.

B) is less frustrating than a broken possession.

C) is never worse than a bad material purchase.

D) can sometimes be remembered favorably.

CONTINUE ➡

16

Which choice provides the best evidence for the answer to the previous question?

A) Lines 40–43 ("It's kind … time")

B) Lines 54–57 ("When it … something")

C) Lines 59–60 ("That's a … you")

D) Lines 69–70 ("Buy this … it")

17

Which statement from the passage is best supported by figure 1?

A) Lines 20–21 ("Essentially, when … experience")

B) Lines 38–40 ("Looking back …possessions")

C) Line 53 ("Even a … story")

D) Lines 78–79 ("So there … people")

18

Figure 2 provides support for which point made in the passage?

A) Purchasing experiences brings more happiness than purchasing material goods.

B) Anticipation is a large part of the happiness an experience brings an individual.

C) Experiences contribute more to an individual's identity and social interactions than do material goods.

D) Even terrible experiences can turn into good memories.

CONTINUE

Questions 19-28 are based on the following passage and supplementary material.

This passage is excerpted from Lore Thaler and Liam Norman, "Learning How to Be a Human Bat." Reproduced with permission. Copyright © 2017 Scientific American, a division of Nature America, Inc. All rights reserved.

Echolocation is probably most associated with bats and dolphins. These animals emit bursts of sounds and listen to the echoes that bounce back to detect objects
Line   in their environment and to perceive properties of the
5   objects (e.g. location, size, material)....

People, remarkably, can also echolocate. By making mouth clicks, for example, and listening for the returning echoes, they can perceive their surroundings. Daniel Kish, who is blind and is a well-known
10   expert echolocator, is able to ride his bicycle, hike in unfamiliar terrain, and travel in unfamiliar cities on his own. Daniel is the founder and president of World Access for the Blind, a non-profit charity in the US that offers training in echolocation alongside training in
15   other mobility techniques such as the long cane.

Since 2011, the scientific interest in human echolocation has gained momentum. For example, technical advances have made it feasible to scan people's brains while they echolocate. This research has
20   shown that people who are blind and have expertise in echolocation use 'visual' parts of their brain to process information from echoes. It has also been found that anyone with normal hearing can learn to use echoes to determine the sizes, locations, or distance of objects
25   or to use [them] to avoid obstacles during walking. Remarkably, both blind and sighted people can improve their ability to interpret and use sound echoes within a session or two.

Marina Ekkel and colleagues from Radboud
30   University in the Netherlands showed recently that sighted people learned to echolocate size, and that people's attentional capacity was related to their learning success....

In their study Ekkel and colleagues trained sighted
35   people to echolocate whilst they wore a blindfold. They did not ask people to make mouth clicks, but people were allowed to use a loudspeaker mounted on their head. People could press a button so that the loudspeaker made a brief (10ms) sound. People then
40   made judgments about the relative sizes of objects using echoes that came back from those objects. Participants came into the lab on four separate

occasions and each time the researchers measured their ability to do the task. The researchers also
45   measured participants' hearing ability, spatial ability, working memory and attention.

What Ekkel and colleagues found was that people's increase in echolocation ability from session 1 to 4 was positively correlated with their attentional measures.
50   That is, those people who had higher attentional capacity scores also showed greater improvement in their echolocation ability.

During the early days of echolocation research, in the 1940s and 1950s, the ability of people to echolocate
55   was referred to as "facial vision" or "obstacle sense." Scientists were not sure how it worked, but many believed that some select blind people were able to mysteriously detect subtle changes in air pressure on their skin, as they approached a wall or some other
60   large obstacle. A series of early experiments conducted at Cornell University, however, made it clear that blind people were actually listening to the echoes of sounds bouncing off surfaces in their immediate surroundings. Subsequent research went on to show that both blind
65   and sighted people can learn to avoid obstacles without vision, as long as they are able to use their hearing....

Ekkel and colleagues' paper follows in this line of research, confirming the learnability of echolocation, and suggesting that people's attentional capacity might
70   be an aspect driving the acquisition of this skill. To date, research into the cognitive variables involved in learning echolocation has been conducted with people who are sighted. Yet, loss of vision is associated with many behavioral and neural changes. We need research
75   to determine if the variables that affect learning in sighted people are the same as those for people who are blind. Blindness affects people worldwide. Finding out more about how echolocation is learned by people who are blind, and how it affects their wellbeing, will
80   answer important questions about how the brain adapts to vision loss. The research may also help establishing echolocation alongside other tools and techniques for people who are blind.

CONTINUE ➡

Figure 1

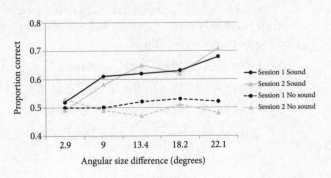

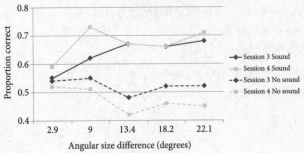

Figure 2

PASAT Score versus Increase in Echolocation Ability

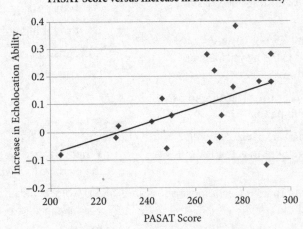

19

Over the course of the passage, the main focus shifts from

A) a historical look at research to contemporary applications of that research.

B) a general discussion of a skill to instructions on how to acquire that skill.

C) an introduction of a concept to an explanation of research on that concept.

D) a personal anecdote to an academic discussion.

20

The primary purpose of the second paragraph (lines 6–15) is to

A) support an unexpected claim.

B) defend a controversial statement.

C) provide support for the previous paragraph.

D) refute the position presented in the previous paragraph.

CONTINUE

It can reasonably be inferred that one of the requirements for most effectively learning echolocation is

A) heightened hearing.

B) normal neural function.

C) strong focus.

D) the ability to click.

Which choice is an assumption the researchers made while conducting the experiment described in the passage?

A) There is no measurable difference between making mouth clicks and using a loudspeaker when learning echolocation.

B) Sighted people have a harder time learning to use echolocation than do blind people.

C) Those who score highest on hearing tests will show the greatest improvement in echolocation ability.

D) Study participants are not practicing echolocation outside of the testing facility.

Which choice best supports the answer to the previous question?

A) Lines 34–35 ("In their … blindfold")

B) Lines 36–38 ("They did … head")

C) Lines 38–39 ("People could … sound")

D) Lines 39–41 ("People then … objects")

As used in line 57, "select" most nearly means

A) elite.

B) specific.

C) delicate.

D) chosen.

25

Which choice best supports the claim that changes in air pressure were not actually helping blind people navigate their surroundings?

A) Lines 47–49 ("What Ekkel… measures")

B) Lines 53–55 ("During the… sense'")

C) Lines 56–60 ("Scientists were… obstacle")

D) Lines 60–63 ("A series… surroundings")

As used in line 70, "driving" most nearly means

A) transporting.

B) provoking.

C) constraining.

D) stimulating.

What purpose do Figures 1 and 2 serve in relation to the passage as a whole?

A) They contradict the findings presented in the passage.

B) They support the conclusions of the researchers in the passage.

C) They offer additional details not mentioned in the passage.

D) They present a different explanation for the outcomes outlined in the passage.

28

Based on the information in the passage and in Figure 1, those who improved the most in learning echolocation were those who

A) completed four trials with no sound.

B) completed two trials with no sound.

C) completed four trials with sound.

D) completed two trials with sound.

CONTINUE

Questions 29-38 are based on the following passage.

The following passage comes from George Washington Cable's *The Silent South*, published in *The Century* in 1885. In the passage, Cable defends attacks against his previous article, "The Freedman's Case in Equity," which advanced full civil rights for the slaves freed in 1865 amid national Civil War.

But now that we have clearly made out exactly what this immovable hostility is, the question follows—and half the nation are asking it today

Line with perplexed brows—why is it? Yet the answer is
5 simple. Many white people of the South sincerely believe that the recognition of rights proposed in the old Civil Rights bills or "The Freedman's Case in Equity" would precipitate a social chaos. They believe Civil Rights means Social Equality. This may seem
10 a transparent error, but certainly any community in the world that believed it, would hold the two ideas in equal abomination; and it is because of the total unconsciousness and intense activity of this error at the South, and the subtle sense of unsafety
15 that naturally accompanies it,—it is because of this, rather than for lack of clearness in its statement of the subject, that the article on "The Freedman's Case in Equity" is so grossly misinterpreted even by some who undoubtedly wish to be fair. That this is the true
20 cause of the misinterpretation is clear in the fact that from the first printing of the article until now the misconstruction has occurred only among those whose thinking still runs in the grooves of the old traditions.
Nothing in that paper touches or seeks to touch
25 the domain of social privileges. The standing of the magazine in which it appears is guarantee against the possibility of the paper containing any such insult to the intelligence of enlightened society. Social equality is a fool's dream. The present writer wants quite as
30 little of it as the most fervent traditionist of the most fervent South. The North, the West, the East, and the rest of the intelligent world, want quite as little of it as the South wants. Social equality can never exist where a community, numerous enough to assert itself,
35 is actuated, as every civilized community is, by an intellectual and moral ambition. No form of laws, no definition of rights, from Anarchy to Utopia, can bring it about. The fear that this or that change will produce it ought never to be any but a fool's fear. And yet there
40 is this to be added; that no other people in America are doing so much for social equality as those who, while

they warmly charge it upon others, are themselves thrusting arbitrary and cheap artificial distinctions into the delicate machinery of society's self-distribution as
45 it revolves by the power of our natural impulses, and of morality, personal interest, and personal preferences. This, of course, is not the intention, and even these persons retard only incidentally, unawares and within narrow limits, nature's social distributions, while taking
50 diligent and absolutely needless pains to hold apart two races which really have no social affinity at all.
Do we charge any bad intention or conscious false pretense? Not at all! They are merely making the double mistake of first classing as personal social
55 privileges certain common impersonal rights of man, and then turning about and treating them as rights definable by law—which social amenities are not and cannot be.
For the sake of any who might still misunderstand,
60 let us enlarge here a moment. The family relation has rights. Hence marital laws and laws of succession. But beyond the family circle there are no such things as social rights; and when our traditionists talk about a too hasty sympathy having "fixed by enactment" the
65 negro's social and civil rights they talk—unwisely. All the relations of life that go by impersonal right are Civil relations. All that go by personal choice are Social relations. The one is all of right, it makes no difference who we are; the other is all of choice, and it makes
70 all the difference who we are; and it is no little fault against ourselves as well as others, to make confusion between the two relations. For the one we make laws; for the other everyone consults his own pleasure; and the law that refuses to protect a civil right, construing
75 it a social privilege, deserves no more regard than if it should declare to be a civil right. Social choice, civil rights; but a civil privilege, in America, is simply heresy against both our great national political parties at once.

CONTINUE ▶

29

The primary purpose of the passage is to

A) contrast two distinct social goals and argue for one and against the other.

B) advocate restrictions against a dangerous social policy.

C) cast doubt on the practicality of establishing an improvement to civil rights.

D) describe the challenges inherent in the struggle for social equality.

The beliefs attributed to people in the South in the first paragraph chiefly serve to

A) introduce a belief that Cable will embrace.

B) provide personal views that Cable will discard.

C) describe a situation that Cable will support.

D) illustrate a position that Cable will reject.

Considering the passage as a whole, the author uses the phrases "total unconsciousness" (line 13) and "grooves of the old traditions" (line 23) primarily in order to

A) show frustration and anger.

B) characterize a faulty assumption.

C) endorse sympathetic understanding and tacit disapproval.

D) call for an investigation into a viewpoint.

32

Cable makes which argument about Southern criticism of "The Freedman's Case in Equity"?

A) It motivates him to improve his plan for Social Equality in order to address those criticisms.

B) It saddens him by illustrating a prejudiced position.

C) It explains why social equality is not yet possible.

D) It reveals to him the disconnect between his intended point and critics' understanding.

Which choice provides the best evidence for the answer to the previous question?

A) Lines 4–5 ("Yet the … simple")

B) Lines 24–28 ("Nothing in … society")

C) Lines 28–31 ("Social equality … South")

D) Lines 39–46 ("And yet … preferences")

Cable suggests that attempting to achieve social equality is

A) invigorating as a means to stand against oppressive traditions.

B) counterproductive considering the necessity of maintaining the established social structure.

C) inspiring because of the many barriers to equality that will need to be overcome.

D) an impossible quest for a misguided outcome.

Which choice provides the best evidence for the answer to the previous question?

A) Lines 1–4 ("But now … it")

B) Lines 19–23 ("That this … traditions")

C) Lines 52–53 ("Do we … pretense")

D) Lines 53–58 ("They are … be")

Cable indicates that a principal difference between himself and his critics is that he

A) recognizes the necessity of social equality, while his critics do not.

B) understands the distinction between regulating social relationships and establishing fundamental rights.

C) sees the absurdity of establishing civil equality.

D) realizes that the struggle for civil rights is futile.

CONTINUE ➤

37

In referring to "a fool's fear" (line 39), Cable implies that he

A) has changed his position from what he held when he wrote "The Freedman's Case in Equity."

B) would reject attempts to engage in establishing rules about social roles.

C) would consider anyone who rejects social equality to be foolish and unintelligent.

D) considers himself to be overly idealistic in his quest for social equality.

38

As used in line 60, "enlarge" most nearly means

A) strengthen.

B) grow.

C) swell.

D) contextualize.

CONTINUE

Questions 39-47 are based on the following passages.

Passage 1 is adapted from Theodore S. Melis, Ed., "Effects of Three High-Flow Experiments on the Colorado River Ecosystem Downstream from Glen Canyon Dam, Arizona," published in 2011 by the U.S. Geological Survey. Passage 2 is adapted from Paul E. Grams, "A Sand Budget for Marble Canyon, Arizona— Implications for Long-Term Monitoring of Sand Storage Change," published in 2013 by the U.S. Geological Survey.

Passage 1

At the time Glen Canyon Dam was constructed (1956–63), little consideration was given to how dam operations might affect downstream resources
Line   in Grand Canyon National Park. In fact, the dam
5   was completed before enactment of the National Environmental Policy Act of 1969 and the Endangered Species Act of 1973. By the late 1950s, public values began to shift, and throughout the 1960s and 1970s recognition of the environmental consequences of
10 Glen Canyon Dam and its operation grew. National Park Service and U.S. Geological Survey scientists and river recreationists observed the physical transformation of the river in Grand Canyon, including the loss of large beaches used for camping,
15 narrowing of rapids so as to reduce navigability, and changes in the distribution and composition of riparian vegetation. The humpback chub and Colorado pikeminnow, species found only in the Colorado River Basin, were listed as endangered in 1967 by
20 the U.S. Fish and Wildlife Service, which concluded in 1978 that the dam and its operation jeopardized the continued existence of humpback chub in Grand Canyon.

Annual spring snowmelt floods were the defining
25 attribute of the pre-dam flow regime. Before the Colorado River was regulated by dams, streamflow gradually increased from mid-December to March, precipitously increased in April and May, and reached its peak in early June.
30 Pre-dam floods disturbed the aquatic ecosystem, and native fish species developed strategies to survive periods when the velocity in the main part of the channel was high and large amounts of suspended sediment were being transported. For example, several
35 of the native fish species share unusual body shapes, including a large adult body size, small depressed skulls, large humps on their backs, and small eyes,

which presumably developed as adaptations to life in a turbid and seasonably variable riverine environment.
40 Sandbars, riverbanks, and their accompanying aquatic habitats were reshaped during floods. Additionally, the increased elevation of the river surface during floods provided water to native riparian vegetation otherwise principally dependent on precipitation.

Passage 2

45 Decline in the size and abundance of sandbars since the pre-Glen Canyon Dam era has been documented by analysis of old aerial and ground-level photographs and by topographic surveys that began in the mid 1970s. Scientists have estimated that sandbar
50 area in the upstream 100 miles of Glen, Marble, and Grand Canyons was 25 percent less in 2000 than in average pre-dam years. This decline occurred because releases of water from Lake Powell are virtually free of sediment. The tributaries that enter the Colorado River
55 downstream from the dam supply only a fraction of the pre-dam sand supply, and the capacity of the post-dam river to transport that sand greatly exceeds this limited supply. Normal dam operations, therefore, tend to erode, rather than build, sandbars.
60 By experimentation, scientists have learned that controlled floods, if released from the reservoir immediately following large inputs of sand from tributaries, can build sandbars. These sandbars are built during controlled floods when sand is carried
65 from the riverbed and temporarily suspended at high concentration in the flow. The suspended sand is transported into eddies where it is then deposited in areas of low stream-flow velocity. Sandbars enlarged by this process provide larger camping beaches for
70 river-rafting trips and create backwater habitats used by native fish. Newly deposited sandbars also provide areas for riparian vegetation to grow and are a source of windblown sand. Windblown sand carried upslope from sandbars helps to cover and potentially preserve
75 some of the culturally significant archeological sites in Grand Canyon.

Scientists have also learned that controlled floods may erode sandbars if the concentration of suspended sand during a controlled flood is too low.
80 The concentration of sand during a flood is directly proportional to the amount of the riverbed covered by sand and the size of that sand. Higher concentrations of suspended sand occur when the sand is relatively fine and large amounts of the riverbed are covered by

CONTINUE ▶

85 sand. These findings are incorporated in the current reservoir-release management strategy for Glen Canyon Dam, which involves releasing controlled floods—administratively referred to as High Flow Experiments (HFEs)—whenever the Paria River
90 has recently delivered large amounts of sand to the Colorado River. The magnitude and duration of the controlled floods is adjusted to transport just the amount of sand that has recently been delivered from the Paria River.

39

The primary purpose of both Passage 1 and Passage 2 is to

A) detail how concerns about a species led to controlled floods.

B) consider the impact of environmental laws.

C) discuss a changing ecosystem through a specific example.

D) illustrate that manmade changes to ecosystems are always beneficial.

40

As used in line 16, "composition" most nearly means

A) writing.

B) song.

C) makeup.

D) creation.

41

As used in line 53, "free" most nearly means

A) lacking.

B) expressive.

C) allowing.

D) vigorous.

42

The author of Passage 2 implies that sand suspended in water is released onto sandbars during which state of the stream-flow?

A) Low stream-flow velocity

B) High stream-flow velocity

C) Pre-dam flow

D) Normal flooding

43

Which choice provides the best evidence for the answer to the previous question?

A) Lines 60–63 ("By experimentation … sandbars")

B) Lines 66–68 ("The suspended … velocity")

C) Lines 71–73 ("Newly deposited … sand")

D) Lines 77–79 ("Scientists have … low")

44

A researcher hypothesized that controlled floods only threaten archaeological sites along the walls of the Grand Canyon. Would the author of Passage 2 most likely agree with the researcher's hypothesis?

A) Yes, because the passage states that controlled floods are more violent than pre-dam floods and may collapse parts of the canyon.

B) Yes, because the passage states that controlled floods cause erosion, which widens the river, and weakens the canyon's walls.

C) No, because the passage states that controlled floods deposit windblown sand, which may protect features of the canyon.

D) No, because the passage states that controlled floods cause erosion, which deepens the river, and strengthens the canyon's walls.

CONTINUE ►

45

In Passage 2, which choice provides the strongest evidence for the author's suggestion that controlled floods can be detrimental?

A) Lines 63–66 ("These sandbars … flow")

B) Lines 71–73 ("Newly deposited … sand")

C) Lines 77–79 ("Scientists have … low")

D) Lines 85–91 ("These findings … River")

46

According to Passage 1, the camping beaches mentioned in line 69 could be part of

A) the Paria River.

B) the Colorado River Basin.

C) the Glen Canyon Dam.

D) Lake Powell.

47

Based on Passages 1 and 2, the controlled floods referenced in line 92 replace floods created by which event?

A) Normal dam operations

B) Snowmelt

C) Rapids

D) Surveys

STOP

If you finish before time is called, you may check your work on this section only.
Do not turn to any other section.

Chapter 9
Reading Test
Drill 3: Answers
and Explanations

ANSWERS AND EXPLANATIONS

Section 1—Reading Test

1. **A** This question asks about the structure of the passage. Since this is a general question, it should be answered after the specific questions. The passage begins by stating that the narrator's mother died two months prior and proceeds with a discussion of her parents' immigration from China and their first years in America. Look for an answer choice that matches this structure. Choices (B), (C), and (D) all mention details from the passage but don't summarize the overall structure and can be eliminated. The correct answer is (A).

2. **C** This question asks about the difference between how the narrator and her father view her mother's death. In paragraph one, the narrator states that her father *thinks she was killed by her own thoughts*. In paragraph three, she states simply that *the doctor said she died of a cerebral aneurysm*. The correct answer will be about using one's own explanation versus using a doctor's explanation. Choices (A) and (B) refer to the emotions of the narrator and her father, which aren't mentioned in the text. Eliminate them. Choice (C) is consistent with the prediction, so keep it. Choice (D) can be eliminated because there is no discussion in the text about who had more difficulty *accepting that… mother died quickly*. The correct answer is (C).

3. **B** This question is the best evidence question in a paired set. Because Q2 was a specific question, simply look at the lines used to answer it. In paragraph one, the narrator states that her father *thinks she was killed by her own thoughts*. In paragraph three, she states that *the doctor said she died of a cerebral aneurysm*. Of these two lines, only the first one is an answer choice. The correct answer is (B).

4. **C** This question asks why the author included the italicized Chinese words. While she knows what the words mean in English, the narrator isn't sure which one her mother used, and *can never remember things [she] didn't understand in the first place*. This indicates a gap in understanding between the narrator and her parents. Choice (A) can be eliminated because it contradicts the passage—the narrator can't remember which word was used and didn't have a good understanding of the words—so eliminate it. Choice (B) can be eliminated because it uses deceptive language. While there is a difference between spoken Chinese and spoken English, this paragraph is only about Chinese words. Choice (C) matches the prediction about a gap between the narrator and her parents, so keep it. Choice (D) can be eliminated because the passage only states that the narrator is unsure of her mother's words, not that these words are commonly confused. The correct answer is (C).

5. **A** This question asks why the narrator's father is moving his hands frantically among the clothes in the trunk. Previously in the paragraph, the narrator states that her *mother and father left China with one stiff leather trunk filled only with fancy silk dresses*, and there was *no time to pack anything else*. Look for an answer that matches this. Choice (A) references the father's clothes, so keep it. Choice (B) is deceptive—he is not literally swimming—so eliminate it. Choice (C) is in the wrong order; they have already packed and thus aren't communicating about what to pack. Eliminate it. Choice (D) contra-

dicts the passage because they are both on the boat; eliminate it. The correct answer is (A).

6. **B** This question is the best evidence question in a paired set. Because Q5 was a specific question, simply look at the lines used to answer it. In lines 27–28 the narrator states that there were only *fancy silk dresses* in her parents' trunk, and her mother said *there was no time to pack anything else*. The correct answer is (B).

7. **D** This question asks what the word *unspeakable* means in line 48. Go back to the text, find the word *unspeakable*, and cross it out. Then read the window carefully, using context clues to determine another word that would fit in the text. The text says *the women of these families also had unspeakable tragedies they had left behind in China*. Therefore, *unspeakable* must mean something like "really bad" or "terrible." *Impossible* and *subtle* don't mean "terrible," so eliminate (A) and (B). *Scandalous* doesn't match the context of *tragedies*, so eliminate (C). The correct answer is (D).

8. **C** This question asks what the word *fragile* means in line 50. Go back to the text, find the word *fragile*, and cross it out. Then read the window carefully, using context clues to determine another word that would fit in the text. The text says the women, who were immigrants from China, had *hopes they couldn't begin to express in their fragile English*. Therefore *fragile* must mean something like "non-fluent" or "unsteady." *Brittle* and *crisp* mean "breakable" and "crumbly" and therefore don't match "non-fluent" or "unsteady"; eliminate (A) and (B). Choice (D), *antiquated,* means "old," so eliminate it. Only (C) matches "non-fluent" or "unsteady," so keep it. The correct answer is (C).

9. **A** This question asks why the author included the final sentence of the passage. The text states that the ending of her mother's story *grew darker, casting long shadows into her life, and eventually into mine*. This indicates that the narrator will describe how she was impacted by the events of her mother's life. Choice (A) matches this prediction, so keep it. Choice (B) is too literal: while the narrator's mother did adjust the ending, it was not a creative endeavor. Eliminate (B). The narrator is not dealing with a *confusing memory*, so eliminate (C). There is no conflict in the text, so eliminate (D). The correct answer is (A).

10. **D** This question asks what the word *material* most nearly means in line 6. Go back to the text, find the word *material*, and cross it out. Then read the window carefully, using context clues to determine another word that would fit in the text. The text says that *experiences bring people more happiness than do possessions*. That contrast is continued into the next sentence as the author says *experiential purchases are more satisfying than material purchases*. The missing word must mean something like "possessions." Choice (A) does not fit and can be eliminated. Choice (B) is another definition of *material* but does not fit this context. Choice (C) does not fit, since experiences can also be actual. Choice (D) fits, as *possessions* are *physical* items. The correct answer is (D).

11. **C** This question asks why the author puts the phrase *provides more enduring happiness* in quotes. Carefully read the window to determine why the author emphasized that phrase. The paragraph begins with an introduction of the idea that research shows experiences bring more happiness than possessions do. The paragraph goes on to discuss the specific research of Gilovich and Killingsworth, saying that they *expanded on the current understanding* that spending money on experiences *provides*

more enduring happiness. The two researchers are going further into an idea that previous research has established. The correct answer should have something to do with the idea of "emphasizing what the researchers wanted to focus on." Choice (A) can be eliminated because the researchers want to *expand* the idea, not *disprove* it. Choice (B) can be eliminated because the phrase in question does not summarize any findings. Choice (C) is consistent with the prediction, so keep it. Choice (D) can be eliminated because there is no intention to *question the current understanding*, but rather to *expand* it. The correct answer is (C).

12. **D** This question asks about a difference in the passage between *waiting for a possession* and *waiting for an experience.* Use the key words to find the window to read. Paragraph 3 begins with a contrast: *Waiting for an experience apparently elicits more happiness and excitement than waiting for a material good.* It then continues to specifically explain the contrast. According to lines 29–30, waiting for a possession is *more likely fraught with impatience than anticipation.* The correct answer should be consistent with that idea. Choice (A) can be eliminated because *efficiency* and *indifference* are not the contrasting ideas from the text. Choice (B) is deceptive by using the word *eerie* from the window, but it doesn't match the prediction. Choice (C) may be tempting because it begins with *happiness*, but it can be eliminated because both words are positive. In (D), *agitation and enthusiasm* are synonyms for *impatience and anticipation*, so keep (D). The correct answer is (D).

13. **C** This question asks for the best evidence for the answer to question 12. That answer was based on lines 29–30 ("By contrast…anticipation") and only (C) contains those lines. The correct answer is (C).

14. **B** This question asks what the word *sweet* most nearly means, as used in line 52. Go back to the text, find the word *sweet*, and cross it out. Then read the window carefully, using context clues to determine another word that would fit in the text. The text references memories that are *imperfect* or *bad*, and then goes on to say that *but…[they] get sweet with time.* The contrast means the correct answer will mean the opposite of "good" or "pleasant." Choices (A), (C), and (D) all mean sweet to the taste, and can be eliminated. Choice (B) has a positive connotation without meaning literally sweet to the taste. The correct answer is (B).

15. **D** This question asks what is true about an experience that is *bad in the moment.* Notice that this is the first question in a paired set, so it can be done in tandem with Q16. Begin with the answers to Q16 first. The lines for (16A) say that a vacation will be *over and gone*, but those lines don't support any of the answers for Q15. Eliminate (16A). The lines for (16B) give an example of a bad moment and a happy memory that came from that moment. These lines support (15D), so draw a line connecting those two answers. The lines for (16C) don't reference an experience at all, so eliminate (16C). The lines for (16D) refer to buying material items, not bad experiences, so these lines don't support any of the answers for Q15. Eliminate (16D). Without support from Q16, (15A), (15B), and (15C) can all be eliminated. The correct answers are (15D) and (16B).

16. **B** (See explanation above.)

17. **B** This question asks which statement from the passage is best supported by Figure 1. First, examine the figure: read the title, axis names, and any other information present. The figure shows that

people who made a material purchase showed little change over the next month in their beliefs that their money was well-spent, whereas people who made an experiential purchase showed a clear increase in their beliefs over the next month that their money was well-spent. The answer will fit both of these ideas. Choice (A) is related to experiential purchases, but only talks about the pre-purchase phase and says nothing about material purchases; eliminate it. Choice (B) fits both predictions; keep it for now. Choice (C) involves a different contrast; eliminate it. Choice (D) has nothing to do with the prediction; eliminate it. The correct answer is (B).

18. **A** This question asks which point made in the passage is supported by Figure 2. First, examine the figure: read the title, axis names, and any other information present. The figure shows that in all four cases, purchase satisfaction is clearly greater for those who made experiential versus material purchases, so the answer will fit this prediction. Choice (A) fits this prediction; keep it for now. Choices (B), (C), and (D), although true statements from the passage, are irrelevant to the figure; eliminate them. The correct answer is (A).

19. **C** This question asks about the shift of the main focus over the course of the passage. Because this is a general question, it should be done after all the specific questions. The passage begins with a general description of echolocation and then moves into a description of a specific experiment designed to teach humans how to echolocate. Eliminate any answers that aren't consistent with this structure. Choice (A) may be tempting, but is a reversal, since the passage begins with contemporary research and later references research from the 1940s and 1950s; eliminate it. The first half of (B) seems possible, but the second half is not addressed in this passage, making this Mostly Right/ Slightly Wrong. No specific instructions about learning to echolocate are provided, so eliminate (B). Choice (C) is consistent with the prediction, so keep it for now. Choice (D) does not match either part of the prediction, so eliminate it. The correct answer is (C).

20. **A** This question asks about the primary purpose of the second paragraph. Read the second paragraph carefully to determine the main point. Note the first sentence: *People, remarkably, can also echolocate*. The word *also* is a clue to look at the first paragraph, which states that echolocation is most associated with certain animals. Thus, the second paragraph emphasizes that humans can also do this. The rest of the paragraph presents an example of a human being who can echolocate. The answer will reflect this prediction. Choice (A), *support an unexpected claim*, fits with the idea of humans learning echolocation, and the fact that it's *remarkable*; keep it for now. Choice (B) can be eliminated, as there is no controversy. Choice (C) may be tempting, but paragraph 2 does not *provide support for* the previous paragraph; it introduces a remarkable/unexpected idea. Eliminate (C). Choice (D) may be tempting, as paragraph 2 introduces something new—that humans can echolocate. However, echolocation is not *a completely new concept*, so eliminate (D). The correct answer is (A).

21. **C** This question asks about one of the *requirements for most effectively learning echolocation*. Eliminate anything that is unnecessary for learning to echolocate. The third paragraph says that *anyone with normal hearing can learn*, so eliminate (A). The last paragraph references *neural changes*, but does not say anything about *normal neural function*. Eliminate (B). The text states that *those people who had higher attentional capacity scores also showed greater improvement in their echolocation ability*. Keep

(C). Choice (D) can be eliminated because the experimenters *did not ask people to make mouth clicks, but allowed [them] to use a loudspeaker mounted on their heads*. The correct answer is (C).

22. **A** Find where the author discusses the specifics of the experiment, which is lines 34–46. Go through each answer choice and eliminate anything not supported by the text. The paragraph says that *people were allowed to use a loudspeaker* instead of making mouth clicks, so keep (A). Choice (B) can be eliminated because there is no mention of sighted versus blind people within the discussion of the experiment. Choice (C) can also be eliminated because there was no *hearing test* administered. Choice (D) might initially look good, because it could be true that researchers are making that assumption. However, compare (A) and (D), and (A) is the only one of the two supported by the text. The correct answer is (A).

23. **B** This is the best-evidence question for the previous question. Simply consider the lines used to answer Q22. The answer came from lines 36–38, *did not ask people to make mouth clicks, but … use a loudspeaker*. The correct answer is (B).

24. **B** This question asks what *select* most nearly means, as used in line 57. Go back to the text, find the word *select*, and cross it out. Then read the window carefully, using context clues to determine another word that would fit in the text. The text refers to *select blind people who were able to…detect subtle changes*. The missing word must mean something like "certain" or "some." Choice (A), *elite*, makes a distinction, but the passage does not support one group of blind people as better than another; eliminate it. Choice (B), *specific*, is possible, so keep it for now. Choice (C), *delicate*, does not match the prediction; eliminate it. Choice (D), *chosen*, makes a distinction, but no one chose the group of blind people, so eliminate it. The correct answer is (B).

25. **D** This question asks which choice best supports a specific claim made in the passage: that changes in air pressure were not actually helping blind people. Because the locations of the possible answers are given, simply go to those lines and eliminate all the ones that don't address the claim. Choice (A) talks about attention, rather than air pressure; eliminate it. Choice (B) simply provides historical information about vocabulary used in early research, so eliminate it. Choice (C) is tempting, because it talks about detecting changes in air pressure, but the correct answer will say that these changes did *not* help; eliminate it. Choice (D) indicates that something other than air pressure was helping blind people, which fits the idea that air pressure was not helping blind people. The correct answer is (D).

26. **D** This question asks what *driving* most nearly means, as used in line 70. Go back to the text, find the word *driving*, and cross it out. Then read the window carefully, using context clues to determine another word that would fit in the text. The text refers to the *learnability of echolocation* and *attentional capacity…driving the acquisition* of the skill. The missing word must mean something like "motivating" or "encouraging." Choice (A), *transporting*, evokes a different meaning of the word *driving*; eliminate it. Choices (B), *provoking*, and (C), *constraining*, do not match the prediction; eliminate them. Choice (D), *stimulating*, is consistent with "motivating" or "encouraging." The correct answer is (D).

27. **B** This question asks what purpose Figures 1 and 2 serve in relation to the passage as a whole. First, examine the figures: read the titles, axis names, and any other information present. Figure 1 shows that the four sessions with sound resulted in better performance than the four sessions with no sound. Figure 2 shows a line of best fit for the data points, indicating a moderate positive correlation between an attentional score and an increase in performance. Thus, Figures 1 and 2 together support the ideas mentioned in the passage that echolocation and attention are important for blind people to navigate in the world. Choice (A) is the opposite of that idea, and (B) fits this idea, so eliminate (A) and keep (B) for now. Choice (C) incorrectly states that the details are *not mentioned in the passage*; eliminate it. Choice (D) incorrectly concludes that the figures *present a different explanation* for the findings; eliminate it. The correct answer is (B).

28. **C** This question asks who improved the most in learning echolocation, based on the passage and on Figure 1. First, examine Figure 1 to see who improved the most. From Session 1 Sound to Session 4 Sound, there seems to have been improvement. From Session 1 No Sound to Session 4 No Sound, there seems to have been a decline in performance. Choices (A) and (B) both state that improvements happened *with no sound*, so they can be eliminated. Choices (C) and (D) both state that improvements happened *with sound*; keep them. Choice (C) mentions *four trials*, which fits the figure; keep it for now. Choice (D) mentions *two trials*, which does not fit the figure; eliminate it. The correct answer is (C).

29. **A** This question asks about the primary purpose of the passage. Because it's a general question, it should be done after all the specific questions. The blurb says that in the passage, Cable *defends attacks against his previous article*. Later in the passage he says that many believe *civil rights mean social equality* and because of that, they misinterpreted his original article. He then goes on to explain the misinterpretation, and the difference between the two ideas. Choice (A) seems to be consistent with this structure, so keep it. Choice (B) can be eliminated, because he is not advocating for restrictions; he's trying to clarify the difference between two ideas. Choice (C) can be eliminated because Cable is against the idea of social rights, not civil rights. Choice (D) relates to the passage, but it's incomplete. While there are definitely challenges to arguing for social equality, that is not the primary purpose of the passage. Eliminate (D). The correct answer is (A).

30. **D** This question asks about beliefs attributable to *people in the South* in the first paragraph. Carefully read the first paragraph to determine how Cable describes their beliefs. He says that they sincerely believe *recognition of rights proposed… would precipitate social chaos*. He goes on to say this is a *transparent error*, so he has a negative view of their beliefs. Eliminate (A) and (C) because those are both positive. Compare (B) and (D). There are no *personal views* presented, so eliminate (B). There is a clear position that Cable goes on to reject, so (D) is supported. The correct answer is (D).

31. **B** This question asks why the author uses the phrases *total unconsciousness* and *grooves of the old traditions*. Locate the phrases and read the entire paragraph to determine what Cable is referring to. In that paragraph, he explains why many white people of the South misunderstand the point of Civil Rights bills and his writings. Eliminate any answer choices that aren't consistent with this prediction. While it Could Be True that the author feels *frustration and anger*, the passage does not state this;

eliminate (A). It is true that the author is describing an *incorrect assumption*, so keep (B) for now. The author does not explicitly endorse *sympathetic understanding*, nor does he *call for an investigation into a viewpoint*, so eliminate (C) and (D). The correct answer is (B).

32. **D** This question asks about the argument Cable makes about the criticism of his "Freedman's Case" from the South. Notice that this is the first question in a paired set, so it can be done in tandem with Q33. Consider the answers to Q33 first. The lines for (33A) simply say *the answer is simple*, which is not an argument. It does not support any of the answers for Q32, so eliminate it. The lines for (33B) say that he did not write anything about *the domain of social privileges* and then go on to say the magazine in which the paper appeared would never publish something that was an *insult to the intelligence of enlightened society*. These lines might initially look good, because he is defending his paper. He isn't, however, addressesing the *Southern criticism* of the paper. Eliminate (33B). The lines for (33C) say that he wants as little of social equality *as the most fervent traditionists of the most fervent South*, or that the Southern criticism is unwarranted because he actually wants the same thing they do. These lines support (32D), so draw a line connecting those two answers. The lines for (33D) do not address Cable's reaction to Southerners' criticism of his piece, so eliminate (33D). Without support from Q33, (32A), (32B), and (32C) can be eliminated. The correct answers are (32D) and (33C).

33. **C** (See explanation above.)

34. **D** This question asks what Cable suggests about *attempting to achieve social equality*. Notice that this is the first question in a paired set, so it can be done in tandem with Q35. Consider the answers for Q35 first. The lines for (35A) refer to identifying the *immovable hostility* and determining *why it is*. These lines don't mention achieving social equality and don't support any of the answers for Q34. Eliminate (35A). The lines for (35B) continue with a discussion of the misinterpretation of civil rights and social equality, but don't mention anything about *attempting to achieve social equality*. Eliminate (35B). The lines for (35C) ask a rhetorical question that does not address the issue. Eliminate (35C). The lines for (35D) specifically address a problem with social equality: classing impersonal rights as social privileges and *treating them as rights definable by law*. These lines describe a negative situation, so they don't support (34A) or (34C). Compare (34B) and (34D). There is no mention of a struggle to *maintain the established social structure*, so the lines don't support (34B). The text does say that social amenities are *not rights and cannot be*, which is strong language to support the strong wording of (34D). The correct answers are (34D) and (35D).

35. **D** (See explanation above.)

36. **B** This question asks about a principal difference Cable sees *between himself and his critics*. Throughout the passage, Cable writes for civil rights and against social equality, so eliminate (A). Choice (B) is consistent with the text, so keep it. Choice (C) can be eliminated, because Cable is against the idea of trying to establish laws for *social equality*, not *civil rights*. Choice (D) can also be eliminated, because Cable encourages the fight for civil rights. The correct answer is (B).

37. **B** This question asks what Cable means about himself when he refers to *a fool's fear*. Go back to the text and carefully read the window to determine what he's referring to. He says that nothing, *no*

form of laws, no definition of rights… can bring [social equality] about. To fear it is nothing but a *fool's fear.* The correct answer will be consistent with the idea that Cable is completely sure that social equality will not happen. Choice (A) can be eliminated because Cable is clarifying his position in this text, not changing it. Choice (B) is consistent with the prediction, so keep it. Choice (C) can be eliminated because Cable himself rejects the idea of social equality. Choice (D) can also be eliminated because Cable is not on a quest for social equality. The correct answer is (B).

38. **D** This question asks what *enlarge* most nearly means, as used in line 60. Go back to the text, find the word *enlarge*, and cross it out. Then read the window carefully, using context clues to determine another word that would fit in the text. Cable says that for anyone *who still might misunderstand,* he is going to *enlarge.* He then goes on to give further examples of his argument in order to clarify the point he wants to make. The missing word must mean something like "explain" or "clarify." Choices (B) and (C) can be eliminated immediately. They are definitions of *enlarge,* but they are not consistent with the context of the passage. Choice (A) might initially look good, but in this part of the text, Cable isn't trying to *strengthen* his argument, he's just trying to "explain" it. Choice (D) is consistent with the prediction. The correct answer is (D).

39. **C** This question asks about the primary purpose of both passages. Because this is a general question about both passages, it should be done after all the other questions. Use POE to eliminate answers by considering one passage at a time. Start with Passage 1. The passage does discuss the effects of controlled floods on animals, so keep (A). Choice (B) is too broad, so eliminate it. Choice (C) also reflects Passage 1, so keep it. Choice (D) can be eliminated because Passage 1 discusses problems with some of the manmade changes. Now consider the remaining answers in the context of Passage 2. The passage does not discuss animal species, so eliminate (A). It does focus on a changing ecosystem through a specific example. The correct answer is (C).

40. **C** This question asks what *composition* most nearly means as used in line 16. Go back to the text, find the word *composition,* and cross it out. Replace it with another word that makes sense based on the text. The passage discusses changes from the dam, listing *loss of beaches, narrowing of rapids,* and *changes in … vegetation.* The vegetation changed both in *distribution* and *composition.* The missing word must have something to do with ways vegetation can be changed, and must mean something like "type" or "arrangement." Choices (A) and (B) are both possible definitions of *composition,* but neither is consistent with the prediction and can be eliminated. Choice (C) is consistent with the prediction, so keep it. Choice (D) can be eliminated, because the vegetation is being changed, not created. The correct answer is (C).

41. **A** This question asks what *free* most nearly means as used in the text. Go back to line 53, find the word *free,* and cross it out. Replace it with another word that makes sense based on the text. The text says the sandbar was *25% less* and that tributaries are supplying *only a fraction of the pre-dam sand supply.* The missing word must mean something like "missing" or "empty." Choice (A) is consistent with this prediction, so keep it. Choice (B) is another definition of *free,* but it isn't consistent with the prediction, so eliminate it. Neither (C) nor (D), "allowing" and "vigorous," means "missing" or "empty," so both of those can be eliminated. The correct answer is (A).

42. **A** This question asks when suspended sand is released by the water, according to Passage 2. Skim for lead words and carefully read the window around those words. In the second paragraph, the author says that sand is *suspended at high concentration in the flow* and then *deposited in… low stream-flow velocity*. Choice (A) is the only answer that is consistent with this information. The correct answer is (A).

43. **B** This question asks for the best evidence to support the previous answer. Simply consider the lines used to answer Q42, *sand… is deposited in areas of low stream-flow velocity*. Choice (B) is the answer that contains these lines. The correct answer is (B).

44. **C** This question asks whether the author of Passage 2 would agree that floods *only threaten archaeological sites along the walls of the Grand Canyon*. Skim for lead words and carefully read the window around those words. At the end of the second paragraph, the author of Passage 2 states that *windblown sand… helps to cover and potentially preserve… archeological sites in the Grand Canyon*. Therefore, the author would not agree with the hypothesis. Eliminate (A) and (B). Choice (C) is consistent with the prediction, while (D) is not. The correct answer is (C).

45. **C** This question asks which answer provides the strongest evidence for floods being detrimental. Because the answers themselves are lines from the text, go straight to the answer choices and eliminate anything that doesn't address detrimental controlled floods. Choice (A) does not contain evidence of detrimental effects; eliminate it. Choice (B) talks about benefits of *newly deposited sandbars,* which is the opposite of what the question asks for. Eliminate (B). Choice (C) says that *controlled floods may erode sandbars.* This is a negative effect of the floods, so keep (C). Choice (D) provides neither a positive nor a negative effect of the floods, so it does not answer the question. The correct answer is (C).

46. **B** This question asks about *camping beaches* mentioned in Passage 2, and what they could be a part of based on Passage 1. First read the window carefully in Passage 2 to find information about camping beaches. They are produced by sandbars enlarged by controlled floods. Eliminate any answer choice that does not mention an area expanded by controlled floods. The Paria River is mentioned in Passage 2, but not in Passage 1, so eliminate (A). Passage 1 mentions the *Colorado River Basin* and the *loss of beaches used for camping,* so keep (B). The beaches are not on the Glen Canyon Dam itself, so (C) can also be eliminated. Lake Powell is mentioned in Passage 2, but not in Passage 1, so it can be eliminated. The correct answer is (B).

47. **B** This question asks about the *controlled floods* mentioned in Passage 2, and what event previously caused flooding, according to Passage 1. The first sentence of the second paragraph says that *spring snowmelt floods were the defining attribute of the pre-dam flow regime*. Therefore, controlled floods replaced floods caused by spring snowmelt. The correct answer is (B).

Part III
Writing and
Language Test

10   Writing and Language Test Drill 1
11   Writing and Language Test Drill 1: Answers and
     Explanations
12   Writing and Language Test Drill 2
13   Writing and Language Test Drill 2: Answers and
     Explanations
14   Writing and Language Test Drill 3
15   Writing and Language Test Drill 3: Answers and
     Explanations

Chapter 10
Writing and Language Test Drill 1

Writing and Language Test

35 MINUTES, 44 QUESTIONS

Turn to Section 2 of your answer sheet to answer the questions in this section.

Questions 1-11 are based on the following passage.

The Economics of the Environment

As each of us tries to be more environmentally conscious, we have to consider certain **1** trade offs. Many of us would love, for instance, to wire our homes for solar electricity, but sometimes it's just not in the budget. We'd love to drive alternative-fuel cars, like those with hydrogen fuel-cells or electric engines, but we may not be able to afford such cars. **2** It would be great to buy sustainably grown vegetables or meats, but sometimes **3** it's just too expensive.

1

Which of the following alternatives to the underlined portion would be LEAST acceptable?

A) concessions

B) compromises

C) allowances

D) swaps

2

A) NO CHANGE

B) We are loving

C) We want to

D) We'd love

3

A) NO CHANGE

B) they're

C) its

D) one's

 CONTINUE

4 Considerations like these occupy many environmentally conscious people, and the answers are by no means simple. On a much larger scale, these considerations occupy environmental economists.

     5 Big questions are like the bread and butter for economists all kinds. First of all, economics doesn't have an obvious relationship to the environment. Second of all, where economics *does* have a relationship to the environment, that relationship seems to be one of conflict rather than conservation. How, we might expect an economist to ask, can a resource be implemented efficiently and with the greatest possible profit margin? There seems to be more emphasis here on **6** how *used* rather than *conserved* environmental resources can be.

4

Which of the following would provide the best transition between the initial discussion in the paragraph and the idea presented in the last line of the paragraph?

A) NO CHANGE

B) Sometimes organic produce can cost twice as much as traditionally farmed produce.

C) Microeconomics is on a small scale; macroeconomics is on a large one.

D) Economists can work in a wide variety of fields and specializations.

5

Which of the following would provide the best introduction to this paragraph?

A) NO CHANGE

B) The job title might seem like a contradiction in terms.

C) There are a few things about environmental economists that are interesting.

D) What are a few things that environmental economists do?

6

A) NO CHANGE

B) conservation rather than usage in the environmental-resource department.

C) how environmental resources can be used rather than conserved.

D) how some of the environment's riches that are used can be conserved.

However, environmental economists cannot be categorized so easily. **7** While they are often interested in the workings of the market, they are interested in finding ways that environmental conservation can work effectively within that market. For **8** instance: if a company is allowed to pollute freely by dumping its waste into a nearby river, that act has negative consequences because it damages other potential market activities: tourist kayaking, camping, clean water, etc. For environmental economists, in fact, pollution is seen as an *anti*-market practice because **9** they have the same selfish effect of cornering the market as do monopolies.

7

Which of the following alternatives to the underlined portion would be LEAST acceptable?

A) Although
B) Whereas
C) Because
D) Though

8

A) NO CHANGE
B) instance, if
C) instance; if
D) instance if:

9

A) NO CHANGE
B) it has
C) the two things have
D) its inefficiency and waste have

CONTINUE ▶

In this sense, environmental economists occupy **10** a middle-ground between hardcore environmentalists and those who think people should be free to pollute as much as they want. In order for pollution to come down to absolute non-existence, the economy would essentially have to shut down. If people were not regulated at all, the consequences (economic and otherwise) could be similarly dire. As a result, environmental economists are in the business of trying to find economically and environmentally reasonable amounts of pollution and to advise businesses and politicians accordingly. **11** As we continue to see changes in how the world thinks about protecting the environment, we will see more of the counterintuitive but absolutely essential work of environmental economists.

10

A) NO CHANGE

B) a middle-ground, between hardcore environmentalists, and those who think people should be free to pollute as much as they want.

C) a middle-ground, between hardcore environmentalists, and those who think people should be free to pollute, as much as they want.

D) a middle-ground between hardcore environmentalists, and those who think people should be free to pollute, as much as they want.

11

The author is considering rewriting the previous sentence as follows:

> As a result, environmental economists are in the business of trying to advise businesses and politicians accordingly.

Should the sentence be kept as it is or rewritten?

A) Kept as is, because the sentence does not have sufficient information otherwise.

B) Kept as is, because the sentence sounds more formal without the deletions.

C) Rewritten, because the sentence contains redundant information as written.

D) Rewritten, because the sentence as written is irrelevant to the paragraph as a whole.

CONTINUE ➡

Questions 12-22 are based on the following passage.

The Runway to Civil Rights

[1]

12 Because it does mark a kind of leap forward for civil rights, the end of the Civil War was by no means the end of cruel treatment toward African Americans in the United States. In 1896, the U.S. Supreme Court ruled in favor of the practice of what was called "separate but equal" treatment for the races in the United States. **13** The fact of the matter was that things were separate but certainly not equal. African Americans were no longer enslaved, but they were still treated like second-class citizens. Even the anti-lynching laws, which **14** punish the mob killings of African Americans that had been rampant and unpunished since the 1860s, did not appear until the 1940s.

[2]

For the early part of the twentieth century, another manifestation of this legal segregation was in the military. Black and white men could not serve in the same companies, and **15** in particular they were barred from assuming certain military positions. For example, during World War I, **16** sometimes called "The Great War," there was not a single African American pilot in the entire air force.

12

A) NO CHANGE

B) It does

C) While it does

D) Really, it does

13

Which of the following would provide the most detailed support for the claim made in the previous sentence?

A) The case started in Louisiana and went all the way to the Supreme Court!

B) The ruling was not to be overturned until *Brown v. Board of Education* in 1954.

C) The defendant in the case was Homer Plessy, who was considered "black" because he had one African-American great grandparent.

D) Train cars, bathrooms, hotels, even water fountains were marked "White" and "Colored."

14

A) NO CHANGE

B) had punished

C) were punishing

D) punished

15

A) NO CHANGE

B) those in particular

C) black men in particular

D) in particular some

16

Which of the following best maintains the focus of this sentence?

A) NO CHANGE

B) a war fought in large part in the air,

C) which the U.S. joined kind of late,

D) during which President Woodrow Wilson declared war on Germany,

CONTINUE

[3]

The Civil Rights decade—the era of [17] Martin Luther King and Malcolm X—is really considered the 1960s. However, that era would not have been possible without the bravery of African American soldiers [18] who fought valiantly in World War II. Radio comedian Jack Benny spoke for many Americans when he said, "When the black man's fight for equal rights and fair play became an issue after the war, I would no longer allow Rochester [a black character on his show] to say or do anything that an audience would consider degrading to the dignity of a modern Afro-American." The bravery of the Tuskegee Airmen and others brought the humanity and patriotism of African Americans to [19] our attention. Even though white Americans should've been much more welcoming much earlier, [20] the Tuskegee Airmen overwhelmed prejudice and led to some real changes.

17

A) NO CHANGE
B) Martin Luther King and Malcolm X, is
C) Martin Luther King, and Malcolm X—is
D) Martin Luther King—and Malcolm X—is

18

A) NO CHANGE
B) who fought with vim and vigor
C) who showed their true guts
D) DELETE the underlined portion.

19

A) NO CHANGE
B) the nation's
C) the national people's
D) people's

20

Which of the following would best conclude this paragraph by restating its main idea?

A) NO CHANGE
B) the Tuskegee Airmen fought hard whether anyone knew it or not.
C) the military is now integrated, and it has been for a while.
D) prejudice still exists in many forms in the United States today.

CONTINUE

[4]

After twenty years of protest, African-American leaders finally began to break down some of this military segregation. In 1939, Appropriations Bill Public Law 18 was passed, allotting some military funding for African American pilots. In time, technical training was available to qualified pilots of all races, and programs like that of Tuskegee, an all-black university in Alabama, came to a new national prominence. With the advanced training they received at Tuskegee, a new crop of pilots, known as the Tuskegee Airmen, were given **21** there rightful place in the Allied victory in the Second World War. **22**

21

A) NO CHANGE

B) they're

C) their

D) DELETE the underlined portion.

22

The best placement for paragraph 4 would be

A) where it is now.

B) before paragraph 1.

C) before paragraph 2.

D) before paragraph 3.

CONTINUE ➤

Questions 23-33 are based on the following passage and supplemental material.

Faces Made for Radio

Critics and historians typically set 1953 as the birth year for the TV revolution in the United States. [23] Between 1950 and 1955, the number of households that owned a TV grew a staggering amount, [24] from 4% to 12% of all American households. As a result, television programs (like Jack Benny's or Sid Caesar's) became part of the national conversation.

23

Which of the following maintains the focus of this paragraph and presents accurate information based on the chart?

A) NO CHANGE

B) From 1950 to 1975,

C) After 1980,

D) Since 2000,

24

Which of the following maintains the focus of this paragraph and accurate information based on the chart?

A) NO CHANGE

B) though after 1965, pretty much everyone had a TV.

C) from a tenth to about two-thirds of all American households.

D) much like cable grew between 1970 and 1975.

Television Set Ownership											
Estimated total number of TV households: 100,800,000											
	1950	1955	1960	1965	1970	1975	1980	1985	1990	1995	2000
% of total households:											
TV households	10	67	87	94	96	97	98	98	98	98	98
% of TV households:											
Multi-set	—	4	12	22	35	43	50	57	65	71	76
Color	—	—	—	7	41	74	83	91	98	99	99
VCR	—	—	—	—	—	—	—	14	66	79	85
Remote control	—	—	—	—	—	—	—	29	77	91	95
Wired pay cable	—	—	—	—	—	—	—	26	29	28	32
Wired cable	—	—	—	—	7	12	20	43	56	63	68

CONTINUE ▶

This birth year doesn't tell the whole story, however. TV did not emerge out of the blue, and the three big stations— 25 NBC, CBS, and also ABC—preexisted TV by a long shot. All three already existed as radio stations throughout the 1930s and 26 1940s; the only change was that ABC used to be known as "NBC Red." 27 In addition, many of the shows on early television were simply visual adaptations of radio plays that had gained significant followings in the previous decades.

25

A) NO CHANGE

B) NBC, CBS, and ABC

C) NBC, CBS, or ABC

D) NBC-CBS-ABC

26

Which of the following alternatives to the underlined portion would NOT be acceptable?

A) 1940s, the only

B) 1940s—the only

C) 1940s. The only

D) 1940s: the only

27

A) NO CHANGE

B) Anyway,

C) Meanwhile,

D) For all that,

CONTINUE

This transition period is fascinating because it provides a [28] concrete instance of how shifts in media actually happen. Although the narrative structures and scripts could often be lifted from radio directly, the visual aspects of TV were more complex than many radio performers anticipated. One of the biggest problems was that while radio comedians' *voices* may not have aged, their faces did, and many comedians were out of work because their images could not properly align with [29] the expectations of the viewer. Jim and Marian Jordan, the creators and stars of *Fibber McGee and Molly*, had no choice in the matter: they sold the identities of the characters in the 1940s when the getting was good, and the network replaced [30] them. With younger actors as soon as the show went to TV.

Which of the following alternatives to the underlined portion would be LEAST acceptable?

A) tangible

B) definitive

C) hard

D) substantial

A) NO CHANGE

B) the expectations of the viewers.

C) the expectation of the viewer.

D) the expectation of the viewer's.

A) NO CHANGE

B) them; with

C) them, with

D) them with

The shift to television had some positive social impact as well. Although the voices on the radio may have been racially and ethnically diverse, the same could not be said for the actors. The practice of minstrelsy, white actors mimicking and mocking the voices of African-Americans, was rampant in the radio era. However, when shows like *The Beulah Show,* [31] who's main character was an African-American woman, came to television, no audience would stand the incongruity between sight and sound. As a result, many of the firsts for non-white actors in show business came during the television era [32] when the new medium forced network executives to change with the times.

There's no telling what our own era's shift will bring, or whether that shift will be so [33] nuts. Still, as much as we think we understand the mediascape in which we live, that golden year of 1953 shows us that there may be more to a simple change of medium than we think.

31

A) NO CHANGE
B) who is
C) whose
D) their

32

Which of the following would provide the most effective conclusion to this paragraph?

A) NO CHANGE
B) though many radio programs would last into the early 1960s.
C) as many white actors were able to handle the transition.
D) despite the obvious lack of non-white talent in the cinema.

33

A) NO CHANGE
B) radical.
C) off the wall.
D) crazy.

CONTINUE ▶

Questions 34-44 are based on the following passage.

Taking the Express Microbiome Downtown

    Anyone who has ever ridden the subway in New York knows that it can be a mysterious and diverse place. People from **34** all walks of life ride the subway, and many have different ideas about what should and shouldn't be done there. If you have food, should you eat it on the subway? Should you sit or stand? **35** I guess it depends: how far are you going to ride?

34

A) NO CHANGE
B) all of life's walks
C) all lives of walking
D) walking all our lives

35

Which of the following would best maintain the style and focus of this paragraph?

A) NO CHANGE
B) Should you hold onto the railings, or is it best to touch nothing at all?
C) How much does it cost to ride the subway versus taking the bus?
D) Does the subway run twenty-four hours a day, seven days a week?

These behavioral questions may never be settled, and there may never be a way to know who is riding next to you. In a recent study, however, a team of scientists **36** have discovered "who" is riding alongside you on the microbial level. **37** A compiled team of researchers led by Christopher Mason, a data geneticist at Weill Cornell Medical College in Manhattan. Mason's team went to all 468 of the stops on the New York subway and the Staten Island Railway, and they swabbed whatever they could find: **38** pretty gross work for most laypeople. They took the swabs back to the lab to discover what life was like on the microbial level in New York's train system.

"The subway kind of looks like skin," said Christopher Mason, by which he meant that most of the bacteria that live on human skin also live on the **39** trains from people's skin. This makes sense, as the human skin and the trains' surfaces are both coated in food particles. No matter how clean you are, your food leaves a trail! **40** Living inside the subway, researchers found traces of mozzarella, chickpeas, and just about anything else you can name.

36
A) NO CHANGE
B) are discovering
C) has discovered
D) was discovered

37
A) NO CHANGE
B) Christopher Mason led a research team, a geneticist at Weill Cornell Medical College in Manhattan, with the data.
C) The data sets was compiled by a research team of Christopher Mason and the Weill Cornell Medical College of Manhattan.
D) A team of researchers led by Christopher Mason, a geneticist at Weill Cornell Medical College in Manhattan, compiled the data.

38
Which of the following would most effectively complete the sentence by providing specific support for the idea presented in the first part of the sentence?
A) NO CHANGE
B) their methods were scientifically sound.
C) there's a lot of disgusting stuff to swab in a subway station.
D) ticket machines, handrails, garbage cans, and seats.

39
A) NO CHANGE
B) trains from homo sapiens.
C) trains.
D) things.

40
A) NO CHANGE
B) In running DNA scans,
C) Fresh off of people's pizza and falafel,
D) Responsible for the subway's foul odor,

CONTINUE ▶

The researchers also turned up some bizarre findings. **41** They found traces of the diseases anthrax and plague, but the cells were found to be totally dead. Then, perhaps most curious of all, the researchers found nearly 1,688 organisms or molecules they couldn't identify, quite an odd **42** compliment to the certainty of all the other research. This has left a long and curious path for the researchers to travel and could lead to a new understanding of New York City's **43** diversity, which is some of the most in the world.

In fact, this seemingly frivolous study could have all kinds of future applications. As the study itself claims, "This baseline metagenomic map of NYC could help long-term disease surveillance, bioterrorism threat mitigation, and health management in the built environment of cities." In other words, understanding how a place works on the cellular level may explain **44** the human level. This is a curious study, but it provides an important reminder that the world around us is much more complex than we could ever acknowledge.

41

A) NO CHANGE

B) They found traces of the diseases anthrax and plague, but they were all totally dead.

C) Anthrax and plague were among the traces of disease that they found, but all of them were dead.

D) They were mostly dead, but anthrax and plague were among some of the traces of disease found.

42

A) NO CHANGE

B) complimentary

C) complement

D) complementary

43

The writer wants to add an idea that will emphasize how the new findings will add information for which previous surveys and studies could not account. Which of the following would most effectively add that information?

A) NO CHANGE

B) diversity that the census simply can't capture.

C) diversity, which is economic as well as racial.

D) diversity that spreads across all five of its boroughs.

44

A) NO CHANGE

B) the level of humans.

C) its workings on the level that humans occupy.

D) how it does so on the human level.

STOP
If you finish before time is called, you may check your work on this section only.
Do not turn to any other section.

Chapter 11
Writing and
Language Test
Drill 1: Answers
and Explanations

ANSWERS AND EXPLANATIONS

Section 2—Writing and Language Test

1. **D** Since the question is asking for the LEAST acceptable alternative to the underlined portion, then the phrase *trade offs* is correctly used. Eliminate any answer choices that are similar to *trade offs*. Get rid of (A), (B), and (C) since each is similar. This leaves (D), which means "exchanges," so it is the best answer.

2. **D** The underlined portion of this sentence contains a pronoun, so make sure it is consistent with the non-underlined portion by finding the other nouns and pronouns. The previous sentence uses the partner third-person pronoun *we* a few times, so eliminate (A). Eliminate (B) and (D) since neither are parallel with the earlier sentence. Choice (D) works because the earlier sentence also uses *we would love*, which makes it parallel. Choice (D) is the best answer.

3. **B** The underlined portion of this sentence contains a pronoun, so make sure it is consistent with the non-underlined portion by finding the other nouns and pronouns. The partner nouns *vegetables or meats* are used earlier in the paragraph, both of which are plural. Eliminate (A), (C), and (D) since each one of them is singular. This leaves (B), which is the best answer.

4. **A** Notice the question and use POE to find an answer consistent with the information in the paragraph. The author begins the first paragraph with *as each of us tries to be more environmentally conscious* and then goes on to discuss the difficulties, so the underlined sentence is consistent with this information. No comparison is made of *organic* and *traditionally farmed produce*, so eliminate (B). Eliminate (C) and (D) since the paragraph does not discuss economics or economists. Choice (A) is the best answer.

5. **B** Notice the question and use POE to find an answer consistent with information in the paragraph. The following sentence states *economics doesn't have an obvious relationship to the environment*, so (B) matches this information. Eliminate (A) since the passage isn't interested in all types of economists. Also, eliminate (C) for its conversational tone. The rest of the paragraph does not discuss what environmental economists do, so eliminate (D) since no answers are given to this question.

6. **C** Since the answer choices do not appear to be testing a consistent grammar rule, use POE to find the answer that is the most consistent and concise with the paragraph. Choice (C) is much more concise than the underlined portion, so eliminate (A). Choice (B) is also very wordy as it uses nouns instead of verbs to discuss the actions of *environmental resources*, so eliminate it. Eliminate (D) since it changes the intended meaning of the sentence. Choice (C) is the best answer.

7. **C** The question is asking for the LEAST acceptable alternative to the underlined portion, and the transition *while* is correctly used. *While* indicates a contrast, so eliminate (A), (B), and (D) since each also indicates a contrast. This leaves (C) as the best answer.

8. **B** Since the answer choices include periods and semicolons, this question is testing STOP punctuation. Draw the Vertical Line Test where the STOP punctuation is and check for complete ideas.

The first phrase is an incomplete idea, so eliminate (C) because STOP punctuation can only separate two complete ideas. Also, eliminate (A) and (D) because colons can only follow a complete idea. Therefore, (B) is the best answer.

9. **D** The underlined portion of this sentence contains a pronoun, so make sure it is consistent with the non-underlined portion by finding the other nouns and pronouns. It is not clear what *they* is referring to, so this is an ambiguous pronoun. Eliminate (A) and (B). Choice (C) is also unclear since the *two things* are not defined. This leaves (D), which clarifies what has an *effect* on the economy.

10. **A** The answer choices contain commas, so find the best answer in which they are correctly used, if at all. In the underlined passage, there is no reason to slow down the ideas in the sentence, so keep (A). Eliminate (B), (C), and (D) since each uses unnecessary commas to break up the flow of ideas in the sentence. Choice (A) is the best answer.

11. **A** Notice the question and use POE to find the best answer consistent with the information in the paragraph. The rewritten sentence is vague since it doesn't state what the economists are trying to advise the politicians and businesses on. Eliminate (C) and (D). Neither sentence sounds more formal than the other, so eliminate (B). This leaves (A), which is the best answer since it clarifies what the economists will advise politicians and businesses on.

12. **C** Look at the answers to see that they contain different conjunctions. Because the two ideas expressed by the sentence are opposites, we should be using a conjunction like *but*. Therefore, (A) can be eliminated. Without any conjunction, however, the sentence has two complete ideas separated by a comma. This would be incorrect. Therefore, you can eliminate (B) and (D). Choice (C) is correct.

13. **D** The previous sentence states that the Supreme Court upheld the practice known as "separate but equal." Choice (A) provides no support for the previous assertion and should be eliminated. Choice (B) discusses the overturning of that ruling, so it cannot support the previous sentence and should be eliminated. Choice (C) mentions the defendant, but it does not explain anything about the ruling, so it should be eliminated. Choice (D) is correct because it provides an example of the practice known as "separate but equal" as a visible consequence of the ruling.

14. **D** The answer choices indicate that verb tense is being tested, so let the non-underlined portions guide your choice of verb. Past tense is seen in *did not appear until the 1940s,* so (D) is consistent. Eliminate (A) because it is present tense, (B) because it is past participle, and (C) because it is present participle.

15. **C** The underlined portion of this sentence contains a pronoun, so make sure it is consistent with the non-underlined portion by finding the other pronouns and nouns. Because the partner noun could either be *white men* or *black men,* (A), (B), and (D) are ambiguous and therefore incorrect. Choice (C) is the best answer.

16. **B** Notice the question and use POE to find the best answer that maintains the sentence's focus on the air force. Choices (A), (C), and (D) make no mention of the air battles fought in WWI, so they are incorrect. Because (B) refers to air combat, it is the best answer.

17. **A** Look at the answers to see that comma usage and dash usage are being tested. Because the non-underlined portion is correct, a dash must be used to surround the unnecessary information in the sentence. First, check to see if *the era of Martin Luther King and Malcolm X* is necessary or unnecessary information. If removed from the sentence, it would still make sense, so it's unnecessary information. Therefore, (A) is a good answer. It places two dashes around unnecessary information. Choice (B) is incorrect because it uses a dash and a comma. Choice (C) is incorrect because it places a comma before *and* in a list of two people. Choice (D) is incorrect because it places a dash before *and,* which breaks up the list. Choice (A) is the best answer.

18. **D** Whenever you are given the option to delete, determine whether the underlined portion serves a precise role within the passage. In fact, the underlined portion is redundant with *bravery* and should therefore be eliminated. Choices (A), (B), and (C) all express the same idea as *bravery*. Therefore, (D) is the best answer.

19. **B** The underlined portion of this sentence is a pronoun, so make sure it is consistent with the non-underlined portion by finding the other pronouns and nouns. There are no other instances of *our* or *we* in the rest of the sentence, so (A) should be eliminated. Because the patriotism of African Americans came to the attention of America, (B) is a good answer. Because (C) expresses the same thing as (B), but is less concise, (C) should be eliminated. Because (D) mentions *people* without any indication of which people, it should be eliminated.

20. **A** The main idea of the paragraph in question is that the exploits of African American soldiers like the Tuskegee airmen helped bring about the civil rights era. Because the underlined sentence expresses the same idea, (A) is a good answer. Because it is vital to the paragraph's argument that people knew how hard the Tuskegee Airmen fought, (B) is incorrect. Choices (C) and (D) should be eliminated because both discuss the present day instead of the eras with which the passage is concerned.

21. **C** Look at the answers to see that each contains a different version of *they're, their,* or *there*. Because the underlined word should indicate the Tuskegee Airmen's rightful place, it should be *their,* the possessive form of *they*. This matches (C).

22. **D** Because paragraph four introduces the Tuskegee Airmen, it should come before any other mentions of that group. Therefore, it cannot be after paragraph three, so (A) is incorrect. Because the first sentence in paragraph four refers to *this military segregation,* it must come after some mention of military segregation. Because the final sentence of paragraph two mentions the segregation of the air force, paragraph four should come after paragraph two. Therefore, (B) and (C) are incorrect. The correct answer is (D).

23. **A** Notice the question and use POE to find an answer consistent with the information in the paragraph and table. Choice (A) matches the information in the graph since the percentages grew from 10% to 67% of households in just five years. Eliminate (B) because, while the percentage of households who own a TV grew in that time period, it began to stagnate around 1965. Eliminate (C) because the percentage of households was flat around this time. No information is given for after 2000, so eliminate (D).

24. **C** Notice the question and use POE to find an answer consistent with the information in the paragraph and table. Choice (A) refers to the wrong time period, and the numbers represent the percentage of households with pay cable. Eliminate (A). Choice (B) is too extreme since the table discusses households, not individual people, so eliminate it. Choice (C) matches the information in the table, so keep it. Eliminate (D) because cable's growth from 1970 to 1975 was much smaller than the growth of households owning televisions. Choice (C) is the best answer.

25. **B** Since there are commas in the answer choices, find the answer that uses them correctly. Choice (B) is correct since a comma is used after each item in the list and before the conjunction *and*. Choice (A) is wordy and not parallel. Because this is a list of the big three stations, "and" is needed rather than "or." Eliminate (C). Hyphens are not used to separate items in a list, so eliminate (D).

26. **A** Since there are periods and semicolons in the answer choices, this question is testing STOP punctuation. The question also wants the LEAST acceptable alternative to the underlined portion, so it must be correct. A semicolon is STOP punctuation, so eliminate (C) since a period is basically the same thing. Also, eliminate (B) and (D) because a colon and dash also serve the same purpose; therefore, both cannot be correct. This leaves (A), which is correct since a comma cannot separate two complete ideas.

27. **A** This sentence uses the phrase *many of the shows on early television were simply visual adaptations of radio plays* as further evidence of the continuity between radio and the early days of television. The underlined portion is correctly used, so keep (A). Each of the other choices are either contrasting or too conversational. Choice (A) is formal, so it is the best answer.

28. **C** Since the question is asking for the LEAST acceptable replacement for the underlined portion, the underlined portion is correct as written. In this context, *concrete* means "something that exists in material form" or "not abstract." Choices (A), (B), and (D) all match this definition. This leaves (C), which is a bit of a trap since it would be a common description of the typical use of *concrete*. Even so, it is the best answer.

29. **B** Notice the answer choices are changing *viewer* from singular to plural. The plural form is correct since television programs would have multiple *viewers* instead of a single *viewer*. Eliminate (A), (C), and (D). Choice (B) is the best answer.

30. **D** Since there are periods and semicolons in the answer choices, this question is testing STOP punctuation. Eliminate (A) and (B) because a semicolon and period are basically the same thing. Eliminate (C) because there is no reason to use a comma to pause the two incomplete ideas. This leaves (D), which is the best answer.

31. **C** Since there are pronouns in the answer choices, look for agreement and ambiguity. Choice (A) is the contraction form of (B), so both cannot be correct. Eliminate (A) and (B). Choice (D) is incorrect since *their* is plural and the subject is *main character*, which is singular. Choice (C) is the best answer.

32. **A** Notice the question and use POE to find the best answer consistent with information in the paragraph. The paragraph primarily focuses on how television could not hide white actors play-

ing non-white characters as radio could. Therefore, major changes occurred during the television era. Choice (A) is consistent with this information, so keep it. The longevity of radio programs is unnecessary, so eliminate (B). No information is given about how non-white actors handled the transition, so get rid of (C) as well. The cinema is not discussed in the passage, so it's unnecessary information. Eliminate (D). Choice (A) is the best answer.

33.   **B**   The change from white to non-white actors playing non-white characters in the television era was a major change, so find an answer that matches this tone. Choices (A), (C), and (D) are incorrect because each basically means the same thing, and each could also be considered offensive since no information indicates that the change was bad. Therefore, (B) is the best answer.

34.   **A**   Since there isn't a consistent grammar rule being tested here, use POE to find the best and most concise answer. Eliminate (B) because it changes the meaning: *life* cannot have possession. Choices (C) and (D) are unnecessarily wordy and awkward. This leaves (A), which is a common figure of speech, so it is the best answer.

35.   **B**   Notice the question and use POE to find an answer most consistent with the information in the paragraph. The previous sentences indicate a choice between two distinct things, so eliminate (A) because no choice is given. Choice (B) shows a choice that would occur on a subway, so keep it. Buses are not discussed in the paragraph, so eliminate (C). Eliminate (D) as well since the operating hours of the subway are unnecessary information. Choice (B) is the best answer.

36.   **C**   Since the answer choices have verbs, use POE to find the answer that has proper agreement and tense with the non-underlined portion of the paragraph. The subject of the sentence is *team*, which is singular, so eliminate (A) because *have* is plural. Eliminate (B) because the present tense is incorrect. Choice (D) is also incorrect because *was* changes the meaning by suggesting that the *team* was discovered. This leaves (C), which is the best answer.

37.   **D**   Since the answer choices each seem to be saying the same thing, use POE and look for an answer that is clear and concise. Eliminate (A) because it is a sentence fragment. Eliminate (B) because it implies that the *team* is the *geneticist,* which is incorrect. The singular verb *was* does not agree with the plural subject *data sets,* so eliminate (C). This leaves (D), which is clear and concise.

38.   **D**   Notice the question and use POE to find an answer that is consistent with the information in the paragraph. Choices (A) and (C) basically say the same thing and are somewhat informal, so eliminate them. Nothing in the paragraph questions how valid the science is, so eliminate (B). Choice (D) works; it describes how the experiment was conducted and would answer some of the questions presented in the first sentence.

39.   **C**   Since the answer choices each seem to be saying the same thing, use POE and look for an answer that is clear and concise. Eliminate (A) and (B) because each contains unnecessary information. Choice (D) is vague so this leaves (C), which is the best, most concise answer.

40.   **B**   Each answer choice is a modifying phrase and the subject—*researchers*—comes right after the comma, so find the answer choice that refers to them. Eliminate (A) and (D) because the *researchers* are

not living on the subway, nor they responsible for the odor. Choice (C) implies that the *researchers* are part of the food, so eliminate this choice as well. This leaves (B), which is the best answer.

41. **A** Since there isn't a consistent grammar rule being tested in this question, use POE to find an answer that is clear and concise. Choice (A) makes sense, so keep it for now. Eliminate (B) because it changes the meaning by implying that the diseases were dead instead of the cells. Choice (C) makes the same error, so eliminate it as well. Eliminate (D) since the pronoun *they* could be referring to the *researchers* from the previous paragraph, and they are certainly not dead. Choice (A) is the best answer.

42. **C** This question is testing proper word use, so use the context of the non-underlined portion of the sentence to find the best answer. Eliminate (B) and (D) since both are adverbs and do not fit the sentence properly. *Compliment* is the "act of saying something nice," which does not make sense within the context of the sentence, so eliminate (A). Choice (C) is the proper use of this word since it means "something that completes something else."

43. **B** Notice the question and use POE to find an answer that is consistent with the information in the paragraph. The correct answer should address a previous survey or study. Only (B) does this, as the census is a particular study. Choices (A), (C), and (D) each have unnecessary information that does not address the question.

44. **D** Notice the sentence is making a comparison between *a place* and *the level*, which is incorrect. All comparisons must be apples to apples. Eliminate (A) and (B). Choice (C) is unnecessarily wordy and passive, so eliminate it as well. Choice (D) makes the correct comparison and is concise.

Chapter 12
Writing and
Language Test
Drill 2

Writing and Language Test

35 MINUTES, 44 QUESTIONS

Turn to Section 2 of your answer sheet to answer the questions in this section.

DIRECTIONS

Each passage below is accompanied by a number of questions. For some questions, you will consider how the passage might be revised to improve the expression of ideas. For other questions, you will consider how the passage might be edited to correct errors in sentence structure, usage, or punctuation. A passage or a question may be accompanied by one or more graphics (such as a table or graph) that you will consider as you make revising and editing decisions.

Some questions will direct you to an underlined portion of a passage. Other questions will direct you to a location in a passage or ask you to think about the passage as a whole.

After reading each passage, choose the answer to each question that most effectively improves the quality of writing in the passage or that makes the passage conform to the conventions of standard written English. Many questions include a "NO CHANGE" option. Choose that option if you think the best choice is to leave the relevant portion of the passage as it is.

Questions 1-11 are based on the following passage and supplementary material.

The Other Brain Doctors

Who is in charge of your medical care? **1** Doctors and nurses play a big part, obviously, but there is more happening behind the scenes than you might think. A hospital is a business and, like any business, it has a complex infrastructure there to make sure that things run as **2** smoothe as possible. The doctors and nurses do the patient-facing work, and a hospital could not run without them, but the work that goes on administratively is often just as important.

1

Which of the following choices would best answer the question posed at the beginning of this paragraph in a way that is in keeping with the main idea of the paragraph?

A) NO CHANGE

B) A hospital can't run without its doctors, but the real heroes are the nurses.

C) The CEO of a private hospital is beholden to his or her shareholders to make a profit.

D) A hospital needs patients, not that anyone wants you to get sick.

2

A) NO CHANGE

B) smooth

C) smoothing

D) smoothly

CONTINUE

Because **3** medical care inflation has leveled off
in the twenty-first century, hospitals feel more and more
that they are forced to practice what is called "defensive
medicine." The risk of such medicine is relatively low, but
it also means that **4** it is not necessarily getting the best
possible care.

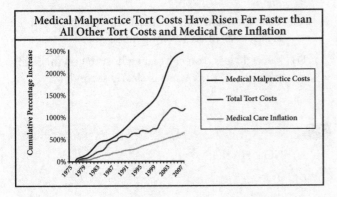

In order to find the balance between risk and safety,
hospitals are more and more reliant on the work of medical
ethicists. **5** Most hospitals have an ethics board that will
draft the hospital's ethical guidelines and advice on those
matters where questions of the medical and legal meet.
Sometimes these boards will intervene on an individual-
patient **6** basis, as when a patient, is terminally ill, but
such patient-facing cases are rare.

3

Which of the following gives accurate information
based on the graph?

A) NO CHANGE

B) total tort costs increased by almost the same
amount as medical-malpractice costs in 2006,

C) medical malpractice costs have risen dramatically
since the 1970s,

D) medical malpractice costs have increased nearly
100% since 1975,

4

A) NO CHANGE

B) they are

C) patients are

D) doctors are

5

The writer is considering deleting the phrase *between
risk and safety* from the previous sentence and placing
the comma after the word *balance*. Should the writer
keep or delete the phrase?

A) Keep the phrase, because it details what medical
ethicists do at work.

B) Keep the phrase, because it clarifies what is
described earlier in the sentence.

C) Delete the phrase, because it adds unnecessary
words to a sentence that is already too long.

D) Delete the phrase, because it is grammatically
incorrect and does not make sense in the context.

6

A) NO CHANGE

B) basis, as when a patient is terminally ill

C) basis as when a patient is terminally ill,

D) basis, as when a patient is terminally ill,

CONTINUE

7 Today, hospitals and universities are beginning to take the question of medical ethics to the next level. Whereas ethics review boards are typically made up of people with a variety of specialties (nurses, social workers, psychologists, lawyers, doctors), a medical ethicist has specific training in **8** their field and usually holds a PhD or an MD/DO. A medical ethicist therefore has a very particularized **9** expertise that gets into the details that allows him or her to comment on a variety of matters, including experimental treatments and high-risk procedures. He or she may be a part of the team of doctors that consults with a family during a hospital stay.

Currently, large academic medical centers **10** of medical ethicists are the primary employers; community hospitals still rely mainly on the ethics board. But this may be changing as more specialization exists for aspiring medical ethicists. After all, the job requires a very specific kind of **11** person—one who can be interested in the one-to-one aspects of patient care but is also interested in the state of the field of medicine and, over and above all of that, the big philosophical questions about right and wrong.

7

Which of the following would best introduce this paragraph by establishing a contrast with the ideas described in the previous paragraph?

A) NO CHANGE

B) However, as mentioned before, the cost of medical malpractice is rising, and the healthcare system is dying.

C) Therefore, a medical ethicist will obviously not see a patient as often as, say, a nurse does.

D) Nevertheless, you can't run a hospital on medical ethicists, so their work is clearly secondary.

8

A) NO CHANGE

B) its

C) they're

D) his or her

9

A) NO CHANGE

B) expertise that is all about the fine-toothed comb

C) expertise that gets him or her into the nitty-gritty

D) expertise

10

The best placement for the underlined portion would be

A) where it is now.

B) after the word *employers* (and before the semi-colon).

C) after the word *hospitals*.

D) after the word *ethics*.

11

A) NO CHANGE

B) person one

C) person; one

D) person. One

CONTINUE ▶

Questions 12-22 are based on the following passage.

Oh, Why No More Weimar?

Germany made some big news in the early part of the twentieth century, but not the kind that most countries hope to make. **12** Germanies' aggression in the First World War played a big role in impelling that conflict, and Hitler's rise to power in 1933 led to one of the bloodiest and widest-ranging conflicts of the twentieth century. What is less known, however, is what happened between those two conflicts. We have a tendency to use wars as the primary motivators of history, **13** and the wars are useful because there are so many of them.

In Germany, that in-between period, 1919 to 1933, is what is known as the era of the Weimar Republic. **14** It got its name from the city of Weimar, where a national convention produced the new German constitution, one that favored democracy and openness. This constitution was crucial in re-establishing Germany's position in the world, and it saved **15** them from having to follow through on many of the articles of the Treaty of Versailles, a largely punitive document in which Germany essentially pled guilty to the international charges that it had caused the First World War.

12
A) NO CHANGE
B) Germanys'
C) Germany's
D) Germans

13
Which of the following choices would provide the most effective transition between this paragraph and the next?
A) NO CHANGE
B) so all history is in a sense a kind of military history.
C) for people are drawn to conflicts in their own lives and in history.
D) but what happens in between is often just as influential.

14
A) NO CHANGE
B) The Republic got its
C) The Republic got their
D) They got their

15
A) NO CHANGE
B) those of Germany
C) the nation
D) it

CONTINUE

[16] Weimar may have had its problems, but it was one of the most culturally effervescent periods of the twentieth century. The shapes that art, architecture, cinema, and philosophy were to take for the rest of the century were determined in this forgotten decade and a half. In particular, the *Goldene Zwanziger* ("Golden Twenties"), the period between 1924 and 1929, [17] stand out.

16

A) NO CHANGE

B) Despite its problems as a culture, Weimar had an effervescent period all the same in the century.

C) In the twentieth century, the Weimar Republic was culturally effervescent and problematic sometimes.

D) With and alongside its cultural effervescence, the Weimar Republic also had some problems in the twentieth century.

17

A) NO CHANGE

B) stands

C) stood

D) standing

CONTINUE

During this period, Gustav Stresemann was foreign minister, and he set as his goal the management of Germany's financial straits, characterized in large part by debts to foreign nations and staggering inflation of the German mark. **18** Germany uses the "euro" now, not the mark. Stresemann, too, helped Germany's economy blossom again with big loans from the American government, which took German products (including the national railways and the national bank) as collateral. **19** Things were looking up, many of the cultural movements that flourished elsewhere found a new home in Weimar Germany. **20** One of the greatest movements of German architecture, the "Bauhaus," flourished in this period.

18

Which of the following sentences would best maintain the paragraph's focus on the consequences of economic improvement?

A) NO CHANGE

B) Stresemann is considered a national hero in Germany.

C) Many German buildings were destroyed in the First World War.

D) With increased financial stability came a cooling of civil unrest.

19

A) NO CHANGE

B) Thus, things

C) Clearly, things

D) As things

20

The writer is considering adding the following parenthetical remark after the word *elsewhere*.

(cinema in the Soviet Union, art in Paris, music in the United States)

Should the writer make this addition here?

A) Yes, because it shows the writer's knowledge of artistic movements.

B) Yes, because it specifies what the writer mentions earlier in the sentence.

C) No, because this information is well-known to all readers.

D) No, because it repeats information given elsewhere in the passage.

CONTINUE

Unfortunately, the renaissance of Weimar could not last forever. The American stock market crash flung Germany into a depression **21** deeper than the United States. With this economic crash, a group of belligerent conservatives, including some led by Adolf Hitler, seized power amid the promise that they could restore Germany to its past glories. The rest is an ugly chapter in history, but the Weimar Republic gives a wonderful **22** interlude that is really nice to think about.

21

A) NO CHANGE

B) deep like the United States.

C) deeper than that of the United States.

D) deeper than the country of the United States.

22

A) NO CHANGE

B) interlude, which is "intermezzo" in Italian.

C) interlude, a term often used in music like that of the Weimar composers.

D) interlude.

CONTINUE

Questions 23-33 are based on the following passage.

The Wondrous Life of Junot Diaz

Although he's not quite the household name that someone like Stephen King is, Junot Diaz is one of the most exciting, most highly regarded authors in contemporary literature. **23** Diaz won the Pulitzer Prize for Fiction in 2008, for his novel, *The Brief Wondrous Life of Oscar Wao*, and in 2012, he was awarded a MacArthur Genius Grant. What is it about Diaz's work that makes it so relatable?

24 [1] I would argue that part of Diaz's power comes from his late twentieth-century "American" story. [2] Stories about immigrants moving to the United States seem to be relegated to the late nineteenth and early twentieth centuries: most of them take place in New York or Chicago. [3] Diaz gives us an updated version. [4] There, Diaz went to public schools as his family dealt with grinding poverty, an absentee **25** father, and the difficulty of assimilation. [5] All the while, Diaz was a voracious reader and became enthralled with the apocalyptic fantasy worlds of *Planet of the Apes* and *The Day of the Triffids*. [6] Born in the Dominican Republic in 1968, **26** Diaz's family moved to Parlin, New Jersey, in 1974. **27**

23

A) NO CHANGE

B) Diaz won the Pulitzer Prize for Fiction in 2008 for his novel *The Brief Wondrous Life of Oscar Wao*,

C) Diaz won, the Pulitzer Prize for Fiction in 2008, for his novel, *The Brief Wondrous Life of Oscar Wao*,

D) Diaz, won the Pulitzer Prize for Fiction in 2008 for his novel, *The Brief Wondrous Life of Oscar Wao*,

24

Which of the following would best introduce this paragraph by stating the author's main idea?

A) NO CHANGE

B) This is a question that has puzzled the ages—I've got the answer.

C) Junot Diaz is a writer from New Jersey who currently teaches at MIT in Massachusetts.

D) Next time you're inclined to read a book by Dan Brown, try one by Junot Diaz instead.

25

A) NO CHANGE

B) father and the difficulty

C) father, and the difficulty,

D) father, and, the difficulty

26

A) NO CHANGE

B) Diaz

C) Diaz's people

D) the Diaz family

27

The best placement for sentence 6 would be

A) where it is now.

B) after sentence 2.

C) after sentence 3.

D) after sentence 4.

CONTINUE

This unique intersection, between the old country and the new, gives Diaz both a particular relatability and a general one. On the one hand, Diaz comes from a newly prominent place: [28] the Dominican Republic is a Spanish-speaking country in the Caribbean Sea. This may seem like an insignificant number, but when we consider how very small the Dominican Republic is and how the same number 20 years ago was below 1%, we cannot help but see its significance. Diaz's story is in this way an updated version of the "rags to riches" story of a century ago. The [29] difficulties of assimilation may have remained largely the same, but [30] there's an entirely new cast of characters trying to navigate them.

28

Which of the following true choices would best support the claim made in the first part of this sentence?

A) NO CHANGE

B) the other country on the island of Hispaniola is Haiti, which suffered a terrible earthquake in 2010.

C) fashion designer Oscar de la Renta is also from the Dominican Republic.

D) Dominican immigrants now make up nearly 3% of new immigrants to the United States.

29

Which of the following alternatives to the underlined portion would be LEAST acceptable?

A) challenges

B) hardships

C) obstructions

D) struggles

30

A) NO CHANGE

B) there've been

C) there was

D) there were

CONTINUE

But the challenge of living in [31] a garbage world is certainly more universal as well. Whether he came from the Dominican Republic or not, Junot Diaz had a tough childhood. His home life was not as steady as it could've been. He got interested in books and movies that no one else seemed to care much [32] about. His family didn't understand or acknowledge his real passions. We all know what it's like to feel isolated or misunderstood, and we've all at times felt like we're entering a world completely alien to our own. [33]

[31]

A) NO CHANGE

B) an unfriendly

C) a major bummer of a

D) a not totally awesome

[32]

A) NO CHANGE

B) about his

C) about, his

D) about his,

[33]

At this point, the writer wants to conclude the essay with a general sentence that captures Diaz's achievements. Which of the following choices would best fulfill that goal?

A) We can expect much more greatness from Junot Diaz in the future.

B) Give his books a chance some time!

C) Junot Diaz has managed to capture that feeling on a number of levels.

D) Let's hope that he inspires more writers who are just as good.

CONTINUE

Questions 34-44 are based on the following passage and supplementary material.

The Change in Climate Change

[1]

It is now fully accepted that human behavior has **34** messed up the global climate. Whether from transportation or industrial waste, our technologies have changed the globe's natural climate, and we can only hope that the consequences are not as dire as **35** everyone says.

[2]

For those who doubt the claims of climate **36** scientists: a series of new findings may be helpful. It seems that air pollution is nearly as old as civilization itself. Led by Celia Sapart of Utrecht University in the Netherlands, a team of scientists analyzed the ice trapped in certain parts of Greenland. **37** By analyzing the chemical content of this ice, the scientists determined that methane levels had risen artificially as early as the Roman era. Around 100 BCE, the scientists reasoned, the Romans began to domesticate animals. The Chinese Han Dynasty expanded its rice fields. Both places **38** had used metallurgical techniques to produce weapons. The level of methane gas in the atmosphere rose in step.

34
A) NO CHANGE
B) messed with
C) altered
D) boggled

35
A) NO CHANGE
B) many scientists predict.
C) all that.
D) people say.

36
A) NO CHANGE
B) scientists; a series
C) scientists. A series
D) scientists, a series

37
Which of the following would best maintain the focus of this paragraph?
A) NO CHANGE
B) Accomplished as they were in collecting scientific data,
C) From a variety of schools,
D) Going to a sparsely populated island nation,

38
A) NO CHANGE
B) were using
C) had been using
D) used

[3]

It has become almost a cliché that air pollution began with the Industrial Revolution of the mid-1800s, but these researchers show that humans have been polluting the air for far longer than that. Still, we should keep these findings in their proper **39** prospective. Between 100 BCE and 1600 AD, methane emissions in the world rose by approximately 31 million tons per year. Those numbers are minuscule, actually, as **40** the United States produced twice that amount in 2014 alone.

39

A) NO CHANGE
B) prospect.
C) perspective.
D) point of view.

40

Which of the following gives accurate information based on the graph?

A) NO CHANGE

B) the United States produced approximately that much in 2014, and the industry of international aviation produced the rest.

C) the United States alone produced more than that in just one year, and some nations produce as much as eight times that much each year.

D) the United States produced nearly 50 million tons in 2014, and China produced almost twenty times that much.

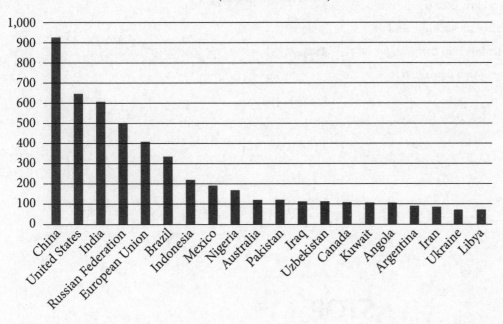

2014 Methane Emissions by Country
(million metric tons)

Data sourced from http://www.wri.org/resources/data-sets/cait-historical-emissions-data-countries-us-states-unfccc.

CONTINUE →

[4]

41 More recently, scientists have analyzed samples from Quelccaya, a glacier in the Andes. The scientists found that prior to the 1530s, there was very little alien material in the ice, apart from the dust and ash from occasional volcanic eruptions. By 1540, however, when colonial mining began to boom in the region, the cores contained a smattering of foreign elements, including chromium, molybdenum, antinomy, and lead. Europeans, especially the Spanish, came to these lands in search of silver, and 42 there technologies for extracting silver came at an environmental cost. For a time, technological advancement and the popularity of mining existed in a loop together, as increases in mining would lead to technological advancement, which would lead to increases in mining… 43

[5]

Therefore, we should not take this ancient data as a free pass for 44 our own polluting ways. The ancient air pollution should show us instead just how fragile our environment is, and if a bit of small-scale farming and technology was able to alter climate levels in the past, we should see all the more clearly how much damage our heavy industry can do.

41
A) NO CHANGE
B) Scientists have been analyzing more recent Quelccaya, a glacier in the Andes, samples.
C) Samples from more recent scientists are those of Quelccaya, a glacier in the Andes.
D) In more recent science have been the samples from Quelccaya, an Andes glacier.

42
A) NO CHANGE
B) their
C) they're
D) our

43
The best placement for paragraph 4 would be
A) after paragraph 1.
B) after paragraph 2.
C) after paragraph 5.
D) where it is now.

44
A) NO CHANGE
B) their
C) one's
D) your

STOP
**If you finish before time is called, you may check your work on this section only.
Do not turn to any other section.**

Chapter 13
Writing and Language Test Drill 2: Answers and Explanations

ANSWERS AND EXPLANATIONS

Section 2—Writing and Language Test

1. **A** Notice the question and use POE to find the best answer that is consistent with the information in the paragraph. Since the main idea of this paragraph is expressed in the final sentence—*the doctors and nurses do the patient-facing work, and a hospital could not run without them, but the work that goes on administratively is often just as important*—find an answer that matches this information. Choice (A) is a good match. Eliminate (B) since the paragraph doesn't address the relative value of doctors and nurses. The CEO and shareholders are unnecessary information, so eliminate (C). Get rid of (D) as well since no mention is made about getting sick.

2. **D** The underlined portion and answer choices indicate the question is interested in the correct use of a similar word. Based on the sentence, an adverb is needed, so (D) is a good answer. Since (A) and (B) are primary and secondary spellings of the same word, eliminate both answer choices. The present participle is unnecessary in this sentence, so eliminate (C) as well.

3. **C** Notice the question and use POE to find an answer with information consistent with the graph. Choice (A) is incorrect since medical care inflation seems to be increasing in the twenty-first century. Medical tort and malpractice costs are very different from each other in 2006, so eliminate (B). Each part of the graph has been rising since the 1970s, so (C) is consistent; keep it. Malpractice costs have increased nearly 2,500% since 1975, so eliminate (D). Choice (C) is the best answer.

4. **C** The underlined portion of the sentence contains a pronoun, so be sure that it is consistent and clear with other nouns and pronouns in the sentence. Since no information is given in the sentence regarding the pronoun, eliminate (A) and (B) since the pronouns are ambiguous. Because *care* is discussed in the paragraph, (C) makes sense since that's what patients receive; keep it. Eliminate (D) since doctors don't receive *care*. Choice (C) is the best answer.

5. **B** Whenever you are given the option to delete, determine whether the underlined portion plays a precise role in the passage. The previous passage describes the *risk of "defensive medicine,"* so this distinction is relevant to the paragraph. Eliminate (C) and (D). The phrase *balance between risk and safety* is too vague to describe specifically what medical ethicists do, so eliminate (A). This leaves (B), which is the best answer.

6. **D** Look at the answers to see that comma usage is being tested. Take a look at the full phrase—*as when a patient is terminally ill*—and you'll notice that this is unnecessary information, so commas must be placed around the whole phrase. Eliminate (A), (B), and (C). Choice (D) is the best answer.

7. **A** Notice the question and use POE to find the best answer that is consistent with the information in the paragraph. The paragraph discusses the specific experience and education many medical ethicists have; therefore, (A) is consistent, so keep it. No mention is made about the death of the healthcare system, so eliminate (B). Nurses are not mentioned in the paragraph, so they are un-

necessary, which means (C) is incorrect. Choice (D) is the direct opposite of what the paragraph is suggesting, so eliminate it. Choice (A) is the best answer.

8. **D** The underlined portion of the sentence is a pronoun, so be sure that it is consistent and clear with other nouns and pronouns in the sentence. The underlined portion is referring to the *medical ethicist,* so a singular pronoun is needed. Eliminate (A) and (C). Choice (B) is incorrect since "its" cannot refer to a person, so (D) is the best answer.

9. **D** The underlined portion mentions *expertise* and *gets into all the details,* which is redundant information, so eliminate (A). Also, eliminate (B) and (C) for the same reason. Choice (D) is the most concise, so it is the best answer.

10. **B** Notice the question and use POE to find the best answer that is consistent with the information in the passage. The medical ethicists are not employers, so eliminate (A). Choice (B) works since the centers are the employers. Choices (C) and (D) would suggest that the hospitals and ethics boards, respectively, were made up of medical ethicists, which is not the case.

11. **A** Since there are periods and semicolons in the answers, check for STOP punctuation. Eliminate (C) and (D) since a period and semicolon are STOP punctuation and both cannot be correct. The information in the underlined portion is referring to the person, so it needs to be separated since it's a descriptive phrase. Eliminate (B). Therefore, (A) is the best answer.

12. **C** The underlined portion in the sentence includes an apostrophe, so look for either contractions or possession. Since the noun *aggression* comes after the apostrophe, look for the answer indicating possession. Eliminate (D). Germany doesn't end with an s, so eliminate (A) and (B). Choice (C) is the best answer.

13. **D** Notice the question and use POE to find the answer that best links these two paragraphs. The next paragraph opens with the phrase *that in-between period.* Choice (D) is a good match with this information. Eliminate (A) since the number of wars is unnecessary information. No information is given in either the first or second paragraph to support (B) and (C), so eliminate them.

14. **B** The underlined portion of this sentence includes pronouns, so make sure it is consistent with the non-underlined portion of the sentence. The first use of *it* is ambiguous since there is no indication of what is being referenced. Eliminate (A) and (D). Compare (B) and (C). Since *republic* is singular, find the singular pronoun to match. Choice (B) is the best answer.

15. **C** The underlined portion of this sentence is a pronoun, so make sure it is consistent with the non-underlined portion of the sentence. There is no plural antecedent before the pronoun *them,* so eliminate (A) and (B). Compare (C) and (D). Eliminate (D) since *it* is ambiguous—it's not clear whether *it* refers to *Germany's position* or its *constitution.* Choice (C) is the best answer.

16. **A** Neither the underlined portion nor the answer choices seem to be testing a consistent grammar rule, so use POE and find the most concise answer without errors. Choice (A) seems okay, so hold onto it. Eliminate (B) since it changes the meaning by suggesting Weimar's culture was a problem.

Choice (C) doesn't show distinction between the country's effervescence and problems, so eliminate it. Choice (D) is very wordy and not as concise as the underlined portion, so (A) is the best answer.

17. **B** The underlined portion of the sentence is a verb, so find the subject and check for agreement. The subject of the sentence is the *Goldene Zwanziger,* which is singular, so find the correct verb tense. Eliminate (A) since it's plural. Neither past perfect nor progressive is necessary, so eliminate (C) and (D). Choice (B) is the best answer.

18. **D** Notice the question and use POE to find the answer most consistent with the information in the paragraph. Eliminate (A) since Germany's current currency is unnecessary information. Choice (B) doesn't indicate any consequences, so eliminate it. Choice (C) is also unnecessary information since the destroyed buildings are not discussed in this paragraph. This leaves (D), which is the best answer.

19. **D** The answer choices include conjunction words, so check for agreement or complete ideas. Choice (A) is incorrect since the comma in the sentence separates two complete ideas, and only STOP punctuation can do this. Eliminate (B) and (C) for the same reason. The conjunction in (D) is correct since it makes the first part of the sentence before the comma incomplete, and a comma can separate a complete and incomplete idea.

20. **B** Notice the question and use POE to find the answer most consistent with the information in the paragraph. The sentence includes the phrase *many of the cultural movements that flourished elsewhere,* so a description of those movements would be necessary information, and (B) looks like a good match; keep it. Eliminate (C) and (D). The writer's knowledge is unnecessary information, so eliminate (A). Choice (B) is the best answer.

21. **C** Notice the comparison word *than* in the sentence, so make sure both things that are compared are the same thing. A *depression* is being compared to the *United States,* which doesn't match, so eliminate (A) and (D). Choice (B) is incorrect since the adjective *deeper* is necessary for the structure of the sentence. Choice (C) works; the pronoun *that* compares to the *depression.*

22. **D** Notice the underlined portion and answer choices contain information after *interlude,* so check to see if this information is necessary for the sentence. Choices (A), (B), and (C) each contain unnecessary information, so eliminate them. Choice (D) is the most concise, so it is the best answer.

23. **B** The underlined portion and answer choices are testing comma usage, so use POE to find an answer with proper use. Eliminate (A) and (D) since there is no reason to stop the flow of ideas after *2008.* Choice (B) works since the name of the book is not unnecessary information, so there's no need to place commas around it. Because of that, eliminate (D) and select (B).

24. **A** Notice the question and use POE to find the best answer consistent with the information in the paragraph. Choice (A) is a good fit because the paragraph discusses Diaz's story, which correlates with the previous paragraph that asks why work is so *relatable.* Eliminate (B) since there is no indication that this is a timeless question. Eliminate (C) and (D) since Diaz's current teaching post and the author Dan Brown are unnecessary information.

25. **A** The underlined portion and answer choices are testing comma usage, so use POE to find an answer with proper use. Since there is a list of items involved, the correct answer will have a comma after each item in the list and before the word *and*. The underlined portion is correct, so (A) works. Eliminate (B), (C), and (D) since each either omits a comma before an item in the list or adds an unnecessary one after *and* or the last item in the list.

26. **B** The underlined portion comes after the descriptive phrase *born in the Dominican Republic in 1968,* so eliminate (A) since it implies that Diaz's entire family was born at that place and time. Choices (C) and (D) make the same mistake. Choice (B) works since it states only Diaz was born at that place and time.

27. **C** Notice the question and use POE to find the proper placement for sentence 6. Since this sentence details when and where Diaz was born, look for other sentences that would come after this time period. Sentence 4 opens with the pronoun *there,* which has to refer to a place. Therefore, it's referring to the *Dominican Republic,* so sentence 6 should come right before sentence 4. Choice (C) is the best answer.

28. **D** Notice the question and use POE to find the best answer that is consistent with the information in the paragraph. Earlier in the sentence, it's stated that Diaz comes from *a newly prominent place,* so (D) is consistent since it discusses the population of the Dominican Republic and the United States (the next sentence further clarifies this relationship); keep it. Eliminate (A) since the language spoken in the Dominican Republic is unnecessary to the paragraph. Choices (B) and (C) are also unnecessary since the passage discusses neither Haiti nor Oscar de la Renta. Choice (D) is the best answer.

29. **C** Since the question is asking for the LEAST acceptable alternative to the underlined word, *difficulties* is correctly used. Eliminate all answer choices that are similar to *difficulties.* Choices (A), (B), and (D) are all similar, so eliminate them. Choice (C) doesn't match; *obstructions* are physical impediments, whereas the others are abstract. Choice (C) is the best answer.

30. **A** Since the underlined portion and answer choices include apostrophes, look for contractions or proper possession. Choice (A) fits since it could be replaced with *there is* and the subject is *a new cast,* so the subject and verb agree with each other. Eliminate (B) because it's a version of *there have,* so the plural, past participle is incorrect. Eliminate (C) and (D) because past tense doesn't work here.

31. **B** Look at the answer choices to see that there isn't a consistent grammar rule being tested. The difference in the answer choices is that *unfriendly* is a proper description of the world Diaz lived in, whereas the other answer choices use slang or hyperbole. Since it's the most clear and direct, (B) is the best answer.

32. **A** Since there is a period in the underlined portion, this question is testing STOP punctuation. The period separates two complete ideas, so it is used correctly. Eliminate (B), (C), and (D) since no STOP punctuation is used. Choice (A) is the best answer.

33. **C** Notice the question and use POE to find the best answer that is consistent with information in the passage. No indication is made of what Diaz will do in the future, so eliminate (A). Choice (B)

doesn't work since the author isn't trying to convince the readers to read Diaz's work. Choice (C) fits since the previous sentence refers to the *feeling* of being *isolated* or *misunderstood*; keep it. The passage never discusses other authors, so (D) is incorrect. Choice (C) is the best answer.

34. **C**   The underlined portion is using slang language, so look at the context within the paragraph and use POE to find the best answer consistent with the information. The paragraph goes on to say that *our technologies have changed the globe's natural climate,* so (C) would be a good match. All other answer choices, when taken literally, wouldn't match the information in the paragraph; (C) is the best answer.

35. **B**   The answer choices alternate between pronouns and nouns, so find the choice that is the most consistent with the information in the paragraph. The following paragraph states that some might *doubt the claims of climate scientists,* so the *predictions* in the previous paragraph must be those of the scientists. Choice (B) is the best answer.

36. **D**   Since there are answer choices with periods and semicolons, the question is testing STOP punctuation. Eliminate (B) and (C) since both a period and semicolon are STOP punctuation, and both cannot be correct. Eliminate (A) as well since a complete idea must precede a colon. This leaves (D), which is the best answer.

37. **A**   Notice the question and use POE to find the best answer consistent with the information in the paragraph. Choice (A) works because the rest of the sentence discusses the rise of *methane levels.* Choice (B) indicates a contrast that is not apparent in the sentence, so eliminate it. No information is given about the types of schools or the population density, so eliminate both (C) and (D).

38. **D**   Since the answer choices have different verb tenses, the question is testing proper verb tense. Use the rest of the paragraph to find information to support the proper tense. The previous sentence uses the simple past tense verb *expanded,* so (D) works. Eliminate (A) and (C) since past perfect should not be used since there are not two events that started and ended in the past. Eliminate (B) since it's present tense.

39. **C**   Since the answer choices keep changing the word choice, use POE to find the best word that matches the context in the sentence. Eliminate (A) and (B) since both are the adjective and noun form of the same word, which basically means something that is "likely to happen." Eliminate (D) since no specific *point of view* is discussed in the passage. Choice (C) means "a way of looking at something," so this fits the sentence, making it the best answer.

40. **C**   Notice the question and use POE to eliminate answers that are not consistent with the graph. Choice (A) can be eliminated because the US produced over 600 million tons in 2014, which is significantly more than twice 31 million tons. Choice (B) can also be eliminated, again because the US produced over 600 millions tons rather than 31 million tons. Choice (C) is consistent with the graph—the US did produce more than 31 million tons in 2014, and multiple countries from Brazil to China produced more than 250 million tons (approximately 31 × 8). Keep (C). Choice (D) can be eliminated because the US produced over 600 million tons, not 50. The correct answer is (C).

41. **A**   The answer choices keep changing the location of the word *recent* or *recently,* so use POE to find the best use. Since *recently* is referring to a time period, (A) works. Choice (B) is incorrect since the glacier Quelccaya is not recent. Eliminate (C) and (D) since neither the scientists nor the science is recent.

42. **B**   The underlined portion of this sentence is a pronoun, so make sure it is consistent with the non-underlined portion by finding the other nouns and pronouns. The *technologies* discussed in the sentence are those of the *Europeans,* which is plural, so *their* should be used as an adjective since it's placed right before a noun. Choice (B) is the best answer.

43. **B**   Notice the question and use POE to find best answer consistent with the information in the passage. Paragraph 4 opens with *more recently* and then discusses another scientific study. Therefore, the correct answer will come after another paragraph that discusses a scientific study. Eliminate (A) and (C) since no studies are discussed. Keep (B) since it mentions that *a team of scientists analyzed the ice trapped in certain parts of Greenland,* and *the scientists determined that methane levels had risen artificially as early as the Roman era.* Keeping it where it is would be awkward since no studies are discussed in paragraph 3. Choice (B) is the best answer.

44. **A**   The underlined portion of this sentence is a pronoun, so make sure it is consistent with the non-underlined portion by finding the other nouns and pronouns. The sentence begins with *we,* and the underlined portion is the possessive form of this pronoun, so (A) is the best answer.

Chapter 14
Writing and
Language Test
Drill 3

Writing and Language Test

35 MINUTES, 44 QUESTIONS

Turn to Section 2 of your answer sheet to answer the questions in this section.

DIRECTIONS

Each passage below is accompanied by a number of questions. For some questions, you will consider how the passage might be revised to improve the expression of ideas. For other questions, you will consider how the passage might be edited to correct errors in sentence structure, usage, or punctuation. A passage or a question may be accompanied by one or more graphics (such as a table or graph) that you will consider as you make revising and editing decisions.

Some questions will direct you to an underlined portion of a passage. Other questions will direct you to a location in a passage or ask you to think about the passage as a whole.

After reading each passage, choose the answer to each question that most effectively improves the quality of writing in the passage or that makes the passage conform to the conventions of standard written English. Many questions include a "NO CHANGE" option. Choose that option if you think the best choice is to leave the relevant portion of the passage as it is.

Questions 1-11 are based on the following passage.

Coming to an Office Near You

A new generation—Generation Z—is reaching adulthood. By 2019, notes *The Washington Post*, tens of millions of Gen Z-ers will have entered the workforce. By 2020 they'll wield an estimated $3 trillion **1** in money to spend on things. As a result, many businesspeople are eager to learn not just what Gen Z-ers want in a product or job, **2** but how their way of experiencing the world will change businesses inside and out.

1

A) NO CHANGE

B) in the amount of money they can purchase things with.

C) in dollars they'll be able to command.

D) in purchasing power.

2

A) NO CHANGE

B) and how

C) but also how

D) yet they also want

CONTINUE ➡

One key is to understand what distinguishes Gen Z-ers from those born just before them. Most demographers include within Gen Z those born between 1995 and the early 2000s. Particularly in the United States, the break **3** up into Millennials and Gen Z-ers separates those who remember the events of September 11, 2001, from those who were too young to remember or were not yet born when the Twin Towers fell.

Gen Z-ers, in other words, are those for whom such events were never inconceivable. They have also always lived in a digital world. Their phones have always enabled them to go shopping, follow trending stories, and **4** instantly interact with a vast network of people—all without getting off the couch. Millennials are often characterized as having an undeserved sense of entitlement that was fostered by the parenting style of the Baby Boomers. **5** Gen Z-ers, by contrast, are portrayed as ambitious, hardworking, independent, and very competitive.

3

A) NO CHANGE
B) among
C) around
D) between

4

A) NO CHANGE
B) instantly interacting
C) to interact instantly
D) in an instant interacting

5

At this point, the writer is considering adding the following sentence:

> That style, often caricatured as the "everybody gets a trophy" mentality, is blamed for giving Millennials the impression that all they have to do is show up to get rewarded.

Should the writer make this addition here?

A) Yes, because it helps the reader to understand a parenting mistake that should be avoided.

B) Yes, because it helps to clarify what aspect of the Baby Boomers' parenting style could have contributed to Millennials' sense of entitlement.

C) No, because the sentence contradicts the characterization of Baby Boomers elsewhere in the passage.

D) No, because the writer should not insert personal opinion into an essay that otherwise maintains an objective tone.

CONTINUE

Their attitudes toward education and jobs are grounded in the cynicism of their Gen X parents and the economic realities of a post-recession world, so many Gen Z-ers **6** <u>don't act like Millennials.</u>

[1] Understanding these and other characteristics of Gen Z-ers **7** <u>matter</u> a great deal, according to Jason Dorsey of the Center for Generational Kinetics. [2] For example, Gen Z's immersion in technology is changing the behavior of older generations. [3] For instance, a Gen Z child's schoolwork might require her Millennial parent to become familiar with an online classroom platform. [4] The idea of the youngest generation wielding power may seem counterintuitive, but examples show how easily such shifts occur. [5] The same child's creation of a blog might prompt her grandmother to learn how to navigate to that site. **8**

6

Which choice provides a supporting example that reinforces the main point of the sentence?

A) NO CHANGE

B) will hold jobs that didn't even exist when their parents were born.

C) regard hard work and academic accomplishment as crucial to survival in a difficult and competitive climate.

D) hope to travel and work in other countries to expand their global awareness.

7

A) NO CHANGE

B) mattered

C) had mattered

D) matters

8

To make this paragraph most logical, sentence 4 should be placed

A) where it is now.

B) before sentence 1.

C) after sentence 1.

D) after sentence 5.

CONTINUE →

Behind all the focus on Gen Z lurks an even larger reason that greater understanding between generations is needed: the increasing rate of technological change is shortening the number of years spanned by a generation. Some predict there will soon be six or seven generations **9** simultaneously existing among the workforce. With so many people operating under different sets of generational **10** perspectives and understanding the effects of those perspectives becomes even more imperative. **11** If we fail to heed the warnings, the future could be perilous indeed.

9

A) NO CHANGE
B) co-existing within
C) being at the same time amid
D) existing at once around

10

A) NO CHANGE
B) perspectives, and understanding
C) perspectives, understanding
D) perspectives: understanding

11

The writer wants a concluding sentence that restates the main argument of the passage. Which choice best accomplishes that goal?

A) NO CHANGE
B) The members of Gen Z may still be young, but they—and the changes they're bringing with them—have much to teach us all.
C) Now more than ever, we need to return to a system that honors the wisdom accrued by our elders as they've journeyed through life.
D) The fact that we've run out of letters to assign to generations seems to be an apt metaphor for the confusion that might lie ahead.

Questions 12-22 are based on the following passage and supplementary material.

Declining Coral Reefs: A Global Threat

Coral reefs are crucial to life in and around the ocean. While reefs occupy just a tiny fraction of the world's oceans, twenty-five percent of marine species—from turtles and fish to colorful **12** algae, call them home. In fact, reefs have earned the nickname "the rainforests of the **13** sea," a nod to the extremely productive ecosystems they form. Reefs also play a key role in supporting human economies and living environments. The significant roles reefs play in maintaining quality of life on Earth make the news that vast swaths of coral reefs are dying particularly alarming. Over the last thirty years, the planet has lost half of its reefs.

Coral reefs are threatened by factors like disease, pollution, overfishing, and, in particular, climate change, with **14** there accompanying rise in oceanic temperatures and acidification levels. Coral reefs' striking colors are a result of symbiotic relationships with algae that live in their tissues. When ocean temperatures rise, the corals expel the algae. **15** It is "bleaching," this expulsion reduces the reef to white coral skeletons. If the water's temperature remains elevated for many months, the bleached coral dies. Changes to global atmospheric conditions **16** also effects the corals' exposure to ocean acidification: as the levels of carbon dioxide in the air increase, more atmospheric carbon dioxide dissolves into the ocean, lowering the pH of the water and making it more acidic. Acidification makes corals less able to absorb the nutrients their skeletons require. Over time, the reefs can weaken and collapse.

12

A) NO CHANGE
B) algae—
C) algae, which
D) algae: these

13

A) NO CHANGE
B) sea; a nod to the extremely productive ecosystems they form.
C) implications, this is a nod to the extremely productive ecosystems they form.
D) implications; this making a nod to the extremely productive ecosystems they form.

14

A) NO CHANGE
B) its'
C) its
D) it's

15

A) NO CHANGE
B) They call it "bleaching,"
C) Known as "bleaching,"
D) It is known as "bleaching,"

16

A) NO CHANGE
B) also affects the corals' exposure
C) also effect the corals' exposure
D) also affect the corals' exposure

CONTINUE →

17 Coral reefs are dying as a result of warming and acidifying oceans. The death of corals also shapes the future of humans living near the ocean. In areas near reefs, the loss of coral hurts key elements of local economies, such as fishing and tourism. **18** Loss of reefs also leaves coastal communities more susceptible to surging waves and severe storms.

17

Which choice most smoothly and effectively introduces the paragraph's discussion of how coral death is linked to the lives of a variety of other species?

A) NO CHANGE

B) As the number of coral reefs decreases, so does the amount of oxygen released into the atmosphere.

C) Given how many marine species live in and among the corals, the loss of so much coral reef threatens the survival of many other sea creatures.

D) DELETE the underlined sentence.

18

At this point, the writer is considering adding the following sentence.

> For example, the Great Barrier Reef, a famous coral formation in the Pacific Ocean, attracts thousands of visitors to the region each year; the death of the reef would decimate the region's tourist income as well as its local fish and algae populations.

Should the writer make this addition here?

A) Yes, because it elaborates on an earlier reference to the Great Barrier Reef.

B) Yes, because it introduces an example that is referenced later in the passage.

C) No, because it contradicts the main argument of the passage.

D) No, because it introduces a tangent that detracts from the main idea of the paragraph.

CONTINUE

In the region stretching from southeast Asia to northern Australia, for example, reefs protect **19** more than ten million people. Even in areas far from the Great Barrier Reef, corals support human habitation: estimates suggest that reefs protect **20** about two million people living in the Middle East.

People Protected by Coral Reefs

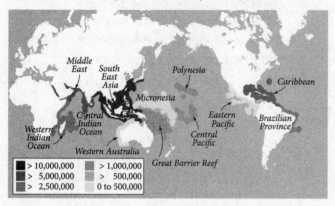

Despite the global risks posed by coral deterioration, instituting some **21** key steps immediately could help to protect the reefs and the populations they support. Decreasing both ocean pollution and CO_2 emissions, increasing scientific monitoring of the oceans, and bolstering the protection of reef refuge areas could help stem the tide of coral destruction. **22**

19

What choice offers the most accurate interpretation of the data in the map?

A) NO CHANGE

B) fewer than ten million people.

C) as many people as are protected by reefs in central America.

D) more than fifteen million people.

20

Which choice offers an accurate interpretation of the data in the map?

A) NO CHANGE

B) more than one million people living on the western coast of North America.

C) fewer than two million people living on the eastern coast of Africa.

D) more than five million people living around the Caribbean Sea.

21

A) NO CHANGE

B) big moves right away

C) crucial stuff as soon as humanly possible

D) really great ideas right now

22

The writer wants a conclusion that describes the ongoing efforts to combat the loss of coral reefs. Which choice results in the passage having the most appropriate concluding sentence?

A) NO CHANGE

B) Coral reefs' status as beacons of biodiversity is at stake if human activities do not change.

C) Scientists and policymakers alike continue to pursue such actions in the hope that a critical mass of people can be persuaded to help prevent still more destruction.

D) Although coral death is only a minor side effect of climate change, the loss of the reefs would be detrimental for many countries' tourist industries.

CONTINUE ▶

Questions 23-33 are based on the following passage.

Eating Prehistorically

In 1985, Melvin Konner and Stanley Boyd Eaton argued in *The New England Journal of Medicine* that humans have not evolved to digest post-industrial foods healthily. They advocated a diet 23 based off of foods available to our prehistoric ancestors before the development of agriculture. Their 24 claims were further popularized by a series of books, and, since 2010, estimates suggest that more than one million Americans have adopted what is now known as a "Paleo" diet.

The theory behind the Paleolithic diet asserts that human metabolism is governed by the genes of our hunter-gatherer ancestors and, though many human populations transitioned to a lifestyle reliant on settled agriculture during the Neolithic Revolution, our bodies have not had enough time to evolve to effectively digest the processed and grain-heavy foods widely available today. The Paleo diet's developers contend, 25 for example, that humans are best able to digest foods like those ancient hunter-gatherers ate: lean meats, fruits, vegetables, nuts, and seeds. The regimen encourages diners to consume about half 26 of their daily calories from meat and fish products.

23
A) NO CHANGE
B) off
C) around
D) on

24
A) NO CHANGE
B) claims that a new dietary regimen is needed
C) claims, which presented a new theory of the evolution of diets,
D) claims, which called for a new dietary regimen,

25
A) NO CHANGE
B) inconsequentially,
C) instead,
D) therefore,

26
A) NO CHANGE
B) these
C) its
D) it's

CONTINUE →

It cautions diners to avoid not only processed foods—no potato chips or cold cuts—but also all dairy products, almost all grains, all added sugar and salt, and legumes (like chickpeas). In return, proponents argue, Paleo eaters experience [27] greater clarity about how to prepare and consume their food.

Skeptics question the hypothesis that [28] human's genetic material has not evolved in response to the Neolithic Revolution. For instance, Professor Anne C. Stone argues that "our diets have changed radically in the last 10,000 years, and, in response, we have changed, too." [29] Some versions of the Paleo diet allow diners to add dairy back into their routines, if their bodies don't respond negatively.

27

Which choice provides the most specific information on the type of health benefits a Paleo diet claims to provide?

A) NO CHANGE

B) increased metabolism, weight loss, and decreased susceptibility to modern chronic illnesses, like diabetes.

C) the satisfaction of knowing they're right about what to eat.

D) a greater confidence that they know where their food comes from and how it will affect their bodies.

28

A) NO CHANGE

B) humans

C) humans's

D) humans'

29

Which choice gives a supporting example that emphasizes the possibility that human genetics have evolved to metabolize foods developed after the Neolithic Revolution?

A) NO CHANGE

B) Paleo cookbooks might, for example, encourage dieters to keep track of how their own tastes and food preferences change over time.

C) Whatever its skeptics say, the Paleo diet has been supported scientifically by some studies that consider the diets and health levels of contemporary hunter-gatherer societies.

D) Humans have clearly evolved some workarounds for foods made available through agriculture: many people can tolerate lactose from dairy, for instance, which would not have been the case for Paleolithic eaters.

CONTINUE ➤

Other nutritionists **30** warn that dieters who don't think carefully about substituting one food for another risk deficiencies in calcium and vitamin D. Finally, some scholars point to the ethical dilemma of **31** giving people such strict requirements about what they should and shouldn't eat.

32 Food has been around as long as humans. In the nineteenth century, for example, a diet dominated by vinegar was believed to cleanse the body; in the early twentieth century, Horace Fletcher instructed eaters to chew each bite of their food at least one hundred times before spitting out what remained. **33** Because some of the Paleo diet's restrictions can also seem extreme, some aspects—such as avoiding excess salt and sugar and limiting processed foods—align with more mainstream nutrition advice. At this point, without further research into the long-term effects of the Paleo diet, evidence of its benefits remains largely in the eyes—and stomachs—of individual eaters.

30

A) NO CHANGE
B) warn:
C) warn,
D) warn—

31

The writer wants to conclude the paragraph effectively while also reinforcing the point that some commentators cast doubt on the Paleo diet's large-scale application. Which choice best accomplishes this goal?

A) NO CHANGE
B) calling the theory of evolution into question by talking about diet and genetics.
C) encouraging billions of people to consume half of their calories through meat, given the finite resources available and the relatively high amount of those required to produce meat.
D) continuing to let people believe that a simple diet can change their lives entirely.

32

Which choice most effectively sets up the paragraph?

A) NO CHANGE
B) Celebrities' endorsements of particular diets, like Paleo, have a big effect on how popular an eating regimen becomes.
C) It's impossible to know how Paleolithic people actually ate.
D) Trends in dietary recommendations famously vary from generation to generation.

33

A) NO CHANGE
B) Supposing that
C) While
D) DELETE the underlined portion and begin the sentence with a capital letter.

CONTINUE

Questions 34-44 are based on the following passage.

Poetic Preservation: The Emily Dickinson Museum

One element of Emily Dickinson's reputation as one of America's great poets is the contrast between the vast scope of her imagination and the limited scope of her physical travels: [34] in her later years, in fact, she rarely left home at all, preferring to entertain guests at home or to stay in touch through letters. For that reason, the house where Dickinson lived in Amherst, Massachusetts—the house where she wrote nearly 1,800 poems—holds great significance for many readers and researchers.

The Emily Dickinson Museum opened in 2003, after Amherst College gained ownership of two houses previously owned by the Dickinson family. The house in which Emily Dickinson lived with her family is called the Homestead. Next door is the Evergreens, where Emily Dickinson's brother lived with his wife and children. Today, visitors can tour one or both of the [35] houses where the Dickinsons used to live, considering firsthand how the poet's surroundings might have had an [36] affect on her poetry.

34

The writer is considering deleting the underlined portion. Should the writer make this deletion?

A) Yes, because the information in the underlined portion is presented later in the paragraph.

B) Yes, because the underlined portion is a digression from the rest of the sentence.

C) No, because the information in the underlined portion explains what makes Dickinson an important American poet.

D) No, because the underlined portion provides an example of the limited scope of her physical travel.

35

A) NO CHANGE

B) houses

C) houses that were home for Emily Dickinson

D) houses of note

36

A) NO CHANGE

B) affect for

C) effect on

D) effect for

CONTINUE

[1] To offer a site that's as historically accurate as possible, extensive archaeology and restoration efforts have been required. [2] The Museum replanted a tall hedge and reconstructed a fence, for example, to match **37** one's that shielded the house from the street in the nineteenth century. [3] Particularly important was the restoration of Emily Dickinson's bedroom, the place where she wrote and compiled her poems. [4] When some floorboards and wallpaper were removed, preservationists found clues regarding the characteristics of the room—**38** furniture arrangement, doorway placement flooring, and wallpaper—when Dickinson occupied it. [5] Replicas of her bureau and writing desk were commissioned, and an artist used scraps found during the room's restoration to create wallpaper whose pattern matches the original. **39**

37

A) NO CHANGE

B) ones

C) them

D) it

38

A) NO CHANGE

B) furniture arrangement, doorway placement,

C) furniture, arrangement, doorway placement

D) furniture, arrangement, doorway, placement,

39

The writer plans to add the following sentence to this paragraph.

> The preservationists even used historically accurate paint samples to make sure the colors of the wallpaper would match.

To make this paragraph most logical, the sentence should be placed

A) after sentence 1.

B) after sentence 2.

C) after sentence 4.

D) after sentence 5.

The work, **40** consequently, is not yet over for Dickinson archaeologists. More recent restoration efforts have used seeds and other artifacts to reconstruct the Homestead's original landscape design and rebuild the greenhouse and **41** are addressed by structural damage to the Evergreens. **42** Instead, the Evergreens presents a particular challenge for preservation. Because of the terms of inheritance, its occupants were not allowed to remove anything from the house, **43** so it remained virtually unchanged for almost one hundred years. As recently as 2014, a visitor could see smoke stains on the wallpaper that were there when Ralph Waldo Emerson sat around the fireplace. Thus, the Museum must **44** strike a balance between maintaining the house's authentic furniture and architecture and making it safe for visitors.

The efforts of the Museum and its historians are clearly paying off. In its first ten years of operation, more than 100,000 people visited, encountering there not only the careful restoration of a century-old household but also the context of Emily Dickinson's poetic prowess.

40

A) NO CHANGE

B) in summary,

C) therefore,

D) nonetheless,

41

A) NO CHANGE

B) will address

C) have addressed

D) had addressed

42

A) NO CHANGE

B) However

C) Indeed

D) Regardless

43

A) NO CHANGE

B) yet

C) but

D) or

44

A) NO CHANGE

B) negotiate an equilibrium

C) navigate the myriad complications

D) introduce a middle path

STOP

If you finish before time is called, you may check your work on this section only. Do not turn to any other section.

Chapter 15
Writing and
Language Test
Drill 3: Answers
and Explanations

ANSWERS AND EXPLANATIONS

Section 2—Writing and Language Test

1. **D** Phrases are changing in the answer choices, so the question is testing precision and concision. Keep (D), the shortest choice, but check the remaining answer choices just to be sure. Choices (A), (B), and (C) are unnecessarily wordy and redundant, so they can be eliminated. The correct answer is (D).

2. **C** Conjunctions are changing in the answer choices, so the question is testing consistency of ideas. The sentence states *businesspeople are eager to learn not just what Gen Z-ers want….* The expression *not just* is synonymous with the idiomatic expression *not only…but also*, which is required to maintain consistency, so (A), (B), and (D) can be eliminated. The correct answer is (C).

3. **D** Prepositions are changing in the answer choices, so the question is testing consistency and precision. The sentence is discussing a break that separates Millennials and Gen Z-ers. To distinguish the two groups, the idiomatic expression of *between 'X' and 'Y'* is required. Choices (A), (B), and (C) can be eliminated. The correct answer is (D).

4. **A** Verb forms are changing in the answer choices, so the question is testing verb consistency. The sentence presents a list with *go…* and *follow…*, so *interact* is the consistent verb form and (B) and (D) can be eliminated. The inclusion of *to* in (C) makes the list inconsistent, as *to* is not included with the second element in the list. Eliminate (C). The correct answer is (A).

5. **B** Note the question! The question is asking whether the writer should add the provided sentence. Begin by reading the surrounding sentences to understand the context. The previous sentence discusses the parenting style of the Baby Boomers and the suggested sentence expands on that specific style, so the addition would be appropriate here. Eliminate (C) and (D). Choice (A) is too strong in referencing a *parenting mistake that should be avoided*, whereas (B) fits the tone of the paragraph. The correct answer is (B).

6. **C** Note the question! The question is asking for the choice that provides a supporting example that reinforces the main point of the sentence. The sentence in question is *Their (Gen Z-ers) attitudes toward education and jobs are grounded in the cynicism of their Gen X parents and the economic realities of a post-recession world, so many Gen Z-ers….* Use POE to identify answer choices that are irrelevant to the requirement posed by the question. Choice (A) does not provide a supporting example, so it can be eliminated. Choices (B) and (D) provide examples that are irrelevant to their attitudes, so (B) and (D) can be eliminated. Choice (C) provides supporting examples that support the point about attitudes. The correct answer is (C).

7. **D** Verb forms are changing in the answer choices, so the question is testing verb consistency. A verb must be consistent in number with the noun and must be consistent with other verbs in the sentence. The subject is *understanding*, which is singular, so a singular verb is required; (A) can be

eliminated. There is no indication of past tense throughout the paragraph, so (B) and (C) can be eliminated. The correct answer is (D).

8. **C** Note the question! The question is asking for the logical placement of sentence 4. Sentence 4 discusses the *idea of the youngest generation wielding power* and *examples show how easily such shifts occur*. Use POE to identify answer choices that are irrelevant to the requirement posed by the question. Where it is now, sentence 4 separates two examples regarding the same Gen Z child, so (A) can be eliminated. Sentence 4 would not introduce the paragraph better than sentence 1 would, so (B) can be eliminated. Sentence 4 could appear after sentence 1 without disrupting the logical flow of ideas, so keep (C) for now. Sentence 4 would not logically lead to sentence 5, so (D) can be eliminated. The correct answer is (C).

9. **B** The length of the phrases is changing in the answer choices, so the question is testing concision. Keep (B), the shortest choice, but check the remaining answer choices just to be sure. Choices (A), (C), and (D) are unnecessarily wordy and redundant, so they can be eliminated. The correct answer is (B).

10. **C** Punctuation is changing in the answer choices, so the question is testing STOP and GO punctuation. Use the Vertical Line Test to identify ideas as complete or incomplete. Draw a vertical line surrounding *and* in the sentence. Before the vertical line is an incomplete idea. Choices (B) and (D) can be eliminated since STOP and HALF-STOP punctuation require a complete idea to precede the punctuation. The sentence, as it is currently, is a run-on sentence and requires a comma to separate the introductory phrase, so (A) can be eliminated. The correct answer is (C).

11. **B** Note the question! The question is asking for the best option to provide a concluding sentence that restates the main argument of the passage. The passage as a whole has been about how Gen Z-ers are growing up and have much to contribute, so look for an option that addresses this idea. Choice (A) is irrelevant to the main point, so it can be eliminated. Choice (B) is relevant, so keep it for now. Choice (C) is also irrelevant, so it can be eliminated. Choice (D) may be tempting, but it only fits the last paragraph, rather than the entire passage, so it can be eliminated. The correct answer is (B).

12. **B** Punctuation is changing in the answer choices, so the question is testing STOP and GO punctuation. Since the sentence contains a long dash between *species* and *from*, another long dash is needed to separate the unnecessary information. Choices (A), (C), and (D) can be eliminated. The correct answer is (B).

13. **A** Phrases and punctuation are changing in the answer choices, so the question is testing precision and STOP and GO punctuation. Choices (C) and (D) create nonsense by starting with *implications*, so they can be eliminated. Choice (B) uses a semicolon to link a complete idea to an incomplete idea, so it can be eliminated. The correct answer is (A).

14. **C** Pronouns and apostrophes are changing in the answer choices, so the question is testing pronoun consistency and apostrophe use. A pronoun must be consistent with the noun it replaces and other pronouns that appear in the sentence. *There* is used to refer to a location, so (A) can be eliminated. Choice (B) is not a word in the English language, so it can be eliminated. *It's* is the contraction of *it is*, which does not appropriately fit into context, so (D) can be eliminated. The correct answer is (C).

15. **C**   Phrases are changing in the answer choices, so the question is testing precision and concision. Keep (B), the shortest choice, but check the remaining answer choices just to be sure. Choices (A), (B), and (D) all introduce an unnecessary pronoun as the subject and produce run-on sentences, so they can be eliminated. The correct answer is (C).

16. **D**   Words are changing in the answer choices, so the question is testing consistency. The sentence requires an action, so the noun, *effect*, is incorrect, and (A) and (C) can be eliminated. The remaining difference is between the singular and plural verb form of *affect*. A verb must be consistent with the subject. The subject of the sentence is *Changes*, which is plural, so (B) can be eliminated. The correct answer is (D).

17. **C**   Note the question! The question is asking which choice most smoothly and effectively introduces the paragraph's discussion of how coral death is linked to the lives of a variety of other species. Use POE to identify answer choices that are irrelevant to the requirement posed by the question. The only answer that is relevant to the question task is (C), since it mentions how *the loss of so much coral reef threatens the survival of many other sea creatures*. Choices (A), (B), and (D) can be eliminated. The correct answer is (C).

18. **B**   Note the question! The question is asking whether the provided sentence should be added to the essay. Begin by reading the surrounding sentences to understand the context. The previous sentence discusses how *losing coral hurts key elements of local economies, such as fishing and tourism*. The provided sentence provides a specific detail in direct reference to the previous sentence, so the addition would be warranted, and therefore (C) and (D) can be eliminated. Choice (A) does not elaborate on an earlier reference to the Great Barrier Reef, so it can be eliminated. The correct answer is (B).

19. **A**   Note the question! The question is asking for the choice that offers the most accurate interpretation of the data in the map. Begin by looking at the map's title and legend. The sentence references the number of people the reefs protect in the region stretching from southeast Asia to northern Australia. This area is marked by the darkest shading, which the legend refers to as more than ten million people, so (B), (C), and (D) can be eliminated. The correct answer is (A).

20. **D**   Note the question! The question is asking for the choice that offers the most accurate interpretation of the data in the map. Use POE to identify answer choices that are irrelevant to the requirement posed by the question. Choice (A) refers to *about two million people living in the Middle East*, but the key shows that more than five million people are protected there, so eliminate (A). Choice (B) references North America, which is not indicated on the map, so eliminate (B). Choice (C) refers to *fewer than two million people living on the eastern coast of Afric*a, but the key indicates this area to be greater than 2.5 million people, so eliminate (C). Choice (D) refers to *more than five million people living around the Caribbean Sea*, which is consistent with the map and the key. The correct answer is (D).

21. **A**   Phrases are changing in the answer choices, so the question is testing precision and concision. Keep (A), the shortest choice, but check the remaining answer choices just to be sure. Choices (B), (C), and (D) are unnecessarily wordy and use slang, so they can be eliminated. The correct answer is (A).

22. **C** Note the question! The question is asking for a conclusion that describes the ongoing efforts to combat the loss of coral reefs. Use POE to identify answer choices that are irrelevant to the requirement posed by the question. Only (C) directly addresses the question task by stating that *scientists and policymakers alike continue to pursue such actions in the hope that a critical mass of people can be persuaded to help prevent still more destruction*, so (A), (B), and (D) can be eliminated. The correct answer is (C).

23. **D** Words are changing in the answer choices, so the question is testing precision and concision. The correct idiomatic expression is *based on*, so (A), (B), and (C) can be eliminated. The correct answer is (D).

24. **A** The number of words after *claims* is changing in the answer choices, so the question is testing concision. Keep (A), the shortest choice, but check the remaining answer choices to be sure. Choices (B) and (D) introduce information already mentioned, so they are redundant. Choice (C) introduces irrelevant information, so it can be eliminated. The correct answer is (A).

25. **D** Transitions are changing in the answer choices, so the question is testing consistency of ideas. Use POE to identify answer choices that are irrelevant to the requirement posed by the question. The previous sentence does not introduce a claim that requires a supporting example, so (A) can be eliminated. The previous sentence does not lead to a negative judgment, so (B) can be eliminated. The previous sentence does not lead to a contrast, so (C) can be eliminated. Choice (D) depicts a summary of the previous sentence, which makes logical sense. The correct answer is (D).

26. **A** Pronouns are changing in the answer choices, so the question is testing pronoun consistency. A pronoun must be consistent in number with the noun it replaces. The noun is *diners*, which is plural, so a plural pronoun is required and (C) and (D) can be eliminated. Since the sentence is discussing the diners' diets, a possessive pronoun is required and (B) can be eliminated. The correct answer is (A).

27. **B** Note the question! The question is asking for the choice that provides the most specific information on health benefits. Use POE to identify answer choices that are irrelevant to the requirement posed by the question. There are no benefits addressed in the original underlined portion, so (A) can be eliminated. Choice (B) specifically names health benefits, so keep it for now. Choices (C) and (D) do not provide any specific benefits, so they can be eliminated. The correct answer is (B).

28. **D** Apostrophes are changing in the answer choices, so the question is testing apostrophe usage. An apostrophe is used to denote either a possession or a contraction. Since the genetic material belongs to the humans, an apostrophe is needed, and (B) can be eliminated. Choice (A) is singular, and can be eliminated. Choice (C) adds an 's to a plural noun, and can be eliminated. The correct answer is (D).

29. **D** Note the question! The question is asking for the choice that gives a supporting example that emphasizes the possibility that human genetics have evolved to metabolize foods developed after the Neolithic Revolution. Use aggressive POE when considering the answers to identify the choice that directly addresses what the question is asking for. Choices (A), (B) and (C) do not provide any evidence of an evolution that has taken place to aid in metabolizing, so they can be eliminated. The correct answer is (D).

30. **A** Punctuation is changing in the answer choices, so the question is testing STOP and GO punctuation. Use the Vertical Line Test to identify ideas as complete or incomplete. Begin by drawing a vertical line between *warn* and *that*. The idea before the vertical line is incomplete, so GO punctuation is needed; (B) and (D) are HALF-STOP punctuation and can be eliminated. Choice (C) adds a comma, but there is neither a list nor unnecessary information, so (C) can be eliminated. The correct answer is (A).

31. **C** Note the question! The question is asking for the choice that best accomplishes the goals of concluding the paragraph effectively and reinforcing the point that some commentators cast doubt on the Paleo diet's large-scale application. Use POE to identify answer choices that are irrelevant to the requirement posed by the question. Choices (A) and (B) do not reinforce the scholars' point about ethics, so they can be eliminated. Choice (C) maintains the focus of the paragraph and references doubt concerning large-scale application by addressing the *finite resources available*, so keep (C) for now. Choice (D) does not reference this doubt, so it can be eliminated. The correct answer is (C).

32. **D** Note the question! The question is asking for the option that most effectively sets up the paragraph. Begin by reading the paragraph to get a general idea of its meaning. The paragraph discusses the changing variety of diets over time, so use POE to identify answer choices that are irrelevant to variety. Choices (A), (B), and (C) do not refer to variety of diets, and can thus be eliminated. The correct answer is (D).

33. **C** Transitions are changing in the answer choices, so the question is testing consistency of ideas. When the option to DELETE appears, check to see if the sentence is logical without the underlined part. Removing the transition would create a run-on sentence, so (D) can be eliminated. Next, check the ideas in the sentence to see if they are similar to or different from one another. The sentence has contrasting details, so (A) and (B) can be eliminated. The correct answer is (C).

34. **D** Note the question! The question is asking whether the writer should delete the underlined portion. The previous sentence addresses the contrast between the *vast scope* of Dickinson's imagination and the *limited scope* of her travels. The underlined portion supports the idea that she did not travel, so the underlined portion should not be deleted, and (A) and (B) can be eliminated. The fact that she rarely left home does not explain why she was important, so (C) can be eliminated. The correct answer is (D).

35. **B** The number of words after *houses* is changing in the answer choices, so the question is testing concision. Keep (B), the shortest choice, but check the remaining answer choices just in case. Choices (A), (C), and (D) are unnecessarily wordy or repetitive, so they can be eliminated. The correct answer is (B).

36. **C** Phrases are changing in the answer choices, so the question is testing consistency. The first choice is between the words *affect* and *effect*. Since the noun form of *affect* means mood, emotion, or feeling, (A) and (B) can be eliminated. The correct noun would be *effect*, and the correct idiomatic expression is *effect...on,* so (D) can be eliminated. The correct answer is (C).

37. **B** Pronouns are changing in the answer choices, so the question is testing pronoun consistency. A pronoun must be consistent with the noun it replaces and the other pronouns in the sentence. The sentence states that a fence and hedge have been reconstructed and replanted to match the fence and hedge that used to shield the house. A plural pronoun is needed for consistency, so (A) and (D) can be eliminated. Also, (A) does not use proper English. The difference between (B) and (C) is that *ones* is a subject, whereas *them* is an object. Since *them shielded the house* is not grammatically correct, (C) can be eliminated. The correct answer is (B).

38. **B** Commas are changing in the answer choices, so the question is testing comma usage. The sentence lists the characteristics of the room, and every element in the list needs a comma following it. Choice (A) can thus be eliminated. Choices (C) and (D) add an additional, unnecessary comma after furniture, so they too can be eliminated. The correct answer is (B).

39. **D** Note the question! The question is asking for the best location of the provided addition. The additional statement discusses the preservationists using *historically accurate paint samples to make sure the colors of the wallpaper would match*. Sentence 5 discusses how *an artist used scraps found during the room's restoration to create wallpaper whose pattern matches the original*, so the additional statement would best follow this. Choices (A), (B), and (C) can be eliminated. The correct answer is (D).

40. **D** Transitions are changing in the answer choices, so the question is testing consistency of ideas. The previous paragraph ended with a discussion of the work already completed by preservationists and this paragraph begins with a discussion of more recent restoration efforts, which means that the work is not actually over. A change in direction is thus needed, and so (A), (B), and (C) can be eliminated. The correct answer is (D).

41. **C** Verbs are changing in the answer choices, so the question is testing verb consistency. A verb must be consistent with the subject and with any other verbs in the sentence. The sentence states that recent restoration efforts *have used seeds*, so the verb form *have addressed* maintains consistency; (A), (B), and (D) can be eliminated. The correct answer is (C).

42. **C** Transitions are changing in the answer choices, so the question is testing consistency of ideas. Begin by reading the previous sentence in conjunction with this sentence to see how the ideas relate to each other. The previous sentence discusses the restoration efforts taken and this sentence continues in the same direction. Choices (A), (B), and (D) all indicate a contrast and can thus be eliminated. The correct answer is (C).

43. **A** Conjunctions are changing in the answer choices, so the question is testing consistency of ideas. Begin by reading the sentence to see how the ideas relate to each other. The sentence states that *its occupants were not allowed to remove anything from the house* and that *it remained virtually unchanged*. Since the first idea leads to the second idea, (B), (C), and (D) can be eliminated. The correct answer is (A).

44.   **A**   Phrases are changing in the answers, so the question is testing precision and concision. Keep (A), the shortest choice, but check the remaining answer choices just to be sure. Choices (C) and (D) are unnecessarily wordy, so they can be eliminated. Choices (A) and (B) are equally concise at three words each, but (B) is awkward, whereas (A) is a common idiom. The correct answer is (A).

Part IV
Math Test

16 Math Test Drill 1
17 Math Test Drill 1: Answers and Explanations
18 Math Test Drill 2
19 Math Test Drill 2: Answers and Explanations
20 Math Test Drill 3
21 Math Test Drill 3: Answers and Explanations

Chapter 16
Math Test Drill 1

Math Test – No Calculator

25 MINUTES, 17 QUESTIONS

Turn to Section 3 of your answer sheet to answer the questions in this section.

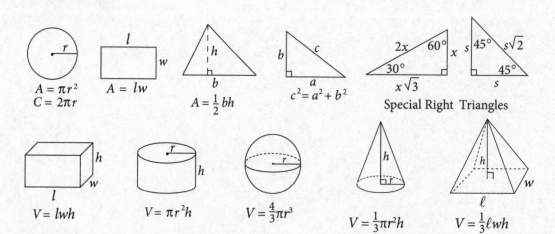

The number of degrees of arc in a circle is 360.
The number of radians of arc in a circle is 2π.
The sum of the measures in degrees of the angles of a triangle is 180.

CONTINUE ➡

1

Given that $3\left(\dfrac{x}{2}+1\right)=9$, what is x ?

A) 2

B) $\dfrac{8}{3}$

C) 3

D) 4

2

The population of Charlotte, NC has risen by about 77,000 people every 5 years since 1990. If the population of Charlotte was 430,000 in 1990, which of the following equations could be used to estimate what the population of Charlotte, in thousands, was in 2011 ?

A) $P = 430 + 21(77)$

B) $P = 430 + \dfrac{21}{5}(77)$

C) $P = 430 + \dfrac{5}{21}(77)$

D) $P = \dfrac{430 + 21(77)}{5}$

3

Given that $f(x) = 2x^2 + 2$, what is $f(3) - f(1)$?

A) 20

B) 16

C) 10

D) 4

4

Sandra discovers that her test scores on biology tests are directly proportional to the number of hours she studies and inversely proportional to the number of classes she misses. She determines that her test score, T, can be calculated with the equation $T = \dfrac{x}{ky}$, where k is a constant. If she studied for 6 hours and got a 90 on her test, which of the following expressions represents the number of classes she missed, in terms of k ?

A) $\dfrac{6}{90k}$

B) $\dfrac{90}{6k}$

C) $90(6k)$

D) $\dfrac{90}{6}k$

CONTINUE

5

$$x^2 - 8x - d = 0$$

In the above polynomial, the constant d is a negative integer. Which of the following could be the roots of the equation?

A) $x = -2$ and $x = -6$

B) $x = -4$ only

C) $x = -9$ and $x = 1$

D) $x = 7$ and $x = 1$

6

$$\frac{x + 6}{x - 2} > 6$$

If x is an integer, which of the following represents the solution set of x?

A)

B)

C)

D)

7

$$\frac{b}{A(x - b)} = \frac{x + b}{bA}$$

If $xb < 0$ and $A \neq 0$, which of the following correctly expresses b in terms of x?

A) $b = \dfrac{-x}{\sqrt{2}}$

B) $b = \dfrac{x}{\sqrt{2}}$

C) $b = \dfrac{x}{4}$

D) $b = \dfrac{x^2}{2}$

CONTINUE

8

James is studying the growth rates of trees and needs to determine the height of a tree. He stands 8 feet from the base of the tree and looks at the top of the tree. If his eyes are tilted up 70 degrees when he focuses on the top of the tree, and his eye level is 5 feet high, how tall is the tree?

A) $8 \sin 70° - 5$

B) $\dfrac{8 \sin 70°}{5}$

C) $8 \tan 70° - 5$

D) $8 \tan 70° + 5$

9

Which of the following is equivalent to $\dfrac{ab^2}{\sqrt[3]{a^4 b^2}}$?

A) $a^{\frac{2}{3}} b^{\frac{4}{3}}$

B) $\dfrac{b^4}{\sqrt[3]{ab}}$

C) $\sqrt[3]{\dfrac{b^4}{a}}$

D) $\dfrac{b^{\frac{4}{3}}}{a^{-\frac{1}{3}}}$

10

Before Annie leaves for a trip, she determines the number of miles she can drive is given by the equation $f(x, y, z) = \dfrac{yz}{2.5} + xy$. The variables x, y, and z in this equation are the amount of money, in dollars, she spends on gas during her trip, the number of gallons of gas in her tank when she starts her trip, and the miles per gallon her car gets for the entire trip, respectively. Given this information, what is the minimum amount of gas, in gallons, that Annie must buy on her trip if she drove 420 miles, her gas mileage was 40 miles per gallon, and she started with 9 gallons in the tank?

A) 16.8

B) 3.75

C) 2.5

D) 1.5

CONTINUE ▶

11

For two integers, p and q, if the positive difference between p and q is no more than 3, and the sum of p and q is between -12 and 30, which of the following describes all possible values of q ?

A) $-7 \leq q \leq 16$

B) $-8 \leq q \leq 17$

C) $-6 < q < 17$

D) $-7 \leq q \leq 13$

12

If three times the sum of the squares of x and y is four more than three times the square of the difference between x and y, what is the value of xy ?

A) -2

B) $-\dfrac{2}{3}$

C) $\dfrac{2}{3}$

D) 2

13

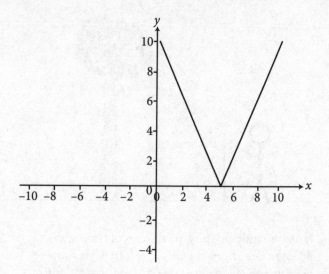

The function $h(x)$ is a reflection of $f(x)$ across the y-axis. If the graph shown above is $h(x) - 5$, which of the following could represent $f(x)$?

A) $f(x) = 2|x - 5| - 5$

B) $f(x) = 2|x + 5| + 5$

C) $f(x) = |x + 5| + 5$

D) $f(x) = |2x - 5| - 5$

CONTINUE ▶

DIRECTIONS

For questions 14-17, solve the problem and enter your answer in the grid, as described below, on the answer sheet.

1. Although not required, it is suggested that you write your answer in the boxes at the top of the columns to help you fill in the circles accurately. You will receive credit only if the circles are filled in correctly.

2. Mark no more than one circle in any column.

3. No question has a negative answer.

4. Some problems may have more than one correct answer. In such cases, grid only one answer.

5. **Mixed numbers** such as $3\frac{1}{2}$ must be gridded as 3.5 or 7/2. (If  is entered into the grid, it will be interpreted as $\frac{31}{2}$, not as $3\frac{1}{2}$.)

6. **Decimal Answers:** If you obtain a decimal answer with more digits than the grid can accommodate, it may be either rounded or truncated, but it must fill the entire grid.

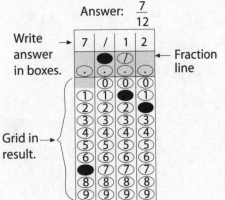

Answer: $\frac{7}{12}$ — Answer: 2.5

Write answer in boxes. ← Fraction line

Grid in result. — Decimal point

Acceptable ways to grid $\frac{2}{3}$ are:

Answer: 201 – either position is correct

NOTE: You may start your answers in any column, space permitting. Columns you don't need to use should be left blank.

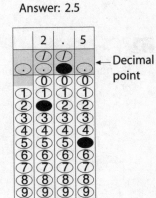

CONTINUE ➤

14

If $x^2 - x = 12$ and $x > 0$, what is the value of x ?

15

If one-third of m is equal to six less than m, what is m ?

16

$$3a - 16 = b$$
$$4a + b = 32$$

What is the value of a in the above system of equations?

17

$$\frac{x}{x-3} + \frac{2x}{x-2} = -\frac{4}{x^2 - 5x + 6}$$

Given the above equation, what is a possible value of $x + 6$?

CONTINUE

THIS PAGE IS LEFT INTENTIONALLY BLANK.

Math Test – Calculator

45 MINUTES, 31 QUESTIONS

Turn to Section 4 of your answer sheet to answer the questions in this section.

For questions **1-27**, solve each problem, choose the best answer from the choices provided, and fill in the corresponding circle on your answer sheet. For questions **28-31**, solve the problem and enter your answer in the grid on the answer sheet. Please refer to the directions before question 28 on how to enter your answers in the grid. You may use any available space in your test booklet for scratch work.

NOTES

1. The use of a calculator **is permitted**.
2. All variables and expressions used represent real numbers unless otherwise indicated.
3. Figures provided in this test are drawn to scale unless otherwise indicated.
4. All figures lie in a plane unless otherwise indicated.
5. Unless otherwise indicated, the domain of a given function f is the set of all real numbers x for which $f(x)$ is a real number.

REFERENCE

$A = \pi r^2$
$C = 2\pi r$

$A = lw$

$A = \frac{1}{2}bh$

$c^2 = a^2 + b^2$

Special Right Triangles

$V = lwh$

$V = \pi r^2 h$

$V = \frac{4}{3}\pi r^3$

$V = \frac{1}{3}\pi r^2 h$

$V = \frac{1}{3}lwh$

The number of degrees of arc in a circle is 360.
The number of radians of arc in a circle is 2π.
The sum of the measures in degrees of the angles of a triangle is 180.

CONTINUE ➡

1

Catherine can swim the length of the 25-yard pool in 12 seconds. At this rate, approximately how long, in seconds, will it take her to swim 50 meters? (Note: 1 yard = 0.91 meters.)

A) 13.2

B) 21.8

C) 24

D) 26.4

2

Nick is working on a project and is supposed to take hourly measurements of the temperature. He records the temperature at 2 P.M. as 78° Fahrenheit, but later realizes that the data needs to be in degrees Celsius. Given that the formula $F = \frac{9}{5}C + 32$ can be used to convert Celsius (C) to Fahrenheit (F), what is the temperature in degrees Celsius at 2 P.M. ?

A) 25.6°

B) 29.3°

C) 61.1°

D) 172.4°

3

Percent of University Community with Health Insurance		
	Male	Female
Undergraduate	75%	83%
Graduate	65%	72%
Faculty and Staff	87%	91%

Roger wants to determine the approximate percentage of residents in his state that have health insurance, so he goes to the state university and asks 500 randomly selected people on campus whether or not they have healthcare. The results are shown in the table above. Which of the following conclusions can be most logically drawn from the data shown above?

A) The number of females at the university with health insurance is greater than the number of males with health insurance at the university.

B) Approximately 76% of males in the state have health insurance.

C) The faculty and staff at this university are more likely to be insured than the graduate students.

D) Graduate students are less likely to have health insurance than the average resident of the state.

4

If $\frac{3x + 2}{7} = \frac{2x + 5}{7}$, then $x = ?$

A) $-\frac{5}{2}$

B) $-\frac{2}{3}$

C) 3

D) 7

CONTINUE

Year	% Unemployed
2005	5.3
2006	4.7
2007	4.6
2008	5.0
2009	7.8
2010	9.8
2011	9.2
2012	8.3
2013	8.0
2014	6.6
2015	5.7

The table above shows the percentage of Americans aged 16 and older who were unemployed in the years 2005–2015 (measured annually at the end of January). According to the data above, what was the average (arithmetic mean) percentage of unemployed Americans aged 16 and older in the years 2008–2011, inclusive?

A) 4.57%

B) 6.82%

C) 7.95%

D) 9.21%

In a certain safari park in Tanzania, the ratio of wildebeest to gazelles is 4 to 3, and the ratio of elephants to hyenas is 3 to 5. If the ratio of gazelles to elephants is 1 to 1, then what is the ratio of hyenas to wildebeest?

A) 5 to 4

B) 4 to 5

C) 5 to 3

D) 3 to 5

Hours since experiment began	Total population of bacteria
0	7
1	14
2	28
3	56

A scientist is studying the growth rate of bacteria in a certain colony. Based on the data in the chart above, she determines that the number of bacteria in the colony at any time in the first 3 hours can be modeled by the expression $7 \times b^c$. What does the quantity b represent in the expression?

A) The initial population of the bacteria colony

B) The factor by which the colony multiplies every hour

C) The hours since the experiment began

D) The total population of the bacteria colony at a given time

8

	5mg dose	10mg dose	15mg dose
Nausea	14%	16%	32%
Insomnia	10%	25%	40%
Nausea and Insomnia	6%	12%	15%

Researchers studying a new medication find that it can cause nausea, insomnia, or both in patients who take it. After studying patients in three different groups, each taking a different dose of the medication, the researchers calculate the chance that a patient on the medication will experience these side effects. The results are shown in the table above. If a patient is chosen at random from those with nausea after taking 10 milligrams of the medication, what is the probability that the patient also has insomnia?

A) 0.50

B) 0.64

C) 0.75

D) 0.80

9

Time (seconds)	Height (feet)
0	10
1	13
2	14
3	13
4	10
5	5

The table above shows the height of a projectile that is shot from a 10-foot tall platform. If $H(t)$ represents the height of the projectile, in feet, and t represents the time, in seconds, then which of the following functions accurately reflects the projectile's trajectory according to the data above?

A) $H(t) = -x^2 + 4x + 10$

B) $H(t) = x^2 - 4x + 10$

C) $H(t) = -x^2 - 4x + 10$

D) $H(t) = x^2 + 4x - 10$

10

During a sale at a certain clothing store, customers receive a discount of 10% off for purchases that are up to $120 at regular price and 15% for purchases that are $120 or more at regular price. A sales tax of 7% is added after the discount. If Sara's total bill is $103.04, what was the original price of the merchandise she bought?

A) $96.70

B) $99.20

C) $107

D) $113.20

CONTINUE ▶

11

Cara has a greenhouse full of pea plants and begins an experiment in which she varies the amount of sunlight that the plants receive. She determines that the average height, in centimeters, of her pea plants t days after she begins the experiment is given by the equation $h = 13 + 0.2t$. Plants that have a height within 15% of this value exhibit "standard" growth. Plants that are taller than this range exhibit "superior" growth, and plants that are shorter than this range exhibit "inferior" growth. If a pea plant has a height of m centimeters after n days it exhibits "superior" growth, but if it has a height of $m - 3$ centimeters, it exhibits "inferior" growth. Which of the following pairs of inequalities could be used to determine possible values of m and n ?

A) $m > 13 + 0.15(0.2n)$

   $m - 3 < 13 - 0.15(0.2n)$

B) $n > 1.15(13 + 0.2m)$

   $n < .85 (13 + 0.2(m - 3)$

C) $m < 1.15 (13 + 0.2n)$

   $m - 3 > .85(13 + 0.2n)$

D) $m > 1.15(13 + 0.2n)$

   $m - 3 < 0.85(13 + .2n)$

12

A function is given by $y = ax + c$, in which a and c are constants and $a > c$. Which of the following could be the graph of y ?

A)

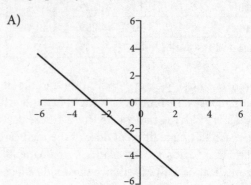

B)

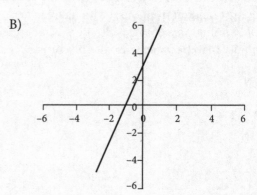

C)

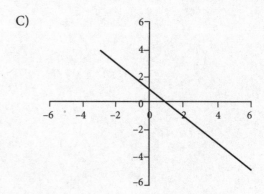

D)

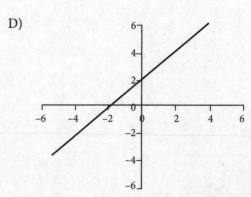

CONTINUE

13

A study group of four students took a midterm exam in Botany class. The students' scores had a high score of 85, a range of 25, and a mode of 70. If a student who scored a 95 on the midterm joined the study group, then what would be the average (arithmetic mean) score of all five students on the midterm?

A) 69

B) 76

C) 78

D) 90

Questions 14-15 refer to the following information.

A scientist places 100 bacteria in a petri dish and observes the increase in the number of bacteria over time. She determines that the number of bacteria triples every hour.

14

If m represents the time, in minutes, then which of the following functions could represent the number of bacteria, $N(m)$, over time?

A) $N(m) = 100(3^{60m})$

B) $N(m) = 100(3^m)$

C) $N(m) = 100(60^{3m})$

D) $N(m) = 100\left(3^{\frac{m}{60}}\right)$

15

Which of the following graphs could accurately represent the growth of bacteria described on the left?

A)

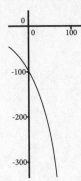

B)

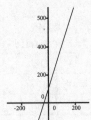

C)

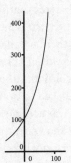

D)

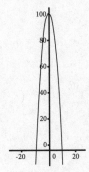

CONTINUE

16

If $3x + 5y = 80$ and $24 - y = x$, then which of the following is equivalent to $\dfrac{x}{y}$?

A) 3

B) 5

C) 7

D) 9

17

	Did donate	Did not donate	Total
Had children present	324	36	360
Did not have children present	66	174	240
Total	390	210	600

A social scientist hypothesizes that people are more likely to donate to charities that benefit children if they have children with them when asked to donate. He set up a booth for a children's charity at a craft fair at a mall and asked for donations. He noted whether each person he asked to donate gave money and whether the person was accompanied by any children. The results are shown in the table above. The probability that a person with children donated is how much greater than the probability that a person without children did NOT donate?

A) 0.175

B) 0.245

C) 0.725

D) 0.900

18

$$y = (x - 5)(x + 6)$$
$$y = x + 6$$

The system of equations above has two solutions in the xy-plane. What is the x-coordinate of the midpoint of the two solutions?

A) −6

B) 0

C) 6

D) 12

19

$$F = 3x - 2$$
$$G = x - 1$$

Given the equations above, which of the following is equivalent to $F^3 - G$?

A) $x^3 - 3x^2 + 1$

B) $8x^3 - 12x^2 + 6x - 1$

C) $27x^3 - 54x^2 + 35x - 7$

D) $27x^3 - 54x^2 + 37x - 9$

CONTINUE

Questions 20-21 refer to the following information.

The scatter plot below shows the relationship between the number of students per third grade class in a metro area and the percentage of the students that read at or above grade level.

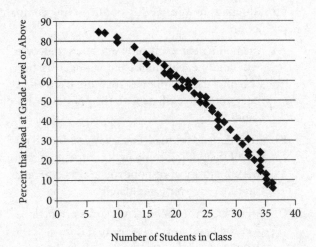

Number of Students in Class

20

For all classes with at least 5 people, which of the following equations, in which n represents the number of students and P represents the percent that read at grade level, most accurately models the above relationship?

A) $P = 85 + 2.5(n)$

B) $P = 85 - 2.5(n - 5)$

C) $P = 88 - \left(\dfrac{n}{4}\right)^2$

D) $P = 88 - \left(\dfrac{n}{2}\right)^2$

21

A school in the metro area has 208 third grade students spread evenly over x classrooms. Approximately 40% of the students in these classes read at a third grade level. If the school had one more third grade classroom, approximately what percent of the students would be expected to read at grade level?

A) 23%

B) 41%

C) 50%

D) 60%

22

Shawn purchases 200 shares of a stock at the beginning of 2009. The stock decreases in value by 15% in 2009, then increases 8% per year in 2010 and 2011, and then the total value of the 200 shares increases by $500 in 2012. If the total value of the stock Shawn owns is $2,750 at the end of 2012, what was the approximate price per share when he purchased it?

A) $11.15

B) $11.35

C) $11.61

D) $12.25

CONTINUE

23

$$\frac{2x - 3}{3} - \frac{5y - 2}{4} = 2$$

$$-4(2x + y) = 27$$

Given the above system of equations, what is the value of $x + y$?

A) $-\frac{39}{8}$

B) -3

C) $\frac{8}{17}$

D) $\frac{9}{8}$

24

On a map Sam's house is 5 centimeters west and 9 centimeters north of Joe's house. If there is a road that runs directly from Sam's house to Joe's house and it takes Sam 45 minutes to drive along this road at 30 miles per hour to Joe's house, approximately how many miles does each centimeter on this map represent?

A) 0.46

B) 1.6

C) 1.8

D) 2.2

25

As part of its effort to predict a recent election, a prominent polling company conducted telephone interviews during which respondents were asked whether they were more likely to vote for Candidate A or Candidate B. Based on the results of this telephone survey, the polling company predicted that Candidate A would likely win the election. Which of the following pieces of information, if true, would cast the most doubt upon the validity of the polling company's prediction?

A) The polling company only interviewed people with landline telephones, but younger voters who only use cell phones are more likely than older voters to affiliate with the political party of Candidate B.

B) An independent mail-in survey conducted by one of the polling company's competitors showed that a majority of respondents claimed to favor Candidate A over Candidate B.

C) Analyses of the polling company's predictions over the past ten years show that it has a very strong record of correctly predicting the results of major elections.

D) The polling company conducted a follow-up telephone interview with the same respondents and asked a more open-ended question: "Which candidate do you plan to vote for in the upcoming election?" and, based on the results of this second interview, concluded that Candidate A was likely to win the election.

CONTINUE

26

In a Brazilian nature conservancy, park rangers have worked over the past few decades to increase the number of howler monkeys living within the grounds of the conservancy. In the year 1980, the conservancy contained 800 howler monkeys; in the year 2010, the conservancy contained 1,200 howler monkeys. In the equation $1,200 = 800 + 30x$, what does the x most likely represent?

A) The total number of howler monkeys added to the conservancy's population from 1980–2010

B) The total number of years that have passed since the park rangers began working to increase the howler monkey population

C) The average yearly increase in the howler monkey population from 1980–2010

D) The minimum number of howler monkeys that must be added for the population in the conservancy to remain constant

27

Which of the following expressions is equivalent to $\dfrac{64^4 - 32^8}{128^2}$?

A) $\dfrac{2^8}{1 + 2^6}$

B) $2^{24} - 2^{-4}$

C) $\dfrac{1 - 2^4}{2^{10}}$

D) $2^{10}(1 - 2^{16})$

CONTINUE

DIRECTIONS

For questions 28-31, solve the problem and enter your answer in the grid, as described below, on the answer sheet.

1. Although not required, it is suggested that you write your answer in the boxes at the top of the columns to help you fill in the circles accurately. You will receive credit only if the circles are filled in correctly.

2. Mark no more than one circle in any column.

3. No question has a negative answer.

4. Some problems may have more than one correct answer. In such cases, grid only one answer.

5. **Mixed numbers** such as $3\frac{1}{2}$ must be gridded as 3.5 or 7/2. (If $\boxed{3\;1\;/\;2}$ is entered into the grid, it will be interpreted as $\frac{31}{2}$, not as $3\frac{1}{2}$.)

6. **Decimal Answers:** If you obtain a decimal answer with more digits than the grid can accommodate, it may be either rounded or truncated, but it must fill the entire grid.

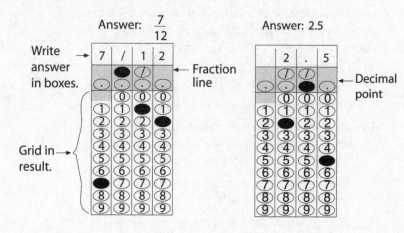

Acceptable ways to grid $\frac{2}{3}$ are:

Answer: 201 – either position is correct

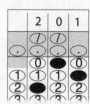

NOTE: You may start your answers in any column, space permitting. Columns you don't need to use should be left blank.

CONTINUE

28

$$3y - 9 = \frac{3}{2}x$$

$$y = ax - 3$$

If the system of equations above has no solutions, what is the value of a ?

29

$$y = 2x + 4$$
$$y = (x - 2)^2$$

The system of equations above has two solutions in the xy-plane. What is the sum of the x- and y-coordinates of the solution in Quadrant I ?

Questions 30-31 refer to the following information.

Brian bought a certain 3D printer that has a maximum build volume of 4 inches × 4 inches × 4 inches. It can print objects at different fill levels, which will make the final object more or less dense without changing the volume.

30

If 1 inch equals 25.4 millimeters and there are 10 millimeters in a centimeter, what is the printer's maximum build volume in cubic centimeters, rounded to the nearest whole number?

31

Brian used the 3D printer to make a tablet stand that weighed 0.2 ounces with a volume of 0.183 cubic inches. If there are 28.35 grams in an ounce and 0.061 cubic inches in a cubic centimeter, at what density did Brian print the stand, in grams per cubic centimeter? (Density = mass / volume)

STOP
**If you finish before time is called, you may check your work on this section only.
Do not turn to any other section.**

Chapter 17
Math Test
Drill 1: Answers
and Explanations

ANSWERS AND EXPLANATIONS

Section 3—Math Test

1. **D** To solve this equation, isolate x on one side of the equation. First, divide both sides by 3, resulting in $\left(\dfrac{x}{2}\right) + 1 = 3$. Subtract 1 from each side to get $\left(\dfrac{x}{2}\right) = 2$. Finally, multiply both sides by 2 to get $x = 4$, or (D). Alternatively, you can use PITA and plug in each of the answer choices into the equation until one of them works.

2. **B** As you work this problem, keep in mind that the question asks for the population in thousands, so we will drop the last three zeroes off the numbers. The population starts at 430,000, so the increase will be added to the base number of 430. Eliminate (D). The population rises 77,000 every five years. Since there are 21 years from 1990 to 2011, divide 21 by 5 and then multiply by the increase of 77, or (B).

3. **B** Plug in 3 and 1 for x in the given function. $f(3)$ is equal to $2(3)^2 + 2$ or 20. $f(1)$ is equal to $2(1)^2 + 2$ or 4. To find the answer, subtract 4 from 20, giving a final answer of 16, or (B).

4. **A** To find the answer, plug in the values given into the equation. Her test score, T, equals 90. She studied 6 hours, which is directly proportional to T, so $6 = x$ (for direct proportion $y = kx$). The equation is now $90 = \dfrac{6}{yk}$. To solve for y, multiply both sides by yk to get $90yk = 6$. Finally, divide both sides by $90k$ to get $y = \dfrac{6}{90k}$, or (A).

5. **D** To find the possible roots that work, try them out. Start with (A). If the roots are -2 and -6, then the factored polynomial is $(x + 2)(x + 6)$. FOIL to get $x^2 + 8x + 12$, which does not fit the polynomial given. Try the other three sets of roots. The constant d is a negative number being subtracted (a double negative), so d will become positive in the polynomial. Only (D) results in -8 for the second term and a positive constant.

6. **C** Because dealing with inequalities is a bit tricky, Plug In the Answers to solve. Choice (A) suggests that 4 is a possible value. Plug 4 into the equation to get $\dfrac{4+6}{4-2} > 6$. Solve the left side of the equation to get $\dfrac{10}{2} > 6$, and $5 > 6$. Since this statement is false, eliminate (A). Choice (B) includes 3 as a possible value. Plug 3 into the equation to get $\dfrac{3+6}{3-2} > 6$. Solve the left side of the equation to get $\dfrac{9}{1} > 6$, and $9 > 6$. This statement is true, so eliminate (D), which does not include 3 as a possible value. The only difference is between (B) and (C) is that (C) includes values above 3. So, plug 3.1

into the equation to get $\dfrac{3.1+6}{3.1-2} > 6$. Solve the left side of the equation to get $\dfrac{9.1}{1.1} > 6$ and $8.27 > 6$. This statement is true, so eliminate (B).

7. **A** Multiply both sides by A to get $\dfrac{b}{x-b} = \dfrac{x+b}{b}$. Cross-multiply: $b^2 = (x-b)(x+b)$. The right-hand side is the difference of squares: $b^2 = x^2 - b^2$. Add b^2 to both sides: $2b^2 = x^2$. Divide both sides by 2: $b^2 = \dfrac{x^2}{2}$. Take the square root of both sides: $\sqrt{b^2} = \sqrt{\dfrac{x^2}{2}}$. Note you get both positive AND negative roots of b: $b = \pm\dfrac{x}{\sqrt{2}}$. Because $xb < 0$, it must be the case that one of x or b is negative (and the other is positive), so you must have the negative root: $b = -\dfrac{x}{\sqrt{2}}$, which is (A).

8. **D** Label the base of the triangle with 8 ft. Use SOHCAHTOA to choose tan as the appropriate trig function; $\tan 70° = \dfrac{x}{8}$, or $x = 8\tan 70°$. Remember to add 5 to the answer to account for James's height. The answer is (D).

9. **C** First, rewrite the denominator. Taking the cube root is the same as raising to the $\dfrac{1}{3}$ power. The new denominator then becomes $a^{\frac{4}{3}} b^{\frac{2}{3}}$. Use the properties of exponents (MADSPM): $\dfrac{a}{a^{\frac{4}{3}}} = a^{-\frac{1}{3}}$ and $\dfrac{b^2}{b^{\frac{2}{3}}} = b^{\frac{4}{3}}$. The b value is the numerator, and the a value is the denominator. The only answer choice equivalent to $\dfrac{b^{\frac{4}{3}}}{a^{\frac{1}{3}}}$ is (C).

10. **D** Be careful with this question; the equation is unnecessary to solve the problem. We know that Annie drove 420 miles total. With the 9 gallons in the tank and a gas mileage of 40 miles per gallon, Annie can drive 360 miles before she needs to stop for more gas. To find how many gallons she purchased, divide the remaining miles (60) by the gas mileage (40), to get 1.5 more gallons, or (D).

11. **A** First, write out the inequalities given in the question: $|p - q| \le 3$ and $-12 < p + q < 30$. Then, Plug In the Answers, using the limits of the ranges you are given in the inequalities listed as possible values for q. Start with the largest possible value of q, which occurs in (B). If q equals 17, then p can equal any number between or equal to 14 and 20 for the first equation to remain true. Then, check to see if any of the p values you get based on the first question will also make the second equation true by testing 14 and 20 in the second equation: neither $17 + 20$ nor $17 + 14$ is less than 30, so eliminate (B). Check $q = 16$ in the first equation: p is between or equal to 19 and 13, which does work in the second equation ($13 + 16 = 29$, which is < 30). Since the answer must include all of the values of q that work, eliminate (D) and choose (A).

12. **C**   Begin by translating the question into an equation: $3(x^2 + y^2) = 4 + 3(x - y)^2$. Distribute the 3 and

FOIL the $(x - y)^2$ to get $3x^2 + 3y^2 = 4 + 3x^2 - 6xy + 3y^2$. Eliminate $3x^2$ and $3y^2$ from both sides to get

$0 = 4 - 6xy$. Isolate xy to get the answer $\dfrac{2}{3}$, or (C).

13. **B**   First, pick a point on the current function. $h(x) - 5$ is the graph of $h(x)$ moved down five units (5 is subtracted from every y-coordinate). If $h(x) - 5$ has the point $(5, 0)$, then that point on $h(x)$ will be $(5, 5)$. Next, translate the point across the y-axis, reversing the sign of the x-value, to get $(-5, 5)$. Now, check to see what functions contain this point by plugging in -5 for x. Two answers, (B) and (C), give us a y-value of 5. Try a new point. $(0, 10)$ becomes $(0, 15)$ for $h(x)$. It's the same point on $f(x)$ as well. Plug in 0 for x in the remaining answer choices. Only (B) gives the correct y-value of 15.

14. **4**   Move the 12 to the other side and factor to get $(x - 4)(x + 3) = 0$, so x equals 4 and -3. The question states $x > 0$, so the correct answer is 4.

15. **9**   Write out the equation: $\left(\dfrac{1}{3}\right) m = m - 6$. Multiply both sides by 3 to get rid of the fraction, resulting in $m = 3m - 18$. Subtract $3m$ from both sides to get $-2m = -18$. Divide by -2 to get $m = 9$.

16. $\dfrac{48}{7}$ **or 6.85 or 6.86**

Rewrite the first equation so it looks like the second equation: $3a - b = 16$. Then add the two equations together. The b's cancel out, leaving $7a = 48$. Divide both sides by 7 to get $a = \dfrac{48}{7}$.

17. $\dfrac{20}{3}$ **or 6.67**

Start by factoring the denominator of the right side of the equation to get

$\dfrac{x}{x-3} + \dfrac{2x}{x-2} = \dfrac{-4}{(x-3)(x-2)}$. With a common denominator of $(x - 3)(x - 2)$, add the

fractions to get $\dfrac{x(x-2) + 2x(x-3)}{(x-3)(x-2)} = \dfrac{-4}{(x-3)(x-2)}$. Distribute the x and the $2x$ to get

$\dfrac{x^2 - 2x + 2x^2 - 6x}{(x-3)(x-2)} = \dfrac{-4}{(x-3)(x-2)}$. Simplify the numerator to get $\dfrac{3x^2 - 8x}{(x-3)(x-2)} = \dfrac{-4}{(x-3)(x-2)}$.

Because the denominators of the two fractions are the same, the numerators of the two fractions

on either side of the equal sign must be equal to each other. Therefore, $3x^2 - 8x = -4$. Bring-

ing all terms over to the left side yields $3x^2 - 8x + 4 = 0$. Factoring $3x^2 - 8x + 4 = 0$ gives us

$(3x - 2)(x - 2) = 0$. From this, you get $x = \dfrac{2}{3}$ or $x = 2$. However, plugging in $x = 2$ back in to the

original equation would result in two of the fractions becoming undefined, so $x = 2$ is discarded.

Therefore, $x = \dfrac{2}{3}$, so $x + 6 = \dfrac{2}{3} + 6 = \dfrac{20}{3}$.

Section 4—Math Test

1. **D** Start by converting 50 meters to yards by using a proportion: $\dfrac{1 \text{ yard}}{0.91 \text{ meters}} = \dfrac{x \text{ yards}}{50 \text{ meters}}$. Cross-multiply to get $0.91x = 50$. Divide both sides by 0.91 to get 54.95 yards. Next, set up a proportion to determine how long it will take Catherine to swim 54.95 yards: $\dfrac{25 \text{ yards}}{12 \text{ seconds}} = \dfrac{54.95 \text{ yards}}{x \text{ seconds}}$. Cross-multiply to get $25x = 659.4$. Divide both sides by 25 to get $x = 26.37$, which is closest to (D).

2. **A** Plug in 78 for F in the equation: $78 = \dfrac{9}{5}C + 32$. Subtract 32 from both sides: $46 = \dfrac{9}{5}C$. Multiply both sides by 5 to clear the fraction: $230 = 9C$. Finally, divide both sides by 9 to get $25.56 = C$, which is closest to (A).

3. **C** Consider each answer choice and use POE. For (A), you would need to know how many males and how many females are at the university. It may be the case that there are many more times as many males as females, which would make the number of males with health insurance greater (despite the lesser percentage). Eliminate (A). Choice (B) would require you to assume that the university is reflective of the state and that averaging the three groups would result in a good reflection of the state as a whole. Each of these alone is a questionable assumption; both together means you should eliminate (B). Choice (D) can similarly be eliminated, as it makes an inference about the average resident of the state. Choice (C) simply compares the groups surveyed and makes a safe inference based on how likely it is a particular member of one group is insured, so it is the best response.

4. **C** Start by multiplying both sides by 7 to clear the fractions. This gives you $3x + 2 = 2x + 5$. Next, subtract $2x$ from both sides: $x + 2 = 5$. Finally, subtract 2 from both sides to get $x = 3$, which is (C).

5. **C** In order to find the average percentage of unemployed Americans in the years 2008–2011, simply find the relevant years in the table and extract the data you need. The average for these four years will be the sum divided by the number of things: $\dfrac{5.0 + 7.8 + 9.8 + 9.2}{4} = \dfrac{31.8}{4} = 7.95$, which matches (C).

6. **A** This question can be solved by plugging in numbers. If you say that there are 4 wildebeest and 3 gazelles and the ratio of gazelles to elephants is 1 to 1, then there would also be 3 elephants (and thus 5 hyenas). The ratio of hyenas to wildebeest would therefore be 5 to 4, (A).

7. **B** Knowing the growth formula can help here. The formula is *final amount = original amount (multiplier)$^{number\ of\ changes}$*, so *b* is the growth multiplier. Without knowing the formula, find the answer using POE and Plugging In. At a time of 0, or when the experiment began, there were 7 bacteria in the colony. The 7 is already represented in the expression, so *b* would not also be 7. Eliminate (A). According to the question, the entire expression $7 \times b^c$ represents the total population at any time, so eliminate (D). Therefore, *b* is either the growth factor or the number of hours. Plug in some numbers from the chart to determine which it is. To test (B), plug in 14 for the total population and 1 for *c*, which would be the time if *b* is the growth factor. The equation becomes $14 = 7 \times b^1$. Divide both sides by 7 to get $2 = b^1$, so $b = 2$. If the growth multiplier is 2, the population would double every hour, and the chart shows that it does. The correct answer is (B).

8. **C** Probability is defined as the number that fits the requirement divided by the total number of things. In this case, there are no numbers, so Plug In. Plugging in 100 on percent questions is the easiest way to go. If 100 people took the medication, 16 of them would have taken the 10 milligram dose and had nausea. This number is the "total" for the probability and is therefore the denominator of the fraction. Of those 16 people, 12 of them would have both nausea and insomnia, so that is the numerator. The probability, then, is $\frac{12}{16} = 0.75$, which is (C).

9. **A** The best way to approach this question is to plug the values from the table into the functions in the answer choices to determine which one matches. Only (A) works for all of the values in the table.

10. **C** Plug In the Answers! Choice (B) is more obnoxious than (C) (because (B) has a decimal), so start with (C). If the item was $107, then Sarah receives a discount of 10%, or $0.10 \times 107 = \$10.70$, making the post-discount price $107 - 10.70 = \$96.30$. Next, you must apply 7% sales tax. 7% of $96.30 is $0.07 \times 96.30 = \$6.74$. This is added to the total: $96.30 + 6.74 = \$103.04$. This matches what the question indicates, so select (C).

11. **D** Start with the "superior" growth scenario. If the average height is $13 + 0.2t$ and superior growth is greater than 15% more than the average, then superior growth is greater than $13 + 0.2t + 0.15 (13 + 0.2t)$, which simplifies to $1.15(13 + 0.2t)$. Because a plant with growth of *m* is superior, then $m > 1.15(13 + 0.2t)$. Only (D) has this inequality. (Note that (B) switches the variables; very tricky!)

12. **A** In the form $y = mx + b$, *m* represents the slope and *b* represents the *y*-intercept. Therefore, if the form is instead $y = ax + c$, *a* is slope and *c* is *y*-intercept. Therefore, the slope must be greater than the *y*-intercept. It's easier to determine the *y*-intercept first, so start there and then determine the slope for each answer choice. In (A), the *y*-intercept is at $(0, -3)$, so the *y*-intercept, and therefore the value of *c*, is –3. The line goes through $(-3, 0)$ and $(0, -3)$, which makes the slope $\frac{-3 - 0}{0 - (-3)} = -1$, so $a = -1$. $-1 > -3$, so (A) works.

13. **B** For the four original students, because the mode was 70, there must be at least two students with a 70. If the highest score was an 85 and the range of scores was 25, then the lowest score was 85 − 25 = 60. This means the original four scores were 60, 70, 70, and 85. With the new student, the five scores are 60, 70, 70, 85, and 95. To find the average, add the scores and divide by (5): $\frac{60 + 70 + 70 + 85 + 95}{5} = 76$, which matches (B).

14. **D** Since the number of bacteria triples every hour, that means that the number of bacteria triples every 60 minutes. Since the m in the functions represents the number of minutes, you need to divide m by 60 to represent the number of hours. Only (D) matches. Alternatively, you could plug in a number, such as 120 minutes, to determine how many bacteria there would be after 2 hours (and then find which answer choice matches your target answer).

15. **C** The question states that the number of bacteria triples every hour; this is an exponential relationship. Choice (B) is linear, and (D) is quadratic, so both can be eliminated. The number of bacteria is increasing, not decreasing, so eliminate (A) and select (C).

16. **B** Start by rearranging the second equation in order to get all of the variables on one side: $x + y = 24$. Next, multiply the second equation by 3: $3(x + y = 24)$ gives you $3x + 3y = 72$. Subtract this equation from the first equation as follows and then solve for y:

$$3x + 5y = 80$$
$$\underline{-(3x + 3y = 72)}$$
$$2y = 8$$
$$y = 4$$

Now that you know the value for y, use $x + y = 24$ to determine that $x = 20$. The value of $\frac{x}{y}$ is thus $\frac{20}{4} = 5$, which is (B).

17. **A** Start by Ballparking—most people with children donated, and most without children did not. Therefore, the difference in probabilities can't be very large, so (C) and (D) are too big. Now, make the two probabilities and find the difference. Probability is defined as the number that fits the requirement divided by the total number of things. For those with children, 324 of the 360 people in that category donated, so the probability is $\frac{324}{360} = 0.9$. For those without children, 174 of the 240 people in that category did not donate, so the probability is $\frac{174}{240} = 0.725$. Now subtract the probabilities to get 0.9 − 0.725 = 0.175, which is (A).

18. **B** Graphing these two equations on a graphing calculator can be a quick way to find the solutions or points of intersection. Another option is to set them equal to each other and solve. The first

equation can be rewritten as $y = x^2 + x - 30$, so when the equations are set equal to each other, it becomes $x^2 + x - 30 = x + 6$. Subtract x and 6 from both sides to get $x^2 - 36 = 0$. Factor the left side to get $(x + 6)(x - 6) = 0$. The values of x that make the equation true are -6 and 6. The x-coordinate of the midpoint will be the average of these two values, so $\frac{-6+6}{2} = \frac{0}{2} = 0$, which is (B). Don't waste time finding the y-coordinates of the solutions if it's not necessary!

19. **C** Don't do all this complicated polynomial multiplication and subtraction; whenever there are variables in the question and answer choices, Plug In! If $x = 2$, then $F = 3(2) - 2 = 6 - 2 = 4$ and $G = 2 - 1 = 1$. Therefore, $F^3 - G = 4^3 - 1 = 64 - 1 = 63$. Plug $x = 2$ into the answer choices to see which equals the target number of 63. Choice (A) becomes $2^3 - 3(2)^2 + 1 = 8 - 12 + 1 = -3$. This does not match the target number, so eliminate (A). Choice (B) becomes $8(2)^3 - 12(2)^2 + 6(2) - 1 = 64 - 48 + 12 - 1 = 27$. Eliminate (B). Choice (C) becomes $27(2)^3 - 54(2)^2 + 35(2) - 7 = 216 - 216 + 70 - 7 = 63$. Keep (C), but check (D) just in case. Choice (D) becomes $27(2)^3 - 54(2)^2 + 37(2) - 9 = 216 - 216 + 74 - 9 = 65$. Eliminate (D) and select (C).

20. **C** Plug in a point from the graph. At 35 students, about 10% of the students read at grade level or above, so make $n = 35$ and eliminate answers that aren't close to 10. (You don't have an exact point nor a line of best fit to go on, so you need to keep answers that are close.) Choice (A) becomes $P = 85 + 2.5(35) = 172.5$; way off, so eliminate (A). Choice (B) becomes $P = 85 - 2.5(35 - 5) = 10$; keep (B). Choice (C) becomes $P = 88 - \left(\frac{35}{4}\right)^2 = 11.44$; close enough, so keep (C). Choice (D) becomes $P = 88 - \left(\frac{35}{2}\right)^2 = -218.25$; definitely wrong, so eliminate (D). Try another point: at 20 students, about 60 percent of students read at grade level. You only need to test (B) and (C). Choice (B) becomes $P = 85 - 2.5(20 - 5) = 47.5$. This is quite far off; eliminate (B) and select (C). Alternatively, you may note that the graph must be a negative exponential function, which allows you to eliminate (A) and (B), as both are linear relationships. This leaves (C) and (D) to plug in on.

21. **C** First, use the graph to determine how many students per classroom would result in 40% of the students reading at grade level. The graph is at 40% at approximately 28 students per classroom. If there are total of 208 students, that means there are approximately $\frac{208}{28} = 7.43$ classrooms. (Obviously there are either 7 or 8 classrooms, but you are dealing with approximate values here, so it's okay.) If another classroom were added, there would be about 8.43 classrooms, meaning there are students $\frac{208}{8.43} = 24.67$ per classroom. Returning to the graph, at about 25 students, approximately 50% of the students read at grade level. This matches (C).

22. **B** Plug In the Answers! Start with (B). If Shawn purchased 200 shares at $11.35 a share, then he has a total value of 200 × 11.35 = $2,270 at the beginning. If the stock decreases by 15%, then its value is 85% of the start, or 0.85 × 2,270 = $1,929.50. If it increases by 8% in 2010, then its value is 108% of the 2009 value, or 1.08 × 1,929.50 = $2,083.86. The value increases again in 2011, so the stock is now worth 1.08 × 2,083.86 = $2,250.57. In 2012, $500 is added to the value to give 2,250.57 + 500 = $2,750.57. Because the problem wanted the approximate price per share when Shawn purchased the stock, this is really close (less than 1% off), so select (B).

23. **A** Start by simplifying the first equation. Multiply the equation by 12 (least common multiple of 3 and 4) to clear the fractions. You get $4(2x - 3) - 3(5y - 2) = 24$. Distribute for each parenthesis: $8x - 12 - 15y + 6 = 24$ (be careful with the negative on the second parenthesis!). Combine like terms: $8x - 15y - 6 = 24$. Add 6 to both sides to get $8x - 15y = 30$. Next, distribute the -4 in the second equation to get $-8x - 4y = 27$. Stack the equations to see what's going on:

$$8x - 15y = 30$$
$$-8x - 4y = 27$$

Note if you add the equations, the x terms will cancel. So do that to get $-19y = 57$. Divide both

sides by -29 to get $y = -3$. Plug this value into the simplified version of the second equation:

$-8x - 4(-3) = 27$. Multiply to get $-8x + 12 = 27$. Subtract from both sides: $-8x = 15$. Divide both

sides by -8: $x = -\dfrac{15}{8}$. Add this to the value of y: $-3 + \left(-\dfrac{15}{8}\right) = -\dfrac{39}{8}$, which matches (A).

24. **D** First, draw a picture of Sam's and Joe's houses:

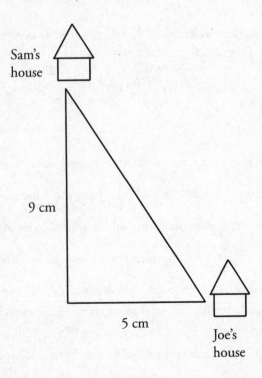

The distance, in centimeters, on the map can by found by using the Pythagorean Theorem:

$5^2 + 9^2 = c^2$, where c is the distance from Joe's house to Sam's house. Solve for c: $25 + 81 = c^2$;

$106 = c^2$; $\sqrt{106} = c$. Next, you need to find the distance in miles from Joe's house to Sam's house:

45 minutes is $\dfrac{45}{60} = 0.75$ hours, so driving at 30 miles per hour means the houses are $0.75 \times 30 =$

22.5 miles apart. Finally, you need to determine how many miles each centimeter represents, so set

up a proportion: $\dfrac{22.5 \text{ miles}}{\sqrt{106} \text{ cm}} = \dfrac{x \text{ miles}}{1 \text{ cm}}$. Divide the left side to get 2.19, which is closest to choice

(D).

25. **A** If (A) is true, then it would provide evidence that calls into question the methodology of the polling company. If the respondents to the initial interview were older and more likely to belong to a particular political party, then the polling company is not basing its predictions on a representative sample of the voting population. This makes (A) the best answer for calling the results into question.

26. **C** Since the period from 1980–2010 encompasses 30 years, you can conclude that in the equation provided, $30x$ represents the number of howler monkeys added to the conservancy's population during that time period. The x itself, however, is the average number of howler monkeys added to the park's population each year for that 30-year time period—(C).

27. **D** The best place to start is to rewrite all parts of the expression such that they have the same base.

Since all of the numbers are multiples of 2, you can rewrite everything in terms of 2 as follows:
$\dfrac{64^4 - 32^8}{128^2} = \dfrac{\left(2^6\right)^4 - \left(2^5\right)^8}{\left(2^7\right)^2} = \dfrac{2^{24} - 2^{40}}{2^{14}} = \dfrac{2^{24}(1 - 2^{16})}{2^{14}} = 2^{10}(1 - 2^{16})$, which is (D).

28. $\dfrac{1}{2}$ **or 0.5**

These are linear equations—no variable has an exponent on it. For two linear equations to have no solutions, they must be parallel. Parallel lines have the same slope. Put the first equation into $y = mx + b$ form to see the slope more easily. Add 9 to both sides to get $3y = \dfrac{3}{2}x + 9$, then divide both sides by 3 to get $y = \dfrac{1}{2}x + 3$. Therefore, for the lines to have the same slope, $a = \dfrac{1}{2}$.

29. **22** Graphing these two equations on a graphing calculator can be a quick way to find the solutions or points of intersection. Another option is to set them equal to each other and solve. The second equation can be rewritten as $y = x^2 - 4x + 4$, so when the equations are set equal to each other, it becomes $x^2 - 4x + 4 = 2x + 4$. Subtract $2x$ and 4 from both sides to get $x^2 - 6x = 0$. Factor the left

side to get $x(x - 6) = 0$. The values for x that make this true are 0 and 6. When $x = 0$, the solution is on the y-axis and not in Quadrant I, so the point in question is at $x = 6$. Plug that value into the first equation to get $y = 2(6) + 4 = 16$. The solution is at $(6, 16)$, and the sum of the coordinates is $6 + 16 = 22$.

30. **1,049** Convert the dimension given in inches to millimeters, using the conversion rate given.

$$\frac{25.4 \text{ mm}}{1 \text{ inch}} = \frac{x}{4 \text{ inches}}$$

Cross-multiply and solve for x to find that the 3D printer can print objects 101.6 millimeters on each side. Now convert this measurement into centimeters by setting up another proportion:

$$\frac{10 \text{mm}}{1 \text{cm}} = \frac{101.6 \text{mm}}{x}$$

Cross-multiply to get $10x = 101.6$, and then divide by 10 to get $x = 10.16$ centimeters per side. Volume = length × width × height, so multiply the three sides in centimeters to get the volume in cubic centimeters. $10.16^3 = 1,048.772$, so rounded to the nearest whole number, the answer is 1,049.

31. **1.89** Convert the ounces to grams using the given conversion rate:

$\frac{1 \text{ ounce}}{28.35 \text{ grams}} = \frac{0.2 \text{ ounces}}{mass}$. Cross-multiply to find that the *mass* of the stand is 5.67 grams. Now convert the cubic inches to cubic centimeters: $\frac{1 \text{ cm}^3}{0.061 \text{ in}^3} = \frac{volume}{0.183 \text{ in}^3}$. Cross-multiply to get $0.061(volume) = 0.183$, and then divide both sides by 0.061 to get *volume* = 3 cm^3. Now plug these values into the formula for density to get $density = \frac{mass}{volume} = \frac{5.67 \text{ grams}}{3 \text{ cm}^3} = 1.89$.

Chapter 18
Math Test Drill 2

Math Test – No Calculator

25 MINUTES, 17 QUESTIONS

Turn to Section 3 of your answer sheet to answer the questions in this section.

DIRECTIONS

For questions **1-13**, solve each problem, choose the best answer from the choices provided, and fill in the corresponding circle on your answer sheet. For questions **14-17**, solve the problem and enter your answer in the grid on the answer sheet. Please refer to the directions before question 14 on how to enter your answers in the grid. You may use any available space in your test booklet for scratch work.

NOTES

1. The use of a calculator **is not permitted**.
2. All variables and expressions used represent real numbers unless otherwise indicated.
3. Figures provided in this test are drawn to scale unless otherwise indicated.
4. All figures lie in a plane unless otherwise indicated.
5. Unless otherwise indicated, the domain of a given function f is the set of all real numbers x for which $f(x)$ is a real number.

REFERENCE

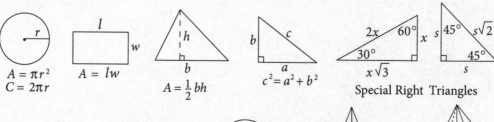

$$A = \pi r^2 \qquad A = lw \qquad A = \frac{1}{2}bh \qquad c^2 = a^2 + b^2$$
$$C = 2\pi r$$

Special Right Triangles

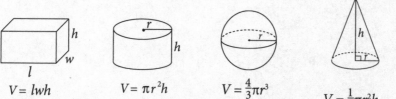

$$V = lwh \qquad V = \pi r^2 h \qquad V = \frac{4}{3}\pi r^3 \qquad V = \frac{1}{3}\pi r^2 h \qquad V = \frac{1}{3}\ell wh$$

The number of degrees of arc in a circle is 360.
The number of radians of arc in a circle is 2π.
The sum of the measures in degrees of the angles of a triangle is 180.

CONTINUE ➡

1

Kate buys a car for $25,000 that depreciates 10% per year. Which of the following shows the value of the car, in dollars, after t years?

A) $25,000(0.9)^t$

B) $25,000 - 10t$

C) $25,000(1.1)^t$

D) $25,000 - 0.1t$

2

John is traveling to Singapore for a days for a conference. He expects to spend 40 Singapore dollars on food per day. Which of the following inequalities shows all the possible values in US dollars, represented by x, that John could exchange for Singapore dollars and have at least enough money to spend on food for the whole conference? (Note: 1 US dollar = 1.3 Singapore dollars.)

A) $1.3x \leq 40a$

B) $x \geq 1.3(40a)$

C) $1.3x \geq 40a$

D) $x \geq 1.3(40 + a)$

3

When Bryan caters a meal, he charges a flat fee to reserve the date plus an additional price per person. He charges a discounted rate for children. The amount that Bryan charges when he caters is given by the function $P = m + 25a + 10b$. What does m represent in this equation?

A) The price per adult that Bryan charges

B) The flat fee Bryan charges

C) The number of hours that Bryan works

D) The price per child

4

The kinetic energy (KE) of an object is calculated by the equation $KE = \frac{1}{2}mv^2$, where m is the mass of the object and v is the velocity. Which of the following equations would solve for the mass of the object in terms of v and KE ?

A) $m = \frac{KE}{2v^2}$

B) $m = \frac{2KE}{v^2}$

C) $m = KE - v^2$

D) $m = KEv^2$

CONTINUE ➡

5

Which of the following is equal to $x^{\frac{2}{3}}$?

A) $\dfrac{x^2}{3}$

B) $\sqrt{x^3}$

C) $\dfrac{x^{\frac{5}{3}}}{x}$

D) $\dfrac{x^2}{x^3}$

6

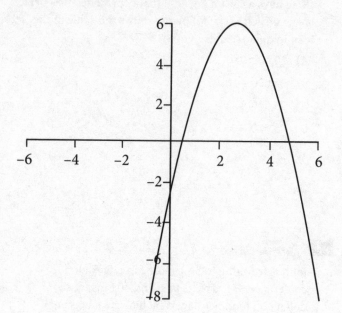

The graph above represents the equation $y = c(x - d)^2 + e$, where c, d, and e are constants. Which of the following must be true?

A) $e > 0 > c > d$

B) $c > 0 > d > e$

C) $e > 0 > d > c$

D) $e > d > 0 > c$

CONTINUE ▶

7

Kelly's car has 12 gallons of gas in it when she starts her trip. After she travels a hours at a speed of b miles per hour, she has 7 gallons left. If Kelly's car averages 29 miles per gallon for this trip, which of the following expresses a in terms of b ?

A) $a = \dfrac{5(29)}{b}$

B) $a = \dfrac{b}{7(29)}$

C) $a = 5(29)b$

D) $a = \dfrac{7(29)}{b}$

8

Given that $\dfrac{y+3}{x-2} = \dfrac{x+2}{y-3}$, which of the following expressions must be equal to 1 ?

A) $\dfrac{(y-3)^2}{(x-2)^2}$

B) $\dfrac{x^2+4}{y^2-9}$

C) $\dfrac{x^2-4}{y^2-9}$

D) $\dfrac{y^2-3}{x^2-2}$

9

If the expression $\dfrac{x^2 - 5x + 6}{x^2 - 6x + 8}$ can be rewritten as $\dfrac{x^2 + 2x - 15}{C}$, what is C ?

A) $x^2 + 9x + 20$

B) $x^2 + x - 20$

C) $x^2 - x - 20$

D) $x^2 - 9x - 20$

10

If c is a constant and the equation $\dfrac{1}{8}cx - 2 = \dfrac{16 - cx}{2c}$ has infinitely many solutions, which of the following is the value of c ?

A) -4

B) 0

C) 2

D) 4

CONTINUE ▶

11

$$-14 \text{ m/s} < V_f < 28 \text{ m/s}$$
$$8 \text{ m/s} < V_i < 14 \text{ m/s}$$

An object travels for 4 seconds with a constant acceleration, and the object's initial and final velocities are represented by the above two inequalities. Which of the following expresses the set of all possible accelerations for the object? (Note: An object's final velocity is given by the equation $V_f = V_i + at$, in which V_i, a, and t represent the object's initial velocity, acceleration, and time, respectively.)

A) $-28 \text{ m/s}^2 < a < 20 \text{ m/s}^2$

B) $-7 \text{ m/s}^2 < a < 5 \text{ m/s}^2$

C) $-5.5 \text{ m/s}^2 < a < 3.5 \text{ m/s}^2$

D) $1.5 \text{ m/s}^2 < a < 3.5 \text{ m/s}^2$

12

$$x^2 - 2ax + 3a = 0$$

Given that $x = 2$ is a solution to the above equation, what is the value of a ?

A) -4

B) $-\dfrac{4}{7}$

C) $\dfrac{4}{7}$

D) 4

13

In the 2008 presidential election, then-Senator Barack Obama received 52.9% of the popular vote; and in 2012, he received approximately 51.1% of the popular vote. Approximately 3.2 million fewer people voted in 2012 than 2008, and 3.5 million more people voted for Obama in 2008 than in 2012. Which of the following sets of equations could be used to solve for the number of voters, in millions, that participated in the 2008 and 2012 elections?

A) $0.529x = 0.511y + 3.5$

$x + 3.2 = y$

B) $0.529x - 3.2 = 0.511y$

$x = y + 3.5$

C) $0.529x = 0.511y + 3.5$

$x = y + 3.2$

D) $0.529x + 0.511y = 3.5$

$x + y = 3.2$

CONTINUE

DIRECTIONS

For questions 14-17, solve the problem and enter your answer in the grid, as described below, on the answer sheet.

1. Although not required, it is suggested that you write your answer in the boxes at the top of the columns to help you fill in the circles accurately. You will receive credit only if the circles are filled in correctly.

2. Mark no more than one circle in any column.

3. No question has a negative answer.

4. Some problems may have more than one correct answer. In such cases, grid only one answer.

5. **Mixed numbers** such as $3\frac{1}{2}$ must be gridded as 3.5 or 7/2. (If 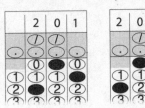 is entered into the grid, it will be interpreted as $\frac{31}{2}$, not as $3\frac{1}{2}$.)

6. **Decimal Answers:** If you obtain a decimal answer with more digits than the grid can accommodate, it may be either rounded or truncated, but it must fill the entire grid.

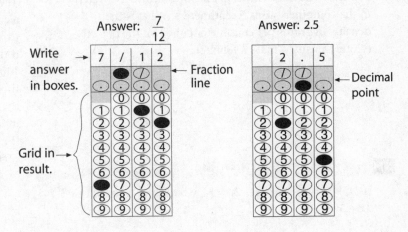

Acceptable ways to grid $\frac{2}{3}$ are:

Answer: 201 – either position is correct

NOTE: You may start your answers in any column, space permitting. Columns you don't need to use should be left blank.

CONTINUE

14

Eugene wants to discover the density of an unknown metal with a mass of 70 grams, so he places it in a rectangular container of water whose base has an area of 8 cm². The metal sinks to the bottom, and the water in the container raises 5 centimeters. What is the density, in grams per centimeter cubed, of the object? (Note: Density = mass / volume)

15

If $2x + 3y = 13$ and $3x + 2y = 12$, what is the value of $3x + 3y$?

16

$$P = 10(10 - d)^2$$

The equation above shows the number of points a contestant in a game of darts can earn per dart thrown. Contestants receive points on a throw only if they hit the circular dartboard that has an area of 100π cm². The points a contestant receives, P, on each throw depend on the distance, d, in centimeters, from the center bulls-eye the dart lands (closer darts receive more points). If a turn consists of 3 throws, what is the maximum number of points that a contestant can earn on a turn?

17

Given that $\left(\dfrac{x^2 + 3x - 10}{x^2 - 4} \right)\left(\dfrac{16x + 32}{x^2 + 10x + 25} \right) = 3$, what is x ?

CONTINUE ▶

THIS PAGE IS LEFT INTENTIONALLY BLANK.

CONTINUE →

Math Test – Calculator

45 MINUTES, 31 QUESTIONS

Turn to Section 4 of your answer sheet to answer the questions in this section.

DIRECTIONS

For questions **1-27**, solve each problem, choose the best answer from the choices provided, and fill in the corresponding circle on your answer sheet. For questions **28-31**, solve the problem and enter your answer in the grid on the answer sheet. Please refer to the directions before question 28 on how to enter your answers in the grid. You may use any available space in your test booklet for scratch work.

NOTES

1. The use of a calculator **is permitted**.
2. All variables and expressions used represent real numbers unless otherwise indicated.
3. Figures provided in this test are drawn to scale unless otherwise indicated.
4. All figures lie in a plane unless otherwise indicated.
5. Unless otherwise indicated, the domain of a given function f is the set of all real numbers x for which $f(x)$ is a real number.

REFERENCE

$A = \pi r^2$
$C = 2\pi r$

$A = lw$

$A = \frac{1}{2}bh$

$c^2 = a^2 + b^2$

Special Right Triangles

$V = lwh$

$V = \pi r^2 h$

$V = \frac{4}{3}\pi r^3$

$V = \frac{1}{3}\pi r^2 h$

$V = \frac{1}{3}\ell wh$

The number of degrees of arc in a circle is 360.
The number of radians of arc in a circle is 2π.
The sum of the measures in degrees of the angles of a triangle is 180.

CONTINUE ➡

1

$$y = x^2 - x - 20$$

The quadratic equation above has two real solutions. Which solution is smaller?

A) $x = -5$

B) $x = -4$

C) $x = 0$

D) $x = 4$

2

	Enrolled in Chemistry	Enrolled in Physics	Enrolled in Biology
11th Grade	62	36	75
12th Grade	24	54	18

What percent of students enrolled in Physics are in the 11th grade?

A) 20%

B) 30%

C) 40%

D) 50%

3

Reaction A: $A + D \rightarrow P$ $P = kt$
Reaction B: $D + C \rightarrow P$ $P = k^t$

Madison is completing two separate chemical reactions to obtain product P. Both reactions start with product P at zero concentration, at $t = 0$ in seconds. In the first reaction, the concentration of P increases linearly with time, with the rate constant $k = 1.3$. In the second reaction, P increases exponentially with the rate constant $k = 1.1$. Which of the following statements best represents the two reactions to form product P?

A) When $t = 10$, Reaction A has produced approximately 5 times as much product as Reaction B.

B) When $t = 10$, Reaction B has produced approximately 5 times as much product as Reaction A.

C) When $t = 10$, Reaction A has produced approximately 10 times as much product as Reaction B.

D) When $t = 10$, Reaction B has produced approximately 10 times as much product as Reaction A.

4

$$y = -\frac{1}{2}x + 4$$

Given the linear equation above, at which value of x does the line cross the x-axis?

A) $x = -2$

B) $x = 2$

C) $x = 4$

D) $x = 8$

CONTINUE ▶

5

If $\dfrac{\left(\sqrt{x}\right)(x+3)(x-2)}{x-2} = 0$, what are all possible real

values of x?

A) −3, 0, 2

B) −3, 0

C) 0, 2

D) 0

6

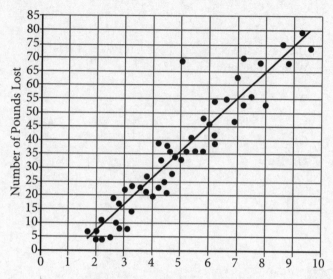

Average Hours of Exercise per Day

A group of medical students studied 50 participants over a two-month period to determine the effects of exercise on weight loss. The scatterplot above shows the relationship between the average number of hours a participant exercised per day and the total weight the participant lost over the two-month period. If x represents the average hours of exercise per day, which of the following expressions gives the line of best fit for the number of pounds lost in two months?

A) $10x - 15$

B) $5x + 15$

C) $15 - 10x$

D) $x^2 + 10$

CONTINUE ➡

Questions 7-8 refer to the information below.

The table shows the employment data for four states for the year 2008. The workforce is the total number of people who could be employed. The unemployment rate is the percentage of the workforce who are not employed.

	Michigan	Minnesota	Ohio	Wisconsin
Unemployment Rate	8.3	5.4	6.6	4.8
Workforce	9,542,000	5,005,000	12,485,000	5,862,000

7

According to the table above, how many people were employed in Michigan in 2008 ?

A)   791,986

B)   8,750,014

C)   9,542,000

D)   114,963,855

8

According to the table, which of the following conclusions can be properly drawn about the employment in the four states in 2008 ?

A) Michigan had the greatest number of unemployed people because it has the highest unemployment rate.

B) Minnesota had both the fewest number of people unemployed and the fewest number of people employed.

C) Ohio did not have the greatest number unemployed people because it did not have the greatest unemployment rate.

D) Wisconsin had the fewest number of unemployed people because it has the lowest unemployment rate.

9

Line l has an x-intercept of 3. Which of the following could be the equation of line l ?

A) $y = 2x - 6$

B) $y = 3x$

C) $y = x + 3$

D) $y = \dfrac{x}{3} + 1$

CONTINUE

10

A class is polled on where to take their next field trip. 45% of the class wants to go to the arboretum, 35% of the class wants to go to the planetarium, and 20% of the class wants to go to the aquarium. If there are 80 students in the class, how many do not want to go to the planetarium?

A) 28

B) 36

C) 52

D) 64

11

A continuous reaction produces carbon dioxide at a rate of 0.02 pounds per minute. After 15 minutes, how many grams of carbon dioxide have been produced? (Note: 1 pound = 453.6 grams)

A)   9.1 grams

B)   30.2 grams

C)   68.0 grams

D)   136.1 grams

12

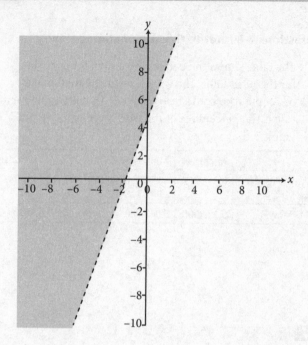

Which of the following equations best represents the chart above ?

A) $y > 3x - 4$

B) $y > 3x + 4$

C) $y < 3x - 4$

D) $y < 3x + 4$

CONTINUE

13

Sara and her partner James studied the population growth of a certain bacterium in petri dishes. They determined that no matter how many bacteria a petri dish initially had, the population tripled every four days. If B represents the population after d days, which of the following expressions represents the population of a petri dish that started with s bacteria?

A) $B = s + 3^{\frac{d}{4}}$

B) $B = 3s^{4d}$

C) $B = s(3)^{\frac{d}{4}}$

D) $B = s + 4^{\frac{d}{3}}$

14

The MacRuff storage facility has decided to conserve energy by limiting the amount of energy for lighting to 22 joules per day. The storage facility has 60 lightbulbs that each consume 110 watts of energy per hour. If 1 joule equals 3,600 watts, what is the maximum number of minutes MacRuff storage facility can keep all the lights on without exceeding its limit?

A)   12

B)   300

C)   720

D) 43,200

15

$$x - \frac{y}{5} = 2$$

$$24x + 2y = 82$$

If (x, y) is a solution to the system of equations above, what is the value of x ?

A) −5

B) 3

C) 5

D) There are no real values of x for the solution.

16

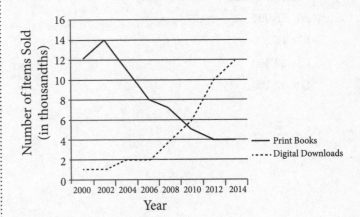

The graph above shows the number of print books and the number of digital downloads sold, in thousands, by the Literary Wonders publishing company from the year 2000 to the year 2014. The number of print books sold in the year for which print book sales were highest was approximately what percent greater than the number of digital download sales in the year for which digital download sales were highest?

A) 14%

B) 17%

C) 67%

D) 71%

CONTINUE

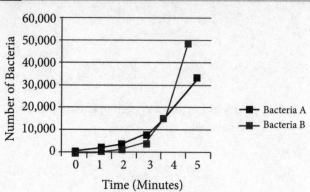

Time (Minutes)

The graph above shows the growth patterns of two different bacteria over time. The growth of Bacteria A is given by the equation $N(t) = 1000(2^t)$, and the growth of Bacteria B is given by the equation $P(t) = 200(3^t)$, where t represents the time, in minutes, since the beginning of the bacteria's growth. At the time for which the number of Bacteria A and the number of Bacteria B were equal, how many total bacteria (A and B) were present?

A) 16,000

B) 16,200

C) 20,400

D) 32,200

Yasmine, a college sophomore, is driving home to visit her parents for winter break. Her college dorm is 225 miles from her parents' house. If she stops at a rest stop one-third of the way to her parents' house and drives at an average speed of 50 miles per hour for the remainder of the trip, then which of the following expressions represents the remaining distance Yasmine still has to drive in terms of t, the time in minutes after leaving the rest stop?

A) $150 - \dfrac{5t}{6}$

B) $225 - 50t$

C) $225 - \dfrac{5t}{6}$

D) $150 - 50t$

Frank is working on a statistics project for his math class. For his project, he categorizes each rubber band in a brand-new bag. 30% of the rubber bands were small length, 40% of the bands were medium length, and 30% were categorized as long. Of the long bands, 15% were single width, 70% were double width, and 15% were triple width. Of the triple width, half were dark brown and the other half were light brown. If Frank counted 9 dark brown, triple width, long rubber bands in the bag, how many bands total did the bag contain?

A) 120

B) 300

C) 400

D) 800

CONTINUE

20

If the equation $\dfrac{2x - 8}{\sqrt{12}}$ is most nearly equal to $C - \dfrac{4\sqrt{3}}{3}$, then what is C in terms of x ?

A) $-\dfrac{\sqrt{3}}{3}x$

B) $\dfrac{\sqrt{3}}{3}x$

C) $x\sqrt{3}$

D) $3x$

21

Census Year	Population
1920	7,989
1930	10,136
1940	11,659
1950	19,056
1960	22,993

The Census data for a rural town in Kansas is shown above. In which of the following decades did the town experience the highest percent growth?

A) 1920–1930, with 21% growth

B) 1920–1930, with 27% growth

C) 1940–1950, with 39% growth

D) 1940–1950, with 63% growth

22

Regina sells cars, for which she receives a yearly salary. Since 2004, Regina has received a raise each year. She also gets a yearly bonus of $500 for each car she sells after the first 300. Her total pay, P, in dollars, for any year after 2004 can be expressed as $P = 35,000 (1 + 0.05y) + 500x$. Which of the following is the best interpretation of the expression?

A) x represents the number of cars sold after the first 300.

B) x must be greater than 300.

C) y must be greater than 2004.

D) y represents the current year.

CONTINUE

23

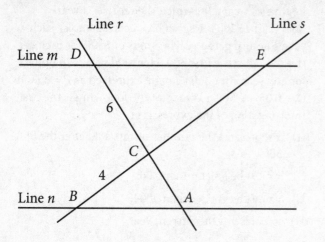

In the figure above, line m is parallel to line n, and line r is perpendicular to line s. If $\overline{DE} = \frac{5}{2}\overline{BC}$, which of the following could be used to find the measure of $\angle BAC$?

A) $\sin^{-1}\left(\dfrac{3}{5}\right)$

B) $\cos^{-1}\left(\dfrac{3}{5}\right)$

C) $\tan^{-1}\left(\dfrac{3}{4}\right)$

D) $\tan^{-1}\left(\dfrac{5}{2}\right)$

24

In a recent election for president, the citizens of the country of Prelandia chose among three different candidates. The ratio of those who voted for Candidate G to those who voted for Candidate H was 4 to 5, while the ratio of those who voted for Candidate H to those who voted for Candidate J was 10 to 17. If half of the people who voted for Candidate H had instead voted for Candidate J, what would have been the ratio of those who voted for Candidate J to those who voted for Candidate G ?

A) 17 to 4

B) 8 to 5

C) 22 to 5

D) 11 to 4

CONTINUE

25

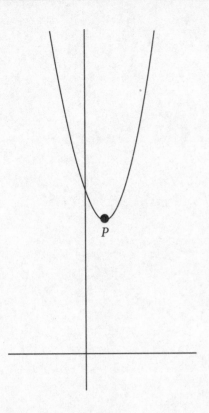

The graph of the function $f(x) = x^2 - 2x + 8$ is shown above. Point P represents the vertex of the graph. If the graph is first reflected across the line $y = 3$ and then reflected across the y-axis, what are the new coordinates of point P?

A) $(-1, 7)$

B) $(1, -1)$

C) $(-1, -1)$

D) $(1, 7)$

26

The equation for line m is $y = -\dfrac{1}{5}x + 9$, and the equation for parabola n is $y = x^2 - 2x - 9$. If line r is perpendicular to line m and has a y-intercept of -21, then what are the points of intersection of parabola n and line r?

A) $(-3, -6)$ and $(-4, -1)$

B) $(-3, 6)$ and $(-4, 1)$

C) $(3, -6)$ and $(4, -1)$

D) $(3, 6)$ and $(4, 1)$

CONTINUE ➤

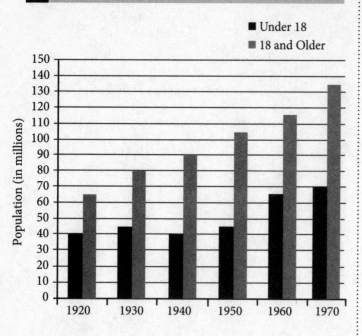

■ Under 18
■ 18 and Older

The data above show the approximate number of United States residents in selected years between 1920 and 1970. The average population of adults 18 years and older from 1940 to 1970, inclusive, was approximately what percent of the mode of the population of children under 18 from 1930 to 1960, inclusive?

A)   2.47%

B)   247%

C)   36%

D)   111.25%

CONTINUE

DIRECTIONS

For questions 28-31, solve the problem and enter your answer in the grid, as described below, on the answer sheet.

1. Although not required, it is suggested that you write your answer in the boxes at the top of the columns to help you fill in the circles accurately. You will receive credit only if the circles are filled in correctly.

2. Mark no more than one circle in any column.

3. No question has a negative answer.

4. Some problems may have more than one correct answer. In such cases, grid only one answer.

5. **Mixed numbers** such as $3\frac{1}{2}$ must be gridded as 3.5 or 7/2. (If 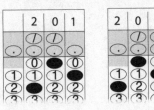 is entered into the grid, it will be interpreted as $\frac{31}{2}$, not as $3\frac{1}{2}$.)

6. **Decimal Answers:** If you obtain a decimal answer with more digits than the grid can accommodate, it may be either rounded or truncated, but it must fill the entire grid.

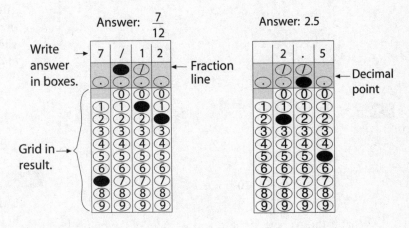

Answer: $\frac{7}{12}$ Answer: 2.5

Write answer in boxes. ← Fraction line

Grid in result. ← Decimal point

Acceptable ways to grid $\frac{2}{3}$ are:

Answer: 201 – either position is correct

NOTE: You may start your answers in any column, space permitting. Columns you don't need to use should be left blank.

28

The amount of solvent, in milliliters, remaining in a beaker can be modeled by the expression $500 - 0.4t$, when t is in seconds. At what value of t will the beaker be empty?

29

$$6x - 4 = \frac{y}{3}$$

$$\frac{y}{2} - 10 = x + 7$$

What is the average of the x- and y-values of the point of intersection of the two equations listed above, rounded to the nearest tenth?

Questions 30-31 refer to the following information

A chocolatier in Los Angeles decides to offer a special gift box for Valentine's Day. The gift box consists of a variety of different chocolates: 20% are dark chocolate, 15% are white chocolate, 35% are mint chocolate, and the rest are chocolate truffle.

30

If there are 6 chocolate truffles in the gift box, then how many mint chocolates does the gift box contain?

31

If the information in question 30 still holds true, then what is the difference between the number of dark chocolates and the number of white chocolates?

STOP
**If you finish before time is called, you may check your work on this section only.
Do not turn to any other section.**

Chapter 19
Math Test
Drill 2: Answers
and Explanations

ANSWERS AND EXPLANATIONS

Section 3—Math Test

1. **A** Though plugging in is preferred when there are variables in the answers, this is not ideal when the calculations aren't easy without a calculator. Utilizing the formula for exponential decay and POE helps eliminate incorrect answers quickly. Recall that the formula for exponential decay is final amount = original amount $(1 - \text{rate})^{\text{number of changes}}$. The original amount is $25,000, so it needs to be multiplied by a quantity. Eliminate (B) and (D) since they do not match the formula. The car depreciates at a rate of 10% per year, so $1 - 0.1 = 0.9$. Eliminate (C). The correct answer is (A).

2. **C** Use process of elimination. The question asks for *at least how much money*. *At least* translates to $\geq$. Therefore, eliminate (A). For *a* days, John needs $40 \times a = \$40a$ Singapore dollars per day. Set up the following proportion to calculate the amount in US dollars: $\dfrac{1\,US}{1.3\,Singapore} = \dfrac{x\,US}{40\,a}$. Cross-multiply to get $1.3x = 40a$. To calculate *at least*, substitute the = sign with $\geq$ to get $1.3x \geq 40a$. Therefore, the correct answer is (C).

3. **B** Use process of elimination to solve. According to the question, the total amount that Bryan charges includes a flat fee plus a charge for each person. The *each person* part of the equation can be further split up into a charge for each adult and a charge for each child. Immediately eliminate choice (C) because there is no information in the question related to the number of hours Bryan works. Looking at the numbers in the equation, the value of $25a$ will change based on what *a* is. Likely *a* stands for the number of adults in attendance. Likewise, the value of $10b$ will change based on the value of *b*. Likely the *b* stands for the number of children in attendance. This leaves *m*, which must be the flat fee. Therefore, the correct answer is (B).

4. **B** Multiply both sides of the equation by 2 to get $2KE = mv^2$. Divide both sides of the equation by v^2 to get $\dfrac{2KE}{v^2} = m$. The correct answer is (B).

5. **C** Use process of elimination to solve. Choice (A) cannot be reduced any further, so eliminate it. For fractional exponents, the numerator is equal to the power, and the denominator is equal to the type of root. Therefore, (B) can be rewritten as $x^{\frac{3}{2}}$. Eliminate (B). When dividing fractions, subtract the exponents. Therefore, (C) can be rewritten as $x^{\frac{5}{3}-1} = x^{\frac{2}{3}}$. The correct answer is (C).

6. **D** The vertex form of a parabola is expressed by the equation $y = a(x - h)^2 + k$, where (h, k) is the vertex. In this problem, the variables have changed so that $y = c(x - d)^2 + e$. Therefore, the vertex is (d, e). Look at the graph and notice that both coordinates of the vertex are positive. Therefore, eliminate (A), (B), and (C) because all of these answers make either d or e, or both, negative. The correct answer is (D).

7. **A** She travels 145 miles, but the question does not ask for the number of miles traveled—that is just the first step. The question asks for the relationship between a and b; a is the number of hours, and b is the speed. Since $d = rt$, $145 = ab$ and $a = 145/b$. Thus, the correct answer is (A).

8. **C** Cross-multiplying the fractions gets $y^2 - 9 = x^2 - 4$. These expressions could then get broken down further into $(y + 3)(y - 3) = (x + 2)(x - 2)$. However, in previewing the answer choices, all of them still have the variables represented with an exponent. Therefore, because $y^2 - 9 = x^2 - 4$, (C) must be correct since any expression that is divided by another that is equal in value will always result in a value of 1.

9. **B** Start by factoring the first fraction to get $\dfrac{x^2 - 5x + 6}{x^2 - 6x + 8} = \dfrac{(x-3)(x-2)}{(x-4)(x-2)}$. Reduce the fraction to get $\dfrac{x-3}{x-4}$. According to the question, $\dfrac{x-3}{x-4} = \dfrac{x^2 + 2x - 15}{C}$. Whenever there are variables in the question and in the answers, think Plugging In. Plug $x = 5$ into the equation to get $\dfrac{5-3}{5-4} = \dfrac{5^2 + 2(5) - 15}{C}$. Solve both sides of the equation to get $\dfrac{2}{1} = \dfrac{25 + 10 - 15}{C}$ and $2 = \dfrac{20}{C}$. Solve for C to get $2C = 20$ and $C = 10$. In the answers, plug 5 in for x to see which answer equals 10. Choice (A) becomes $5^2 + 9(5) + 20 = 25 + 45 + 20 = 90$. Eliminate (A). Choice (B) becomes $5^2 + 5 - 20 = 25 + 5 - 20 = 10$. Keep (B), but check the remaining answers just in case. Choice (C) becomes $5^2 - 5 - 20 = 25 - 5 - 20 = 0$. Eliminate (C). Choice (D) becomes $5^2 - 9(5) - 20 = 25 - 45 - 20 = -40$. Eliminate (D). The correct answer is (B).

10. **A** An equation will have an infinite number of solutions when one side of the equation is equal to the other side. Whenever you have variables in the question and numbers in the answers, think Plugging In the Answers. Start with the middle numbers. Eliminate (B) because plugging in 0 would cause the left side of the equation to have 0 in the denominator of a fraction, which can never happen. Try (C). In (C), $c = 2$, so the equation becomes $\dfrac{1}{8}(2)x - 2 = \dfrac{16 - (2)x}{2(2)}$. Simplify both sides of the equation to get $\dfrac{1}{4}x - 2 = \dfrac{16 - (2)x}{4}$. Multiply both sides of the equation by 4 to get

$x - 8 = 16 - 2x$. Solve for x to get $3x - 8 = 16$, $3x = 24$, and $x = 8$. Eliminate (C). It may not be clear which direction to go from here, so just pick a direction. In (A), $c = -4$, so the equation becomes $\frac{1}{8}(-4)x - 2 = \frac{16-(-4)x}{2(-4)}$. Simplify both sides of the equation to get $-\frac{1}{2}x - 2 = \frac{16+4x}{-8}$. Multiply both sides of the equation by -8 to get $4x + 16 = 16 + 4x$. Because both sides of the equation are identical, the equation has an infinite number of solutions. The correct answer is (A).

11. **B** The equation can be rearranged as $\frac{V_f - V_i}{t} = a$. Since the question says that the object travels for 4 seconds, it can be written as $\frac{V_f - V_i}{4} = a$. Now, in order to find the minimum and maximum values of a, you need to try all four combinations of the inner and outer bounds. So plug in -14 m/s for V_f and try it with both 8 m/s and 14 m/s for V_i : $\frac{-14 - 8}{4} = -5.5$ m/s^2 and $\frac{-14 - 14}{4} = -7$ m/s^2. Now try $V_f = 28$ m/s with both 8 m/s and 14 m/s for V_i : $\frac{28 - 8}{4} = 5$ m/s^2 and $\frac{28 - 14}{4} = 3.5$ m/s^2. Since these represent all of the extremes, we can see that the lowest value is -7 m/s^2, and the highest value is 5 m/s^2, (B).

12. **D** Plug 2 in for x in the equation to get $2^2 - 2(a)(2) + 3a = 0$. Simplify the left side of the equation to get $4 - 4a + 3a = 0$ and $4 - a = 0$. Solve for a to get $a = 4$. The correct answer is (D).

13. **C** In the answers x and y relate to the two years 2008 and 2012. All of the answers put 0.529 with x and 0.511 with y. According to the question, in the 2008 presidential election, Obama received 52.9% of the popular vote; in 2012, he received approximately 51.1% of the popular vote. Therefore, $x = 2008$ and $y = 2012$. According to the question, 3.2 million fewer people voted in 2012 than 2008. This translates to $x = y + 3.2$. Only (C) includes this equation. The correct answer is (C).

14. **1.75 or $\frac{7}{4}$**

If the base of the container has an area of 8 cm^2 and it is rectangular, then when the water level raises by 5 inches, the total volume change is $8 \times 5 = 40$ cm^3. Therefore, the volume of the metal is 40 cm^3. Since density = mass/volume, the density is 70/40, which is 1.75.

15. **15** Whenever there are two equations with the same variables think Simultaneous Equations. Place the two equations on top of each other and add them together to get:

$$2x + 3y = 13$$
$$\underline{+(3x + 2y = 12)}$$
$$5x + 5y = 25$$

Divide the entire equation by 5 to get $x + y = 5$. Multiply the entire equation by 3 to get $3(x + y) = 3(5)$, and $3x + 3y = 15$. The correct answer is 15.

16. **3,000**

The maximum number of points achieved on any throw occurs when $d = 0$. The points when $d = 0$ can be calculated as $P = 10(10 - 0)^2 = 10(100) = 1,000$. Therefore, over 3 throws, the maximum number of points is $3 \times 1000 = 3,000$. The correct answer is 3,000.

17. $\dfrac{1}{3}$ **or .333**

Start by factoring the top and bottom of each fraction to get: $\left(\dfrac{(x+5)(x-2)}{(x+2)(x-2)}\right)\left(\dfrac{16(x+2)}{(x+5)(x+5)}\right) = 3$.

Reduce the left fraction to get $\left(\dfrac{(x+5)}{(x+2)}\right)\left(\dfrac{16(x+2)}{(x+5)(x+5)}\right) = 3$. Reduce diagonally to get $\dfrac{16}{x+5} = 3$.

Multiply both sides by $x + 5$ to get $16 = 3(x + 5)$. Distribute the 3 to get $16 = 3x + 15$. Solve for x to

get $1 = 3x$ and $x = \dfrac{1}{3}$. The correct answer is $\dfrac{1}{3}$.

Section 4—Math Test

1. **B** Factor the equation to get $0 = (x - 5)(x + 4)$. Therefore, either $x - 5 = 0$ and $x = 5$, or $x + 4 = 0$ and $x = -4$. The smaller of the two possible x-values is -4. Therefore, the correct answer is (B).

2. **C** The total number of students enrolled in Physics can be calculated as $36 + 54 = 90$. The question can be translated as $\dfrac{x}{100} \times 90 = 36$. Solve for x to get $\dfrac{x}{10} \times 9 = 36$, $\dfrac{x}{10} = 4$, and $x = 40$. The correct answer is (C).

3. **A** Each of the answer choices asks about what happens when $t = 10$. Start by working out each reaction with this value. Reaction A would yield a concentration of $1.3 \times 10 = 13$. Reaction B would yield $(1.1)^{10} \approx 2.593$. $13 \div 2.593 \approx 5$. Therefore, the correct answer is (A).

4. **D** When the line crosses the x-axis, the y-value is equal to 0, and the line equation becomes $0 = -\dfrac{1}{2}x + 4$. Solve for x to get $-4 = -\dfrac{1}{2}x$ and $x = 8$. The correct answer is (D).

5. **D** Use POE to solve this question. The denominator of a fraction can never be 0. Therefore, x cannot be equal to 2. Eliminate (A) and (C). The square root of a negative number yields a result that is an imaginary number. Therefore, x cannot be –3 since one of the terms in the numerator is $\sqrt{x}$. On this basis, eliminate (B). Therefore, the correct answer is (D).

6. **A** Use POE. You can see that the graph is linear, so eliminate (D). Also, the slope is positive, so you cannot have a negative coefficient in front of x. Eliminate (C). Lastly, if you extend the line of best fit over to the y-axis, you can see that the y-intercept is negative. Therefore, eliminate (B), so the answer must be (A).

7. **B** Use POE to solve this question. According to the table, the total number of people who could be employed in Michigan is 9,542,000. On this basis, eliminate (D) since the number of people employed cannot be larger than the number of people who could be employed. Also, eliminate (C) because Michigan has an unemployment rate of 8.3%, which means that not all people who could be employed are employed. Since the unemployment rate is less than 10%, (A) is too small a number to equal over 90% of close to 10 million. The best answer is (B).

8. **B** Use POE to solve this question. Having the highest unemployment rate does not automatically imply that the state has the most number of people unemployed. Remember that to find the number of people unemployed, the unemployment rate is multiplied by the workforce. Therefore, the final value is driven as much by the unemployment rate as it is the number of people in the workforce. On this basis, eliminate (A) and (C). Likewise, the lowest unemployment rate does not automatically equate with the fewest number of unemployed people. On this basis, eliminate (D). The correct answer is (B).

9. **A** The x-intercept is where the line crosses the x-axis. At that point, the y-value is 0. Plug the point $(3, 0)$ into each of the answer choices to see which equation works. Choice (A) becomes $0 = 2(3) - 6$. Solve the right side of the equation to get $0 = 6 - 6$, and $0 = 0$. This equation works, so the correct answer is (A).

10. **C** According to the question, 45% of the class wants to go to the arboretum, and 20% of the class wants to go to the aquarium. This means that $45 + 20 = 65$% of the class does not want to go to the planetarium. $0.65 \times 80 = 52$. Therefore, the correct answer is (C).

11. **D** After 15 minutes, $0.02 \times 15 = 0.3$ pounds of carbon dioxide is produced. To convert to grams, set up the following proportion: $\dfrac{1 \text{ pound}}{453.6 \text{ grams}} = \dfrac{0.3 \text{ pounds}}{x \text{ grams}}$. Cross-multiply to get $x = 453.6 \times 0.3 = 136.08$. Therefore, the correct answer is (D).

12. **B** Use POE. Shading above the line means the equation should include the > sign. On this basis, eliminate (C) and (D). The equation of a line is $y = mx + b$, where b denotes the y-intercept. In the graph, the y-intercept is 4. Therefore, eliminate (A). The correct answer is (B).

13. **C** Whenever the question and the answer choices include variables, think Plugging In. If $s = 2$ and $d = 4$, then the value of B will be 6. Plug 2 in for s and 4 in for d in the answers to see which equation equals 6. Choice (A) becomes $B = 2 + 3^{\frac{4}{4}} = 2 + 3 = 5$. Eliminate (A). Choice (B) becomes $B = 3(2)^{4(4)} = 3(2)^{16} = 3(65,536) = 196,608$. Eliminate (B). Choice (C) becomes $B = 2(3)^{\frac{4}{4}} = 2(3) = 6$. Keep (C), but check the remaining answer just in case. Choice (D) becomes $B = 2 + \left(4^{\frac{4}{3}}\right) = 2 + 6.3496 = 8.3496$. Eliminate (D). The correct answer is (C).

14. **C** 60 lightbulbs will use $60 \times 110 = 6,600$ watts per hour. Set up the following proportion to convert the wattage to joules: $\dfrac{1 \text{ joule}}{3,600 \text{ watts}} = \dfrac{x \text{ joules}}{6,600 \text{ watts}}$. Cross-multiply to get $3,600x = 6,600$. Solve for x to get $x \approx 1.83$. Therefore, the 60 lightbulbs at the MacRuff storage facility use approximately 1.83 joules per hour. The maximum amount of energy MacRuff has is 22 joules. $22 \div 1.83 \approx 12$ hours, and $12 \times 60 = 720$ minutes. Therefore, the correct answer is (C).

15. **B** Whenever there are variables in the question and numbers in the answers, think Plugging In the Answers. Start with (B). If $x = 3$, then the second equation becomes $24(3) + 2y = 82$. Solve for y to get $72 + 2y = 82$, $2y = 10$, and $y = 5$. Plug 3 in for x and 5 in for y in the first equation to get $3 - \dfrac{5}{5} = 2$. Solve the left side of the equation to get $3 - 1 = 2$ and $2 = 2$. Since the numbers work, the correct answer is (B).

16. **B** According to the graph, print book sales were highest in 2002. The number of print books sold in 2002 was 14,000. Digital download sales were highest in 2014. The number of digital download sales in 2014 was 12,000. This question is asking for percent change, which can be calculated as follows: $\dfrac{14,000 - 12,000}{12,000} = \dfrac{2,000}{12,000} = \dfrac{1}{6} \approx 17\%$. Therefore, the correct answer is (B).

17. **D** The number of Bacteria A and Bacteria B are equal at 4 minutes. At 4 minutes, the graph shows each of the bacteria populations to be equal to approximately 16,000. $16,000 + 16,000 = 32,000$. Choice (D) is the closest possible answer.

18. **A** The rest stop is $\dfrac{1}{3}$ of the way to Yasmine's parents' house, so the rest stop is 75 miles from her dorm. Therefore, Yasmine still has 150 miles to drive. Now, plug in a value for t. Since t represents the min-

utes that Yasmine has driven since leaving the rest stop and Yasmine's speed is given in miles per hour, plug in $t = 60$. After 60 minutes, Yasmine will have driven an additional 50 miles, so she would have 100 miles left to drive. If you plug in $t = 60$ into the answers, only (A) will equal 100.

19. **C** Whenever the question includes unknown quantities and the answers are numbers, think Plugging In the Answers. Start with choice (B). If the bag contains a total of 300 rubber bands, then the bag contains $0.3 \times 300 = 90$ long rubber bands of which $0.15 \times 90 = 13.5$ are triple width. Since it is impossible to have half of a rubber band, eliminate (B). Try (C). If the bag contains 400 rubber bands, then there are $0.3 \times 400 = 120$ long rubber bands of which $0.15 \times 120 = 18$ are triple width. Half of these or $\frac{1}{2} \times 18 = 9$ are dark brown. This matches the information in the question, so the answer is (C).

20. **B** First, rationalize the expression by multiplying both the numerator and the denominator by $\sqrt{12}$. This yields $\frac{(2x - 8)\sqrt{12}}{12}$. You can also rewrite $\sqrt{12}$ as $\sqrt{4(3)} = 2\sqrt{3}$. Distribute this on the numerator to get $\frac{4x\sqrt{3} - 16\sqrt{3}}{12}$. Split the numerator to make two terms: $\frac{4x\sqrt{3}}{12} - \frac{16\sqrt{3}}{12}$. Since the second term simplifies to $\frac{4\sqrt{3}}{3}$, the first term must be C. Reduce the fraction by dividing the numerator and denominator by 4, so C equals $\frac{x\sqrt{3}}{3}$, which is (B).

21. **D** Since we're asked for the period with the highest percentage growth, start by testing (D). Between 1940 and 1950, the population grew by 7,397 people. The percent change for this decade would be 7,397/11,659 times 100, which is 65%. Since the table supports (D) and that is the answer choice with the highest percentage growth, it must be the answer.

22. **A** Use POE to solve this question. The current year, e.g., 2015, would not be a number used to calculate her total pay. Therefore, eliminate (D). Likewise, the year Regina started getting raises would not be included in the equation to calculate her total pay. Therefore, eliminate (C). The $500 bonus, which is connected to x in the equation, is paid out after the first 300 cars she sells. If Regina sold 290 cars, x would be equal to 0 because she would not have sold more than 300 cars; therefore, the bonus would not apply. On this basis, eliminate (B). The correct answer is (A).

23. **B** First, since the problem says that line r is perpendicular to line s, angles DCE and BCA are both right angles. Also, since $DE = \frac{5}{2}BC$ and $BC = 4$, DE must be 10. You now have both the adjacent side and the hypotenuse for angle EDC, so set up the following equation: $\cos EDC = \frac{6}{10}$. Since lines m and n are parallel, angle BAC is equivalent to angle EDC. Therefore, $\cos BAC = \frac{3}{5}$, which is (B).

24. **D** Whenever the question includes unknown values, think Plugging In. According to the question $\frac{G}{H} = \frac{4}{5}$ and $\frac{H}{J} = \frac{10}{17}$. Since both ratios include H, plug in a number for H that will make both ratios easy to work with. Try H = 10. The number of votes for each candidate would be as follows:

Votes for G	Votes for H	Votes for J
8	10	17

Therefore, if half of the votes given to H were moved to J, the new vote tallies would be:

Votes for G	Votes for H	Votes for J
8	5	22

The ratio of those who voted for J to those who voted for G would be 22 to 8, which reduces to 11 to 4. Therefore, the correct answer is (D).

25. **C** First, get the parabola into vertex form of $(x-1)^2 + 7$ by completing the square, so the vertex is (1, 7). Then, do the two reflections. The first brings the point to (1, –1), and the second brings it to (–1, –1).

26. **C** Lines that are perpendicular to each other have slopes that are the negative reciprocal of each other. The equation of a line is $y = mx + b$, where m denotes the slope and b denotes the y-intercept. Therefore, the equation for line r, which is perpendicular to line m, is $y = 5x - 21$. To find the x-values of the points of intersection between line r and the parabola, set the two equations equal to each other to get $x^2 - 2x - 9 = 5x - 21$. Set the equation to 0 to get $x^2 - 7x + 12 = 0$. Factor the right side of the equation to get $(x-3)(x-4) = 0$. Solve for x to get $x = 3$ and $x = 4$. Eliminate choices (A) and (B) because the x-value in those answer choices is incorrect. Plug x into the equation for line r to get $y = 5(3) - 21 = 15 - 21 = -6$. Therefore, one of the points of intersection is (3, –6). Eliminate (D). The correct answer is (C).

27. **B** First, solve for the average population of adults 18 and older from 1940–1970 by adding up the four values and dividing by 4. The average is 111.25. The mode is the value that occurs most frequently between 1930 and 1960, inclusive. Since 45 occurs twice for children under the age of 18, the mode is 45. Lastly, the question asks what percent 111.25 is of 45, so divide 111.25 by 45 and multiply by 100. The answer is (B).

28. **1,250**

The beaker will be empty when $0.4t = 500$. Solve for t to get $t = 1,250$. The correct answer is 1,250.

29. **21.3** Start by eliminating the fractions in the two equations. Multiply the first equation by 3 to get $18x - 12 = y$. Multiply the second equation by 2 to get $y - 20 = 2x + 14$. Solve the equation for y to get $y = 2x + 34$. To find the x-value of the point of intersection, set the two equations equal to each other to get $18x - 12 = 2x + 34$. Solve for x to get $16x = 46$ and $x = 2.875$. Plug 2.875 in for x into the equation $y = 2x + 34$ to get $y = 2(2.875) + 34 = 39.75$. Calculate the average of x and y

as follows: $\dfrac{39.75 + 2.875}{2} = \dfrac{42.625}{2} = 21.3125$. Calculated to the nearest tenth, the value becomes 21.3. The correct answer is 21.3.

30. 7 According to the question, 20% of the chocolates are dark chocolate, 15% are white chocolate, and 35% are mint chocolate. 20 + 15 + 35 = 70%, which means that 30% of the total number of chocolates are chocolate truffle. The total number of chocolates in the box can be calculated as follows: 6 = 0.3 × total, so there are 20 chocolates. Therefore, the number of mint chocolates in the box is 0.35 × 20 = 7. The correct answer is 7.

31. 1 There are 20 chocolates in the box. (See question 30 for an explanation of how to arrive at this information). Therefore, the number of dark chocolates is 0.2 × 20 = 4, and the number of white chocolates is 0.15 × 20 = 3. The difference is 4 − 3 = 1. The correct answer is 1.

Chapter 20
Math Test Drill 3

Math Test – No Calculator

25 MINUTES, 17 QUESTIONS

Turn to Section 3 of your answer sheet to answer the questions in this section.

DIRECTIONS

For questions **1-13**, solve each problem, choose the best answer from the choices provided, and fill in the corresponding circle on your answer sheet. For questions **14-17**, solve the problem and enter your answer in the grid on the answer sheet. Please refer to the directions before question 14 on how to enter your answers in the grid. You may use any available space in your test booklet for scratch work.

NOTES

1. The use of a calculator **is not permitted**.
2. All variables and expressions used represent real numbers unless otherwise indicated.
3. Figures provided in this test are drawn to scale unless otherwise indicated.
4. All figures lie in a plane unless otherwise indicated.
5. Unless otherwise indicated, the domain of a given function *f* is the set of all real numbers *x* for which *f(x)* is a real number.

REFERENCE

$A = \pi r^2$
$C = 2\pi r$

$A = lw$

$A = \frac{1}{2}bh$

$c^2 = a^2 + b^2$

Special Right Triangles

$V = lwh$

$V = \pi r^2h$

$V = \frac{4}{3}\pi r^3$

$V = \frac{1}{3}\pi r^2h$

$V = \frac{1}{3}\ell wh$

The number of degrees of arc in a circle is 360.
The number of radians of arc in a circle is 2π.
The sum of the measures in degrees of the angles of a triangle is 180.

CONTINUE ▶

1

Which of the following equations has the solution set $\{-5, 5\}$?

A) $5x^2 - 125 = 0$

B) $5x^2 - 3,125 = 0$

C) $25x^2 - 125 = 0$

D) $25x^2 - 3,125 = 0$

2

A snail is travelling in a straight line at a speed of 8 centimeters per minute. If it travels a total of 1.5 meters to reach a certain plant, which function can be used to estimate how many <u>centimeters</u>, $R(m)$, it still has to travel to reach the plant after m minutes?

(1 meter = 100 centimeters)

A) $R(m) = 8 - 150m$

B) $R(m) = 800 - 1.5m$

C) $R(m) = 150 - 8m$

D) $R(m) = 1.5 - 800m$

3

$$4 + \frac{5}{2}a = \frac{5}{6}a + 14$$

What is the value of a in the equation above?

A) $\frac{6}{5}$

B) $\frac{27}{5}$

C) 6

D) 8

4

Which of the following is a possible solution of $y > \frac{1}{7}(2y + 10)$?

A) 3

B) 2

C) 1

D) 0

5

Which of the following is equivalent to the expression $2f^2 - 3f + 4fg - 6g$?

A) $f(2f - 3 - g)$

B) $(2f - 3)(f + 2g)$

C) $(f + 2)(2g - 3)$

D) $2f(f + 3) - 2g(2f + 3g)$

CONTINUE

6

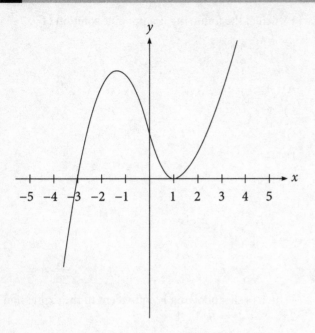

Which of the following could be the equation for the graph shown in the *xy*-plane above?

A) $y = x(x + 1)(x - 3)$

B) $y = (x + 1)^2(x - 3)$

C) $y = (x - 1)(x + 3)$

D) $y = (x - 1)^2(x + 3)$

7

Which of the following is the intersection of the lines $6x = 9 - 2y$ and $4x + 3y = 11$ in the *xy*-plane?

A) $\left(\dfrac{1}{2}, 3\right)$

B) $\left(1, \dfrac{3}{2}\right)$

C) $(2, 1)$

D) $\left(3, \dfrac{9}{2}\right)$

8

$$14 + (2 + x)(3 - x)$$

The expression above is equivalent to which of the following?

A) $8 + 3x - 2x - x^2$

B) $(4 + x)(5 - x)$

C) $20 - x - x^2$

D) $(4 - x)(5 + x)$

9

$$\dfrac{\dfrac{1}{2k-4} - \dfrac{1}{3k}}{2}$$

For all $k \neq 0$ and $k \neq 2$, which of the following is equivalent to the expression above?

A) $\dfrac{12k^2 - 24k}{k + 4}$

B) $\dfrac{k + 4}{12k^2 - 24k}$

C) $k + 4$

D) $12k^2 - 24k$

CONTINUE ➡

10

$$g(x) = 2 + |x - 2|$$

In the function g shown above, $g(-2) = g(b)$ and $b \neq -2$. What is the value of b ?

A) 0

B) 2

C) 4

D) 6

11

$$a = 0.09(f - s)$$

A physics student is studying the acceleration of an object for a certain amount of time it is in motion. The equation above gives the amount of acceleration a, in centimeters per second squared, of an object based on a final velocity of f centimeters per second and an initial velocity of s centimeters per second. If an object accelerates at 540 centimeters per second squared with a final velocity of 15,000 centimeters per second, what was the initial velocity, in centimeters per second?

A) 1,350

B) 6,000

C) 9,000

D) 14,460

12

$$R = 5,690 + 1.75n$$

The equation above estimates the total revenue R, in <u>thousands of dollars</u>, of a particular private company n days after the stock was first offered to the public. Which of the following accurately describes the meaning of the coefficient 1.75 ?

A) Each day the company's revenue increases by $1,750.

B) Each day the company's revenue increases by $1.75.

C) For every $1.75 increase in the revenue, the company's overall budget increases by $5,690.

D) For every $1,750 increase in the revenue, the company's overall budget increases by $5,690.

13

$$\sqrt[3]{x^4} = \frac{x^y}{\sqrt{x^3}}$$

If the expression above is true for all $x > 0$, what is the value of y ?

A) $\dfrac{7}{5}$

B) 2

C) $\dfrac{7}{3}$

D) $\dfrac{17}{6}$

CONTINUE

DIRECTIONS

For questions 14-17, solve the problem and enter your answer in the grid, as described below, on the answer sheet.

1. Although not required, it is suggested that you write your answer in the boxes at the top of the columns to help you fill in the circles accurately. You will receive credit only if the circles are filled in correctly.

2. Mark no more than one circle in any column.

3. No question has a negative answer.

4. Some problems may have more than one correct answer. In such cases, grid only one answer.

5. **Mixed numbers** such as $3\frac{1}{2}$ must be gridded as 3.5 or 7/2. (If $\boxed{3\ 1\ /\ 2}$ is entered into the grid, it will be interpreted as $\frac{31}{2}$, not as $3\frac{1}{2}$.)

6. **Decimal Answers:** If you obtain a decimal answer with more digits than the grid can accommodate, it may be either rounded or truncated, but it must fill the entire grid.

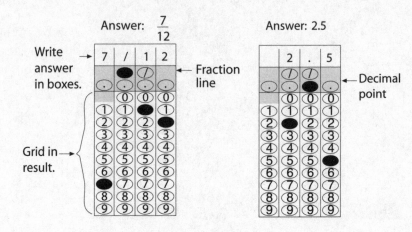

Answer: $\frac{7}{12}$ Answer: 2.5

Write answer in boxes. Fraction line. Grid in result. Decimal point.

Acceptable ways to grid $\frac{2}{3}$ are:

Answer: 201 – either position is correct

 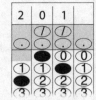

NOTE: You may start your answers in any column, space permitting. Columns you don't need to use should be left blank.

14

$$3a - 2b = 10$$
$$4a + 2b = 11$$

What value of a makes the above system of equations true?

15

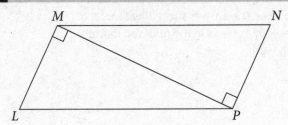

In the figure above, the measure of angle LPM is 25°. If angle MLP is congruent to angle MNP, what is the measure of angle MNP? (Disregard the degree sign when gridding your answer.)

16

A bakery sells medium-sized regular cakes and ice cream cakes. An ice cream cake costs $45, and a regular cake costs $27. If the bakery sells 40 medium-sized cakes for a total of $1,332, how many ice cream cakes does the bakery sell?

17

If $5x = 6y$ and x and y are negative numbers, what is the value of $\dfrac{x-y}{x}$?

CONTINUE

Math Test – Calculator

45 MINUTES, 31 QUESTIONS

Turn to Section 4 of your answer sheet to answer the questions in this section.

DIRECTIONS

For questions **1-27**, solve each problem, choose the best answer from the choices provided, and fill in the corresponding circle on your answer sheet. For questions **28-31**, solve the problem and enter your answer in the grid on the answer sheet. Please refer to the directions before question 28 on how to enter your answers in the grid. You may use any available space in your test booklet for scratch work.

NOTES

1. The use of a calculator **is permitted**.
2. All variables and expressions used represent real numbers unless otherwise indicated.
3. Figures provided in this test are drawn to scale unless otherwise indicated.
4. All figures lie in a plane unless otherwise indicated.
5. Unless otherwise indicated, the domain of a given function f is the set of all real numbers x for which $f(x)$ is a real number.

REFERENCE

$A = \pi r^2$
$C = 2\pi r$

$A = lw$

$A = \frac{1}{2}bh$

$c^2 = a^2 + b^2$

Special Right Triangles

$V = lwh$

$V = \pi r^2 h$

$V = \frac{4}{3}\pi r^3$

$V = \frac{1}{3}\pi r^2 h$

$V = \frac{1}{3}lwh$

The number of degrees of arc in a circle is 360.
The number of radians of arc in a circle is 2π.
The sum of the measures in degrees of the angles of a triangle is 180.

CONTINUE ➡

1

Which of the following is equivalent to $4 + 2(y - 7)$?

A) $2y + 3$

B) $2y - 10$

C) $2y - 3$

D) $14y + 4$

2

A certain species of freshwater crayfish can grow to a length of 11.5 centimeters. Approximately how long can it grow in <u>inches</u>? (1 inch ≈ 2.54 centimeters)

A) 29.21

B) 8.96

C) 4.53

D) 1.45

3

Every 10 seconds, a secretary can type 2 lines of a memo. Working at this rate, how many lines can she type in 3 <u>minutes</u>?

A) 60

B) 36

C) 20

D) 12

4

As part of a research project, a student analyzes the growth of an algal bloom on a pond on campus. Using a computer program, she is able to track the percentage of the pond that is covered by the algal bloom over the course of 40 days. The data are graphed below with the time on the x-axis and the percent of the pond covered by the algal bloom on the y-axis.

Data from Study of Algal Bloom Coverage

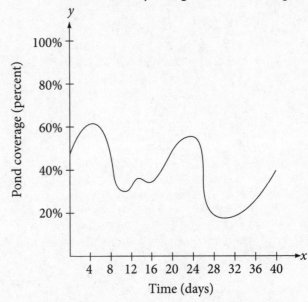

Based on the data shown, which of the following statements is true?

A) The algal bloom reaches its minimum coverage about 10 days into the observation period.

B) The percent of the pond that the algal bloom covered increased steadily between the 10th and 24th days after the observation began.

C) The x-intercept represents the portion of the pond covered by the algal bloom at the beginning of the observation period.

D) The maximum coverage in the second half of the observation period occurs around the 24th day of the observation period.

CONTINUE ➡

5

If $12b = 5$, what is the value of $24\left(\dfrac{2}{3} - b\right)$?

A) $\dfrac{39}{12}$

B) $\dfrac{17}{3}$

C) 6

D) 11

6

$$(z - 4)^3 + 27 = 0$$

Which of the following is a solution to the equation above?

A) −7

B) −1

C) 1

D) 13

CONTINUE

Questions 7-9 refer to the following information.

A polling company conducts a survey of 400 likely voters in a county to determine voter opinion of a new bill. Each participant selects one of five options that best represents his opinion of the bill. The results are shown in the table below.

	Voters aged 18–35	Voters over age 35	Total
Strongly Agree	32	74	106
Slightly Agree	18	52	70
Neutral	29	33	62
Slightly Disagree	33	51	84
Strongly Disagree	28	50	78
Total	140	260	400

7

What is the approximate probability that a voter selected at random stated that he or she was neutral about the bill, if that voter was over the age of 35 ?

A) 0.13

B) 0.16

C) 0.21

D) 0.33

8

How many voters over the age of 35 indicated that they slightly agree, are neutral, or slightly disagree with the bill?

A) 158

B) 136

C) 80

D) 52

9

Based on the information collected by the survey, what is the predicted number of voters aged 18–35 in the county that would indicate that they strongly agree with the bill, if the sample is representative of the 4,800 registered voters in the county?

A) 32

B) 106

C) 384

D) 1,272

10

Keko ordered a refrigerator, a dishwasher, and a food processor online. The combined weight of the three appliances was 360 pounds. If the refrigerator weighed 40 percent less than the dishwasher and food processor combined, how much did the refrigerator weigh, in pounds?

A) 82

B) 90

C) 135

D) 257

Questions 11 and 12 refer to the following information.

A player of an online game receives points for completing four different actions in the game. His score sheet is shown below.

> <u>Score sheet</u>
> 8 Experience Events
> 12 Skills Sessions
> 8 Character Classes
> 7 Wealth Winnings
> Bonus: 33.91
> Total Points: 342.16

The bonus is given when a player has a total of 35 or more actions and is calculated as a percentage of the score at that point. The total points are the sum of the score and the bonus.

11

The player completed 35 actions and received the bonus. What percentage of the score was used to calculate the bonus?

A) 11%

B) 16%

C) 21%

D) 26%

12

The total points the player earned for all Skills Sessions and Character Classes was 254. If the combined score for completing one Skills Session and one Character Class is 24, how many points does a player earn for completing a Skills Session?

A) 8.5

B) 9.6

C) 14.4

D) 15.5

13

$$\text{Line } m: -2x + 3y = 12$$

$$\text{Line } n: y = \frac{2}{3}x + 3$$

The system of equations above represents two lines, m and n, that are graphed in the xy-plane. Which of the following statements is true regarding lines m and n ?

A) Line n intersects line m at $(-3, 1)$.

B) Line n and line m are perpendicular.

C) Line n and line m are the same line.

D) Line n is parallel to line m.

CONTINUE ▶

14

Carl received some money for his birthday and decided to use it to start saving up to buy a video game console. The amount of money he has saved is given by the equation $y = 45x + 100$, where y is the amount of money he has saved, and x is the number of weeks since he started saving for the console. Which of the following accurately describes the meanings of the coefficients in this equation?

A) It will take Carl 45 weeks to save up the $100 he needs to purchase the console.

B) The number 45 is the rate of decrease, in dollars per week, of the money Carl has saved, which started at $100.

C) The number 45 is the rate of increase, in dollars per week, of the money Carl has saved, which started at $100.

D) The number 45 is the rate of increase, in dollars per week, of the amount that Carl saves to put towards the cost of the $100 console.

▼

Questions 15 and 16 refer to the following information.

A children's choir is selling boxes of two types of cookies, Skinny Mints and Grand Goldens, to raise money for an upcoming trip. Both flavors cost the same amount, but family members of the children in the choir receive a discount. Boxes sold to neighbors cost the same as boxes sold at a public location, and there is no discount for purchasing more than one box. The table below shows data collected about the boxes sold to family members, neighbors, and at public locations.

	Boxes of Skinny Mints	Boxes of Grand Goldens	Total boxes sold	Total sales, in dollars	Customers purchasing multiple boxes
Family Members	196	336	532	$6,118	65
Neighbors	175	237	412	$5,974	54
General Public	420	573	944	$12,092	119
Total	791	1,146	1,888	$24,184	238

15

What is the cost of one box of cookies sold to a family member of a child in the choir?

A) $11.50

B) $12.80

C) $14.50

D) $15.10

16

Based on the information shown, if one of the boxes of cookies sold to someone other than a family member is selected at random, what is the approximate probability that it is a box of Skinny Mints?

A) 0.48

B) 0.44

C) 0.42

D) 0.37

▲

CONTINUE ▶

17

$$P = I^2R$$

When current runs through a material with electrical resistance, heat is produced in a process known as joule heating. The formula above represents the process of joule heating, in which P is the power in watts, converted from electrical to thermal energy, I is the current in amperes, and R is the resistance of the material in ohms. Which of the following would convert 3 watts of power from electrical to thermal energy?

A) A current of 6 amperes passing through a material with a resistance of 0.5 ohms

B) A current of 1 ampere passing through a material with a resistance of 3 ohms

C) A current of 3 amperes passing through a material with a resistance of 1 ohm

D) A current of 0.5 amperes passing through a material with a resistance of 6 ohms

18

Rick takes his son Chris to see a play. An adult ticket costs A dollars, and the cost of a child's ticket is 40 percent less than the cost of an adult ticket. If the online service Rick uses to purchase the tickets gives a 6 percent discount, what is the total cost that Rick pays for the two tickets?

A) $0.94(A + 0.60A)$

B) $0.94(A - 0.40A)$

C) $0.94A + 0.60A$

D) $0.94(2(0.60A))$

19

A botanist runs three trials of an experiment to determine the number of flowers on each plant in a group of 24 plants. The histograms below show the results of each trial. Which of the trials resulted in a range of 6, a median of 2, and a mode equal to the mean?

Trial I.

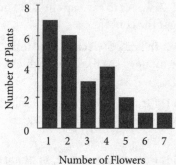

Trial II.

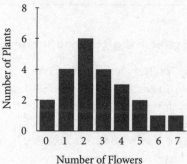

Trial III.

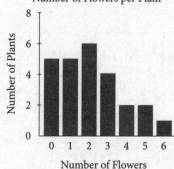

A) Trial I only

B) Trials I and II only

C) Trials I and III only

D) Trial III only

CONTINUE

20

A jewelry maker is melting down gold coins to create a gold alloy. He has two different types of coins: W and Z. Coins of type W are 27% gold and coins of type Z are 43% gold. He wants to melt down no more than 20 ounces to produce a mixture that is at least 35% gold. If a represents the number of ounces of type W coins and b represents the number of ounces of type Z coins, which of the following systems could be used to solve for all the possible values of a and b that meet the jewelry maker's conditions?

A) $\begin{cases} 0.27a + 0.43b \geq 0.35 \\ a + b \leq 20 \\ a > 0 \\ b > 0 \end{cases}$

B) $\begin{cases} 0.27a + 0.43b \leq 0.35 \\ a + b = 20 \\ a > 0 \\ b > 0 \end{cases}$

C) $\begin{cases} 0.27a + 0.43b \geq 0.35(a + b) \\ 0 < a < 10 \\ 0 < b < 10 \end{cases}$

D) $\begin{cases} 0.27a + 0.43b \geq 0.35a + 0.35b \\ a + b \leq 20 \\ a > 0 \\ b > 0 \end{cases}$

21

The chart below shows the distribution of grades in Biology at a high school. If 72 more students received B's than A's, how many students are taking Biology at the school?

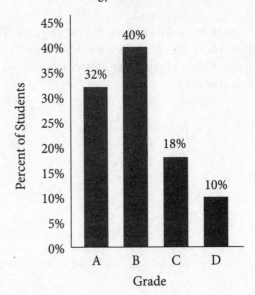

Biology Grade Distribution

A) 900

B) 560

C) 225

D) 180

CONTINUE

22

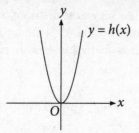

The graph of $y = h(x)$ is shown in the xy-plane above. If $p(x) = h(x - a) + b$, where a and b are positive constants, then which of the following could be the graph of $h(x)$?

A)

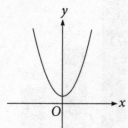

B)

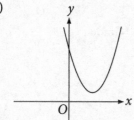

C)

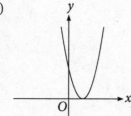

D)

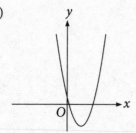

23

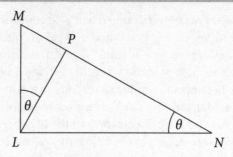

Note: Figure not drawn to scale

In the figure shown above, the measure of angle LNP is equal to the measure of angle MLP. If $LM = 6$, and the length of $\overline{MN}$ is four times the length of $\overline{MP}$, what is the length of $\overline{MP}$?

A) 12

B) 4

C) 3

D) $\dfrac{1}{4}$

24

A scientist studying acid rain at a particular location determines that the measured parts per billion of sulfur dioxide in the atmosphere has increased by 5% every year since the study began. Which of the following is true regarding the relationship between the number of years since the study began and the level of sulfur dioxide in the atmosphere?

A) The relationship is quadratic with the minimum value at the beginning of the study.

B) The relationship is exponential with the minimum value at the beginning of the study.

C) The relationship is linear with a graph having a positive slope.

D) The relationship is exponential with the maximum value at the beginning of the study.

25

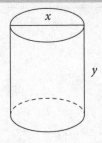

$$\text{Surface Area} = 2\pi\left(\frac{x^2}{4}\right) + \pi xy$$

The surface area of the tin can shown can be calculated using the above formula, where x is the diameter of the lid and base of the can, and y is the height of the can. The can is wrapped with a rectangular label that covers everything except the base and the lid. What does the expression $\frac{1}{2}\pi x^2$ represent?

A) The area of the base of the can

B) The area of the rectangular label wrapped around the can

C) One half of the area of the base of the can

D) The sum of the areas of the base and the lid of the can

26

Which of the following is equivalent to in the expression $(3x - 3) + (3x - 3)^2$?

A) $(3x - 3)(3x - 2)$

B) $(3x - 3)^3$

C) $9x - 9$

D) $9x^2 - 15x - 12$

27

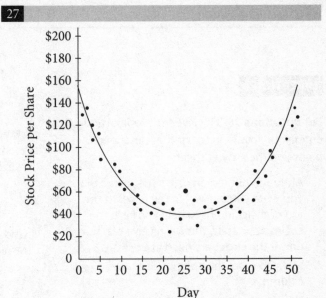

An investment broker tracks the stock price of Stock A for 50 days. The scatterplot above shows the price at the close of each of the 50 days. A quadratic model of best fit is also shown. On day 25, the observed stock price was approximately what percent more than the predicted stock price based on the model?

A) 33%

B) 50%

C) 66%

D) 150%

CONTINUE

DIRECTIONS

For questions 28-31, solve the problem and enter your answer in the grid, as described below, on the answer sheet.

1. Although not required, it is suggested that you write your answer in the boxes at the top of the columns to help you fill in the circles accurately. You will receive credit only if the circles are filled in correctly.

2. Mark no more than one circle in any column.

3. No question has a negative answer.

4. Some problems may have more than one correct answer. In such cases, grid only one answer.

5. **Mixed numbers** such as $3\frac{1}{2}$ must be gridded as 3.5 or 7/2. (If ⌗ is entered into the grid, it will be interpreted as $\frac{31}{2}$, not as $3\frac{1}{2}$.)

6. **Decimal Answers:** If you obtain a decimal answer with more digits than the grid can accommodate, it may be either rounded or truncated, but it must fill the entire grid.

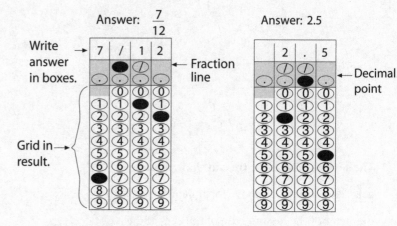

Acceptable ways to grid $\frac{2}{3}$ are:

Answer: 201 – either position is correct

NOTE: You may start your answers in any column, space permitting. Columns you don't need to use should be left blank.

CONTINUE ▶

28

A pool in the shape of a rectangular prism has a depth of 3 meters and a volume of 288 cubic meters. If the pool is 4 meters longer than it is wide, what is the perimeter, in meters, of the base of the pool?

29

If (a, b) is the solution to the following system of equations, what is the value of b ?

$$7a - 6b = 4$$
$$-3a + 2b = -12$$

Questions 30-31 refer to the following information.

At an art gallery opening, the ratio of attendees that were friends of the artist to other attendees was 3 to 2. During the evening, many attendees bought a piece of art. Among the attendees who were friends of the artist, the ratio of buyers to non-buyers was 1 to 3, and among the other attendees, the ratio of buyers to non-buyers was 1 to 7.

30

What was the ratio of the buyers who were friends of the artist to buyers who were not? (When entering your answer, express the ratio as a fraction or a decimal.)

31

What was the ratio of the attendees at the gallery that bought a piece of art to those that did not? (When entering your answer, express the ratio as a fraction or a decimal.)

STOP
If you finish before time is called, you may check your work on this section only.
Do not turn to any other section.

CONTINUE ➜

Chapter 21
Math Test
Drill 3: Answers
and Explanations

ANSWERS AND EXPLANATIONS

Section 3—No Calculator Math Test

1. **A**   Plug the given values of x into the answer choices to see which equation is true. Start with the easiest equation, which is in (A). When $x = 5$, (A) becomes $5(5)^2 - 125 = 0$, or $5(25) - 125 = 0$. This becomes $125 - 125 = 0$, which is true. Try $x = -5$ in (A), which becomes $5(-5)^2 - 125 = 0$, or $5(25) - 125 = 0$. This becomes $125 - 125 = 0$, which is true. Since both values of x work in (A), that equation has the given solutions. The correct answer is (A).

2. **C**   There is a variable in the question and the answer choices, so plug in. Pick a value of m that will make the math easier, such as $m = 10$. If the snail travels at 8 centimeters per minute, it will travel 80 centimeters in 10 minutes. The distance is 1.5 meters, but the question asks for the equation in centimeters, so convert meters to centimeters by setting up a proportion: $\dfrac{1 \text{ meter}}{100 \text{ centimeters}} = \dfrac{1.5 \text{ meters}}{x}$. Cross-multiply to get $x = 150$ centimeters. If the snail has traveled 80 of the 150 centimeters, it has 70 centimeters left to travel to reach the plant line. This is the target number: circle it. Plug $m = 10$ into the answer choices to see which one equals the target value of 70. Choice (A) becomes $8 - 150(10)$. This will be a negative value, so eliminate (A). Choice (B) becomes $800 - 1.5(10) = 800 - 15 = 785$. This does not match the target value, so eliminate (B). Choice (C) becomes $150 - 8(10) = 150 - 80 = 70$. Keep (C), but check (D) just in case. Choice (D) becomes $1.5 - 800(10)$, which is negative, so eliminate it. The correct answer is (C).

3. **C**   With all the fractions in the equation and the answer choices, plugging in the answers could get messy. Solve the equation instead. Start by multiplying the entire equation by 6 to clear the fractions. The equation becomes $24 + 15a = 5a + 84$. Subtract $5a$ from both sides to get $24 + 10a = 84$, then subtract 24 from both sides to get $10a = 60$. Divide both sides by 10 to get $a = 6$. The correct answer is (C).

4. **A**   Start by multiplying the entire inequality by 7 to get rid of the fraction. The inequality becomes $7y > 2y + 10$. Subtract $2y$ from both sides to get $5y > 10$, then divide both sides by 5 to get $y > 2$. The only choice that is greater than 2 is 3. The correct answer is (A).

5. **B**   There are variables in the question and answer choices, so plug in. Make $f = 2$ and $g = 3$. The expression becomes $2(2^2) - 3(2) + 4(2)(3) - 6(3)$, which equals $8 - 6 + 24 - 18 = 2 + 24 - 18 = 26 - 18 = 8$. Now plug the values for f and g into the answer choices to see which one equals the target value of 8. Choice (A) becomes $2[2(2) - 3 - 3] = 2(-2) = -4$. This does not match the target value, so eliminate (A). Choice (B) becomes $[2(2) - 3][2 + 2(3)] = (1)(8) = 8$. Keep (B), but check (C) and (D) just in case. Choice (C) becomes $(2 + 2)[2(3) - 3] = (4)(3) = 12$, and (D) becomes $2(2)(2 + 3) - 2(3)[2(2) + 3(3)] = 4(5) - 6(13) = 20 - 78 = -58$. Eliminate (C) and (D). The correct answer is (B).

6. **D** Without a calculator to graph the equations in the answer choices, the best option is to plug in points from the graph to see what equations could be true. The graph goes through the point at $(1, 0)$, so plug $x = 1$ into the answer choices to see which makes $y = 0$. Choice (A) becomes $y = 1(1 + 1)(1 - 3) = 1(2)(-2) = -4$. This does not equal 0, so eliminate (A). Choice (B) becomes $y = (1 + 1)^2(1 - 3) = 2^2(-2) = -8$. Eliminate (B). Choice (C) becomes $y = (1 - 1)(1 + 3) = (0)(4) = 0$. Keep (C), but check (D) just in case, Choice (D) becomes $y = (1 - 1)^2(1 + 3) = (0)^2(4) = 0$. Since both (C) and (D) work for $x = 1$, try another point. The graph also goes through $(-3, 0)$, but that won't help differentiate between (C) and (D), which both have an $(x + 3)$ term. Try something like $x = -1$. The graph does not show the exact y-value for this x-value, but it must be positive. Choice (C) becomes $(-1 - 1)(-1 + 3) = (-2)(2) = -4$. This does not match the graph, so eliminate (C). The correct answer is (D).

7. **A** There are specific points in the answer choices, so plug in. Start with (A) and see if the given point works in both equations. The first equation becomes $6\left(\dfrac{1}{2}\right) = 9 - 2(3)$ or $3 = 9 - 6$. This is true, so check the second equation, which becomes $4\left(\dfrac{1}{2}\right) + 3(3) = 11$ or $2 + 9 = 11$. This is also true. The correct answer is (A).

8. **B** There is a variable in the question and answer choices, so plug in. Make $x = 2$. The expression becomes $14 + (2 + 2)(3 - 2)$, or $14 + (4)(1) = 18$. Plug $x = 2$ into the answer choices to see which one equals the target value of 18. Choice (A) becomes $8 + 3(2) - 2(2) - 2^2 = 8 + 6 - 4 - 4 = 6$. This does not match the target value, so eliminate (A). Choice (B) becomes $(4 + 2)(5 - 2) = (6)(3) = 18$. Keep (B), but check (C) and (D) just in case. Choice (C) becomes $20 - 2 - 2^2 = 20 - 2 - 4 = 14$, and (D) becomes $(4 - 2)(5 + 2) = (2)(7) = 14$. Eliminate (C) and (D). The correct answer is (B).

9. **B** There is a variable in the question and answer choices, so plug in. Pick a number that fits the conditions, such as $k = 3$. The expression becomes $\dfrac{\dfrac{1}{2(3) - 4} - \dfrac{1}{3(3)}}{2}$ or $\dfrac{\dfrac{1}{2} - \dfrac{1}{9}}{2}$. Use the bowtie to combine the fractions in the numerator as $\dfrac{\dfrac{9}{2 \times 9} - \dfrac{2}{9 \times 2}}{2} = \dfrac{\dfrac{9 - 2}{18}}{2} = \dfrac{\dfrac{7}{18}}{2}$. Dividing by a number is the same as multiplying by its reciprocal, so this becomes $\dfrac{7}{18} \times \dfrac{1}{2} = \dfrac{7}{36}$. Plug $k = 3$ into the answer choices to see which one equals this target value. Choice (A) becomes $\dfrac{12(3^2) - 24(3)}{3 + 4} = \dfrac{108 - 72}{7} = \dfrac{36}{7}$. This does

not match the target value, so eliminate (A). Choice (B) is the reciprocal of (A), and the result with (A) was the reciprocal of the target value. Therefore, (B) will give the target value. Check (C) and (D) just in case. Choice (C) becomes 3 + 4 = 7, and (D) becomes $12(3^2) - 24(3) = 108 - 72 = 36$. Eliminate (C) and (D). The correct answer is (B).

10. **D** Start by finding the value of $g(-2)$ by plugging -2 in for x in the function, which becomes $g(-2) = 2 + |-2 - 2| = 2 + |-4| = 2 + 4 = 6$. Now plug in the answers for b to see which one also gives a value of 6 when put into the g function. Start with (B). The function becomes $g(2) = 2 + |2 - 2| = 2 + |0| = 2 + 0 = 2$. This does not result in a g value of 6, so eliminate (B). A larger value of b is needed, so try (D). If $b = 6$, then $g(6) = 2 + |6 - 2| = 2 + |4| = 2 + 4 = 6$. The correct answer is (D).

11. **C** This is a plugging in question in which two of the three values to plug in are given. The question defines a as acceleration and f as final velocity. Plug $a = 540$ and $f = 15,000$ into the equation, which becomes $540 = 0.09(15,000 - s)$. Now solve the equation for s. Start by multiplying both sides by 100 to get rid of the decimal. The equation becomes $54,000 = 9(15,000 - s)$. Now divide both sides by 9 to get $6,000 = 15,000 - s$. Add s to both sides to get $6,000 + s = 15,000$. Finally, subtract 6,000 from both sides to get $s = 9,000$. The correct answer is (C).

12. **A** Start by reading the full question. The question asks about *the meaning of the coefficient 1.75*. Next, label the parts of the equation. The variable R represents *the total revenue…in thousands of dollars*, and the variable n represents the number of days after the stock was first offered to the public. This makes the equation *revenue = $5,690 + $1.75(days)*. As the number of days increases, the revenue will increase. Next, go through the answers and use process of elimination. Choices (C) and (D) can be eliminated because they bring in the idea of the overall budget, which is not included in the equation. Compare the remaining answers. The difference between (A) and (B) is the amount by which the revenue increases. The equation gives the revenue <u>in thousands</u>, so the coefficient 1.75 is really multiplied by 1,000 to get the actual numbers. Eliminate (B), which does not do this. The correct answer is (A).

13. **D** When dealing with an equation that has both root and exponents, work to write everything with the same base and in the same form. Here, since the question asks for the value of exponent y, re-write the left side of the equation with only exponents. When there is both an exponent and a root on a variable, remember "power over root." This means that $\left(\sqrt{x^3}\right)$ can be written as $x^{\frac{3}{2}}$ and $\left(\sqrt[3]{x^4}\right)$ can be written as $x^{\frac{4}{3}}$. These x-values are multiplied together; according to MADSPM rules, that means to add the exponents. The left side of the equation then becomes $x^{\frac{3}{2} + \frac{4}{3}}$. Use the bowtie to get a common denominator for the exponents: $\frac{3}{2} + \frac{4}{3} = \frac{3(3)}{2(3)} + \frac{4(2)}{3(2)} = \frac{9}{6} + \frac{8}{6} = \frac{17}{6}$. Now the full equation is $x^{\frac{17}{6}} = x^y$. Since the bases are the same, the exponents are equal, and $y = \frac{17}{6}$. The correct answer is (D).

14. **3** When solving a system of equations, stack and add them to see if that gives the value the question asks for. Often, it is necessary to multiply one or both equations by a constant to make the other variable disappear. In this case, however, the *b* terms have the same value coefficient with opposite signs, so adding the equations together will make the *b* terms disappear. The result is $7a = 21$. Divide both sides by 7 to get $a = 3$. The correct answer is 3.

15. **65** Mark angle *LPM* as 25°. Because angle *LMP* is a right angle and every triangle contains 180°, angle *MLP* must be 65°. Opposite angles of a parallelogram are congruent, so angle *MNP* must also be 65°.

16. **14** When given two sets of information about a situation, set up a system of equations. Translate the English to math one piece at a time, starting with the most straightforward piece. The bakery sells 40 cakes. If regular cakes are represented by *r* and ice cream cakes are represented by *i*, this can be written as $r + i = 40$. The cost of a regular cake is 27, so the income from those can be written as $27r$. Similarly, the income from ice cream cakes can be written as $45i$. Together, the income from these cakes is \$1,332, so $27r + 45i = 1,332$. The question asks for the number of ice cream cakes sold, so solve the system for *i*. To do this, multiply the first equation by –27 so that the *r* terms will disappear when the equations are added together. The first equation becomes $-27r - 27i = -1,080$. Stack and add the two equations.

$$27r + 45i = 1,332$$
$$\underline{-27r - 27i = -1,080}$$
$$18i = 252$$

Divide both sides by 18 to get $i = 14$. The correct answer is 14.

17. $\dfrac{1}{6}$, **.166, or .167**

There are variables in relation to each other, so plug in. The equation will be true if $x = -6$ and $y = -5$. Plug these values into the expression to get $\dfrac{-6 - (-5)}{-6} = \dfrac{-6 + 5}{-6} = \dfrac{-1}{-6} = \dfrac{1}{6}$. The correct answer is $\dfrac{1}{6}$.

Section 4—Calculator Math Test

1. **B** Plugging in could work on this question, but it may be more straightforward and efficient to just distribute the 2 and combine like terms. Distributing the 2 makes the expression become $4 + 2y - 14$ or $2y - 10$. The correct answer is (B).

2. **C** Set up a proportion, making sure to match the units in the numerators and denominators. The proportion is $\dfrac{1 \text{ inch}}{2.54 \text{ centmeters}} = \dfrac{x}{11.5 \text{ centimeters}}$. Cross-multiply to get $2.54x = 11.5$, then divide both sides by 2.54 to get 4.5276. This is closest to 4.53. The correct answer is (C).

3. **B** To answer this question, set up a proportion, making sure to match the units in the numerators and in the denominators. Convert the 3 minutes to seconds by multiplying by 60 to get 180 seconds. Set up the proportion $\frac{2 \text{ lines}}{10 \text{ seconds}} = \frac{x}{180 \text{ seconds}}$. Cross-multiply to get $10x = 360$, then divide both sides by 10 to get $x = 36$. The correct answer is (B).

4. **D** When dealing with a figure in one of the Math sections, note the title and the axis labels to determine what is represented with the data. This graph shows the percent of the pond covered over time in days. Next, go right to the answer choices and use process of elimination. Choice (A) says that the minimum coverage is seen at Day 10. The line on the graph reaches its lowest point between day 28 and day 32, so (A) is not true; eliminate it. Choice (B) indicates a steady increase between days 10 and 24, which would be shown as a line with a positive slope. The line of the graph goes up and down in this period, so eliminate (B). Choice (C) mentions the x-intercept, but the graph does not cross the x-axis. Eliminate (C). The correct answer is (D).

5. **C** Divide both sides of the first equation by 12 to get $b = \frac{5}{12}$. Put this value into the expression to get $24\left(\frac{2}{3} - \frac{5}{12}\right)$. It is possible to get a common denominator inside the parentheses, but it will be more efficient to distribute the 24 to both fractions, whose denominators will cancel. The expression becomes $24\left(\frac{2}{3}\right) - 24\left(\frac{5}{12}\right) = (8)(2) - (2)(5) = 16 - 10 = 6$. The correct answer is (C).

6. **C** The question asks for a specific value, so plug in the answers to see which value of z will make the equation true. Start with (B). If $z = -1$, the equation becomes $(-1 - 4)^3 + 27 = 0$ or $(-5)^3 + 27 = 0$. This simplifies to $-125 + 27 = 0$, which is not true. Eliminate (B). A bigger value of z is needed, so try (C). If $z = 1$, the equation becomes $(1 - 4)^3 + 27 = 0$ or $(-3)^3 + 27 = 0$. This simplifies to $-27 + 27 = 0$, which is true. The correct answer is (C).

7. **A** Probability is defined as $\frac{\# \text{ of outcomes that fit the requirements}}{\text{total } \# \text{ of outcomes}}$. In this case, the total number of outcomes is all voters over the age of 35, of which there are 260. There are 33 people in that group that fit the requirement of being neutral. The probability is $\frac{33}{260} = 0.1269 \approx 0.13$. The correct answer is (A).

8. **B** Look up the numbers on the chart, being careful to find the correct ones. In the row labeled "Voters over age 35," the number that slightly agree is 52, the number that are neutral is 33, and the number that slightly disagree is 51. Add these together to get $52 + 33 + 51 = 136$. The correct answer is (B).

9. **C** Start by looking up the number of voters in the survey that fit the requirements. In the "Voters aged 18–35" category, there were 32 who strongly agreed. That number was out of 400 in the survey, so set up a proportion to see how many of 4,800 would fit the requirements. The proportion is

$\dfrac{32 \text{ strongly agree}}{400 \text{ total}} = \dfrac{x}{4{,}800}$. Cross-multiply to get $400x = 153{,}600$, then divide both sides by 400 to get $x = 384$. The correct answer is (C).

10. **C**   The question asks for a specific value, so plug in the answers. Start with (B). If the refrigerator weighed 90 pounds, there are $360 - 90 = 270$ pounds left for the other two appliances. The refrigerator weighed *40 percent less* than the other appliances, which can be written as $270 - \dfrac{40}{100}(270) = 270 - 108 = 162$. This does not equal 90, so eliminate (B). A larger number is needed for the weight of the refrigerator, so try (C). If the refrigerator weighed 135 pounds, there are $360 - 135 = 225$ pounds left for the other two appliances. Forty percent less than 225 can be written as $225 - \dfrac{40}{100}(225) = 225 - 90 = 135$. This matches the weight of the refrigerator. The correct answer is (C).

11. **A**   The question states that the total points are the sum of the score and the bonus. Therefore, the score was $342.16 - 33.91 = 308.25$. To determine the percent that 33.91 is of this score, divide 33.91 by 308.25 to get 0.11, then multiply this by 100 to get 11%. The correct answer is (A).

12. **D**   The question asks for a specific value, so plug in the answers. Start with (B). If a Skills Session is worth 9.6 points, then a Character Class is worth $24 - 9.6 = 14.4$ points. The 12 Skills Sessions would be worth $12(9.6) = 115.2$ points, and the 8 Character Classes would be worth $8(14.4) = 115.2$ points. Together, these two actions would be worth a total of $115.2 + 115.2 = 230.4$. This does not match the 254 points that the question says the player earned. Eliminate (B). To get a larger number of points, the number of Skills Sessions needs to be greater, since the player did more Skills Sessions than Character Classes. Try (C). If a Skills Session is worth 14.4 points, then a Character Class is worth $24 - 14.4 = 9.6$ points. The 12 Skills Sessions would be worth $12(14.4) = 172.8$ points, and the 8 Character Classes would be worth $8(9.6) = 76.8$ points. Together, these two actions would be worth a total of $172.8 + 76.8 = 249.6$. This is still not enough, so eliminate (C). The correct answer is (D).

13. **D**   When given a system of equations, there are many ways to solve it, so look for the most efficient way. Choices (B) through (D) reference things that can be determined by comparing the slopes of the two lines, so that's a good place to start. Line n is already in $y = mx + b$ form, in which m is the slope. Therefore, the slope of line n is $\dfrac{2}{3}$. Now get the equation of line m into $y = mx + b$ form. Add $2x$ to both sides of the equation to get $3y = 2x + 12$. Divide both sides by 3 to get $y = \dfrac{2}{3}x + 4$. Line m also has a slope of $\dfrac{2}{3}$. The lines are not the same, since the equations do not match, so eliminate (C). Because the lines have the same slope, they are parallel. The correct answer is (D).

14. **C** Start by reading the full question. The question asks about *the meanings of the coefficients*. Next, label the parts of the equation. The variable *y* represents *the amount of money he has saved*, and the variable *x* represents *the number of weeks since he started saving*. This makes the equation *amount he has saved = 45(weeks) + 100*. As the number of weeks increases, the amount he has saved will increase. Next, go through the answers and use process of elimination. Choice (A) can be eliminated because it says the 45 represents the number of weeks, but the question states that *x* is the number of weeks. Choice (B) can be eliminated because it refers to a decrease in the amount saved. Choice (C) says the equation is about the money Carl has saved, which started at $100. To see if this is true, plug in *x* = 0 to find that Carl started with 45(0) + 100 = 100 dollars. This fits the question, so keep (C), but check (D) just in case. Choice (D) refers to the cost of the console, but the question does not provide that information. Eliminate (D). The correct answer is (C).

15. **A** Look on the chart for the numbers needed to answer this question. In the Family Members row, the total number of boxes sold is 532 and the total sales, in dollars, is $6,118. To find the cost per box, divide the dollar amount by the number of boxes to get $11.50. The correct answer is (A).

16. **B** Probability is defined as $\dfrac{\text{\# of outcomes that fit the requirements}}{\text{total \# of outcomes}}$. In this case, the total number of outcomes is all boxes sold to non-family members. In the Neighbors row, the total boxes sold was 412, and in the General Public row, the number was 944. Therefore, the total number of outcomes is 412 + 944 = 1,356. There are 175 boxes of Skinny Mints sold to Neighbors and 420 boxes sold to the General Public, so there were 175 + 420 = 595 boxes that fit the requirements. The probability is $\dfrac{595}{1,356} = 0.4388 \approx 0.44$. The correct answer is (B).

17. **B** When given an equation and different possible values for the variables in the equation, plug in those given values to determine which set gives the needed result. In this question, the variables are measured in units with names that don't correspond to the variable name, so be careful to plug each number into the correct place. Choice (A) gives a current of 6 amperes and a resistance of 0.5 ohms, so *I* = 6 and *R* = 0.5. The equation becomes $P = (6^2)(0.5) = (36)(0.5) = 18$. This is much more than the required 3 watts of power, so eliminate (A). Choice (B) becomes $P = (1^2)(3) = (1)(3) = 3$. The correct answer is (B).

18. **A** There are variables in the answer choices, so plug in. Since the question deals with a percent, plug in *A* = $100. If an adult ticket is $100, a child's ticket is 40% less than that, or $40 less, so a child's ticket is $60. Rick would pay $100 + $60 = $160 for the tickets before the discount of 6%. To find the discount, take 6% of $160 by multiplying $160 by $\dfrac{6}{100}$ to get $9.60. Therefore, the total with the discount is $160 − $9.60 = $150.40. Plug *A* = $100 into the answer choices to see which one equals this target value. Choice (A) becomes 0.94[100 + (0.60)(100)] = 0.94(100 + 60) = 0.94(160) = 150.40.

Keep (A), but check the remaining answers just in case. Choice (B) becomes $0.94[100 - (0.40)(100)] = 0.94(100 - 40) = 0.94(60) = 56.40$, so eliminate (B). Choice (C) becomes $0.94(100) + 0.60(100) = 94 + 60 = 154$, so eliminate (C). Choice (D) becomes $0.94[2(0.60)(100)] = 0.94(120) = 112.80$, so eliminate (D). The correct answer is (A).

19. **D** When dealing with Roman numeral questions, pick a straightforward piece, determine if it is true, and use process of elimination on the answers before checking out another piece. In the case of bar graphs, range is easy to determine. Range is defined as the difference between the greatest value and the least, so the range of Trial I is $7 - 1 = 6$. This works, so Trial I meets the range requirements. Trial II has a range of $7 - 0 = 7$, which is not what the question asks for. Trial II is listed in (B), so eliminate (B). Trial III has a range of $6 - 0 = 6$, so it also meets the range requirements. Next check the median. In a list of numbers, the median is the middle number or the average of the two middle numbers in a list with an even number of items. Here, the median would be the average of the 12th and 13th number of flowers when all the numbers of flowers are listed in order. In Trial I, there are 7 plants with 1 flower and 6 more with 2 flowers, so the 12th and 13th numbers are both 2. Again, this fits the requirements. Trial III has 5 plants with 0 flowers and 5 more with 1 flower, so the first 10 numbers are 0s or 1s. There are 6 plants with 2 flowers, so the 12th and 13th numbers are both 2. This also fits the requirements. Move on to the mode, which is also easy to determine from a bar graph. The mode is the number that occurs most often, or has the tallest bar. For Trial I, the mode is 1, and for Trial III, the mode is 2. Comparing this with the mean takes a bit more work, though. The mean or the average is the total divided by the number of things. There are 24 plants, so that is the number of things. To find the total, multiply each Number of Flowers by the Number of Plants that had that many flowers, then add them all up. The total in Trial I is $1(7) + 2(6) + 3(3) + 4(4) + 5(2) + 6(1) + 7(1) = 7 + 12 + 9 + 16 + 10 + 6 + 7 = 67$. The mean is $67 \div 24 = 2.79$. This is not equal to the mode, so Trial I does not fit the final requirement. Eliminate (A) and (C), which include Trial I. The correct answer is (D).

20. **D** When asked to create a system of equations or inequalities, translate one piece of information at a time, starting with the most straightforward one, and use process of elimination. The question states that the jeweler *wants to melt down no more than 20 ounces*. The number of ounces of each type of coins is represented by a and b, and *no more than* can be represented by $\leq$. Therefore, one inequality must be $a + b \leq 20$. Eliminate (B) and (C), which do not contain this inequality. Compare the remaining answers: both have a final inequality with the same left-hand side and only differ in the right-hand side of the inequality. The numbers in these two final inequalities relate to the percent of gold in the coins, which was 27% for coin W and 43% for coin Z. The final mixture must be 35% gold. Choice (A) relates the percent multiplied by the ounces of coins on the left side of the inequality to just the percent on the right side. The 35% must be multiplied by a total, which in this case is $a + b$, so $0.35(a + b)$ or $0.35a + 0.35b$ must be part of the inequality. The correct answer is (D).

21. **A** The question asks for a specific amount, so plug in the answers. Start with (B). If there are 560 students taking Biology, then 40% of 560 got a B and 32% of 560 got an A. The number of students that got a B would be $\frac{40}{100}(560) = 224$, and the number that got an A would be $\frac{32}{100}(560) = 179.2$. It is not possible to have 179.2 students, so eliminate (B). The values given for (B) had a difference of $224 - 179.2 = 44.8$, but the question states that 72 more students got B's than A's. Therefore, a larger total is needed. Try (A). If there are 900 Biology students, then $\frac{40}{100}(900) = 360$ got B's and $\frac{32}{100}(900) = 288$ got A's. The difference is $360 - 288 = 72$. The correct answer is (A).

22. **B** When dealing with transformation questions, take one transformation at a time and use process of elimination. When a number is added outside the parentheses of a function, the whole function moves up by that many units. The constant b is positive, so the graph needs to move up. Look at the graphs in each answer choice and see if this is happening. Choice (A) contains a graph that does move up from the origin. Since the graph in (A) *could* be $p(x)$, keep (A). The graph in (B) also moves up, so keep (B). The graph in (C) moves sideways but not up, so eliminate (C). The graph in (D) moves down, so eliminate (D). Compare the graphs (A) and (B). The graph in (A) only moves up, while the graph in (B) moves up and to the right. When a number is subtracted inside the parentheses, the graph moves right. The correct answer is (B).

23. **C** Follow the steps of the geometry basic approach. Label the given information on the figure. The equal angles are already marked, so just label LM as 6 and MN as $4(MP)$. When there are multiple triangles in a question, it is likely testing similar triangles. Since information is given about sides of the large triangle LMN and the small triangle LMP, focus on those. It may be hard to see if they are similar with no angles labeled, so plug in a value for θ and angle m and figure out the remaining angles from there. Make $\theta = 30$ and angle $m = 60$. There are 180 degrees in a triangle, so angles LPM and MLN each equal 90 degrees. Since triangles LMN and LMP now both have a right angle, a 30-degree angle, and a 60-degree angle, they are similar. Similar triangles have proportional sides, so set up a proportion, making sure to match up corresponding sides. In triangle LPM, MP is between the right angle and 60-degree angle. This side corresponds to ML in triangle MLN. The hypotenuses of the two triangles also correspond. If all this is hard to see with the overlapping shapes, redraw the two triangles separately. Now it is possible to set up the proportion $\frac{MP}{ML} = \frac{ML}{MN}$. Plug the information given in the question into the proportion to get $\frac{MP}{6} = \frac{6}{4(MP)}$. Cross-multiply to get $4MP^2 = 36$, then divide both sides by 4 to get $MP^2 = 9$. Take the square root of both sides to get $MP = 3$. The correct answer is (C).

24. **B** If something increases or decreases by a set amount over time, the graph forms a line with a positive (if increasing) or negative (if decreasing) slope. If something changes by a multiple or a percent of its value over time, it forms a curve. To see how this is true, plug in a number for the level of the sulfur dioxide, such as 100 parts per billion. After one year, the level will be 1.05(100 ppb) = 105 ppb; after two years, it will be 1.05(105 ppb) = 110.25 ppb; after three years, it will 1.05(110.25 ppb) = 115.7625 ppb. The graph of this data will form a curve. This is an exponential relationship, not a linear one, so eliminate (C). Choice (A) can also be eliminated, since a quadratic equation forms a parabola, not a curve. The difference between (B) and (D) is the level at the beginning of the study. Looking at the values that resulted from plugging in, the level increased from its starting value and would continue to do so. Therefore, the minimum value occurs at the beginning of the study. The correct answer is (B).

25. **D** Start by reading the full question. The question asks about the expression $\frac{1}{2}\pi x^2$. This resembles the first part of the surface area equation: $2\pi\left(\frac{x^2}{4}\right)$, so focus on that part. If the 2π is distributed to the part in parentheses, the expression becomes $\frac{2\pi x^2}{4} = \frac{1}{2}\pi x^2$. Therefore, the question is asking about the first part of the surface area equation. The surface area is made up of the areas of the circular lid and base and the area covered by the label. Because the term in question originally had a 2 in front of it, it likely represents the sum of the areas of the lid and the base. The formula for the area of a circle is $A = \pi r^2$, and these circles have a diameter of x and a radius of $\frac{x}{2}$. The area of one circle is then $A = \pi\left(\frac{x}{2}\right)^2 = \pi\left(\frac{x^2}{4}\right)$. This doesn't quite match the term in question, but if it is multiplied by 2 to reflect the area of the lid and the base, it becomes $2\pi\left(\frac{x^2}{4}\right)$. Therefore, the term represents the sum of the areas of the base and lid of the can. The correct answer is (D).

26. **A** There are variables in the answer choices, so plug in. If $x = 2$, the expression becomes $[3(2) - 3] + [3(2) - 3]^2 = (6 - 3) + (6 - 3)^2 = 3 + 3^2 = 3 + 9 = 12$. Now plug $x = 2$ into the answer choices to see which one matches this target value. Choice (A) becomes $[3(2) - 3][3(2) - 2] = (6 - 3)(6 - 2) = (3)(4) = 12$. Keep (A), but check the remaining answers just in case. Choice (B) becomes $[3(2) - 3]^3 = (6 - 3)^3 = 3^3 = 27$, which does not match the target value, so eliminate (B). Choice (C) becomes $9(2) - 9 = 18 - 9 = 9$, so eliminate (C). Choice (D) becomes $9(2)^2 - 15(2) - 12 = 9(4) - 30 - 12 = 36 - 42 = -6$, so eliminate (D). The correct answer is (A).

27. **B**   When asked to compare the percent that a value differs from another value, use the percent change

formula: $\dfrac{difference}{original} \times 100$. Use the graph to find the numbers needed to fill in the formula. At day

25, the curve predicts a stock price of $40, but the dot is actually at $60 on that day. The difference

between the two numbers is $60 − $40 = $20. In this question, it can be a little tricky to determine

what the "original" value is, but there are two clues. The question asks for the *observed stock price*

in comparison to *the predicted stock price*, specifically asking what percent more it is. Therefore,

the "original" is the predicted price of $40. The percent change is $\dfrac{\$20}{\$40} \times 100 = \dfrac{1}{2} \times 100 = 50\%$.

The correct answer is (B).

28. **40**   Follow the geometry basic advice by first drawing a rectangular solid shape for the pool. Label all
the information given in the question, such as *depth* = 3 and *length* = *width* + 4. Now write out the
formula for the volume of a rectangular solid, $V = lwd$ and plug in the given information. The formula becomes $288 = (w + 4)(w)(3)$. Divide both sides by 3 to get $96 = (w + 4)(w)$, then distribute on
the right side to get $96 = w^2 + 4w$. To solve for w, set the equation equal to 0 and factor it. Subtract
96 from both sides to get $0 = w^2 + 4w − 96$. This factors into $0 = (w + 12)(w − 8)$, so $w = −12$ or 8.
Since measurements of distance can't be negative, $w = 8$ and $l = 8 + 4 = 12$. The perimeter of the
base is 8 + 12 + 8 + 12 = 40. The correct answer is 40.

29. **18**   When given a system of equations, there are many ways to solve it, so look for the most efficient
way. To find the value of b in this system, try to make the a terms disappear. Multiply both sides
of the first equation by 3 and both sides of the second one by 7 to get matching coefficients with
opposite signs on the a terms. The first equation becomes $3(7a − 6b) = 3(4)$, which simplifies to $21a$
$− 18b = 12$. The second equation becomes $7(−3a + 2b) = 7(−12)$, which simplifies to $−21a + 14b =$
$−84$. Now stack and add the two equations together.

$$
\begin{array}{r}
21a - 18b = 12 \\
\underline{-21a + 14b = -84} \\
-4b = -72
\end{array}
$$

Divide both sides by −4 to get $b = 18$. The correct answer is 18.

30. **3** When a question asks about a ratio within an unknown total, plug in 100 for that total. If 100 people attended the opening, there were 3 friends of the artist for every 2 other attendees. Set up a ratio box to determine the numbers in each group. Put the ratio in the top line, adding the parts to fill in the Total column, and put the total number of attendees in the lower right box.

	Friends	Other attendees	Totals
Ratio	3	2	5
Multiplier			
Actual numbers			100

The 5 in the Ratio row under Totals must be multiplied by 20 to get 100 people, so 20 is the multiplier. The complete ratio box looks like this:

	Friends	Other attendees	Totals
Ratio	3	2	5
Multiplier	20	20	20
Actual numbers	60	40	100

Now take the 60 friends and use that as the Total Actual Number in a new ratio box to determine how many friends bought art. Follow the same steps as above to complete the ratio box.

	Bought	Didn't Buy	Totals
Ratio	1	3	4
Multiplier	15	15	15
Actual numbers	15	45	60

Finally, do the same thing for the 40 other attendees.

	Bought	Didn't Buy	Totals
Ratio	1	7	8
Multiplier	5	5	5
Actual numbers	5	35	40

Given these numbers, the ratio of friends that bought art to other buyers was 15:5. This can be entered as the fraction $\frac{15}{5}$ or reduced to 3. The correct answer is 3.

31. $\frac{1}{4}$ **or 0.25**

Use the information above from the previous explanation regarding how many people fit into each of the four categories—friends versus other attendees and people who purchased art versus those who did not. To find the ratio of buyers to non-buyers, add the friends who bought art to the other attendees who bought art to get 15 + 5 = 20 buyers. The non-buyers are the other 80 people who attended the opening, so the ratio is 20:80. This can be reduced to 1:4. The question says to enter the ratio as a fraction or decimal. The correct answer is $\frac{1}{4}$ or 0.25.

Part V
Practice Test

22 Practice Test
23 Practice Test: Answers and Explanations

Chapter 22
Practice Test

Reading Test

60 MINUTES, 47 QUESTIONS

Turn to Section 1 of your answer sheet to answer the questions in this section.

Questions 1–9 are based on the following passage.

That same morning, a police officer named David Delinko was sent to the future site of another Mother
Line Paula's All-American Pancake House. It was a vacant
5　lot at the corner of East Oriole and Woodbury, on the eastern edge of town.

Officer Delinko was met by a man in a dark blue pickup truck. The man, who was as bald as a beach ball, introduced himself as Curly. Officer Delinko
10　thought the bald man must have a good sense of humor to go by such a nickname, but he was wrong. Curly was cranky and unsmiling.

"You should see what they done," he said to the policeman.

15　"Who?"

"Follow me," the man called Curly said.

Officer Delinko got in step behind him. "The dispatcher said you wanted to report some vandalism."

"That's right," Curly grunted over his shoulder.

20　The policeman couldn't see what there was to be vandalized on the property, which was basically a few acres of scraggly weeds. Curly stopped walking and pointed at a short piece of lumber on the ground. A ribbon of bright pink plastic was tied to one end of the
25　stick. The other end was sharpened and caked with gray dirt.

Curly said, "They pulled 'em out."

"That's a survey stake?" asked Officer Delinko.

"Yep. They yanked 'em out of the ground, every damn one."

30　"Probably just kids."

"And then they threw 'em every which way," Curly said, waving a beefy arm, "and then they filled in the holes."

"That's a little weird," the policeman remarked.
35　"When did this happen?"

"Last night or early this morning," Curly said. "Maybe it don't look like a big deal, but it's gonna take a while to get the site marked out again. Meantime, we can't start clearin' or gradin' or nuthin'. We got
40　backhoes and dozers already leased, and now they gotta sit. I know it don't look like the crime of the century, but still—"

"I understand," said Officer Delinko. "What's your estimate of the monetary damage?"

45　"Damage?"

"Yes. So I can put it in my report." The policeman picked up the survey stake and examined it. "It's not really broken, is it?"

"Well, no—"

50　"Were any of them destroyed?" asked Officer Delinko. "How much does one of these things cost—a buck or two?"

The man called Curly was losing his patience. "They didn't break none of the stakes," he said gruffly.

55　"Not even one?" The policeman frowned. He was trying to figure out what to put in his report. You can't

CONTINUE

have vandalism without monetary damages, and if nothing on the property was broken or defaced....

"What I'm tryin' to explain," Curly said irritably, "it's not that they messed up the survey stakes, it's them screwing up our whole construction schedule. That's where it'll cost some serious bucks."

Officer Delinko took off his cap and scratched his head. "Let me think on this," he said.

Walking back toward the patrol car, the policeman stumbled and fell down. Curly grabbed him under one arm and hoisted him to his feet. Both men were mildly embarrassed.

"Stupid owls," said Curly.

The policeman brushed the dirt and grass burrs off his uniform. "You say owls?"

Curly gestured at a hole in the ground. It was as big around as one of Mother Paula's famous buttermilk flapjacks. A mound of loose white sand was visible at the entrance.

"That's what you tripped over," Curly informed Officer Delinko.

"An owl lives down there?" The policeman bent over and studied the hole. "How big are they?"

"'Bout as tall as a beer can."

"No kidding?" said Officer Delinko.

"But I ain't never seen one, officially speakin'."

Back at the patrol car, the patrolman took out his clipboard and started writing the report. It turned out that Curly's real name was Leroy Branitt, and he was the "supervising engineer" of the construction project. He scowled when he saw the policemen write down "foreman" instead.

Officer Delinko explained to Curly the problem with filing the complaint as a vandalism. "My sergeant's going to kick it back down to me because, technically, nothing really got vandalized. Some kids came on the property and pulled a bunch of sticks out of the ground."

"How do you know it was kids?" Curly muttered.

"Well, who else would it be?"

"What about them fillin' up the holes and throwin' the stakes, just to make us lay out the whole site all over again. What about that?"

It puzzled the policeman, too. Kids usually didn't go to that kind of trouble when pulling a prank...

The policeman put on his sunglasses and slid into his patrol car, which was as hot as a brick oven. He quickly turned on the ignition and cranked the air conditioner up full blast. As he buckled his seatbelt, he said, "Mr. Branitt, there's one more thing I wanted to ask. I'm just curious."

"Fire away," said Curly, wiping his brow with a yellow bandanna.

"It's about those owls."

"Sure."

"What's gonna happen to them?" Office Delinko asked. "Once you start bulldozing, I mean."

Curly the foreman chuckled. He thought the policeman must be kidding.

"What owls?" he said.

1

As used in line 20, "basically" most nearly means

A) formerly.

B) mostly.

C) especially.

D) notably.

2

Based on the passage, how did Delinko react to Curly's vandalism complaint?

A) He was upset about the extent of the damage.

B) He was angry at Curly for calling in a silly report.

C) He was mostly confused about the situation.

D) He was amused that Curly was upset about some stakes.

3

What does the author indicate about Curly's chief complaint about the vandalism?

A) The stakes will be expensive to replace.

B) The owls' habitat was disturbed by the vandals.

C) The construction timeline will have to be pushed back.

D) The vandals created large holes in the parking lot that will have to be filled.

CONTINUE

4

Which choice provides the best evidence for the answer to the previous question?

A) Lines 43–44 ("I understand … damage")

B) Lines 55–56 ("Not even … report")

C) Lines 60–61 ("it's not … schedule")

D) Lines 72–74 ("Curly gestured … flapjacks")

5

In the context of the construction project, Curly's comment in line 82 ("But I … speakin'") mainly serves to

A) present a fact about Curly's interactions with the owls.

B) prove that the owls' safety is a large concern to Curly.

C) introduce a complication that will stop the construction project.

D) show that he doesn't intend to worry about the owls.

6

Based on the passage, which character would most likely agree that something must be physically damaged in order to classify as vandalism?

A) Delinko's sergeant

B) Delinko

C) Curly

D) Mother Paula

7

Which choice provides the best evidence for the answer to the previous question?

A) Lines 50–52 ("Were any … two")

B) Lines 53–54 ("The man … gruffly")

C) Lines 78–79 ("An owl … they")

D) Lines 90–92 ("My sergeant … vandalized")

8

Based on the context of the passage, "grunted" (line 18) and "muttered" (line 95) mainly serve to show Curly's

A) exhaustion.

B) irritation.

C) fury.

D) despair.

9

Based on the passage, when Curly says, "What owls?" (line 116)

A) he doesn't want to acknowledge the owls.

B) he hasn't heard about the owls.

C) he was surprised Delinko knew about the owls.

D) he was worried about the owls.

CONTINUE ➡

Questions 10-18 are based on the following passage and supplementary material.

Originally published on *The Huffington Post,* copyright 2017 of Andrea Friedman. Excerpt reprinted with permission of the author.

In modern violent conflicts the victims are 90%
civilian, mainly women and children (a century ago
that number was 10%). Rape and sexual violence have
Line become an increasingly popular method of warfare,
5 reaching new levels of brutality. Women constitute
an average of 18% of legislatures and parliaments
worldwide. In short, when violence breaks out, women
are substantially less likely to have started or to carry
out the conflict and substantially more likely to suffer
10 at the hands of those who did.

Conflicts leave governing bodies weakened or in
shambles and those who are left must rebuild. Yet too
often the same people are put right back into power
and too often the violence repeats itself. A movement
15 has begun to undermine this cycle of devastation.
Women who have been denied some of their most
basic rights are using these transitions, when the
governance system is in flux and the world is more
likely to be paying attention, to demand that their
20 voices are heard. Security Council Resolution 1325
has increased their leverage. The resolution, adopted
unanimously in October 2000, mandates that women
be included in all aspects of conflict prevention,
reconciliation and post-conflict reconstruction.
25 Change is at hand—and the women of Rwanda are
leading the way.

Rwanda is primarily known as the site of a horrific
genocide during which approximately 800,000 people,
mostly ethnic Tutsis, were brutally murdered in only
30 100 days. It is now the first country to have a majority
of women in the legislature at 56%, up from a high of
18% before the conflict. Women also hold one-third of
the cabinet level posts. This dramatic result came about
because well-organized women crossed party lines to
35 advocate for change, and President Paul Kagame and his
party, the Rwanda Patriotic Front, supported that effort.

The 2003 Rwandan Constitution included a quota
providing for 30% reserved seats for women in all
decision making bodies. In 2008 women filled the 30%
40 quota and then gained another 26% of the seats in the
legislature via the political party ballot, for a total of
56%. The process and quota system is discussed in detail

in a 2004 paper for International IDEA by Elizabeth
Powley, who was in Rwanda tracking these advances
45 for the Initiative for Inclusive Security. According to
Powley, of the 24 women who held the reserved quota
seats from 2003 to 2008, only a small number ran for
those seats again. Some choose not to continue in
politics. Most chose to run on political party ballots in
50 the 2008 election, competing with the men—and many
were successful, which is what catapulted the percentage
of women to 56%. The reserved seats had served as an
incubator for women who might otherwise have been
excluded from the process, giving them the experience
55 and confidence to run in the general election.

Even though Rwanda still faces many barriers to
democratic governance and gender equality, there are
already indications that the women-led legislature is
making an impact. For example, according to a recent
60 report, the parliamentary women's caucus (the Forum
des Femmes Rwandaises Parlementaires or FFRP) led
a successful effort to pass ground-breaking legislation
on gender-based violence in part by involving and
garnering support from their male colleagues.

65 Democracy is an ever-changing and imperfect
experiment. We need to learn from the women of
Rwanda and the men who supported them. Using
quotas to support gender equality not only enables
more representative leadership in struggling nations,
70 but it fosters change—a change that may lead to more
effective leadership and increase the chances for
sustainable peace. And that is good for democracy.

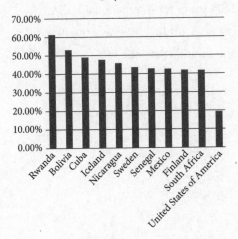

**Percentage of Women in National Parliaments
(July 2017)**

Data sourced from the Inter-Parliamentary Union. July 2017.

CONTINUE ➤

10

Over the course of the passage, the main focus shifts from

A) anecdotes about men in political office to anecdotes about women in political office.

B) a description of an international problem to the way one country is trying to fix that problem.

C) an overview of several different countries' approaches to gender equality to a summary of the barriers they all face.

D) a step-by-step process of how one country solved a problem to an implementation guide for other countries to use that same process.

11

As used in line 15, "undermine" most nearly means

A) weaken.

B) bankrupt.

C) demote.

D) excavate.

12

Which of the following is cited as being the most direct cause for the increase in female legislators in Rwanda?

A) 2003 Rwandan Constitution

B) 2004 paper for International IDEA

C) Initiative for Inclusive Security Act

D) The Rwanda Patriotic Front

13

As used in line 44, "tracking" most nearly means

A) covering.

B) capturing.

C) expelling.

D) hounding.

14

The passage characterizes the women's quota in government decision-making bodies as helpful in that

A) the quotas allowed all the women who held seats in 2003 to keep them in 2008.

B) women who might never have run for office otherwise had the opportunity to do so.

C) complete gender equality was established in Rwandan government.

D) the quota in Rwanda created a plan for gender equality that was easy for other countries to follow.

15

Which choice provides the best evidence for the answer to the previous question?

A) Lines 30–32 ("It is...conflict")

B) Lines 37–39 ("The 2003...bodies")

C) Lines 45–48 ("According to... again")

D) Lines 52–55 ("The reserved... election")

CONTINUE

16

Which of the following best supports the claim that a female-led legislature can make differences that might not be seen with a male-led legislature?

A) Lines 39–42 ("In 2008… 56%")

B) Lines 49–52 ("Most chose…56%")

C) Lines 56–59 ("Even though…impact")

D) Lines 59–64 ("For example… colleagues")

17

According to the graph, which country has just under triple the percentage of women in national government as the United States?

A) Bolivia

B) Finland

C) Iceland

D) Senegal

18

According to the graph, the percentage of women in Nicaragua's government is less than the percentage of women in the government of

A) Mexico

B) Sweden

C) Cuba

D) United States of America

CONTINUE

Questions 19–28 are based on the following passage.

This passage is adapted from "Yellowstone Wolf Project: Annual Report, 2012."

Although wolf packs once roamed from the Arctic tundra to Mexico, they were regarded as dangerous predators, and gradual loss of habitat and
Line deliberate extermination programs led to their demise
5 throughout most of the United States. By 1926, when the National Park Service (NPS) ended its predator control efforts, there were no gray wolf (*Canis lupus*) packs left in Yellowstone National Park (YNP).

In the decades that followed, the importance of
10 the wolf as part of a naturally functioning ecosystem came to be better understood, and the gray wolf was eventually listed as an endangered species in all of its traditional range except Alaska. Where possible, NPS policy calls for restoring native species that have been
15 eliminated as a result of human activity. Because of its large size and abundant prey, the greater Yellowstone area was identified in the recovery plan as one of three areas where the recovery of wolves had a good chance of succeeding.
20 At the end of 2012, at least 83 wolves in 10 packs (6 breeding pairs) occupied YNP. This is approximately a 15% decline from the previous three years when numbers had stabilized at around 100 wolves. Breeding pairs declined slightly from eight the previous year. Wolf
25 numbers in YNP have declined by about 50% since 2007, mostly because of a smaller elk population, the main food of wolves in YNP. State-managed wolf hunts harvested 12 wolves that lived primarily in YNP when these animals moved into Montana and Wyoming.
30 The number of wolves living in the park interior has declined less, probably because they supplement their diet with bison. The severity of mange continued to decline in 2012, although some packs still showed signs of the mite. There was no evidence that distemper
35 was a mortality factor in 2012 as it was in 1999, 2005, and 2008. Pack size ranged from 4 (Blacktail and Snake River) to 11 (Lamar Canyon, Cougar, and Yellowstone Delta) and averaged 10, which is the long-term average. Seven of 11 (64%) packs had pups. The number of
40 wolves observed spending most of their time in the park was significantly fewer than the parkwide peak of 174 in 2003, a decline that was brought about by disease and food stress, and suggests a long-term lower equilibrium for wolves living in YNP, especially on the northern

45 range. Northern range wolves have declined 60% since 2007 compared to only 23% for interior wolves during the same period. Northern range wolves are more dependent on elk as a food source, and elk have declined 60% since 2007. Wolf packs in the interior also prey on
50 bison, which were still widely available in 2012. Disease impacts have also likely played a larger role in the wolf decline on the northern range because of higher canid density (wolves, coyotes, and foxes) than in the interior where density was lower.
55 Wolf–prey relationships were documented by observing wolf predation directly and by recording the characteristics of prey at kill sites. Wolf packs were monitored for two winter-study sessions in 2012 during which wolves were intensively radio-tracked
60 and observed for 30-day periods in March and from mid-November to mid-December. The Blacktail, Agate Creek, and Lamar Canyon packs were the main study packs monitored by three-person ground teams and aircraft during the March session, with the Junction
65 Butte pack replacing the Agate Creek pack for the November–December session. Additionally, other park packs (Canyon, Cougar Creek, Mary Mountain, Mollie's, Quadrant, 8-mile) were monitored from only aircraft. The Delta pack was monitored less intensively
70 because of logistical constraints and the Bechler pack (no radio collars) was unable to be located. Data from downloadable GPS collars was also utilized to detect predation events for wolves from the Agate Creek, Blacktail, Lamar Canyon, and Junction Butte packs
75 during winter studies and also during a spring–summer (May–July) monitoring period. During these established predation studies, and opportunistically throughout the year, project staff recorded behavioral interactions between wolves and prey, kill rates, total time wolves
80 fed on carcasses, percent consumption of kills by scavengers, characteristics of wolf prey (e.g., sex, species, nutritional condition), and characteristics of kill sites.

Given the controversy surrounding wolf impacts on ungulate populations, wolf and elk interactions
85 continue to be a primary focus of predation studies in YNP. The northern Yellowstone elk population has declined since wolf reintroduction. In addition to wolves, factors affecting elk population dynamics include other predators, management of elk outside
90 the park, and weather patterns (e.g., drought, weather severity). Weather patterns influence forage quality

CONTINUE ➡

and availability, ultimately impacting elk nutritional condition. Consequently, changes in prey selection and kill rates through time result from complex
95 interactions among these factors.

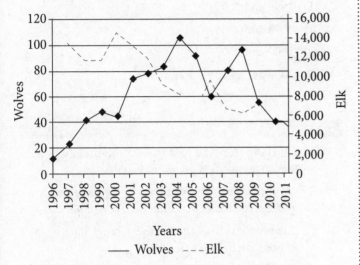

Yellowstone National Park Northern Range Elk-Wolf Populations, 1995–2010.

The main purpose of the passage is to

A) evaluate causes of a disturbance.

B) present detailed scientific observations.

C) suggest a solution to a population decline.

D) reject an alternative ecological proposal.

Which choice most closely captures the meaning of the "predator control efforts" referred to in lines 6–7?

A) Natural outcome

B) Animal extinction

C) Only solution

D) Pest removal

The main purpose of the second paragraph of the passage is to

A) apologize for the unfortunate eradication of wolves in Yellowstone National Park.

B) reconcile past evidence with contemporary knowledge about wolf populations.

C) explain a change of policy affecting wolves and the manner in which it was pursued.

D) demand that wolf populations be reinstated to their historical peak.

According to the passage, one potential cause of wolf population decline is proximity to

A) other canines.

B) elk.

C) tundra.

D) kill sites.

Which choice provides the best evidence for the answer to the previous question?

A) Lines 1–5 ("Although wolf…States")

B) Lines 32–34 ("The severity…mite")

C) Lines 50–54 ("Disease impacts…lower")

D) Lines 55–57 ("Wolf-prey relationships…sites")

CONTINUE

24

According to the passage, what was true of the wolf packs in the 2012 study?

A) A few were primarily responsible for elk predation.

B) Some responded more favorably to the tracking collars.

C) All experienced a decline in population.

D) Some were easier to track than others.

25

Which choice provides the best evidence for the answer to the previous question?

A) Lines 45–47 ("Northern range…period")

B) Lines 61–66 ("The Blacktail…session")

C) Lines 69–71 ("The Delta…located")

D) Lines 78–82 ("project staff…sites")

26

As used in line 88, "dynamics" most nearly means

A) changes.

B) explosions.

C) fates.

D) gains.

27

According to the table, the northern range wolf population experienced the largest change between which of the following years?

A) 1999 and 2001

B) 2004 and 2006

C) 2007 and 2009

D) 2008 and 2010

28

Which claim from the passage is most directly supported by the data given in the table?

A) Wolf numbers have declined by a greater percentage than elk numbers have overall.

B) Elk numbers in in the northern range have been more than halved since 2007.

C) Wolf numbers and elk numbers have reached similar peaks, but in different years.

D) Elk numbers continue to be studied as a result of reintroducing wolves into the environment.

CONTINUE

Questions 29–38 are based on the following passages.

Passage 1 is adapted from John Locke, "On Slavery and Natural Liberty." Originally published in 1690. Passage 2 is adapted from a speech made by Frederick Douglass, "Abolition Fanaticism in New York." Locke wrote his treatise in the United Kingdom before the founding of the United States. Douglass's speech was made in the Tabernacle in New York, NY on May 11, 1847.

Passage 1

Slavery is so vile and miserable an estate of man, and so directly opposite to the generous temper and courage of our nation, that it is hardly to be conceived
Line that an "Englishman," much less a "gentleman," should
5 plead for it. And truly I should have taken this, as any other treatise which would persuade all men that they are slaves, and ought to be so, for such another exercise of wit as was his who writ the encomium of Nero, rather than for a serious discourse meant in earnest,
10 had not the gravity of the title and epistle, the picture in the front of Sir Robert's book, and the applause that followed it, required me to believe that the author and publisher were both in earnest. I therefore took the Patriarcha of Sir Robert Filmer into my hands with
15 all the expectation, and read it through with all the attention, due to a treatise that made such a noise at its coming abroad, and cannot but confess myself mightily surprised that, in a book which was to provide chains for all mankind, I should find nothing but a rope of
20 sand, useful, perhaps, to such whose skill and business it is to raise a dust, and would blind the people the better to mislead them, but is not of any force to draw those into bondage who have their eyes open, and so much sense about them as to consider that chains are
25 but an ill wearing, how much care soever hath been taken to file and polish them.

If any one think I take too much liberty in speaking so freely of a man who is the great champion of absolute power, and the idol of those who worship it, I
30 beseech him to make this small allowance for once to one who, even after the reading of Sir Robert's book, cannot but think himself, as the laws allow him, a freeman, and I know no fault it is to do so, unless any one better skilled in the fate of it than I, should have
35 it revealed to him that this treatise, which has lain dormant so long, was, when it appeared in the world, to carry by strengths of its arguments all liberty out of it, and that from thenceforth our author's short model was to be the pattern in the Mount and the

40 perfect standard of politics for the future. His system lies in a little compass. It is no more but this, "That all government is absolute monarchy." And the ground he builds on, is this, "That no man is born free."

Passage 2

I am very glad to be here. I am very glad to be
45 present at this Anniversary—glad again to mingle my voice with those with whom I have stood identified, with those with whom I have labored, for the last seven years, for the purpose of undoing the burdens of my brethren, and hastening the day of their emancipation.

50 I do not doubt but that a large portion of this audience will be disappointed, both by the *manner* and the *matter* of what I shall this day set forth. The extraordinary and unmerited eulogies which have been showered upon me, here and elsewhere, have done
55 much to create expectations which, I am well aware, I can never hope to gratify. I am here, a simple man, knowing what I have experienced in Slavery, knowing it to be a bad system, and desiring, by all Christian means, to seek its overthrow. I am not here to please you with
60 an eloquent speech, with a refined and logical address, but to speak to you the sober truths of a heart overborne with gratitude to God that we have in this land, cursed as it is with Slavery, so noble a band to second my efforts and the efforts of others in the noble work of undoing
65 the Yoke of Bondage, with which the majority of the States of this Union are now unfortunately cursed.

You are aware, doubtless, that my object in going from this country, was to get beyond the reach of the clutch of the man who claimed to own me as his
70 property. I had written a book giving a history of that portion of my life spent in the gall and bitterness and degradation of Slavery, and in which I also identified my oppressors as the perpetrators of some of the most atrocious crimes. This had deeply incensed them
75 against me, and stirred up within them the purpose of revenge, and my whereabouts being known, I believed it necessary for me, if I would preserve my liberty, to leave the shores of America, and take up my abode in some other land, at least until the excitement occasioned by
80 the publication of my Narrative had subsided. I went to England, Monarchical England, to get rid of Democratic Slavery, and I must confess that, at the very threshold, I was satisfied that I had gone to the right place. Say what you will of England—of the degradation—of the

CONTINUE ➡

poverty—and there is much of it there—say what you will
85 of the oppression and suffering going on in England at
this time, there is Liberty there—there is Freedom there,
not only for the white man, but for the black man also.

Weapons of war we have cast from the battle: Truth
is our armor—our watchword is Love; Hushed be the
90 sword, and the musketry's rattle,

All our equipments are drawn from above. Praise
then the God of Truth, Hoary age and ruddy youth.

Long may our rally be Love, Light and Liberty;
Ever our banner the banner of Peace.

29

As used in line 16, "noise" most nearly means

A) impact.

B) crash.

C) announcement.

D) sound.

30

Locke makes which point about the effectiveness of
the argument in the Patriarcha?

A) It is limited in its ability to convince
knowledgeable men such as himself.

B) It was poorly based upon archaic Roman writing
that has been proven incorrect.

C) It reasonably defends the position that no man is
ever truly free.

D) It demands a critical rethinking of conventional
English political wisdom.

31

Which choice provides the best evidence for the
answer to the previous question?

A) Lines 1–5 ("Slavery is … it")

B) Lines 5–9 ("I should … earnest")

C) Lines 19–23 ("I should … open")

D) Lines 38–40 ("thenceforth our … future")

32

As used in line 45, "mingle" most nearly means

A) converse.

B) share.

C) modulate.

D) shout.

33

According to Douglass, slavery as an institution
should not be

A) practiced by a minority of the States in the Union.

B) viewed as less detrimental to a free society than
monarchy.

C) accepted silently while waiting for an inevitable
emancipation.

D) escaped by any means available if it endangers
others.

34

Which choice provides the best evidence for the
answer to the previous question?

A) Lines 47–49 ("I have … emancipation")

B) Lines 56–59 ("I am … overthrow")

C) Lines 76–79 ("I believed … land")

D) Lines 80–83 ("I went … place")

35

The primary purpose of each passage is to

A) demand immediate governmental change by
citing a higher authority.

B) challenge a contemporary opinion using personal
experience as evidence.

C) suggest leaving one's country is the best way to
pursue individual freedom.

D) attack the legitimacy of divine absolute monarchy.

CONTINUE

36

In the passages, a significant difference in how the two authors discuss England is that Douglass views it as

A) completely lacking the oppression and suffering existing in the United States.

B) a justly ruled land that proves the benevolence of a king.

C) fundamentally flawed and beset by numerous social problems.

D) a society that can provide the oppressed an opportunity for freedom.

37

Both authors would most likely agree with which statement about all men?

A) They yearn for the perfect authority of an undemocratic government.

B) They must all rise in unison to end the tyranny of slavery.

C) They are not naturally subjected to the chains of bondage.

D) They are incapable of ending slavery without assistance from the government.

38

Based on his statements in Passage 1, Locke would most likely view Douglass's observations regarding England in Passage 2 as

A) an ineffective proclamation for slavery to end worldwide.

B) a terrible attack on the honor of the English people.

C) a justified plea for a corrupt monarchy to be overthrown.

D) a welcome indication of major social progress.

CONTINUE

Questions 39–47 are based on the following passage.

Each year, scientists publish roughly 17,000 detailed descriptions of newly discovered animals. Recently, in the journal Breviora, researchers described yet another,

Line a new species of lizard called *Aspidoscelis neavesi.*

5   At first glance, this seems to be a run-of-the mill lizard: a small, slender creature with spots along its back and a bluish tail. In fact, *Aspidoscelis neavesi* is quite exceptional. The lizard was produced in the laboratory by mating two other species, and its creation defies

10 conventional ideas about how new species evolve.

The evolution of a new animal species is usually a drawn-out affair. Typically, an existing animal population is somehow divided, and the newly isolated populations reproduce only among themselves. Over

15 thousands of generations, the animals may become genetically distinct and can no longer interbreed.

Of course, scientists have long known that some related species sometimes interbreed. But the hybrid progeny generally were thought to be evolutionary

20 dead-ends—sterile mules, for instance. In recent decades, however, researchers have learned that these hybrids may represent new species.

Some of the most striking examples occur among whiptail lizards, which live in the southwestern United

25 States. In the 1960s, scientists noticed that some whiptail lizard species had a strange genetic makeup. They have two copies of each chromosome, just as we do, but each copy is very different from its counterpart. The genes look as if they come from different species.

30   Perhaps stranger, many species produce no males. The eggs of the females hatch healthy female clones, a process known as parthenogenesis.

Normally, unfertilized animal eggs have only one set of chromosomes. But parthenogenic female

35 whiptail lizards can duplicate the chromosomes in their offspring without males.

These findings led scientists to a hypothesis for how these strange species came about: Sometimes individuals from two different species of whiptail

40 lizards interbreed, and their hybrid offspring carry two different sets of chromosomes.

Somehow, this triggers a switch to parthenogenesis. The female hybrids start to produce clones distinct from either parental species. In other words, they

45 instantly become a new species of their own.

But it gets even more bizarre. Some species of whiptail lizards carry three sets of genes, rather than two.

How can that be? Scientists hypothesized that male lizards from sexually reproducing species sometimes

50 mated with parthenogenic females. Sometimes, their sperm succeeded in fertilizing a female's eggs, which already contained two sets of chromosomes. The egg now had three sets, and voilà: yet another a new species.

The strangeness doesn't end there. In 1967, a

55 Harvard graduate student named William B. Neaves was searching for whiptails around Alamogordo, N.M., when he found one with *four* sets of chromosomes.

Dr. Neaves didn't follow up on this finding, instead pursuing a career researching fertility and stem cells.

60 But at a dinner in 2002, he mentioned the whiptail lizards to Peter Baumann, a molecular biologist at Stowers Institute for Medical Research, where Dr. Neaves served as president.

Dr. Baumann decided it was high time to use new

65 scientific tools to study whiptail lizards, and he and Dr. Neaves started making road trips to New Mexico to catch them and take them back to Stowers. As they came to understand the biology of the lizards better, they and their colleagues began to bring different

70 species together to see if they could hybridize. Most of the time, their experiments failed.

In 2008, the scientists tried to recreate the hybrid with four sets of chromosomes. They put female *Aspidoscelis exsanguis* (the parthenogenic species with

75 three sets of chromosomes) and male *Aspidoscelis inornata* in the same containers. In short order, the lizards started mating, and the females laid eggs. When the eggs hatched, the scientists examined the genes of the baby lizards and found four sets of chromosomes.

80   Four of the new hybrids were females. To the delight of the scientists, the females could clone themselves—and the offspring could produce clones of their own. Today, the scientists have a colony of 200 of these lizards….

CONTINUE ▶

39

Over the course of the passage, the main focus shifts from

A) a description of how scientists discover new species to how those scientists publish their findings.

B) an explanation of typical animal reproduction to a study concerning atypical reproduction.

C) a general overview of cloning to a specific look at different forms of cloning.

D) the introduction of a newly-discovered species to a series of increasingly surprising discoveries about that species.

40

The phrase "At first glance" (line 5) mainly serves to

A) indicate the author is beginning a visual description.

B) offer a non-scientific observation before providing a more detailed clinical one.

C) how what scientists believed absolutely true prior to their research.

D) present an impression that will later be disproven.

41

The central claim of the fourth paragraph (lines 17–22) is that

A) further research into these lizards will lead to a dead-end.

B) the genetic capabilities of the new lizard species are more complex than researchers first believed.

C) what researchers believe about genetic hybrids is changing because of this new species.

D) the mule is more likely to die out than the whiptail lizard.

42

As used in line 23, "striking" most nearly means

A) painful.

B) wonderful.

C) impressive.

D) alarming.

43

According to the passage, one difference between the whiptail lizards and other species of hybrids is that the hybrid female lizards

A) are sterile, much like mules and other hybrid species.

B) are able to reproduce on their own, creating genetically exact copies of themselves.

C) are able to reproduce, but only with males that have the same chromosomes as the females.

D) always have three sets of chromosomes, rather than two.

44

Which choice provides the best evidence for the answer to the previous question?

A) Lines 18–20 ("But the … instance")

B) Lines 31–32 ("The eggs … parthenogenesis")

C) Lines 46–47 ("Some species … two")

D) Lines 48–50 ("Scientists hypothesized … females")

CONTINUE

45

The main idea of the eleventh paragraph (lines 48–53) is that

A) every hybrid species is incomparably more complex than scientists originally hypothesized.

B) evidence provided more questions than answers regarding the reproductive capabilities of hybrids.

C) further study of the whiptail lizard might ultimately enable scientists to clone other animals.

D) parthenogenesis is the primary reason the whiptail lizard is flourishing in a desert environment.

46

According to the passage, progress in genetic research of the whiptail lizard in the 21st century came about as a result of

A) advancements in research technology.

B) teamwork between scientists who were previously professional rivals.

C) the discovery of the whiptail lizard in New Mexico.

D) the discovery and classification of parthenogenesis.

47

Which choice provides the best evidence for the answer to the previous question?

A) Lines 34–36 ("But parthenogenic … males")

B) Line 46 ("But it … bizarre")

C) Lines 54–57 ("In 1967 … chromosomes")

D) Lines 64–67 ("Dr. Baumann … Stowers")

STOP
**If you finish before time is called, you may check your work on this section only.
Do not turn to any other section in the test.**

No Test Material On This Page

CONTINUE

Writing and Language Test

35 MINUTES, 44 QUESTIONS

Turn to Section 2 of your answer sheet to answer the questions in this section.

DIRECTIONS

Each passage below is accompanied by a number of questions. For some questions, you will consider how the passage might be revised to improve the expression of ideas. For other questions, you will consider how the passage might be edited to correct errors in sentence structure, usage, or punctuation. A passage or a question may be accompanied by one or more graphics (such as a table or graph) that you will consider as you make revising and editing decisions.

Some questions will direct you to an underlined portion of a passage. Other questions will direct you to a location in a passage or ask you to think about the passage as a whole.

After reading each passage, choose the answer to each question that most effectively improves the quality of writing in the passage or that makes the passage conform to the conventions of standard written English. Many questions include a "NO CHANGE" option. Choose that option if you think the best choice is to leave the relevant portion of the passage as it is.

Questions 1–11 are based on the following passage.

A Pie Rich with Flavor—and History

In the British region of Cornwall, the hand-held pie called a pasty has been a culinary staple for centuries. **1** Descended from the meat pies of medieval England, the Cornish pasty had gained widespread popularity by the nineteenth century. It was a common meal for laborers, especially miners, in the region.

Which choice most effectively combines the underlined sentences?

A) Descended from the meat pies of medieval England, the Cornish pasty by the nineteenth century was in the region a common meal for laborers, especially miners, and had gained widespread popularity.

B) Descended from the meat pies of medieval England, the Cornish pasty had gained widespread popularity by the nineteenth century as a meal for laborers, especially miners, in the region.

C) Descended from the meat pies of medieval England, the Cornish pasty had gained widespread popularity for laborers, especially miners, by the nineteenth century as a common meal in the region.

D) The Cornish pasty was a common meal in the region, and had gained widespread popularity by the nineteenth century, descending from the meat pies of medieval England, for laborers, especially miners.

CONTINUE →

Today, the pasty—a semi-circular pastry stuffed with meat, onions, and root vegetables—is so deeply associated with Cornwall that **2** it had earned from the European Union a designation as a protected regional food, like Champagne or Provolone cheese. The shape and ingredients of the pasty do more, though, than simply link the pastries to those **3** whom live in Cornwall. The composition of the pasty (whose name rhymes with "nasty," not "hasty") also **4** reflects the social history of the region, and the hand-pie's global popularity today echoes broader historical trends in labor and migration.

5 For example, the shape made a pasty **6** conveniently easy to carry and eat without cutlery or to reheat over a candle if it had gotten cold by lunchtime. The thick crimped crust that seals the pie along its curved edge might also have played a role in the pie's popularity.

2

A) NO CHANGE

B) it has

C) they have

D) they had

3

A) NO CHANGE

B) who live

C) which live

D) who lives

4

A) NO CHANGE

B) which reflects

C) reflecting

D) reflected

5

Which choice best introduces the paragraph?

A) In Cornwall, pasties were prepared for miners to take for lunch each day.

B) Not all diners in Cornwall agree about the best pasty shape.

C) Traditional pasty-making involves spreading the filling in the center of the pastry, then folding the pie in half and crimping together the curved edges to make a D-shape.

D) Contemporary diners might take the pasty's distinctive shape for granted, but in centuries past, the pie's form was key to its success as a miner's meal.

6

A) NO CHANGE

B) easy and convenient

C) simple and easy

D) easy

CONTINUE

Some historians speculate that miners would hold the crust [7] like a handle: for instance, then discard it when they were finished eating to avoid ingesting any dust (or arsenic) from their fingers. Others, however, point to photographs that show pasties were eaten end-to-end, arguing that the pasties were often carried in cloth, which kept away dust, and that it is unlikely that hungry miners would willingly waste food.

The pasty's stuffing was also crucial to the pie's popularity across the centuries, since it combines vegetables, carbohydrates, and protein for a complete, compact meal. [8] Because the EU's definition of the "official" Cornish pasty calls for the pie to contain at least 12.5% beef, the earliest recipes for pasties involved venison, and the working-class bakers responsible for preparing the pies in previous centuries used whatever meat was most affordable—often pork. [9] This diversity of options continues today: in Cornwall and elsewhere, contemporary pasty fillings can include fish, rabbit, vegetarian proteins, or even sweet ingredients like apple or chocolate.

7

A) NO CHANGE
B) like a handle, for instance,
C) like a handle for instance,
D) like a handle for instance—

8

A) NO CHANGE
B) Moreover,
C) Despite this convenience,
D) While

9

At this point, the writer is considering adding the following sentence.

> The EU defines protected regional foods to ensure that only foods that genuinely originate in a particular area or have particular distinguishing characteristics can be marketed as such.

Should the writer make this addition here?

A) Yes, because it clarifies what makes the EU's definition "official."

B) Yes, because it adds to the paragraph's explanation of why the term "Cornish pasty" is popular.

C) No, because it digresses from the paragraph's discussion of the variety of pasty fillings available in the past and in the present.

D) No, because it should be placed at the beginning of the paragraph instead.

CONTINUE

Since **10** collapsing Cornwall's mining industry in the mid-nineteenth century, many laborers immigrated elsewhere in search of work— **11** which is why today the pasty flourishes in locations from Australia to Montana to Mexico. Whether we encounter the pasty at a street festival in Michigan or a bakery in western England, however, the Cornish pie's global influence should remind us of the rich social histories underlying the substance and structure of the foods we eat.

10

A) NO CHANGE

B) they collapsed Cornwall's mining industry

C) Cornwall's mining industry collapsed

D) their collapsing of Cornwall's mining industry

11

Which choice most clearly connects the statement made earlier in the sentence to the theme of the rest of the paragraph?

A) NO CHANGE

B) which is interesting, since many other nations already had traditional hand-pie recipes.

C) leading to the decline of the pasty in Cornwall.

D) which contributed to a global mining boom.

CONTINUE

Questions 12-22 are based on the following passage and supplementary material.

Studies in Dog Evolution

From the Chihuahua to the [12] Newfoundland, domestic dogs inhabit our homes and trot along sidewalks in an array of sizes, colors, personalities, and body shapes. Domestication from their wolf ancestors has clearly involved temperamental as well as physical changes over the course of many [13] generation after generation. Recent studies show that wild foxes can be domesticated within several decades through selective [14] breeding and anecdotal evidence suggests that individual fox pups raised from birth by humans can behave remarkably like domesticated dogs. Wolves, however, do not respond similarly to domestication efforts. This fact led some scientists to wonder if it is possible that some ancient wolves possessed an unusual potential to socialize or bond with others that made possible a closer relationship with humans.

A recent study by animal behaviorist Monique Udell and geneticist Bridgett vonHoldt supports this "survival of the friendliest" idea. The scientists compared the behavior of 10 wolves that had been raised in captivity with that of 18 dogs (some purebred, some not) to confirm that the dogs [15] were, across the board, significantly friendlier toward humans than even hand-raised wolves.

[12]

A) NO CHANGE
B) Newfoundland, however,
C) Newfoundland, of course,
D) Newfoundland, moreover,

[13]

A) NO CHANGE
B) generations that resulted from breeding.
C) generations.
D) generations bred from the previous generations.

[14]

A) NO CHANGE
B) breeding, and anecdotal evidence suggests
C) breeding: and anecdotal evidence suggests
D) breeding and anecdotal evidence suggesting

[15]

A) NO CHANGE
B) were across the board,
C) were: across the board
D) were, across the board

CONTINUE

16 The dogs spent much more time interacting with the people than the wolves did. They did so when confronted with strangers. Next, the researchers looked at the canine equivalent of a genetic sequence that, when altered in humans, can lead to very trusting, hypersocial behavior. In dogs, this sequence is located on **17** chromosome 6. Whose important role in canine evolution more generally had already been established. The scientists found that the dogs in their study had more disruptions to that genetic sequence than did the wolves. Udell and vonHoldt concluded that these kinds of **18** genetic disruptions might have contributed to some ancient wolves' willingness to interact with humans at the beginning of the domestication process.

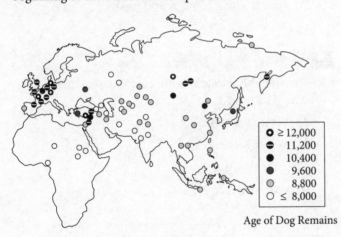

◔	≥ 12,000
◑	11,200
●	10,400
●	9,600
●	8,800
○	≤ 8,000

Age of Dog Remains

16

Which choice most effectively combines the underlined sentences?

A) Interacting with strangers is what dogs do, and this meant they spent much more time interacting with people than the wolves did.

B) Even when confronted with strangers, the dogs spent much more time interacting with the people than the wolves did.

C) The dogs spent much more time interacting with people than the wolves did; in addition, they were confronted with strangers.

D) The dogs spent much more time interacting with people than the wolves did, and they were confronted with strangers.

17

A) NO CHANGE

B) chromosome 6; whose

C) chromosome 6, whose

D) chromosome 6,

18

A) NO CHANGE

B) genetic disruption's

C) genetics disruptions

D) genetic disruptions'

CONTINUE

[1] Their findings are particularly interesting in light of fossil records. [2] In the areas between those locations, the fossil record dates to significantly later—the bones found around what is now India and Greece are **19** 7,000 years old. [3] The earliest fossil evidence indicates that dogs were present in specific areas of both eastern and western Eurasia: bones that are around 12,000 years old have been found in **20** central and western Africa. [4] A team led by archaeologist and geneticist Greger Larson has argued that this evidence suggests that humans domesticated dogs independently in two regions, and that one population of humans and dogs subsequently migrated west from eastern Asia. **21**

However one interprets the migration patterns underlying the fossil record, though, Udell and vonHoldt's study **22** is pointing to one component of the animal genome that seems to have contributed to the powerful bonds so many people have with their dogs.

19

Which choice makes the writer's description of data represented in the figure most accurate?

A) NO CHANGE

B) fewer in number than the bones found elsewhere.

C) less than 9,000 years old.

D) no less than 10,000 years old.

20

Which choice makes the writer's description of data represented in the figure most accurate?

A) NO CHANGE

B) both France and western Russia

C) only the coasts of Asia

D) only northern Europe and Iceland

21

To make this paragraph most logical, sentence 2 should be placed

A) where it is now.

B) before sentence 1.

C) after sentence 3.

D) after sentence 4.

22

A NO CHANGE

B) has pointed

C) pointed

D) points

CONTINUE ▶

Questions 23-33 are based on the following passage.

Making Music For One World

In 1963, six musicians in Kingston, Jamaica, formed a band called the Wailing Wailers. Their sound drew from Jamaica's shifting music scene, at a time when the up-tempo rhythms of ska were slowing into reggae using elements not only 23 the Caribbean's traditional music but also of American jazz and R&B. The Wailers' socially- and politically-inflected lyrics reflected 24 the musicians' experiences. Within three years, the band had 25 increased some local success but was not making much money, and only three band members remained: Peter Tosh, Neville Livingston, and Bob Marley.

The Wailers pushed reggae's boundaries with an integration of rock 'n' roll elements and honest lyrics about violence, faith, and poverty. In the early 1970s, they started working with producer Chris Blackwell; their next two albums, released in 1973, received much critical and popular acclaim. However, amidst a reception that amounted to the band's big 26 breakthrough. Creative and personal differences among the members were magnified, and the Wailers disbanded in 1974.

23

A) NO CHANGE
B) traditional music of the Caribbean
C) traditionally Caribbean music
D) of traditional Caribbean music

24

The writer is considering revising the underlined portion to the following.

> the musicians' experiences of turmoil, racism, and hardship in the recently decolonized country.

Should the writer make this revision?

A) Yes, because it further clarifies the nature of the experiences the musicians drew on.
B) Yes, because it helps the reader to understand what decolonization is.
C) No, because it digresses from the paragraph's main point about the Wailing Wailers' formation.
D) No, because it paints an unnecessarily negative picture of the band members' lives.

25

A) NO CHANGE
B) weighed heavily
C) added onto
D) gained

26

A) NO CHANGE
B) breakthrough, creative
C) breakthrough: creative
D) breakthrough—creative

27 Debate still rages about the elements that played a role in Marley's success, particularly since his disagreements with Tosh and Livingston **28** centered on, through revolving, his willingness, in pursuit of a wider audience, to accept concessions that his bandmates refused to make. What is not in doubt is that Marley's music stayed inextricably linked to his religious faith as a Rastafarian and that his lyrics called for peace and compassion among conflicting groups.

In the U.S., Marley's genre-blending approach to music affected how the music industry positioned his songs within existing categories like "rock," "R&B" and "pop." Indeed, his success contributed to the creation of the new category "world music" to accommodate artists whose influences and music lay outside the industry's conventional divisions. By 1980, with worldwide fame, strong record sales, and a recent tour of Europe, Marley was firmly taking **29** a hold to the opportunities presented to him. Then, while jogging, he suffered a **30** collapse, it heralded his decline and death from melanoma at age 36.

27

At this point, the writer is considering adding the following sentence.

> After parting ways with Livingston and Tosh, Bob Marley embarked on a very successful solo career, touring and recording with his backup band and backup singers as Bob Marley and the Wailers.

Should the writer make this addition here?

A) Yes, because it explains what roles Livingston and Tosh played in Marley's new band.

B) Yes, because it establishes that the success discussed in the next sentence extended beyond Marley's time in the Wailing Wailers.

C) No, because it distracts from the paragraph's focus on the material in the albums made in 1973.

D) No, because it simply repeats an idea mentioned in the previous paragraph.

28

A) NO CHANGE

B) centered on and revolved around

C) centered on

D) were at their center about

29

A) NO CHANGE

B) ahold of

C) a whole of

D) a hold of

30

A) NO CHANGE

B) collapse, that

C) collapse that

D) collapse which

CONTINUE

31 Because Marley was talented and charismatic, his influence endures. The reggae historian Roger Steffens estimates that at least 500 books have been written about Marley, and *Forbes* calculated that his estate's earnings in 2014 made him the sixth-highest-earning dead celebrity in that year. His biggest legacy, **32** therefore, might be the doors he helped to open for artists outside the U.S. and Europe. In 2010, *Rolling Stone* placed him 11th on its list of the 100 Greatest Artists, identifying him as the musician **33** who "almost single-handedly brought reggae to the world." Singing of his own experiences and deep faith, he led the way for others to add their voices to the stories popular music tells.

31

The writer wants a transition that makes a connection to the final idea of the previous paragraph. Which choice best accomplishes this goal?

A) NO CHANGE

B) Since Bob Marley stood for peace even when violent factions threatened his life,

C) Because so many musicians still cite Bob Marley as an inspiration,

D) Almost 40 years after Bob Marley's death,

32

A) NO CHANGE

B) necessarily,

C) though,

D) thus,

33

A) NO CHANGE

B) who:

C) who,

D) who—

CONTINUE

Questions 34-44 are based on the following passage.

A Multimedia Approach to Artistic Success

In decades past, the primary path for aspiring artists was through art galleries. Artists worked to secure space in galleries **34** hopefully attracting the attention of art critics and wealthy collectors. In turn, that attention might lead to some museum shows that would gain the artist a broader popular following. These days, however, many artists seeking a wider audience are utilizing a different means—the Internet—to maximize **35** their visibility to more people.

In the old model, individual critics and curators mediated which arts and crafts the general public **36** bumped into and where and how that happened. Now, artists have more control. Internet venues provide more opportunities for artists to showcase their work—and more options for art buyers as well. A website called Saatchi Art, **37** however, markets itself as an "online gallery" where customers can shop for art by medium and by price point—with prices in the thousands for high-end works by artists with formal training and burgeoning careers. At the other end of the spectrum, the flourishing of the "maker movement" and the popularity of DIY crafts have inspired online venues featuring works **38** by artists who focus on collaboration.

34

A) NO CHANGE
B) hoping to
C) in hopes of
D) DELETE the underlined portion.

35

A) NO CHANGE
B) the number of people who see their work.
C) their visibility.
D) how visible their work is to many people.

36

A) NO CHANGE
B) happened to stumble across
C) encountered
D) apprehended

37

A) NO CHANGE
B) moreover,
C) instead,
D) for example,

38

Which choice most effectively completes the contrast between the productions mentioned in this sentence and those mentioned in the previous sentence?

A) NO CHANGE
B) by artists famous for their gallery shows.
C) by artists who charge exorbitant prices.
D) by part-time or amateur artists.

CONTINUE ➡

Many social-media platforms allow artists to share not only the photos that showcase finished products but also **39** those that capture the chaos and inspiration of the creation process. **40** Other websites offer craftspeople a platform to start and grow their own businesses according to their own business models. When an artist opens an online shop, he or she controls what kinds of items are offered, how they are priced, and how they are presented **41** to the public, through photos and written listings).

39

A) NO CHANGE

B) those the chaos' and inspiration's

C) those the chaos and inspiration

D) those that capturing the chaos and inspiration

40

At this point, the writer is considering adding the following sentence.

> Most potential buyers will already be familiar with the options to "like" or "share" an image, which are quick ways for people to respond to things they see posted.

Should the writer add this sentence here?

A) Yes, because it supports the writer's claim that social-media outlets provide artists with more control over how their works reach an audience.

B) Yes, because it defines all the ways that a consumer can interact with an artist's work on these websites.

C) No, because it should be placed instead at the end of the paragraph to support the claim that the artwork must speak for itself.

D) No, because it presents information that distracts from the writer's focus in this paragraph on the increased control that Internet venues offer to artists.

41

A) NO CHANGE

B) to the public (through

C) to the public—through

D) to the public: through

[1] In some ways, the abundance of artists now listing their work on Internet sites mirrors the saturation of artists vying for gallery space. [2] Thus, to most effectively build a base of customers, artists must learn how to make their work readily findable through a digital search. [3] For example, a social media outlet helps its sellers maintain a multimedia presence by allowing them to link <u>there</u> 42 business pages to accounts on other social media platforms. [4] The key difference is that instead of physical geography dictating which gallery walls a potential buyer encounters, search engine serendipity and savvy determine what pops up first in an Internet search. [5] Maintaining multiple accounts can take a fair amount of time and energy, but such efforts are becoming essential to effective Internet marketing. 43

Understandably, some people might shy away from the degree of self-promotion required to make the best use of the Internet. Nevertheless, if you're an aspiring craftsperson or artist trying to find 44 <u>your</u> audience, the resources and benefits of online platforms are hard to discount.

42

A) NO CHANGE
B) its
C) it's
D) their

43

To make this paragraph most logical, sentence 4 should be placed

A) before sentence 1.
B) after sentence 1.
C) after sentence 3.
D) after sentence 5.

44

A) NO CHANGE
B) his or her
C) their
D) one's

STOP
**If you finish before time is called, you may check your work on this section only.
Do not turn to any other section in the test.**

No Test Material On This Page

Math Test – No Calculator

25 MINUTES, 17 QUESTIONS

Turn to Section 3 of your answer sheet to answer the questions in this section.

DIRECTIONS

For questions 1–13, solve each problem, choose the best answer from the choices provided, and fill in the corresponding circle on your answer sheet. **For questions 14–17,** solve the problem and enter your answer in the grid on the answer sheet. Please refer to the directions before question 14 on how to enter your answers in the grid. You may use any available space in your test booklet for scratch work.

NOTES

1. The use of a calculator **is not permitted**.
2. All variables and expressions used represent real numbers unless otherwise indicated.
3. Figures provided in this test are drawn to scale unless otherwise indicated.
4. All figures lie in a plane unless otherwise indicated.
5. Unless otherwise indicated, the domain of a given function f is the set of all real numbers x for which $f(x)$ is a real number.

REFERENCE

$A = \pi r^2$
$C = 2\pi r$

$A = \ell w$

$A = \frac{1}{2}bh$

$c^2 = a^2 + b^2$

Special Right Triangles

$V = \ell w h$

$V = \pi r^2 h$

$V = \frac{4}{3}\pi r^3$

$V = \frac{1}{3}\pi r^2 h$

$V = \frac{1}{3}\ell w h$

The number of degrees of arc in a circle is 360.
The number of radians of arc in a circle is 2π.
The sum of the measures in degrees of the angles of a triangle is 180.

CONTINUE

1

$$y = x - 3$$

$$y = x^2 + 5x - 8$$

Which of the following ordered pairs (x, y) is a solution to the system of equations shown above?

A) $(-5, -8)$

B) $(-1, -12)$

C) $(4, 1)$

D) $(6, 3)$

2

Which of the following expressions is equivalent to $12mn + 20n$?

A) $32(m + n)$

B) $(12m + 20)n$

C) $32mn$

D) $(3m + 4)n$

3

The density of a material is calculated using the equation $d = \dfrac{m}{v}$, where m is the mass and v is the volume. According to the formula, what is the mass, m, in terms of d and v ?

A) $m = d + v$

B) $m = \dfrac{d}{v}$

C) $m = \dfrac{v}{d}$

D) $m = dv$

4

$$2x + 7y = 5$$

$$-3x - 3y = 15$$

What value of y satisfies the system of equations above?

A) -3

B) 3

C) 5

D) 8

CONTINUE

5

There is a value a for which $x = a$ satisfies the equation $3 + 2x = x^2 - 5$. Which of the following could be the value of a ?

A) -4

B) -2

C) 1

D) 5

6

Point C lies on a line with the equation $y = ax + b$ and is graphed in the xy-plane. If $a < 0 < b$, which of the following cannot be the coordinates of point C ?

A) $(-2, -4)$

B) $(-2, 4)$

C) $(2, -4)$

D) $(2, 4)$

7

The relationship between the value of a car in dollars, y, and the number of miles, x, it has been driven since it was purchased is modeled by the equation $y = 14{,}000 - 0.2x$. What does the y-intercept of this graph in the xy-plane represent?

A) The decline in value of the car for every mile driven

B) The average number of miles the car is driven per year

C) The total number of miles the car has been driven since it was purchased

D) The value of the car when it was purchased

8

During a sale, a shoe store gives a 15% discount on the total purchase. Chris purchases three pairs of sandals at a regular price of $21.10 per pair. If he also buys n pairs of sneakers at a regular price of $32.70 per pair, which of the following equations correctly calculates the total cost in dollars, c, of his purchase after the discount?

A) $63.30 + 32.70n = 1.15c$

B) $63.30 + 32.70n = 0.85$

C) $(63.30 + 32.70n)0.85 = c$

D) $(63.30 + 32.70n)1.15 = c$

CONTINUE

9

A theater sells tickets for their Matinee and Nighttime showings. The Matinee tickets cost $8 each and the Nighttime tickets cost $14 each. The theater needs to sell at least 10 tickets of each type and needs to receive at least $200 in revenue from ticket sales for the day. If m represents the number of Matinee tickets sold and n represents the number of Nighttime tickets sold, which of the following systems of inequalities correctly expresses these restrictions?

A) $\begin{cases} 8m+14n \leq 200 \\ m \geq 10 \\ n \geq 10 \end{cases}$

B) $\begin{cases} 8m+14n \leq 200 \\ m+n \geq 10 \end{cases}$

C) $\begin{cases} 8m+14n \geq 200 \\ m \geq 10 \\ n \geq 10 \end{cases}$

D) $\begin{cases} 8m+14n \geq 200 \\ m+n \geq 10 \end{cases}$

10

A cat eats more than 290 calories but less than 340 calories every day for a week. If the cat consumes a total of c calories in the week, which of the following inequalities represents all of the possible values of c ?

A) $2{,}330 < c < 2{,}380$

B) $2{,}030 < c < 2{,}380$

C) $2{,}030 < c < 2{,}080$

D) $290 < c < 340$

11

If the ordered pair (a, b) represents the vertex in the xy-plane of the parabola given by the equation $y = (x + 4)(x - 8)$, what is the value of a ?

A) -10

B) -2

C) 2

D) 10

12

$$\frac{\left(x^n y^n\right)^{\frac{1}{4}}}{\left(x^3 y^3\right)^{\frac{1}{2}}} = (xy)^{\frac{1}{4}}$$

If n is a constant in the equation above, which value of n makes the equation true for all positive values of x and y ?

A) 1

B) 7

C) 9

D) 13

13

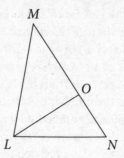

In the figure above, $\angle LMO = \angle OLN$. Which of the following statements must be true?

A) $\dfrac{LN}{LM} = \dfrac{ON}{LO}$

B) $\dfrac{LN}{LM} = \dfrac{LO}{NO}$

C) $\dfrac{LN}{LM} = \dfrac{LM}{MN}$

D) $\dfrac{LN}{LM} = \dfrac{ON}{LN}$

CONTINUE

No Test Material On This Page

DIRECTIONS

For questions 14–17, solve the problem and enter your answer in the grid, as described below, on the answer sheet.

1. Although not required, it is suggested that you write your answer in the boxes at the top of the columns to help you fill in the circles accurately. You will receive credit only if the circles are filled in correctly.

2. Mark no more than one circle in any column.

3. No question has a negative answer.

4. Some problems may have more than one correct answer. In such cases, grid only one answer.

5. **Mixed numbers** such as $3\frac{1}{2}$ must be gridded as 3.5 or 7/2. (If 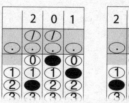 is entered into the grid, it will be interpreted as $\frac{31}{2}$, not as $3\frac{1}{2}$.)

6. **Decimal Answers:** If you obtain a decimal answer with more digits than the grid can accommodate, it may be either rounded or truncated, but it must fill the entire grid.

Answer: $\frac{7}{12}$ Answer: 2.5

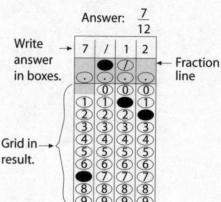

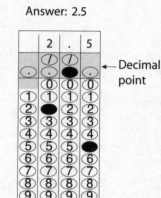

Acceptable ways to grid $\frac{2}{3}$ are:

Answer: 201 – either position is correct

NOTE: You may start your answers in any column, space permitting. Columns you don't need to use should be left blank.

CONTINUE ➡

14

Sarah and Lizzie each plant bamboo stalks. After a week, Sarah's bamboo stalk is three times as tall as Lizzie's bamboo stalk. If the sum of the heights of the two stalks of bamboo is 4 feet and 4 inches, how tall, in inches, is Sarah's bamboo stalk?

16

$$(3x + ny)(5x - my) = ax^2 + bxy + cy^2$$

In the equation above, n, m, a, b, and c are non-zero constants. If $b = 14$ and $c = -8$, what is the value of $5n - 3m$?

15

$$c(2n - 5) = 14n - 35$$

If c is a constant, for what value of c does the equation above have an infinite number of solutions?

17

For what integer value of c is $5x - c$ a factor of the expression $10x^2 - x - 3$?

STOP

If you finish before time is called, you may check your work on this section only.
Do not turn to any other section in the test.

Math Test – Calculator

45 MINUTES, 31 QUESTIONS

Turn to Section 4 of your answer sheet to answer the questions in this section.

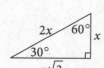

CONTINUE

1

A standard 8-ounce cup of coffee contains 95 milligrams of caffeine. If Jason were to drink 26 ounces of coffee over the weekend, how many milligrams of caffeine will he have consumed?

A)   29.23

B)   113.00

C)   285.00

D)   308.75

2

During the month of October, leaves fall from a maple tree. The graph above shows the number of leaves that remain on the tree as a function of the day of the month. On which of the following days did more leaves fall than had fallen during the previous two days combined?

A) Day 3

B) Day 9

C) Day 16

D) Day 26

3

The number of logs F in Shawn's firewood supply after d days can be modeled with the equation $F = -23d + 1,235$. In this equation, what is represented by the number 23 ?

A) The number of logs Shawn burns each day

B) The number of logs Shawn started with

C) The number of days Shawn has been burning wood

D) The total number of logs Shawn has burned thus far

CONTINUE

Questions 4-5 refer to the following information.

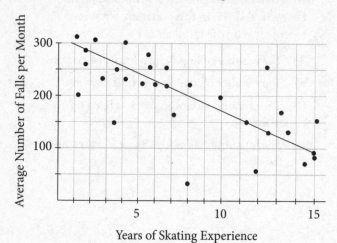

Years of Skating Experience

The scatterplot above shows the number of years of experience of 30 competitive ice skaters and their average number of falls on the ice per month, along with the line of best fit.

4

For the skater with 10 years of experience, how many more falls on average occur each month than would be expected for someone with this level of experience?

A)   0

B)   5

C)   50

D)   200

5

Which of the following accurately describes the relationship between years of experience and average number of falls per month?

A)   As the number of years of experience decreases, the average number of falls per month decreases.

B)   As the number of years of experience increases, the average number of falls per month decreases.

C)   As the number of years of experience increases, the average number of falls per month increases.

D)   There is no relationship between the number of years of experience and the average number of falls per month.

6

A line in the standard xy-plane has the equation $y = bx - 6$ and crosses the x-axis at the point $(3, 0)$. What is the value of b ?

A)   −3

B)   −2

C)   2

D)   18

CONTINUE

7

Month	Sales
January	43,120
February	45,276
March	47,431
April	49,588
May	51,741
June	53,899

Monthly sales of LED lightbulbs have been increasing over the last 6 months, as demonstrated in the data shown above. Which of the following best describes the trend in the data?

A) Sales are increasing linearly by approximately 2,156 bulbs per month.

B) Sales are increasing an exponential rate of 0.05% per month.

C) Sales are increasing at an exponential rate of 5% per month.

D) Sales are increasing each month, but the rate of increase is falling over time.

8

$$(mn^2 - 2n^2 + 3mn) - (2n^2 + 3mn^2 - mn)$$

Which of the following is equivalent to the expression shown above?

A) $-2mn^2 - 4n^2 + 4mn$

B) $-mn^2 - 5n^2 + 4mn$

C) $4mn^2 + 2mn$

D) $-2m^2n^4 - 4n^4 + 4m^2n^2$

9

Beatrix has been running each morning at a pace of 1 mile per 7 minutes. What is her pace measured in <u>kilometers per hour</u>? (1 mile is approximately 1.61 kilometers.)

A) 0.19

B) 5.32

C) 11.27

D) 13.80

10

	Students' Scores									
Mr. Sulu's Students	90	81	21	67	99	82	75	71	85	82
Ms. Picard's Students	75	82	98	55	89	74	94	68	79	100

In the table above, Mr. Sulu's and Ms. Picard's students' scores on a test are given. Both teachers believe their own students have outperformed those in the other class. Based on the given scores, what would be an accurate description of the results?

A) Mr. Sulu's students did better when considering the mean score of each class, while Ms. Picard's students did better when considering the median score of each class.

B) Ms. Picard's students did better when considering both the mean and median scores of each class.

C) Mr. Sulu's students did better when considering both the mean and median scores of each class.

D) Ms. Picard's students did better when considering the mean score of each class, while Mr. Sulu's students did better when considering the median score of each class.

CONTINUE

11

Pet Ownership in the Town of Labradoodle

	Small Breeds	Medium Breeds	Large Breeds
Cats	54	82	99
Dogs	90	210	305

A newspaper conducted a survey of homes in the town of Labradoodle to determine how many domestic cats and dogs lived in the area. Based on the survey results above, the number of medium and large breed dogs is what percent of all cats and dogs in the town of Labradoodle?

A) 21.5

B) 61.3

C) 85.1

D) 72.0

12

$$3x - 6y = 15$$
$$x = 5 + 2y$$

Which of the following describes the solution set to the system of equations shown above?

A) $(5, 3)$

B) $(-3, 5)$

C) The system has no solutions.

D) The system has an infinite number of solutions.

13

If the equation $(x - 1)^2 + (y + 7)^2 = 4$ were graphed in the xy-plane, the resulting graph would be a circle with which of the following attributes?

A) Center $(1, -7)$; radius = 4

B) Center $(-1, 7)$; radius = 2

C) Center $(1, 7)$; radius = 16

D) Center $(1, -7)$; radius = 2

14

Jamie needs to make 85 batches of chocolate chip cookies, each of which takes 20 minutes to prepare. How many <u>hours</u> will it take Jamie to prepare all 85 batches?

A)   4.25

B)   12.75

C)   28.33

D)   255

CONTINUE

15

Daily Temperature (°F)	
Sunday	45
Monday	54
Tuesday	58
Wednesday	52
Thursday	54
Friday	55
Saturday	60

The table above shows the temperatures for a week in mid-April. How many degrees greater is the mean of these temperatures than the mode?

A) 0

B) 0.5

C) 6

D) 15

16

The Better Bubble Soda Company carbonates its beverages using the formula $C = \dfrac{V}{6} + 0.427$, where V is the volume of the beverage being carbonated in fluid ounces, and C is the grams of carbon dioxide that are added. If the company wishes to increase the grams of carbon dioxide in all of its beverages by 10 percent, which of the following adjustments to the formula would achieve this?

A) Change 0.427 to 0.470

B) Change 6 to 6.6

C) Multiply the right side of the equation by 1.1

D) Multiply the left side of the equation by 1.1

Questions 17–19 refer to the following information.

An art museum sponsors its second annual statewide art competition for children ages 5–14. Participants are broken up into three age brackets, and each must submit a piece of artwork that demonstrates something special about his or her local community. Participants are given three themes to choose from: The Natural World, Historical Figures, or Food and Fun. The number of submissions in each category is displayed in the table below.

Art Fair Submissions

	Age 5–7	Age 8–11	Age 12–14
Natural World	49	103	75
Historical Figures	24	58	67
Food and Fun	173	69	54

17

If a child in the 8–11 age bracket were selected at random, what would be the probability that their submission fell into either the Natural World or Historical Figures categories?

A) $\dfrac{3}{10}$

B) $\dfrac{3}{7}$

C) $\dfrac{7}{10}$

D) $\dfrac{3}{4}$

CONTINUE

18

Approximately what percentage of the Food and Fun submissions were from students aged 11 and younger?

A) 23%

B) 58%

C) 71%

D) 82%

19

After the contest was concluded, the director of the museum compared the contest records to the submissions form the previous year and found that there were 96 entrants this year who had also had a submission the previous year. Which of the following is the ratio of the number of first time entrants this year to the number of repeat entrants?

A) 1:7

B) 1:6

C) 6:1

D) 7:1

20

Marcus has a square garden surrounded on all sides by a fence. The garden is smaller than he would like, and he wishes to enlarge it by adding 3 feet of fencing to each side. He determines that this will increase the area of the garden by 69 square feet. What is the perimeter of his garden before the increase, measured in feet?

A) 13

B) 40

C) 52

D) 100

21

$$f(x) = \frac{x-3}{2x-8}$$

The graph of the function above has one vertical asymptote. Which of the following functions has a vertical asymptote at the same x-value as the function above and also has a second vertical asymptote located seven units to the left of the first?

A) $f(x) = \dfrac{x-10}{x^2 - 15x + 44}$

B) $f(x) = \dfrac{x-3}{(2x-8)(2x-1)}$

C) $f(x) = \dfrac{x-7}{x^2 - x - 12}$

D) $f(x) = \dfrac{(x-10)(x-3)}{2x-8}$

CONTINUE

22

Allie's Alliterative Appetizers packages its Barbecued Beets in a cylindrical can. If the company decides to increase the radius of the can from 2 centimeters to 4 centimeters, by what factor will the volume of the can increase?

A) 0.5

B) 2

C) 4

D) 8

23

The graph of a quadratic function t contains the points $(-3, 5)$ and $(9, 5)$. If the coefficient of the x^2 term is negative, at what value of x will the maximum value occur?

A) −15

B) 0

C) 3

D) 21

24

Vincent is planting tomatoes in his garden, and purchases his plants at an average height of 10 centimeters. Over the course of the summer, his plants follow a linear model of growth, and 72 days after planting, the average plant height is 120 centimeters. Which of the following functions best models the average height $h(t)$ of his plants t days after planting?

A) $h(t) = 1.67t + 10$

B) $h(t) = 1.53t + 110$

C) $h(t) = 1.53t + 10$

D) $h(t) = 0.65t + 10$

25

The function g is defined by the equation $g(x) = 2x^2 + 3x - 6$. Which of the following represents $g(x + 2)$?

A) $g(x + 2) = 2x^2 + 11x + 8$

B) $g(x + 2) = 2x^2 + 3x + 8$

C) $g(x + 2) = 2x^2 + 3x - 4$

D) $g(x + 2) = 2x^2 + 7x + 4$

26

$$y = -2x + 27$$

$$x = -2y + 27$$

If the system of equations shown above were graphed in the xy-plane, at what point would the lines intersect?

A) $(9, 9)$

B) $(-13.5, -13.5)$

C) The two lines are parallel and will never intersect.

D) The two lines intersect at an infinite number of points.

27

A magician notices that his audience has grown bored with his "pull a rabbit out of the hat" trick, so he decides to change his performance by pulling 2 rabbits out of his hat, followed by 4, 8, 16, and 32 rabbits on each successive night. Which of the following best describes the type of equation that would correctly model this growth?

A) Constant, since each night the number of rabbits grows by the same percentage

B) Linear, since each night the number of rabbits increases by the same amount

C) Quadratic, since each night's number of rabbits is the square of the previous night's

D) Exponential, since each night the number of rabbits grows by the same percentage

CONTINUE

DIRECTIONS

For questions 28–31, solve the problem and enter your answer in the grid, as described below, on the answer sheet.

1. Although not required, it is suggested that you write your answer in the boxes at the top of the columns to help you fill in the circles accurately. You will receive credit only if the circles are filled in correctly.

2. Mark no more than one circle in any column.

3. No question has a negative answer.

4. Some problems may have more than one correct answer. In such cases, grid only one answer.

5. **Mixed numbers** such as $3\frac{1}{2}$ must be gridded as 3.5 or 7/2. (If $\boxed{3\ 1\ /\ 2}$ is entered into the grid, it will be interpreted as $\frac{31}{2}$, not as $3\frac{1}{2}$.)

6. **Decimal Answers:** If you obtain a decimal answer with more digits than the grid can accommodate, it may be either rounded or truncated, but it must fill the entire grid.

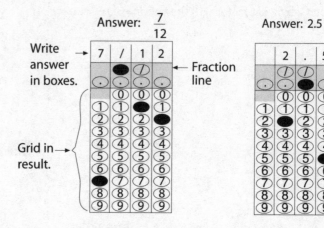

Answer: $\frac{7}{12}$ Answer: 2.5

Write answer in boxes.   Fraction line   Decimal point

Grid in result.

Acceptable ways to grid $\frac{2}{3}$ are:

Answer: 201 – either position is correct

NOTE: You may start your answers in any column, space permitting. Columns you don't need to use should be left blank.

CONTINUE

28

$$y = 5x - 18$$
$$y = x^2 - 5x + 6$$

The graphs of the two equations above intersect at two points. What is the product of the *y*-values of the two points?

29

	Audition Candidates	
Years of Experience	Female	Male
>12	17	16
<12	8	7

A long-running science-fiction television show is casting a new lead actor, and the producers have 36 audition slots available. They wish to divide the time equally between male and female candidates from the table above. They also want to devote at least 80 percent of the slots to actors with at least 12 years of professional experience. If they decide to audition all but 2 of the female candidates with more than 12 years of experience, what is the maximum number of male candidates with less than 12 years of experience that can be auditioned?

Questions 30–31 refer to the following information.

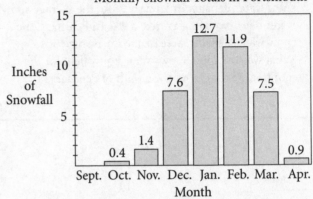

Monthly Snowfall Totals in Portsmouth

The bar graph above shows the monthly snowfall totals for the town of Portsmouth for the winter of 2015-16. For months not shown, the monthly total was 0 inches.

30

The average amount of snowfall in November over the past 15 years is equal to the amount of snowfall in November 2015. If the cumulative snowfall for November in the past 15 years is *s* inches, how many years will it take for the cumulative snowfall for March, at the rate it fell in 2016, to reach *s* inches?

CONTINUE

31

Snow Water Equivalent is a measure of the amount of water from fallen snow and is determined by multiplying the depth of the snow in inches by the snow water density. In January 2016, the average snow water density was measured at 9%. In February, the snow water density increased to an average of 13%. What was the total Snow Water Equivalent for the month of January and the month of February?

▲

STOP
**If you finish before time is called, you may check your work on this section only.
Do not turn to any other section in the test.**

Chapter 23
Practice Test:
Answers and
Explanations

PRACTICE TEST ANSWER KEY

Section 1:
Reading

1.	B	25.	C
2.	C	26.	A
3.	C	27.	C
4.	C	28.	B
5.	D	29.	A
6.	A	30.	A
7.	D	31.	C
8.	B	32.	B
9.	A	33.	B
10.	B	34.	D
11.	A	35.	B
12.	A	36.	D
13.	A	37.	C
14.	B	38.	D
15.	D	39.	D
16.	D	40.	D
17.	A	41.	C
18.	C	42.	C
19.	B	43.	B
20.	D	44.	B
21.	C	45.	B
22.	A	46.	A
23.	C	47.	D
24.	D		

Section 2:
Writing & Language

1.	B	23.	D
2.	B	24.	A
3.	B	25.	D
4.	A	26.	B
5.	D	27.	B
6.	D	28.	C
7.	B	29.	D
8.	D	30.	C
9.	C	31.	D
10.	C	32.	C
11.	A	33.	A
12.	A	34.	C
13.	C	35.	C
14.	B	36.	C
15.	A	37.	D
16.	B	38.	D
17.	C	39.	A
18.	A	40.	D
19.	C	41.	B
20.	B	42.	D
21.	C	43.	B
22.	D	44.	A

Section 3:
Math (No Calculator)

1.	A	10.	B
2.	B	11.	C
3.	D	12.	B
4.	B	13.	A
5.	B	14.	39
6.	A	15.	7
7.	D	16.	14
8.	C	17.	3
9.	C		

Section 4 :
Math (Calculator)

1.	D	17.	C
2.	B	18.	D
3.	A	19.	C
4.	B	20.	B
5.	C	21.	C
6.	C	22.	C
7.	A	23.	C
8.	A	24.	C
9.	D	25.	A
10.	D	26.	A
11.	B	27.	D
12.	D	28.	24
13.	D	29.	4
14.	C	30.	2.8
15.	A	31.	2.69
16.	C		

ANSWERS AND EXPLANATIONS

Section 1: Reading

1.   **B**   This question asks what *basically* most nearly means as used in line 20. Go back to the text, find the word *basically*, and cross it out. Replace it with another word that makes sense based on the text. The author describes a property that doesn't have much on it, just weeds. The missing word must mean something like "only" or "pretty much." Eliminate (A) because it has nothing to do with the prediction. Choice (B) is consistent with "pretty much," so keep it. Choices (C) and (D) can be eliminated, because there's nothing special about the weeds. They're simply the only things in the lot. The correct answer is (B).

2.   **C**   This question asks about Delinko's reaction to Curly's vandalism complaint. Carefully read the interactions between the two men to determine Delinko's reaction. Toward the beginning of the passage, the author says *the policeman couldn't see what there was to be vandalized*. Later, Delinko tries to *figure out what to put in his report* because *nothing on the property was broken or defaced*. Delinko is perplexed about the complaint. Eliminate any answers that aren't consistent with this prediction. Choice (A) can be eliminated because he can't find anything that's been damaged. Choice (B) can be eliminated because there's no evidence Delinko is *angry*; he's just trying to figure out what's going on. Choice (C) is consistent with the prediction, so keep it. Choice (D) can be eliminated because there is no evidence that Delinko is *amused*. The correct answer is (C).

3.   **C**   This question asks about Curly's *chief complaint* about the vandalism. He's aggravated that the stakes have been pulled up, and as he talks to Delinko about it, he says, "*It's not that they messed up the survey stakes, it's them screwing up our whole construction schedule. That's where it'll cost some serious bucks.*" Curly isn't upset about the stakes themselves, but rather the effect of the uprooted stakes on the construction schedule. Choice (A) isn't consistent with the prediction. The cost is not from the stakes themselves, but from changing the schedule. Choice (B) can be eliminated because Curly never shows any concern for the owls' habitat. Choice (C) is consistent with the prediction, so keep it. Choice (D) can be eliminated because the owls created the holes, not the vandals. The correct answer is (C).

4.   **C**   This is a best evidence question, so simply look at the lines used to answer the previous question. The support came from Curly's explanation in lines 60–62 that by removing the stakes, the vandals had *screw[ed] up [the] whole construction schedule*. Choice (C) contains those lines. The correct answer is (C).

5.   **D**   This question asks about Curly's comment *in the context of the construction project*. When he says he *ain't never seen one, officially speakin'*, he's talking to Delinko about the owls. He clearly knows about the owls, because he explains to Delinko that the owls are responsible for the holes and that they're '*bout as tall as a beer can*. Eliminate (A), because it isn't true that he's *never seen one*. Choice (B) can also be eliminated, because Curly is worried about the construction schedule, not the owls.

Choice (C) could be true: if the owls are protected, that might mess up the project, but there's no indication in the text that the owls *will stop the ... project*. Choice (D) is consistent with what Curly tells Delinko. The correct answer is (D).

6. **A** This question asks which character would agree that something must be damaged for the complaint to count as vandalism. Notice that this is the first question in a paired set, so it can be answered in tandem with Q7. Consider the answers for Q7 first. In (7A), Delinko asks if any of the stakes were destroyed and how much a stake costs. His questions aren't answered, and there's no mention of whether or not it's vandalism, so these lines don't support any of the answers for Q6. Eliminate (7A). The lines for (7B) are Curly's statement to Delinko that *they didn't break none of the stakes*. There is no damage and no mention of whether or not the claim is vandalism, so eliminate (7B). In the lines for (7C), Delinko asks Curly about the owls. Because there is no mention of either damage or vandalism, these lines do not support any of the answer choices for Q6. Eliminate (7C). In the lines for (7D), Delinko tells Curly that because nothing was damaged, *technically, nothing really got vandalized*, and because of that, he says his *sergeant's going to kick it back down*. Therefore, according to Delinko's sergeant, if there's no damage, there's no vandalism. These lines support (6A), so draw a line connecting them. Without support from Q7, (6B), (6C), and (6D) can all be eliminated. The correct answers are (6A) and (7D).

7. **D** (See explanation above.)

8. **B** This question asks what the use of the words *grunted* and *muttered* show about Curly's character. The author describes him as *cranky and unsmiling*. There's no evidence of *exhaustion*, so eliminate (A). Choice (B) is consistent with someone muttering because they're cranky, so keep (B). Choices (C) and (D) can be eliminated because there's no evidence of extreme anger or sadness, just crankiness. The correct answer is (B).

9. **A** This question asks what Curly means when he says, "What owls?" Based on Q5, Curly knows the owls exist. When Delinko trips over one of their holes, Curly describes how they look and what they do. Choices (B) and (C) can be eliminated immediately. Choice (A) could be a possibility: Curly has already expressed frustration with a delayed construction schedule, and owls would not make things easier. Keep it. Choice (D) is less of a possibility. Curly never expresses concern or worry about the owls. In fact, he seems much more annoyed by them than anything else, calling them *stupid owls*. Between (A) and (D), (A) is best supported by the text. The correct answer is (A).

10. **B** This question asks how the main focus of the passage shifts. Because it is a general question, it should be done after all the specific questions. The passage begins with an overview of what can happen to women during times of war. The passage then gets more specific about how one country, Rwanda, is trying to change those statistics by putting more women in positions of political power. Eliminate any answer choices that aren't consistent with this structure. Choice (A) can be eliminated because the passage does not begin with *anecdotes about men in political office*. Choice (B) is consistent with the prediction, so keep it. Choice (C) can be eliminated because the majority of the passage specifically talks about Rwanda, not *different countries* and the *barriers they all face*. Choice (D) can also be eliminated because there is no *step-by-step process* listed in the passage. The correct answer is (B).

11. **A** This question asks what *undermine* means in line 15. Go back to the text, find *undermine*, and cross it out. Then use the surrounding text to put in another word that makes sense based on the context. A cycle of violence is described and attributed to the *same people… put back into power*. The text goes on to say that in order to *undermine the cycle of devastation*, a movement has been started to get more women into power. Therefore, the missing word must mean something like "stop" or "lessen." Eliminate anything that's not consistent with this prediction. Choice (A), *weaken*, is a clear match with the prediction, so keep it. Choices (B), (C), and (D) are all potential definitions of *undermine*, but none are consistent with "stop" or "lessen," so they can be eliminated. The correct answer is (A).

12. **A** This question asks about the most direct cause of the increase in Rwandan female legislators. Use chronology and the lead words in the answers to skim for relevant information in the text. Choice (A) is in line 37, which states that the Rwandan Constitution *included a quota providing for 30% reserved seats for women*. This directly caused an increase in female legislators, so keep (A). Choice (B), the paper for International IDEA, is in line 43. This paper *discussed in detail… the quota system*, but it didn't actually affect the quota system. Eliminate (B). Choice (C), the Initiative for Inclusive Security, is mentioned in line 45; this group is *tracking the [political] advances [for women]*, not directly affecting the advances. Eliminate (C). Choice (D) can be eliminated because although the Rwanda Patriotic Front *supported the effort*, the text does not mention its direct effect on the increase. The correct answer is (A).

13. **A** This question asks what *tracking* most nearly means in line 44. Go back to the text, find the word *tracking*, and cross it out. Then read the window carefully, using context clues to determine another word that would fit in the text. The window refers to a paper that *discussed… the process and quota system in detail* by an organization that was *tracking these advances*. Therefore, the missing word must mean something like "paying attention to" or "gathering information about." Choice (A) is consistent with this prediction, so keep it. Choices (B) and (D) can both be eliminated because those deal with meanings of *tracking* more closely related to hunting rather than gathering information. Choice (C) can be eliminated because the group is paying attention to the advances, not *expelling* anything. The correct answer is (A).

14. **B** This question asks why the women's quota in government is helpful. Notice that this is the first question in a paired set, so it can be done in tandem with Q15. Consider the answers for Q15 first. The lines for (15A) say that Rwanda is the *first country to have a majority of women in the legislature*. There is no mention of the quota or why it was helpful, so these lines don't support any of the answers for Q14. Eliminate (15A). The lines for (15B) provide a fact: the Constitution included a *quota providing for 30% reserved seats for women*. Again, these lines give information about the quota, but no mention of why it was helpful. Eliminate (15B). The lines for (15C) say that of the women who held the reserved seats, *only a small number ran for those seats again*. This is the opposite of helpful, because it doesn't show the quota working to keep women in government. Eliminate (15C). The lines for (15D) say that the reserved seats *served as an incubator for women who might otherwise have been … giving them … experience and confidence*. These lines support (14B), so draw a line connecting the two answers. Without support from Q15, (14A), (14C), and (14D) can all be eliminated. The correct answers are (14B) and (15D).

15. **D** (See explanation above.)

16. **D** This question asks which of the answer choices best supports the claim that a female-led legislature *can make differences that might not be seen with a male-led legislature*. Because the support text is already provided in the answer choices, simply eliminate any answers that don't address the question. Choice (A) gives a fact about the number of women in the legislature, with no mention of any difference in the legislation from male and female legislators. Eliminate (A). Choice (B) states that women were *competing with the men—and many were successful*, but there's no mention of the differences between male-led and female-led legislatures. Eliminate (B). Choices (C) and (D) both discuss outcomes of a female-led legislature, so compare the answers to see which *best supports* the claim. Choice (C) states that the *women-led legislature is making an impact*, while (D) gives a specific example of *ground-breaking legislation on gender-based violence*. With the specific example, (D) gives stronger support for the claim. The correct answer is (D).

17. **A** This question asks which country has *just under triple the percentage* as the United States. Go back to the figure and find the United States. The United States has a national government with just under 20% females. The correct answer will be something between 50% and 60%. Bolivia is between 50% and 60%, so keep it. Finland, Iceland, and Senegal are all between 40% and 50%, which is too low. The correct answer is (A).

18. **C** This question asks which country has a higher percentage of women in government than does Nicaragua. Go back to the figure and find Nicaragua. Nicaragua's national government is approximately 45% female, so eliminate anything below 45%. Mexico, Sweden, and the United States are all below Nicaragua and can be eliminated. Cuba's national government is approximately 49% female. The correct answer is (C).

19. **B** This question asks about the main purpose of the passage. Since this is a general question, it should be answered after all the specific questions. The passage begins by discussing how the gray wolf population in Yellowstone National Park has changed over time. The passage then goes on to discuss the documentation of *wolf-prey relationships*. Although the passage does briefly mention the factors affecting elk population dynamics, it is not the main purpose of the passage. Eliminate (A). Choice (B) is consistent with the prediction, so keep it. The passage is neither *suggesting a solution* nor *rejecting an alternative proposal*, so eliminate (C) and (D). The correct answer is (B).

20. **D** This question asks what the phrase *predator control efforts* most nearly means in lines 6–7. Go back to the text and carefully read the window to determine what the phrase means. The text says that *deliberate extermination programs...* left no gray wolves in Yellowstone National Park. Therefore, *predator control efforts* must mean something like "removal of wolves." *Natural outcome, extinction*, and *only solution* do not mean "removal," so eliminate (A) (B), and (C). Choice (D), *pest removal*, fits this prediction, so keep (D). The correct answer is (D).

21. **C** This question asks about the main purpose of the second paragraph. The second paragraph describes a modern approach to the gray wolf where the animal was regarded as important to a *naturally functioning ecosystem*. This is neither an apology nor a demand, so eliminate (A) and (D). Although (B) may be tempting, the paragraph doesn't compare past knowledge to present knowledge. Instead, it

says *NPS policy calls for restoring native species* and *the gray wolf was eventually listed as an endangered species*. These represent policies that were implemented affecting wolves. The correct answer is (C).

22. **A** This question asks about one potential cause of wolf population decline as a result of proximity to something. Notice that this is the first question in a paired set, so it can be done in tandem with Q23. Look at the answer choices for Q23 first. Choice (23A) mentions *demise* of wolves, which looks pretty good, but these lines don't support any of the answers for Q22. Eliminate (23A). Choice (23B) mentions *decline of mange*, which has nothing to do with the decline of the wolf population. Eliminate it. Choice (23C) mentions *wolf decline* due to *higher canid density*. These lines support (22A), so draw a line connecting those two answers. The lines for (23D) mention *wolf-prey relationships* at *kill sites*, which don't relate to declining wolf populations. Eliminate (23D). Without support from Q23, (22B), (22C), and (22D) can all be eliminated. The correct answers are (22A) and (23C).

23. **C** (See explanation above.)

24. **D** This question asks *what was true of the wolf packs in the 2012 study*. Notice that this is the first question in a paired set, so it can be done in tandem with Q25. Look at the answer choices for Q25 first. Choice (25A) refers to information about wolves from 2007, not from the 2012 study. Eliminate (25A). Choice (25B) describes the locations of the packs studied, which does not support any of the answers for Q24. Eliminate (25B). Choice (25C) says that one of the packs was monitored *less extensively* and another pack was *unable to be located*. This supports (24D), so draw a line connecting those two answers. Choice (25D) simply lists the stats researchers recorded about the wolves. This does not support any of the answers from Q24, so eliminate (25D). The correct answers are (24D) and (25C).

25. **C** (See explanation above.)

26. **A** This question asks what the word *dynamics* most nearly means in line 88. Go back to the text, find the word *dynamics*, and cross it out. Then read the window carefully, using context clues to determine another word that would fit in the text. The text says elk populations have declined since wolf reintroduction and that other factors also influence the elk population. Therefore, *dynamics* must mean something like "ups and downs" or "changes." *Changes* fits this prediction, so keep (A). Neither *explosions* nor *fates* means "changes," so eliminate (B) and (C). *Gains* doesn't capture the full meaning of "ups and downs," so eliminate (D). The correct answer is (A).

27. **C** This question asks when *the northern range wolf population experienced the largest change*. Locate the trend line for wolves in the chart and the correct *y*-axis (on the left). Find the change in wolf population for each range in years by finding the number of wolves on the *y*-axis at the beginning year in the range then find the number of wolves on the *y*-axis for the final year in the range. Subtract the two numbers to find the change in wolf populations. The largest change, or biggest difference, will be the best answer. The differences are as follows: (A) 1999 (45) to 2001 (75) = change of 30; (B) 2004 (90) to 2006 (60) = change of 30; (C) 2007 (95) to 2009 (55) = change of 40; (D) 2008 (55) to 2010 (40) = change of 15. The largest difference is (C), so the correct answer is (C).

28. **B** This question asks which statement is supported by the chart. Work through each answer choice using the figure. Pay attention to the axis labels! Choice (A) is more difficult to assess, so assess the other choices first. Choice (B) is supported by the chart, since elk numbers were roughly 10,000 in 2007 and 5,000 in 2011. Keep it. Choice (C) can be eliminated because although the graph peaks for wolves and elk reach the same height, they correspond to two different *y*-axes, meaning their numbers reached very different peak values. Choice (D) can be eliminated because the chart does not address the reason elk populations were studied. Finally, (A) can be eliminated because overall, elk numbers have only declined whereas wolf numbers have risen and declined, and ultimately ended higher than where they began. So, wolf numbers haven't declined by a greater percentage then elk numbers overall. The correct answer is (B).

29. **A** This question asks what the word *noise* most nearly means in line 16. Go back to the text, find the word *noise*, and cross it out. Then read the window carefully, using context clues to determine another word that would fit in the text. The text says that the book *made such a noise at its coming abroad*. He also says that the book had *applause that followed it*, indicating the book was important. Therefore, noise must mean something like "uproar" or "public display." Choice (A), *impact*, is consistent with the prediction, so keep it. *Crash* and *sound* are both definitions of *noise*, but have the wrong meaning for the text. Eliminate (B) and (D). Choice (C) can be eliminated because the book itself is not making an announcement. The correct answer is (A).

30. **A** This question asks which point Locke makes *about the effectiveness of the argument in Patriarcha*. Notice that this is the first question in a paired set, so it can be done in tandem with Q31. Look at the answer choices for Q31 first. The lines for (31A) fiercely denounce slavery, but there is no mention of the Patriarcha. These lines don't support any of the answers for Q30, so eliminate (31A). The lines for (31B) say the Patriarcha states that *all men … are slaves*. It's a straightforward description of the content of the book, with no reference to Locke's opinion. Eliminate (31B). Choice (31C) presents Locke's opinion that the book that he was expecting to be *a chain* turned out to be *a rope of sand* useful only to *blind people the better to mislead them*. He goes on to say that the book does not have *any force to draw … into bondage* those who have *their eyes open*. These lines support (30A), so draw a line connecting them. The lines for (31D) do not support any of the answers for Q30 and can be eliminated. Without support from Q31, (30B), (30C), and (30D) can all be eliminated. The correct answers are (30A) and (31C).

31. **C** (See previous explanation.)

32. **B** This question asks what the word *mingle* most nearly means in line 45. Go back to the text, find the word *mingle*, and cross it out. Then read the window carefully, using context clues to determine another word that would fit in the text. The text says *I am very glad to be present … with those with whom I have labored, for the last seven years…* Therefore, *mingle* must mean something like "mix" or "share." Choices (C) and (D) can be eliminated because neither *modulate* nor *shout* are consistent with the prediction. Choices (A) and (B) might both initially seem to fit the context of the sentence, so make sure to read carefully. Douglass says he wants to *mingle his voice* with the others. That whole phrase could mean *converse*, but a voice is not *conversed*. A voice can, however, be *shared*. The correct answer is (B).

33. **B** This question asks how Douglass does *not* view *slavery as an institution*. Notice that this is the first question in a paired set, so it can be done in tandem with Q34. Passage 2 describes the author's desire to overthrow slavery in the *States of the Union* and how he traveled to the monarchy of England to *preserve* his *liberty*. The lines for (34A) discuss his work to undo slavery, but don't mention what slavery should *not* be. Eliminate (34A). The lines for (34B) continue with the idea that slavery is bad and should be overthrown. These lines might initially seem to support (33C), as Douglass agrees that slavery should not be *accepted silently*. However, there is no mention in the lines of *inevitable emancipation*, so eliminate (34B). The lines for (34C) do not support any of the answers for Q33 and can be eliminated. The lines for (34D) say that he went to England to *get rid of Democratic Slavery* and discovered he had *gone to the right place*. Therefore, the monarchy is not worse than slavery. Pay attention to the negatives in Q33. These lines support (33B) because the question asks what is *not* true about slavery. Draw a line connecting these two answers. Without support from Q34, (33A), (33C), and (33D) can all be eliminated. The correct answers are (33B) and (34D).

34. **D** (See explanation above.)

35. **B** This question asks about the primary purpose of each passage. Since this is a general question, it should be answered after the specific questions. In Passage 1, Locke begins by introducing a popular book and his high expectations of the book, and then continues by talking about how disappointed, as an educated man, he was by the book. In Passage 2, Douglass begins by expressing desire for the overthrow of slavery and continues by recounting how a trip to *Monarchical England, to get rid of Democratic Slavery* showed him that *there is Liberty there—there is Freedom there*. Look for an answer choice that matches this information. Neither passage demands *immediate governmental change* nor *attack[s] the legitimacy of ... monarchy*. Eliminate (A) and (D). In Passage 1, Locke challenges the contemporary idea that Filmer made a good argument in his book, and in Passage 2, Douglass mentions his personal experience with slavery. Keep (B). Passage 1 didn't reference leaving the country at all, so eliminate (C). The correct answer is (B).

36. **D** This question asks about how Douglass viewed England differently than Locke did. In Passage 2, Douglass says that in England, *there is Liberty there—there is Freedom there*. Eliminate (C) since he doesn't have a negative opinion of England. Douglass does mention *the oppression and suffering going on in England*, so eliminate (A). He never mentions the *benevolence of a king*, so eliminate (B). Choice (D) is a clear paraphrase of what Douglass says about England. The correct answer is (D).

37. **C** This question asks which statement about all men both authors would most likely agree with. Because this is a general question, it should be done after the other specific questions. In Passage 1, Locke states that *slavery is so vile an estate of man* that he *should have taken this, as any other treatise which would persuade all men that they are slaves,... for such another exercise of wit*. In Passage 2, Douglass states that *this land, cursed as it is with Slavery, so noble a band to second my efforts and the efforts of others in the noble work of undoing the Yoke of Bondage, with which the majority of the States of this Union are now unfortunately cursed*. Neither author mentions a desire for an *undemocratic government*. Eliminate (A). Although both authors condemn slavery, Locke doesn't suggest a rise to end slavery. Eliminate (B).

Choice (C) is consistent with both passages, so keep it. Neither author suggests that men are incapable of ending slavery without assistance from the government and Douglass specifically mentions that *all our equipments are drawn from above*. Eliminate (D). Choice (C) is the best answer.

38. **D** This question asks how Locke would view Douglass's observations regarding England. Locke believes that *slavery ... is vile and miserable* and *directly opposite to the generous temper and courage of [his] nation*. Douglass is also anti-slavery, and said that he *went to England to get rid of Democratic slavery* and that when he got there, he was *satisfied that [he] had gone to the right place*. The correct answer will be consistent with Locke agreeing with Douglass and being glad he found a welcome environment in England. Eliminate (A) and (B) because both of those answers are negative. There is no plea to overthrow a *corrupt monarchy*, so eliminate (C). Choice (D) is consistent with the prediction. The correct answer is (D).

39. **D** This question asks how the main focus of the passage shifts. Because this is a general question, it should be answered after all the specific questions are completed. The passage begins with an introduction of a newly-discovered species of lizard and then continues by describing how unusual it is. Choice (A) is not consistent with the passage because there is no discussion about how scientists *discover new species* nor about how they *publish their findings*. Eliminate (A). Choice (B) can be eliminated because, although the passage discusses *atypical reproduction*, there is no discussion in the passage about *typical animal reproduction*. Choice (C) can be eliminated because the passage focuses on a species of lizard, not on cloning. Choice (D) is consistent with the structure of the passage. The correct answer is (D).

40. **D** This question asks what the phrase *at first glance* serves to do in the passage. Use the line reference to find the window and then read carefully. The phrase connects two ideas: *seems to be a run-of-the-mill lizard* and *in fact, [the lizard] is quite exceptional*. The phrase *at first glance* introduces the first idea, which is almost immediately contradicted by the second idea. Eliminate any answer choices that are inconsistent with this prediction. Choice (A) can be eliminated; although *beginning with a visual description* might initially seem to match *at first glance*, the two phrases actually mean very different things. There is no contrast between *scientific* and *non-scientific* observations, so eliminate (B). Eliminate (C) because there is no mention of either *scientists* or what they believe *absolutely true* in the window. Choice (D) is a clear paraphrase of the prediction. The correct answer is (D).

41. **C** This question asks about the central claim of the fourth paragraph. Carefully read the paragraph to determine the main point the author makes there. He says that scientists have known *some species... interbreed*, but the offspring were thought to be *evolutionary dead-ends*. An example of this dead-end is given, but then the author goes on to say that *in recent decades, however*, the scientists have discovered some hybrids *may represent new species*. Therefore, the author's central claim is that scientists thought they knew something until recent discoveries changed that belief. Eliminate any answers that aren't consistent with this prediction. Choice (A) can be eliminated because, although *dead-end* is in the text, the paragraph is not suggesting the *research* is the dead-end. Choice (B) might initially look attractive because there is a contrast between what scientists did believe and what they now believe, but the text doesn't say anything about *complex genetic capabilities*. Eliminate (B). Choice (C) is consistent with the prediction, so keep it. Choice (D) does not match the prediction at all, so eliminate it. The correct answer is (C).

42. **C** This question asks what the word *striking* most nearly means in line 23. Go back to the text, find the word *striking*, and cross it out. Then read the window carefully, using context clues to determine another word that would fit in the text. The text says that the hybrids represent *new species* and goes on to say that the lizard has a *strange genetic makeup*. This missing word must mean something like "stands out" or "noticeable." Eliminate (A) right away. While all three remaining answers could be "noticeable" for different reasons, the text doesn't provide any support for the lizard being noticeable for a really good reason or a really bad reason. Eliminate (B) and (D). Choice (C), *impressive*, is consistent with the prediction. The correct answer is (C).

43. **B** This question asks about a difference between *whiptail lizards* and *other species of hybrids,* specifically asking what's relevant to the *female whiptail lizard*. Notice that this is first question in a paired set, so it can be done in tandem with Q44. Look at the answers to Q44 first. Choice (44A) mentions *sterile mules* and *hybrid progeny…dead-ends*. There is no mention of female whiptail lizards, so this answer cannot support any of the answers for Q43. Eliminate (44A). The lines in (44B) reference the eggs hatching *healthy female clones*. This answer supports (43B), so draw a line connecting those two answers. Choice (44C) mentions that some whiptail lizards carry *three sets of genes, rather than two*. This might initially seem to support (43D), but notice the extreme language. Choice (43D) uses the word *always*, while the text says *some species*. Eliminate (44C). Choice (44D) states that male lizards sometimes mate with female lizards. This is not anything different from any other species of animal, so it will not support any of the answers for Q43. Eliminate (44D). Without any support from Q44, (43A), (43C), and (43D) can all be eliminated. The correct answers are (43B) and (44B).

44. **B** (See explanation above.)

45. **B** This question asks about the main idea of the eleventh paragraph. Find the eleventh paragraph and carefully read to determine the author's main point. The paragraph begins with a question (*How can that be?*) that stems from the preceding statement that some species of whiptail lizard have three sets of genes rather than two. After asking the question, the author goes on to offer a hypothesis, explaining that a possible explanation is that male lizards mating with a parthenogenic female could create an egg with three sets of genes. Immediately after the eleventh paragraph, the author says that *the strangeness doesn't end there*. This paragraph is another example of a question scientists have about the strangeness of the whiptail lizards. Eliminate anything that isn't consistent with the prediction of explaining a phenomenon. Choice (A) might initially look attractive, because the lizard is definitely complicated, but the main point of the paragraph is the whiptail lizard, not all hybrids in general. Eliminate (A). Choice (B) is true, so keep it. Choice (C) can be eliminated because there is no mention of cloning *other animals* in the text. Choice (D) can also be eliminated because the paragraph discusses a hypothesis about the genetic makeup of the lizard, not why or why not the lizard survives. The correct answer is (B).

46. **A** The question asks why progress happened in 21st century genetic research of the whiptail lizard. Notice that this is the first question in a paired set, so it can be done in tandem with Q47. Read the answers for Q47 first. Choice (47A) says that the female lizards can *duplicate the chromosomes in their*

offspring without males. This has nothing to do with the research of the 21st century and will therefore not support any of the answers for Q46. Eliminate (47A). Choice (47B) states that *it gets more bizarre*, which does not support any of the answers for Q46. Eliminate (47B). Both (47C) and (47D) reference research, so look at the answers for Q46 to see if there are any matches. Neither (47C) nor (47D) mentions anything about *professional rivals* or *parthenogenesis*, so eliminate (46B) and (46D). Choice (47C) might initially seem to support (46C), but read carefully. The lines say that Neaves was *searching for whiptails* when he discovered one with *four chromosomes*. He already knew the lizards were there, so he wasn't discovering them. Eliminate (46C) and (47C). Choice (47D) supports (46A) because it mentions *new scientific tools*. The correct answers are (46A) and (47D).

47. **D** (See above explanation).

Section 2: Writing and Language

1. **B** Note the question! The question is asking for the most effective combination of the underlined sentences. Start with (B), the shortest. This option is both precise and concise, and it effectively combines the two sentences, so (A), (C), and (D) can be eliminated. The correct answer is (B).

2. **B** Pronouns and verbs are changing in the answers, so the question is testing consistency. Start with the pronouns. A pronoun must be consistent with the noun it replaces. The noun that is replaced is *the pasty*, which is singular, so (C) and (D) can be eliminated. The difference between (A) and (B) is the verb tense. The sentence references *Today*, so (A) can be eliminated. The correct answer is (B).

3. **B** Pronouns and verbs are changing in the answers, so the question is testing consistency. Start with the pronouns. The sentence is referencing *those* as a subject just before the underlined portion, so (C) can be eliminated since *which* cannot be used to reference people. Since the phrase *live in Cornwall* does not have a subject, one must be introduced in the form of *who*, and (A) can be eliminated. The difference between (B) and (D) is a singular or plural verb. Since *those* is plural, it requires a plural verb, and (D) can be eliminated. The correct answer is (B).

4. **A** Verbs are changing in the answers, so the question is testing verb consistency. A verb must be consistent with the subject and with other verbs. The subject of the sentence is *The composition*, a singular subject, which is consistent with each answer choice. Check for other verbs in the sentence. Later in the sentence is the verb *echoes* so look for an answer choice that is consistent. Choice (A) is consistent, so keep it. Choice (B) can be eliminated for the unnecessary inclusion of *which*, which makes the sentence incomplete. Choices (C) and (D) are not consistent, so eliminate them. The correct answer is (A).

5. **D** Note the question! The question is asking for the best introduction to the paragraph. Begin by reading to get a gist of the key topic in discussion. The paragraph starts out with *For example*, and then discusses the shape of the pasty and ties this into how miners would hold the crust of the pasty. Use POE to look for an answer relevant to the topic of discussion. Choice (A) seems relevant, so keep it for now. Choice (B) references *diners in Cornwall*, but not the miners, so eliminate it. Choice (C) makes no mention of the miners, so eliminate it. Choice (D) references both the *distinctive shape* and the miners, so it is the best introduction, and (A) can be eliminated. The correct answer is (D).

6. **D** The number of words are changing in the answers, so the question is testing concision. Keep (D), the shortest, but check the remaining choices just to be sure. Choices (A), (B), and (C) are each unnecessarily wordy or redundant, so they can be eliminated. The correct answer is (D).

7. **B** Commas are changing in the answers, so the question is testing the four ways to use a comma. Since (B) has commas surrounding *for instance*, check for unnecessary information. When *for instance* is removed from the sentence, the sentence still preserves its original intent. Since this is the case, commas (or dashes) must surround *for instance*, and (A), (C), and (D) can be eliminated. The correct answer is (B).

8. **D** Transitions are changing in the answers, so the question is testing consistency of ideas. Begin by reading the sentence to determine the context. The sentence discusses that *the EU's definition of the "official" Cornish pasty calls for the pie to contain at least 12.5% beef, the earliest recipes for pasties involved venison, ... often pork*. Since the two ideas are in contrast, (A) and (B) can be eliminated. There is no evidence of a *convenience*, so (C) can be eliminated. The correct answer is (D).

9. **C** Note the question! The question is asking whether the writer should add the provided sentence. The provided sentence discusses what the EU defines as protected regional foods, but the paragraph is discussing various ingredients of pasties, so the addition would not make sense here and (A) and (B) can be eliminated. Use POE to compare the reasons in the remaining choices. Choice (C) is supported, so keep it. Choice (D) suggests placing the sentence at the beginning of the paragraph, but it still would not have relevance there. Eliminate (D). The correct answer is (C).

10. **C** Phrases are changing in the answers, so the question is testing precision. Choice (A) produces a meaning that *many laborers* collapsed Cornwall's mining industry and is not what is intended. Choice (A) can be eliminated. Choices (B) and (D) also produce the meaning that the many laborers collapsed the mining industry, so eliminate (B) and (D). The correct answer is (C).

11. **A** Note the question! The question is asking for the clearest connection of the statement to the theme of the rest of the paragraph. Begin by reading the surrounding details to get the gist of what is discussed. The previous sentence states *many laborers immigrated elsewhere in search of work* and the following sentence references the different locations to encounter the Cornish pie and its global influence. Keep (A) since this is relevant to the discussed topics, but check the other answers to be sure. Choice (B) references other traditional hand-pie recipes, a detail irrelevant to the paragraph, so it can be eliminated. Choices (C) and (D) can be eliminated as well since the *decline of the pastry in Cornwall* and *a global mining boom* are not relevant details to the paragraph. The correct answer is (A).

12. **A** The additional wording after *Newfoundland* is changing in the answers, so the question is testing concision. Keep (A), the shortest, but check the remaining choices to be sure. There is no need for a transition to link the thoughts, so (B), (C), and (D) can be eliminated. The correct answer is (A).

13. **C** The number of words after *generations* is changing, so the question is testing concision. Keep (C), the shortest, but check the remaining choices to be sure. Choices (A), (B), and (D) are each either unnecessarily wordy or redundant and can be eliminated. The correct answer is (C).

14. **B** Punctuation is changing in the answers, so the question is testing STOP/GO punctuation. One of the FANBOYS, *and,* appears after a comma, so use the Vertical Line Test and draw two vertical lines surrounding *and.* Check to see if the ideas are complete or incomplete. Both before and after the set of vertical lines are complete ideas, so either STOP or HALF-STOP punctuation is needed and (A) and (D) can be eliminated. The inclusion of a colon before the *and* in (C) makes it incorrect as the *and* is not necessary to join the two ideas. The correct answer is (B).

15. **A** Commas surrounding a phrase are changing in the answers, so the question is testing the four ways to use a comma. Removing *across the board* from the sentence does not change the original intent of the sentence, so commas (or dashes) need to surround the phrase to denote unnecessary information. Choices (B) and (D) can be eliminated. Choice (C) contains a colon, so check with the Vertical Line Test. Draw a vertical line between *were* and *across.* The idea before the vertical line is incomplete. Since HALF-STOP punctuation requires starting with a complete idea, (C) can safely be eliminated. The correct answer is (A).

16. **B** Note the question! The question is asking for the most effective combination of the underlined sentences. Start with (D), the shortest. The sentences are combined, but there is a precision error with the ambiguous pronoun *they,* which could refer to *dogs, wolves,* or *people.* Eliminate (D). Move to the next shortest answer, (B). The phrase in the beginning, *Even when confronted with strangers,* correctly modifies *the dogs,* and there is a consistency in comparison with *the dogs spent much more time than the wolves did.* The correct answer is (B).

17. **C** Punctuation is changing in the answers, so the question is testing STOP/GO punctuation. Use the Vertical Line Test to identify ideas as complete or incomplete. Begin by drawing a vertical line between *chromosome 6* and *whose.* Before the vertical line is a complete idea and after is an incomplete idea, so HALF-STOP or GO punctuation is needed and (A) and (B) can be eliminated. In (D), *whose* is removed, which makes the second idea complete and requires STOP or HALF-STOP punctuation, so it can be eliminated. The correct answer is (C).

18. **A** Apostrophes are changing in the answers, so the question is testing apostrophe usage. An apostrophe is necessary to denote possession or a contraction. Since *disruptions* is a noun, check for possession. The disruptions are not possessing anything, so no apostrophe is needed and (B) and (D) can be eliminated. The singular or plural form of *genetic* is the next difference, so check for consistency in the non-underlined parts. The previous sentence references *genetic sequence,* so eliminate (C) for inconsistency. The correct answer is (A).

19. **C** Note the question! The question is asking for the choice that describes the represented data most accurately. Begin by referencing the map and the legend. The map provides data points regarding the age of bones found. Choice (A) can be eliminated since 7,000 years old is unable to be determined, and (B) is irrelevant. Choice (C) is verified by the legend, so keep it for now and check (D). The data is not greater than 10,000 years old, so (D) can be eliminated. The correct answer is (C).

20. **B** Note the question! The question is asking for the choice that describes the represented data most accurately. Use POE to check the answers to the data presented in the map. Choice (A) can be eliminated since Central Africa had ages of around 8,000 years old. According to the key, 12,000 years old is the darkest markings, and those are mostly populated around France and western Russia. Choices (C) and (D) can be eliminated. The correct answer is (B).

21. **C** Note the question! The question is asking where sentence 2 should be logically placed. Begin by reading sentence 2 to determine the details. Sentence 2 references *those locations*, so it needs to be placed after a sentence referencing locations. Choice (A) can be eliminated since there is no mention of locations. Choice (B) can be eliminated since sentence 2 would begin the paragraph and there is no mention of locations in the last sentence of the previous paragraph. After sentence 3 would make logical sense due to references of locations and fossil evidence, so keep it for now. Choice (D) can be eliminated since the end of it discusses migrating west from eastern Asia and would not logically lead into sentence 2. The correct answer is (C).

22. **D** Verbs are changing in the answers, so the question is testing verb consistency. A verb must be consistent with its subject and other verbs in the text. The subject of the sentence is *study*, which is singular. All of the answer choices are consistent with the subject, so look for other verbs in the sentence. Appearing earlier in the sentence is *However one interprets*, and the form of *interprets* is most consistent with *points*, so (A), (B), and (C) can be eliminated. The correct answer is (D).

23. **D** Phrases are changing in the answers, so the question is testing consistency of ideas. The sentence is discussing where the Wailing Wailers got their sound from. The elements were drawn from two discussed references: the Caribbean's traditional music and American jazz and R&B. The connecting phrase for these two elements is *not only...but also*, which requires parallel construction. The non-underlined part states *but also of American...*, so *not only of Caribbean...* is required and (A), (B), and (C) can be eliminated. The correct answer is (D).

24. **A** Note the question! The question is asking whether the author should make the proposed revision. The proposed revision expands upon the socially- and politically-inflected lyrics, so the revision would be appropriate in the context. Eliminate (C) and (D). The revision does not help the reader to understand what decolonization is, so (B) can be eliminated. The correct answer is (A).

25. **D** Words are changing in the answers, so the question is testing word choice and concision. The sentence states *Within three years, the band had (increased) some local success but was not making much money*. In context, the word should reference how the band started earning recognition. Choices (A), (B), and (C) can be eliminated for not matching the prediction. The correct answer is (D).

26. **B** Punctuation is changing in the answers, so the question is testing STOP/GO punctuation. Use the Vertical Line Test and identify ideas as complete or incomplete. Begin by drawing a vertical line between *breakthrough* and *creative*. Before the vertical line is *However, amidst a reception that amounted to the band's big breakthrough*, which is an incomplete idea. Choices (A), (C), and (D) can be eliminated right now since only GO punctuation can have an incomplete idea preceding it. The correct answer is (B).

27. **B** Note the question! The question is asking whether the writer should make the provided addition. Begin by reading the surrounding text to determine the topic of the paragraph. The previous paragraph ends with the Wailers disbanding in 1974, and this paragraph begins to introduce and discuss Marley's success. The proposed addition provides a seamless transition to introduce the new topic, so the addition would be appropriate, and (C) and (D) can be eliminated. Choice (A) can be eliminated because the proposed addition does not explain roles of Livingston and Tosh. The correct answer is (B).

28. **C** The number of words is changing in the answers, so the question is testing concision. Keep (C), the shortest, but check the remaining choices just to be sure. Choices (A), (B), and (D) are either redundant or unnecessarily wordy and can safely be eliminated. The correct answer is (C).

29. **D** Words are changing in the answer choices, so the question is testing idiom. Neither *taking a hold to* nor *taking ahold to* are correct usage, so eliminate (A) and (B). *Taking a whole of* is not an English phrase, so eliminate (C). *Taking a hold of* is the correct idiom. The correct answer is (D).

30. **C** Punctuation and pronouns are changing in the answers, so the question is testing comma usage and precision. Begin with the punctuation. There is no reason to slow down the ideas here, so a comma is not necessary and (A) and (B) can be eliminated. To use *which* in context, a comma would be necessary, so (D) can be eliminated. The correct answer is (C).

31. **D** Note the question! The question is asking for the best transition to connect to the final idea of the previous paragraph. The final idea of the previous paragraph was that Bob Marley collapsed while jogging and died at age 36. The only answer relevant to Bob Marley's death is (D), so (A), (B), and (C) can be eliminated. The correct answer is (D).

32. **C** Transitions are changing in the answers, so the question is testing consistency of ideas. Begin by reading the sentence to get the gist of the ideas discussed. The sentence states *His biggest legacy, (therefore), might be the doors he helped to open for artists outside the U.S. and Europe.* The previous sentence discusses the amount of money his estate earned in 2014 to make him the sixth-highest-earning dead celebrity that year. The two ideas are not similar, so a contrasting transition is required and (A), (B), and (D) can be eliminated. The correct answer is (C).

33. **A** Punctuation is changing in the answers, so the question is testing STOP/GO punctuation. Use the Vertical Line Test to identify ideas as complete or incomplete. Begin by drawing a vertical line between *who* and *almost*. Before the vertical line is an incomplete idea, so (B) and (D) can be eliminated. Since there is no appropriate reason to use a comma, either unnecessary info or listing, (C) can be eliminated. The correct answer is (A).

34. **C** Phrases are changing in the answer choices, and the option to DELETE appears, so the question is testing consistency and concision. Begin by checking to see if the underlined portion can be removed from the sentence. Removing *hopefully* would and introduce a grammar error, so eliminate (D). Choices (A) and (B) would also introduce a grammar error, so eliminate them. The correct answer is (C).

35. **C** The number of words is changing in the answer choices, so the question is testing concision. Keep (C), the shortest, but check the other answers just in case. Choices (A), (B), and (D) are unnecessarily wordy and repetitive, so eliminate them. The correct answer is (C).

36. **C** Words are changing in the answer choices, so the question is testing consistency of ideas. Begin by reading the relevant sentence to get an idea of the word that would best fit. The sentence states that *individual critics and curators mediated which arts and crafts the general public (bumped into) and where and how that happened.* The underlined portion should mean something like *came across.* Choice (D) does not match the prediction, so eliminate it. Choice (B) is excessively wordy, so eliminate it. Choice (A) is overly informal, and thus inconsistent with the tone of the passage; eliminate it. The correct answer is (C).

37. **D** Transitions are changing in the answer choices, so the question is testing consistency of ideas. Begin by reading the previous sentence and the current sentence to get a sense of direction and relationship between the two sentences. The previous sentence discusses *Internet venues* providing *more opportunities…* and the sentence in question provides a specific example of such a venue. Choices (A) and (C) offer a contrast, so eliminate them. Choice (B), *moreover*, is not the correct transition word, so eliminate it. Choice (D), *for example*, fits the prediction. The correct answer is (D).

38. **D** Note the question! The question is asking for the choice that most effectively completes the contrast between the productions mentioned in this and the previous sentences. Begin by reading the sentences to get a sense of the topic discussed. The previous sentence references *artists with formal training and burgeoning careers* and the current sentence starts with *At the other end of the spectrum*, so the underlined contrast should refer to non-formally trained artists. Carefully consider the answers and use POE. Choices (A), (B), and (C) do not address this issue of training, so eliminate them. The correct answer is (D).

39. **A** Phrases and apostrophes are changing in the answer choices, so the question is testing consistency and precision. Begin by reading the sentence to get an idea of the topic being discussed. The sentence references that *Platforms…allow artists to share not only the photos…but also….* The non-underlined *not only… but also* phrasing requires parallel construction for consistency. Choices (B) and (C) begin with *those the*, which introduces a grammatical error, so eliminate them. Choices (A) and (D) begin with *those that*, which provides parallel construction. Choice (A) refers to the photos as *those that capture*, which is correct, whereas (D) refers to the photos as *those that capturing*, which is incorrect. Eliminate (D). The correct answer is (A).

40. **D** Note the question! The question is asking whether the writer should add the proposed sentence. Begin by reading the relevant surrounding text to get an idea of the topic discussed. The previous sentence discussed various platforms that help artists share photos. The following sentence continues the discussion of another such website. The proposed addition would not fit in context with the surrounding information, so it should not be added. Eliminate (A) and (B). There is no support for the claim that the artwork must speak for itself, so eliminate (C). The correct answer is (D).

41. **B** Punctuation is changing in the answer choices, so the question is testing consistency of punctuation. The end of the non-underlined sentence contains a close parenthesis, so the answer must contain an open parenthesis. Eliminate (A), (C), and (D). The correct answer is (B).

42. **D** Pronouns are changing in the answer choices, so the question is testing pronoun consistency. A pronoun must be consistent with the noun it refers to and with other pronouns that appear. The subject of the sentence is *sellers*, which is plural, so eliminate (B) and (C). Because *there* refers to location, eliminate (A). The correct answer is (D).

43. **B** Note the question! The question is asking for the best location for sentence 4. Begin by reading sentence 4 to get an idea of the topic discussed and use process of elimination to determine the logical placement of the sentence. Sentence 4 begins with *The key difference*, but the previous paragraph did not end with a similarity, so Sentence 4 should not come before Sentence 1; eliminate (A). Sentence 4 could logically follow the comparison in Sentence 1 between *the abundance of artists now listing their work on Internet sites* and *the saturation of artists vying for gallery space*, so keep (B) for now. Sentence 4 does not logically follow either Sentence 3 or Sentence 5, so eliminate (C) and (D). The correct answer is (B).

44. **A** Pronouns are changing in the answer choices, so the question is testing pronoun consistency. A pronoun must be consistent with the noun it refers to and with other pronouns that appear. The sentence states *If you're an aspiring…*, so a form of *you* would be needed to remain consistent. Eliminate (B), (C), and (D). The correct answer is (A).

Section 3: Math (No Calculator)

1. **A** The question is asking for the ordered pair that represents the solution to the provided system of equations. Since the choices represent the specific possible solutions, Plugging In the Answers will be able to help here. Label the answers as (x, y). Since there's no specific order, start with (A), $(-5, -8)$ and plug it into the first equation: $(-8) = (-5) - 3$, and $-8 = -8$, a true statement. Check $(-5, -8)$ in the second equation: $(-8) = (-5)^2 + 5(-5) - 8$, $-8 = 25 - 25 - 8$, and $-8 = -8$, a true statement. Since the $(-5, -8)$ holds true for both equations, this must be the solution. The correct answer is (A).

2. **B** The question is asking for an equivalent form of the provided expression. Previewing the answer choices reveals that the expression needs to be factored. Factor out an n from both terms: $12mn + 20n = (12m + 20)n$. Alternatively, the question and answer choices contain variables, so Plugging In could be used. Keep the numbers small since the calculator cannot be used. The correct answer is (B).

3. **D** The question is asking for an expression for mass, m, in terms of d and v. Write down the provided equation and isolate m by multiplying v to the other side: $d = \dfrac{m}{v}$, and $dv = m$. Alternatively, there are variables in the question and answer choices, so Plugging In could be used. The correct answer is (D).

4. **B** The question is asking for the value of y that satisfies the system of equations. Since the question is asking for the value of y, manipulate the equations to make the x terms cancel out. Multiply the first equation by 3 to get $3(2x + 7y = 5) = 6x + 21y = 15$ and the second equation by 2 to get $2(-3x - 3y = 15) = -6x - 6y = 30$. Stack the equations and add to get $15y = 45$. Solve for y by dividing both sides by 15 to get $y = 3$. Alternatively, the question is asking for a specific value and the answers are numbers in increasing order, so Plugging In the Answers could be used. The correct answer is (B).

5. **B** The question is asking for the value of a that satisfies the provided equation. Since the question is asking for a specific value and the answers are smaller numbers in increasing order, Plugging In the Answers will be able to help. Label the answers as a and start with (B). Plug $x = a = -2$ into the equation and simplify: $3 + 2(-2) = (-2)^2 - 5$, $3 - 4 = 4 - 5$, and $-1 = -1$, a true statement. Alternatively, combine like terms and solve the quadratic either by factoring or using the quadratic formula. The correct answer is (B).

6. **A** The question is asking for the coordinate that cannot represent point C. The question provides the equation $y = ax + b$ and that $a < 0 < b$, or a is negative and b is positive. In a linear expression in the form $y = mx + b$, m represents the slope and b represents the y-intercept. It can be concluded that in $y = ax + b$ form, the y-intercept, b, is positive and the slope, a, is negative. The line would cross the y-axis above the x-axis and would travel down and to the right, as well as up and to the left, meaning that the line would pass through quadrants I, II, and IV, but not quadrant III. So any coordinate in quadrant III could not be point C. In quadrant III, both the x- and y-coordinates are negative, so look for a point with both a negative x- and y-coordinate. The correct answer is (A).

7. **D** The question is asking what the y-intercept of the provided equation represents. Begin by writing the equation and labeling what is known from the question. In the equation $y = 14,000 - 0.2x$, y is the value of the car in dollars and x is the number of miles it has been driven since it was purchased. The y-intercept occurs when $x = 0$. It can be concluded then that when it was purchased, at $x = 0$ miles, $y = \$14,000$. Use process of elimination in the answers. Choice (A) can be eliminated because this would be represented by 0.2. Choice (B) can be eliminated since this is not represented in the equation. Choice (C) can be eliminated as this is x. The correct answer is (D).

8. **C** The question is asking for the equation that correctly calculates the total cost of the purchase after the discount. Read the question carefully using bite-sized pieces to translate the information. The question states that there is a 15% discount applied, so the total cost after discount would be 85%, or $0.85 \times$ total cost. This allows (A), (B), and (D) to be eliminated. The correct answer is (C).

9. **C** The question is asking for the system of inequalities that correctly represents the provided information. Begin by reading the question carefully. Translate using bite-sized pieces, and use process of elimination. The question states that the theater needs to sell at least 10 tickets of each type: Matinee, m, and Nighttime, n. This can be translated as $m \geq 10$ and $n \geq 10$, so (B) and (D) can be eliminated. The question also states that the theater needs to receive at least \$200, which can be translated as ≥ 200 and (A) can be eliminated. The correct answer is (C).

10. **B** The question is asking for the inequality that represents all possible values of the calories, c, the cat consumes in the week. Begin by eliminating (D) since this is the range each day, while the question asks for the entire week. At minimum, the cat will consume more than 290 calories per day, so for the week this is $7 \times 290 = 2{,}030$ calories, so eliminate (A). Also, (C) could be safely Ballparked out here since the greater value will not be only 50 calories more for the entire week. The maximum number of calories consumed for the week must be less than $7 \times 340 = 2{,}380$. The correct answer is (B).

11. **C** The question is asking for the value of a, the x-coordinate of the vertex of the parabola. The equation provided is the factored form of a quadratic which provides the x-intercepts as $x = -4$ and $x = 8$. The vertex of a parabola is centrally located between the intercepts, so find the distance between the intercepts and divide by two: $\frac{8 - (-4)}{2} = \frac{12}{2} = 6$. This means that the vertex will be 6 units away from either x-intercept, so $a = -4 + 6 = 2$, or $a = 8 - 6 = 2$. The correct answer is (C).

12. **B** The question is asking for the value of n. The provided equation includes terms with bases and exponents, so MADSPM will need to be applied. The question asks for a specific value for n, and the answers are numbers in increasing order, so Plugging In the Answers will be able to help. Label the answers as n and start with (B), $n = 7$. Begin with the left-side of the equation. When raising a power to another power, multiply the exponents. Begin with the numerator and distribute: $\left(x^7 y^7\right)^{\frac{1}{4}} = x^{\frac{7}{4}} y^{\frac{7}{4}}$. Repeat this process in the denominator: $\left(x^3 y^3\right)^{\frac{1}{2}} = x^{\frac{3}{2}} y^{\frac{3}{2}}$. When dividing exponential terms with the same bases, subtract the exponents: $\frac{x^{\frac{7}{4}} y^{\frac{7}{4}}}{x^{\frac{3}{2}} y^{\frac{3}{2}}} = x^{\frac{7}{4} - \frac{3}{2}} y^{\frac{7}{4} - \frac{3}{2}} = x^{\frac{1}{4}} y^{\frac{1}{4}} = \left(xy\right)^{\frac{1}{4}}$, which matches the equation provided. Alternatively, use algebra and MADSPM to rewrite the left-hand side to match the right-hand side. The correct answer is (B).

13. **A** The question is asking for the statement that must be true based on the provided figure. The figure contains two triangles, $\triangle MLN$ and $\triangle LON$. Both triangles share $\angle N$, and the question states that $\angle LMO = \angle OLN$, so it can be concluded that the two triangles are similar. It can be helpful to redraw the triangles separately. Draw $\triangle LON$ as it appears in the figure, but when redrawing $\triangle MLN$, it must be drawn with L at the top of the triangle and M and N on the left and the right corners of the base, respectively.

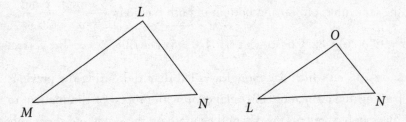

This reveals the sides that will be proportional and process of elimination can be used in the answers to eliminate (B), (C), and (D). The correct answer is (A).

14. **39** The question is asking for the height, in inches, of Sarah's bamboo stalk. The combined height is given as 4 feet 4 inches tall. Use the conversion 1 foot = 12 inches to figure out the height in inches as 4 × 12 = 48 inches + 4 inches = 52 inches total. Sarah's bamboo stalk is three times as tall as Lizzie's, so let Lizzie = x and Sarah = $3x$. An equation can be created as $x + 3x = 52$. Combine like terms and solve for x: $4x = 52$, and $x = 13$. Since Sarah = $3x$, the total height of the bamboo is $3(13)$ = 39 inches. The correct answer is 39.

15. **7** The question is asking for the value of c that will produce an equation with an infinite number of solutions. The expressions on both sides of the equal sign are each linear, and for linear expressions to have an infinite number of solutions, they must be the exact same. Begin by factoring 7 out of the right-hand expression to get $c(2n - 5) = 7(2n - 5)$. Therefore, $c = 7$. The correct answer is 7.

16. **14** The question is asking for the value of $5n - 3m$. Begin by using FOIL to expand out the left-hand side of the equation: $(3x + ny)(5x - my) = 15x^2 - 3mxy + 5nxy - mny^2 = 15x^2 + (5n - 3m)xy - mny^2$. The question states that $b = 14$, so the middle term on the right-hand side is $14xy$. Determine the value of $5n - 3m$ by setting the middle terms equal to each other: $(5n - 3m)xy = 14xy$. It can be concluded that $5n - 3m = 14$. The correct answer is 14.

17. **3** The question is asking for the value of c to make $5x - c$ a factor of the quadratic. Use the provided clue of $5x - c$ to begin factoring out the quadratic. The first term in the expression is $10x^2$, so the other factor must begin with $2x$. The last term in the expression is -3, so the numbers in the factors must be either -1 and 3 or 1 and -3. Use FOIL to confirm the factors if needed. $10x^2 - x - 3 = (5x - 3)(2x + 1)$, so $c = 3$. The correct answer is 3.

Section 4: Math (Calculator)

1. **D** The question asks for how many milligrams of caffeine Jason would consume were he to drink 26 ounces of coffee. Begin by reading the question to identify a relationship between ounces and milligrams. The question states that 8 ounces of coffee contain 95 milligrams of caffeine. Use this to set up a proportion to determine the number of milligrams in 26 ounces of coffee, being sure

to keep the same units on top and bottom of both fractions: $\dfrac{95 \text{ mg}}{8 \text{ oz}} = \dfrac{x \text{ mg}}{26 \text{ oz}}$. Cross-multiply and solve for x: $(95)(26) = 8x$. Consequently, $2{,}470 = 8x$ and $308.75 = x$. The correct answer is (D).

2. **B** The question asks on which day more leaves fell than did during the previous 2 days combined. Use ballparking and estimation, in conjunction with process of elimination, to narrow down the choices. The graph represents the day of the month on the x-axis and the number of leaves remaining, in thousands, on the y-axis. For more leaves to have fallen on one day than the combined total of the previous two days, the graph would need to have a steep decline to show a significant decrease in the number of leaves remaining. This only occurs around days 9 to 10, so (A), (C), and (D) can be eliminated. The correct answer is (B).

3. **A** The question asks for the meaning of the number 23 in the equation. Begin by writing the equation and labeling what is known from the question. In the equation, F represents the number of logs remaining in Shawn's firewood supply and d represents the number of days that have passed. Choice (C) can safely be eliminated, since this is the description of d. Plug in values for d, like $d = 0$ and $d = 1$, to see what happens to F. When $d = 0$, $F = -23(0) + 1{,}235 = 1{,}235$ logs and when $d = 1$, $F = -23(1) + 1{,}235 = 1{,}212$ logs. Since after one day the remaining logs decreased by 23, keep (A) and check the remaining answers. Choice (B) is represented by 1,235, which was proven by plugging in $d = 0$. Choice (D) refers to the number of logs burned so far. This will change each day, as seen from plugging numbers into the function. Therefore, this quantity cannot be represented by a constant like 23. Eliminate (D). The correct answer is (A).

4. **C** The question asks for the difference between the actual average number of falls and the expected average number of falls for a skater with 10 years of experience. Begin by going to the graph and gathering the relevant data. For 10 years of experience, the actual plotted average number of falls is at about 200, and the line of best fit predicts the average number of falls to be approximately 150. The difference is $200 - 150 = 50$. The correct answer is (C).

5. **B** The question asks for an accurate description of the relationship between the years of experience and the average number of falls on the ice per month. Begin by looking at the graph to spot a trend and use process of elimination when considering the answer choices. The scatterplot shows that as the number of years of skating experience increases, the average number of falls seems to decline. This is also supported by the line of best fit, which is an indication of an inverse relationship, which means that (D) can be eliminated. Choices (A) and (C) can be eliminated as these would be direct relationships. The correct answer is (B).

6. **C** The question asks for the value of b in the provided equation. The question states that the line crosses the x-axis at the point $(3, 0)$, meaning that the line contains this point. Plug the point in to the equation $y = bx - 6$ to determine the value for b: $0 = b(3) - 6$, $6 = 3b$, and $2 = b$. The correct answer is (C).

7. **A** The question asks for the best description of the trend in the provided data. Use process of elimination when considering the answer choices. Start with (A). For sales to be increasing linearly, the total sales should be increasing by approximately 2,156 bulbs each month. Check the months using

a calculator carefully. January to February: 43,120 + 2,156 = 45,276, February to March: 45,276 + 2,156 = 47,432, March to April: 47,431 + 2,156 = 49,588, April to May: 49,588 + 2,156 = 51,744, and May to June: 51,741 + 2,156 = 53,897. Since all the calculations were either exact or only differing by at most 3 bulbs, (B), (C), and (D) could safely be ruled out. The correct answer is (A).

8. **A** The question asks for an equivalent form of the provided expression. Use bite-sized pieces and process of elimination to tackle this question. Begin with the first term, mn^2, and combine it with the like term in the second set of parentheses, paying attention to sign changes: $mn^2 - (3mn^2) = -2mn^2$. Choices (B), (C), and (D) can be ruled out since they do not contain this result in the expression. Alternatively, the question and the answer choices contain variables, so Plugging In could have been used. The correct answer is (A).

9. **D** The question asks for the running pace in kilometers per hour. Begin by reading the question to find information on the running pace. The question states that Beatrix has been running each morning at a pace of 1 mile per 7 minutes and that 1 mile = 1.61 kilometers. This means that the pace is 1.61 kilometers per 7 minutes. There are 60 minutes in an hour, so set up a proportion to see how far she'll go in 60 minutes: $\dfrac{1.61 \text{ km}}{7 \text{ minutes}} = \dfrac{x \text{ km}}{60 \text{ minutes}}$. Cross-multiply to solve for x: 96.6 = 7x. Divide both sides of the equation by 7 to get 13.80. The correct answer is (D).

10. **D** The question asks for an accurate description of the results provided in the table. Inspection of the answer choices reveals that the concern needs to be mean and median. Begin by arranging the provided data from smallest to largest to get the median. For Mr. Sulu this is 21, 67, 71, 75, 81, 82, 82, 85, 90, and 99, and for Ms. Picard this is 55, 68, 74, 75, 79, 82, 89, 94, 98, and 100. Since there is an even list of elements in both classes, the median will be the average of the middle two data points. In Mr. Sulu's class, the median is $\dfrac{81+82}{2}$ = 81.5 and for Ms. Picard's class the median is $\dfrac{79+82}{2}$ = 80.5. The median is greater in Mr. Sulu's class than in Ms. Picard's class, so (A) and (B) can be eliminated. Next, calculate the average of each class by adding up all scores to get a total and dividing by the number of scores. Mr. Sulu's class average is $\dfrac{21+67+71+75+81+82+82+85+90+99}{10} = \dfrac{753}{10}$ = 75.3, and Ms. Picard's class average is $\dfrac{55+68+74+75+79+82+89+94+98+100}{10} = \dfrac{814}{10}$ = 81.4. Since Ms. Picard's class average is greater than Mr. Sulu's class average, (C) can be eliminated. The correct answer is (D).

11. **B** The question asks for what percent of all cats and dogs is represented by medium and large breed dogs. Begin by reading the table provided to determine the required values. The table shows that there are 210 medium breed dogs and 305 large breed dogs. This represents a total of 210 + 305 = 515 dogs. Find the total number of cats and dogs by adding all provided values in the table: 54 + 82 + 99 + 90 + 210 + 305 = 840 cats and dogs. Find the percentage by taking the total number of medium and large breed dogs divided by the total number of cats and dogs and multiplying by 100: $\frac{515}{840} \times 100 = 61.3\%$. The correct answer is (B).

12. **D** The question asks for the description of the solution set for the provided system of equations. Begin by getting the two equations to look like each other by subtracting $2y$ over to the left side of the second equation: $x - 2y = 5$. Inspection of the system reveals that multiplying the second equation by 3 results in $3x - 6y = 15$, which is identical to the first equation, and this means that there are infinite solutions to the system. Be careful with Plugging In the Answers here: In (A), (5, 3) is not a solution to either equation, so it may be tempting to eliminate (D). This just means that (5, 3) is not a point contained on the lines provided. The correct answer is (D).

13. **D** The question asks for the correct properties of the provided circle equation. The equation of a circle in standard form is $(x - h)^2 + (y - k)^2 = r^2$, where (h, k) is the center and r is the radius. Since $r^2 = 4$, the radius is 2 and (A) and (C) can be eliminated. Be careful of the sign changes in the equation when getting the center. In $(x - 1)^2 + (y + 7)^2$, the center is at $(1, -7)$, so (B) can be eliminated. The correct answer is (D).

14. **C** The question asks for how long it will take Jamie to prepare all 85 batches of cookies, in hours. Begin by reading the question carefully to find information about the batches and prep time. The question states that it takes 20 minutes to prepare 1 batch of cookies, so use this to set up a proportion, being sure to keep the consistent units on top and bottom of the fraction: $\frac{20 \text{ minutes}}{1 \text{ batch}} = \frac{x \text{ minutes}}{85 \text{ batches}}$. Cross-multiply to solve for x, the number of minutes: $(20)(85) = x$, and $x = 1,700$ minutes. Use the conversion of 60 minutes in 1 hour to get the time in hours: $\frac{1 \text{ hour}}{60 \text{ minutes}} = \frac{x \text{ hours}}{1,700 \text{ minutes}}$, $1,700 = 60x$, and $28.333 = x$. The correct answer is (C).

15. **A** The question asks for the difference, in degrees, between the mean and the mode of the provided data. Begin by going to the table to find the required values. The mode is the element of data that appears most frequently. The most frequent temperature is 54. Find the mean by adding up all temperatures and dividing by the total number of temperatures: $\frac{45 + 54 + 58 + 52 + 54 + 55 + 60}{7} = \frac{378}{7} = 54$. The mean is the same as the mode, so the difference is $54 - 54 = 0$ degrees. The correct answer is (A).

16. **C** The question asks for which adjustment to the provided formula would result in the overall grams of carbon dioxide increasing by 10 percent. The question provides the formula $C = \dfrac{V}{6} + 0.427$ in which C is grams of carbon dioxide and V is the volume of the beverage being carbonated. Use process of elimination when considering the answer choices. Choices (A) and (B) can safely be eliminated, as those do not apply to the overall change in grams of carbon dioxide. Choice (D) can be eliminated as well since that only changes the grams of carbon dioxide, and has nothing to do with altering the formula to increase the grams. When trying to illustrate a 10% increase in a quantity, add 10% of the quantity to 100% of the quantity, for a total of 110%, or 1.1. The correct answer is (C).

17. **C** The question asks for the probability that a submission for a child aged 8–11 would fall into either the Natural World or Historical Figures categories. Probability is defined as $\dfrac{\textit{\# of outcomes that fit the requirements}}{\textit{total \# of possible outcomes}}$, or, in this question, $\dfrac{\textit{8–11 Natural World or Historical Figures}}{\textit{total 8–11 children}}$. Begin by using the provided table to find the total number of children 8–11 for Natural World and Historical Figures. This total is 103 + 58 = 161, and this will be the numerator of the fraction. The total number of children from 8–11 is 103 + 58 + 69 = 230, and this will be the denominator of the fraction. Perform the division to find the probability: $\dfrac{161}{230} = 0.70 = \dfrac{7}{10}$. The correct answer is (C).

18. **D** The question asks for the percentage of Food and Fun submissions that were from students aged 11 and younger. Begin by going to the table to locate the totals for students in Food and Fun aged 5–7 and 8–11, which are 173 and 69, respectively, and the total submissions are 173 + 69 = 242. The total number of all submissions for Food and Fun are 173 + 69 + 54 = 296. Find the percentage by taking the Food and Fun submissions from the 5–7 and 8–11 age groups, dividing by the total number of Food and Fun submissions from all age groups, and multiplying by 100: $\dfrac{242}{296} \times 100 \approx 81.76\%$, which is closest to 82%. The correct answer is (D).

19. **C**   The question asks for the ratio of the number of first time entrants to the number of repeat entrants. Begin by reading the question carefully to find information regarding the various entrants. The question states that the director found that there were 96 entrants this year who also had a submission from the previous year, meaning that there are 96 repeat entrants. Find the number of first time entrants by finding the total number of entrants and subtracting the repeat entrants. The total number of entrants is $49 + 103 + 75 + 24 + 58 + 67 + 173 + 69 + 54 = 672$, and then the number of first time entrants is $672 - 96 = 576$. Since the number of first time entrants is greater than the number of repeat entrants, (A) and (B) can be ballparked out. The ratio of first-time entrants to repeat entrants is 576:96, or 6:1. The correct answer is (C).

20. **B**   The question asks for the perimeter of the garden, in feet, before the increase. Since the question asks for a specific value and the answers contain numbers in increasing order, Plugging In the Answers is helpful in tackling this question. Begin by labeling the answers as the original perimeter and start with (B), 40 feet. The garden is a square, so the length of each side is 10 feet. The formula for area of a square is $A = s^2$, so $A = (10)^2 = 100$. Marcus enlarges the garden by adding 3 feet of fencing to each side, so the new lengths of the sides will be $10 + 3 = 13$ feet, and the new area will be $A = (13)^2 = 169$. The resulting increase is $169 - 100 = 69$ square feet, which matches the target in the question, so stop here. Alternatively, translate the question into algebraic equations and solve for the length of the sides to arrive at the perimeter. The correct answer is (B).

21. **C**   The question asks for the function, of the ones provided, that contains two vertical asymptotes, one of which is the same as the one in the provided equation and another that is located seven units to the left of the common asymptote. For a rational function to have a vertical asymptote, the denominator must equal zero for some value of x. Since two x-values are required, (D) can be eliminated. Begin by identifying the vertical asymptote in the provided function. Find the value of x by setting the denominator equal to zero and solving: $2x - 8 = 0$, $2x = 8$, and $x = 4$. Next, determine the x-values of the answer choices to match the requirements of the question. The denominator of (A) is $x^2 - 15x + 44$ and can be factored as $(x - 4)(x - 11)$, resulting in x-values of $x = 4$ and $x = 11$. Since $x = 11$ is located 7 units to the right of $x = 4$, (A) can be eliminated. The denominator of (B) is already factored, so set each factor equal to zero and solve. The first factor was already solved from the original function, so solve the second factor: $2x - 1 = 0$, $2x = 1$, and $x = \frac{1}{2}$. Since $x = \frac{1}{2}$ is not 7 units to the left, (B) can be eliminated, leaving only one choice remaining. Either stop here or check (C) to confirm. The denominator of (C), $x^2 - x - 12$, can be factored as $(x - 4)(x + 3)$. Setting each factor equal to zero and solving results in $x = 4$ and $x = -3$, which satisfies the restrictions of the question. The correct answer is (C).

22. **C** The question asks what factor the volume of the can will increase by with the provided changes. Since the question is describing a relationship, Plugging In will be able to help tackle this question. The radius of each can is provided, so plug in for a uniform height of each can, such as $h = 2$. The formula for the volume of a cylinder is $V = \pi r^2 h$, so plug in the values to determine the volume of each can. The first can's volume is $V = \pi(2)^2(2) = 8\pi$ and the second can's volume is $V = \pi(4)^2(2) = 32\pi$. Find the factor of increase by dividing the larger volume by the smaller volume: $\frac{32\pi}{8\pi} = 4$. The correct answer is (C).

23. **C** The question asks for the x-value that the maximum value of the quadratic function will occur at. A quadratic function has symmetry around the vertex, meaning that for x-values evenly spaced away from the vertex, the corresponding y-coordinate, or value, will be the same. The question states that the quadratic function t contains the points $(-3, 5)$ and $(9, 5)$. Since the y-coordinates are the same, the maximum value of the parabola must occur at the x-value located centrally between the provided x-values of the coordinates. Find this by taking the average of the x-values: $x = \frac{-3+9}{2} = \frac{6}{2} = 3$. Alternatively, plot the points and use the negative x^2 fact to roughly sketch the parabola and plot the answers to ballpark. The correct answer is (C).

24. **C** The question asks for the function that best models the average height of the plants t days after planting. Begin by reading the question carefully to find information regarding the number of days and height. The question states that 72 days after planting, the height is 120 centimeters. Let $t = 72$ and $h(t) = 120$ to see which answer provides the relationship. In (A), $1.67(72) + 10 = 120.24 + 10 = 130.24$, which doesn't approximately equal 120 cm, so it can be eliminated. In (B), $0.65(72) + 10 = 46.8 + 10 = 56.8$ and can be eliminated. In (C), $1.53(72) + 10 = 110.16 + 10 = 120.16$, fairly close to 120 cm, so keep (C), but check (D) just in case. Choice (D) could safely be ballparked out since instead of adding 10, it adds 110. Checking (D) results in $1.53(72) + 110 = 110.16 + 110 = 220.16$, which is too large. The correct answer is (C).

25. **A** The question asks for the expression that represents $g(x + 2)$. Since both the question and answer choices contain the variable x, Plugging In will be able to help tackle this question. Begin by plugging in a simple number for x, such as $x = 2$. This means that $g(2 + 2) = g(4) = 2(4)^2 + 3(4) - 6 = 32 + 12 - 6 = 38$. This is the target, so circle 38 and check the answers with $x = 2$ to see which matches. Choice (A) becomes $g(2 + 2) = 2(2)^2 + 11(2) + 8 = 8 + 22 + 8 = 38$. Keep (A) but check the remaining answers just in case. Choice (B) becomes $g(2 + 2) = 2(2)^2 + 3(2) + 8 = 8 + 6 + 8 = 22$ and can be eliminated. Choice (C) becomes $g(2 + 2) = 2(2)^2 + 3(2) - 4 = 8 + 6 - 4 = 10$ and can be eliminated. Choice (D) becomes $g(2 + 2) = 2(2)^2 + 7(2) + 4 = 8 + 14 + 4 = 26$ and can be eliminated. The correct answer is (A).

26. **A** The question asks for the point that the two lines would intersect. Since the question asks for a specific solution and the choices provide possible solutions, Plugging In the Answers will be able to help tackle this question. Begin by labeling the answers as (x, y) and start with (A), (9, 9). Plugging in this coordinate to the first equation yields $(9) = -2(9) + 27$, $9 = -18 + 27$, and $9 = 9$. Since this is true, check the coordinate in the second equation: $(9) = -2(9) + 27$, which also yields $9 = 9$. Since (9, 9) is a solution, (C) can safely be eliminated. Checking (B) is not helpful, as the two equations could be the same line, but not cross through that point, and there cannot be more than one correct answer to the question. Proceed to checking (D) to determine whether the two equations represent the same line. The first equation is already in slope-intercept form. Change the second equation to slope-intercept form by subtracting 27 from both sides to get $x - 27 = -2y$. Then divide both sides by -2 to get $-\dfrac{x}{2} + \dfrac{27}{2} = y$. Because this does not match the first equation, they do not describe the same line. Eliminate (D) The correct answer is (A).

27. **D** The question asks for the best type of equation to model the growth. Begin by reading the question carefully to identify information regarding the growth. The question states that the magician decides to pull rabbits out of a hat, over successive nights, in values of 2, 4, 8, 16, and 32 for each performance. Use process of elimination when considering the answer choices. Since the number of rabbits is doubling with each performance, the relationship is neither constant nor linear, so (A) and (B) can be eliminated. For (C), $2^2 = 4$, but $4^2 \neq 8$, so it can be eliminated, leaving only (D), which is correct since the number of rabbits each evening exactly doubles, therefore increasing by 100% each night. The correct answer is (D).

28. **24** The question asks for the product of the y-values of the points of intersection. Since the question provides both equations solved for y, set the expressions equal to solve for x. This becomes $5x - 18 = x^2 - 5x + 6$. Subtract $5x - 18$ from both sides to get $0 = x^2 - 10x + 24$. Factor the right side to solve for x: $0 = (x - 6)(x - 4)$, and $x = 6$ and $x = 4$. Plug the values of x into the first equation to determine the corresponding y-values. When $x = 6$, $y = 5(6) - 18 = 30 - 18 = 12$, and when $x = 4$, $y = 5(4) - 18 = 20 - 18 = 2$. The resulting product of y-values is $12 \times 2 = 24$. The correct answer is 24.

29. **4** The question asks for the maximum number of male candidates with less than 12 years of experience that can be auditioned. Begin by reading the question carefully for information about the audition process. The question states that the producers have a total of 36 audition slots available. The producers want to devote at least 80% of the slots to actors with at least 12 years of experience, or $0.80 \times 36 = 28.8$, so 29 spots. This leaves $36 - 29 = 7$ spots to devote to actors with less than 12 years of experience. The question also states that the producers want to divide the time equally in auditions between male and female candidates, and that all but 2 of the female candidates with more than 12 years of experience receive an audition. This means that for candidates with at least

12 years of experience, 15 of the 29 are female, and 29 − 15 = 14 are male. In order to audition an equal number of male and female candidates, the remaining 7 spots for the candidates with less than 12 years of experience must be split 3 female and 4 male. The correct answer is 4.

30. **2.8** Read the question carefully and work in bite-sized pieces. Start with the information about November. Look up the snowfall for November, which was 1.4 inches. To find the cumulative snowfall for November, multiply this by the number of years, 15, to get (1.4)(15) = 21. This is the value of s. To find the number of years it will take for the cumulative snowfall for March to reach s or 21 inches, see how much fell in March in 2016. This was 7.5 inches, so 7.5 × *years* = 21. Divide both sides by 7.5 to get *years* = 2.8. The correct answer is 2.8.

31. **2.69** Read the question carefully and work in bite-sized pieces. Start with the information about January. Look up the snowfall for January, which was 12.7 inches. To find the Snow Water Equivalent, multiply this by the density in January, 9%, to get (12.7)(0.09) = 1.143. For February, the snowfall was 11.9 and the density was 13%, so the Snow Water Equivalent then was (11.9)(0.13) = 1.547. Add these values together to get the total Snow Water Equivalent: 1.143 + 1.547 = 2.69. The correct answer is 2.69.

RAW SCORE CONVERSION TABLE — SECTION AND TEST SCORES

Raw Score (# of correct answers)	Reading Test Score	Writing and Language Test Score	Math Section Score	Raw Score (# of correct answers)	Reading Test Score	Writing and Language Test Score	Math Section Score
0	8	8	160	25	26	25	560
1	9	9	190	26	26	26	570
2	10	10	210	27	27	27	580
3	11	11	240	28	27	27	580
4	12	12	270	29	28	28	590
5	14	13	290	30	28	28	600
6	15	14	320	31	29	29	610
7	16	14	340	32	29	29	620
8	16	15	360	33	30	30	630
9	17	15	370	34	30	30	640
10	18	16	390	35	31	31	650
11	18	16	400	36	31	32	670
12	19	17	420	37	32	32	680
13	19	18	430	38	32	33	690
14	20	18	440	39	33	34	710
15	20	19	460	40	34	35	720
16	21	20	470	41	34	36	730
17	21	20	480	42	35	37	730
18	22	21	490	43	36	37	740
19	22	21	500	44	37	38	740
20	23	22	510	45	37		750
21	23	23	520	46	38		750
22	24	24	530	47	38		760
23	24	24	540	48			760
24	25	25	550				

Please note that the numbers in the table may shift slightly depending on the PSAT's scale from test to test; however, you can still use this table to get an idea of how your performance on the practice tests will translate to the actual PSAT.

CONVERSION EQUATION — SECTION AND TEST SCORES

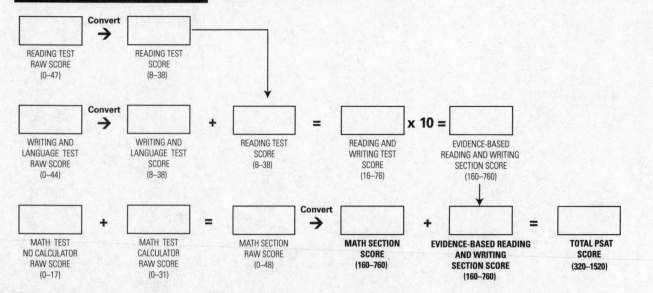

Appendix
Reading Tips

READING BASIC APPROACH

Here's a breakdown of some of the shortcuts and strategies that we refer to in our explanations.

1. Read the Blurb

The text at the beginning of the passage provides the title of the piece, the author, and the year of publication. Occasionally, the blurb will also provide a little bit of background information about the passage. Although there isn't a lot in the blurb, it will give you an idea of what to expect in the passage. It can help you make a decision about which passages to do and in what order.

2. Answer Specific Questions First

You don't have to answer each question in order. We recommend that you skip the general questions that usually begin each question set (stuff like "What is the main idea" or an open-ended look at the "main focus") and start with the specific questions. Because these questions are often arranged in chronological order and reference specific lines or paragraphs, you can get a solid idea of the general purpose and structure of the passage as you go.

3. Understand the Question

Once you've selected a question, reframe it as a *What?* or *Why?* question. The questions are usually written in a weird, open-ended way, and rephrasing them can help you focus on the information you need in the passage.

4. Read Only What You Need

Do not read the entire passage from start to finish before you start on the questions. You don't get points for reading the passage, only for answering questions, so read only as much as you need. If a question refers you to a paragraph, read that paragraph. If it refers you to a specific line, read about 5 lines above and 5 lines below the given reference.

5. Predict the Correct Answer

Remember that the PSAT Reading section is a straightforward test of reading comprehension. There is no analysis or interpretation. You don't get to write 500 words to convince someone why your answer is the best. Look for something specific in the text that answers the question. Underline it if you can. Your prediction should come from the text, not from your head.

6. Use Process of Elimination

Go through each answer, comparing it to your prediction. If the answer is inconsistent with the prediction, eliminate it. If it is consistent, or if you don't see a clear reason to get rid of it, keep it. Once you've eliminated everything you know is wrong, compare what's left. Don't ask yourself, "Which one do I like better?" Ask yourself, "Which one is best supported by the text?" Find evidence in the passage to keep or eliminate remaining answers.

COMMON WRONG ANSWERS

PSAT question writers are very good at creating attractive trap answers and awkward-looking right answers. Make sure you're reading the text carefully, considering exactly what the author says and comparing that to exactly how the answer choices are crafted. Wrong answers often fall into one of three categories:

1. Deceptive Language

These answers use words from the text that look familiar, but the words are mixed up in a way that changes the meaning. Make sure you read carefully for context: don't just look for familiar words.

2. Mostly Right/Slightly Wrong

These answer choices are similar to Deceptive Language in that the words may look familiar, but rather than being mixed up, they actually seem to be consistent with the prediction. However, while these answer choices *almost* look right, there will be a word or two that allow you to eliminate them. Watch out for extreme words like *all*, *never*, *must*, *only* and *always*. While these words don't automatically indicate a wrong answer, they will only be in a right answer if the text contains equally strong wording. (For instance, if the text says something *rarely happens*, the answer will not be that it *never happens*.)

3. Could Be True

If you've narrowed things down to two choices and think "Both of these could work," one of those is a Could Be True answer. This sort of trap answer makes sense and seems logical based on the text, but isn't actually supported by the passage. Be sure that the evidence for an answer is in the text, not in your head. (This is why we recommend underlining predictions in Basic Approach #5.)

PAIRED SETS

Most passages have two paired sets: a standard question followed by a question that asks which set of lines *provides the best evidence for the answer to the previous question*. If the first question is specific, we recommend using the Basic Approach: the lines that you used for your prediction will be the ones that answer the following best-evidence question. (Earn One Point, Get One Free!) If the first question is general, or tricky to answer, try using Parallel POE.

Step 1:   Begin with the first answer choice for the best-evidence question. Find the given lines in the text, underline them, and read carefully. (Just read the given lines, not the window.)

Step 2:   Consider the answers for the first question. Do the lines you've underlined support any of the answers for the first question? If so, draw a line connecting the two answers. (Because questions sometimes break across pages, you can just do this in the margins.) If not, eliminate the best-evidence answer. If the lines don't support any of the answers for the first question, it cannot be the answer, regardless of the question.

Step 3:   Repeat Steps 1 and 2 for the remaining three best evidence answers.

Step 4:   Once you've worked your way through all the best evidence answers, eliminate any of the answers from the first question that don't have support from the best-evidence question. If it doesn't have any support, it can't be the right answer.

Step 5:   If you have only one pair of connected answers remaining, this is your answer! If you have two pairs, go back to the question and carefully reread it. Determine which pair of answers best addresses the question or has the strongest connection based on the text.

VOCABULARY IN CONTEXT

Almost every passage on the test will have at least one question that asks you to determine the meaning of a word based on the context in which it's used. The words themselves will not be particularly challenging (words like *basic*, *sharp*, or *raise*), but you're not being asked just to define these words. You're being asked what they mean *as used in the text*. The best way to answer these questions is to go back to the text, cross out the word in question, and use the surrounding context to put in another word that makes sense. Use that prediction to eliminate answer choices.

SYNTHESIS QUESTIONS

On the PSAT, three of the five Reading passages will test your ability to synthesize information from two different sources. On one passage, these two sources will be two shorter passages about the same topic, and the other two passages will have a graphic (chart, table, or figure) that connects to the content of the passage.

Dual Passages

One of the passages will be two shorter passages about the same topic. Rather than trying to attempt both passages at the same time, simply follow the Basic Approach for each passage, one at a time.

1. Do the specific questions for Passage 1 followed by the general questions for Passage 1.
2. Do the specific questions for Passage 2 followed by the general questions for Passage 2.
3. Do the questions that ask about both passages.

Graphics

When you have a passage that includes a chart, table, or figure, spend a little time with the figure. Pay attention to the labels, the units, and the direction of the lines or numbers. Consider how the information fits within the context of the passage. When you use the graphic to answer questions, try to put your pencil on the exact data point you need. If you can't, eliminate that choice. Don't make any assumptions.

International Offices Listing

China (Beijing)
1501 Building A,
Disanji Creative Zone,
No.66 West Section of North 4th Ring Road Beijing
Tel: +86-10-62684481/2/3
Email: tprkor01@chol.com
Website: www.tprbeijing.com

China (Shanghai)
1010 Kaixuan Road
Building B, 5/F
Changning District, Shanghai, China 200052
Sara Beattie, Owner: Email: sbeattie@sarabeattie.com
Tel: +86-21-5108-2798
Fax: +86-21-6386-1039
Website: www.princetonreviewshanghai.com

Hong Kong
5th Floor, Yardley Commercial Building
1-6 Connaught Road West, Sheung Wan, Hong Kong
(MTR Exit C)
Sara Beattie, Owner: Email: sbeattie@sarabeattie.com
Tel: +852-2507-9380
Fax: +852-2827-4630
Website: www.princetonreviewhk.com

India (Mumbai)
Score Plus Academy
Office No.15, Fifth Floor
Manek Mahal 90
Veer Nariman Road
Next to Hotel Ambassador
Churchgate, Mumbai 400020
Maharashtra, India
Ritu Kalwani: Email: director@score-plus.com
Tel: + 91 22 22846801 / 39 / 41
Website: www.score-plus.com

India (New Delhi)
South Extension
K-16, Upper Ground Floor
South Extension Part–1,
New Delhi-110049
Aradhana Mahna: aradhana@manyagroup.com
Monisha Banerjee: monisha@manyagroup.com
Ruchi Tomar: ruchi.tomar@manyagroup.com
Rishi Josan: Rishi.josan@manyagroup.com
Vishal Goswamy: vishal.goswamy@manyagroup.com
Tel: +91-11-64501603/ 4, +91-11-65028379
Website: www.manyagroup.com

Lebanon
463 Bliss Street
AlFarra Building - 2nd floor
Ras Beirut
Beirut, Lebanon
Hassan Coudsi: Email: hassan.coudsi@review.com
Tel: +961-1-367-688
Website: www.princetonreviewlebanon.com

Korea
945-25 Young Shin Building
25 Daechi-Dong, Kangnam-gu
Seoul, Korea 135-280
Yong-Hoon Lee: Email: TPRKor01@chollian.net
In-Woo Kim: Email: iwkim@tpr.co.kr
Tel: + 82-2-554-7762
Fax: +82-2-453-9466
Website: www.tpr.co.kr

Kuwait
ScorePlus Learning Center
Salmiyah Block 3, Street 2 Building 14
Post Box: 559, Zip 1306, Safat, Kuwait
Email: infokuwait@score-plus.com
Tel: +965-25-75-48-02 / 8
Fax: +965-25-75-46-02
Website: www.scorepluseducation.com

Malaysia
Sara Beattie MDC Sdn Bhd
Suites 18E & 18F
18th Floor
Gurney Tower, Persiaran Gurney
Penang, Malaysia
Email: tprkl.my@sarabeattie.com
Sara Beattie, Owner: Email: sbeattie@sarabeattie.com
Tel: +604-2104 333
Fax: +604-2104 330
Website: www.princetonreviewKL.com

Mexico
TPR México
Guanajuato No. 242 Piso 1 Interior 1
Col. Roma Norte
México D.F., C.P.06700
registro@princetonreviewmexico.com
Tel: +52-55-5255-4495
+52-55-5255-4440
+52-55-5255-4442
Website: www.princetonreviewmexico.com

Qatar
Score Plus
Office No: 1A, Al Kuwari (Damas)
Building near Merweb Hotel, Al Saad
Post Box: 2408, Doha, Qatar
Email: infoqatar@score-plus.com
Tel: +974 44 36 8580, +974 526 5032
Fax: +974 44 13 1995
Website: www.scorepluseducation.com

Taiwan
The Princeton Review Taiwan
2F, 169 Zhong Xiao East Road, Section 4
Taipei, Taiwan 10690
Lisa Bartle (Owner): lbartle@princetonreview.com.tw
Tel: +886-2-2751-1293
Fax: +886-2-2776-3201
Website: www.PrincetonReview.com.tw

Thailand
The Princeton Review Thailand
Sathorn Nakorn Tower, 28th floor
100 North Sathorn Road
Bangkok, Thailand 10500
Thavida Bijayendrayodhin (Chairman)
Email: thavida@princetonreviewthailand.com
Mitsara Bijayendrayodhin (Managing Director)
Email: mitsara@princetonreviewthailand.com
Tel: +662-636-6770
Fax: +662-636-6776
Website: www.princetonreviewthailand.com

Turkey
Yeni Sülün Sokak No. 28
Levent, Istanbul, 34330, Turkey
Nuri Ozgur: nuri@tprturkey.com
Rona Ozgur: rona@tprturkey.com
Iren Ozgur: iren@tprturkey.com
Tel: +90-212-324-4747
Fax: +90-212-324-3347
Website: www.tprturkey.com

UAE
Emirates Score Plus
Office No: 506, Fifth Floor
Sultan Business Center
Near Lamcy Plaza, 21 Oud Metha Road
Post Box: 44098, Dubai
United Arab Emirates
Hukumat Kalwani: skoreplus@gmail.com
Ritu Kalwani: director@score-plus.com
Email: info@score-plus.com
Tel: +971-4-334-0004
Fax: +971-4-334-0222
Website: www.princetonreviewuae.com

Our International Partners

The Princeton Review also runs courses with a variety
of partners in Africa, Asia, Europe, and South America.

Georgia
LEAF American-Georgian Education Center
www.leaf.ge

Mongolia
English Academy of Mongolia
www.nyescm.org

Nigeria
The Know Place
www.knowplace.com.ng

Panama
Academia Interamericana de Panama
http://aip.edu.pa/

Switzerland
Institut Le Rosey
http://www.rosey.ch/

All other inquiries, please email us at
internationalsupport@review.com